Two Score And Thirteen

Third Marine Division
Association History
1949 - 2002

U. S. Marine Corps

Turner Publishing Company

Co-published by
Mark A. Thompson, Associate Publisher

For book publishing write to:
M.T. Publishing Company, Inc.
P.O. Box 6802
Evansville, Indiana 47719-6802

Pre-Press work by
M.T. Publishing Company, Inc.
Graphic Designer: Jason E. Stoermer

Copyright © 2002
Turner Publishing Company

The historical information contained in the association history
section is taken from the pages of *CALTRAP*, the official
publication of the Third Marine Division Association. A complete
CALTRAP collection dating to 1952 was provided to Turner
Publishing for reference. The *Caltrap* issues from 1952 to 1987
were donated to the Association by the late LtGen. Edward A. Craig
USMC(Ret), subsequent issues came from Harold J. Melloy and
Association archives. Photographs were provided by the Third
Marine Division Association.

Library of Congress
Control Number: 2002102274

ISBN: 978-1-68162-170-8

Limited Edition

Table of Contents

Introduction

Throughout its storied history, the 3d Marine Division has earned a stellar reputation for its dedication to the highest values and principles of the United State Marine Corps; for its extraordinary bravery on the battlefields of Bougainville, the Northern Solomon Islands, Guam, and Iwo Jima in World War II and in the jungles of Southeast Asia during the Vietnam War; for its loyalty and sacrifice to country; and for the esprit de corps for which the Marine Corps is renowned.

Division veterans of the Pacific battles of World War II formed the Third Marine Division Association in 1949. Fifty-three years later, the ranks of the Association number more than 5,000 Division veterans of three wars as well as Marines and Navy personnel who have served with the Division "between wars." Through the Third Marine Division Association, friendships forged on far-flung battlefields or in places far from the comforts of home and family are maintained. With its many programs, the Association honors the Division Marines of the past, supports the Division Marines of the present, and provides continuity to the Division Marines of the future.

The roll call of Marines who have served with the 3d Division includes 42 men who were awarded the Medal of Honor for exceptional heroism – 10 from World War II and 32 from the Vietnam War. The Division itself has also been the recipient of numerous honors, including two Presidential Unit Citation Streamers with Bronze Star, the first in World War II for the battle at Iwo Jima and the second for the Vietnam War; the Navy Unit Commendation Streamer for Iwo Jima; the Asiatic-Pacific Campaign Streamer with four Bronze Stars; the World War II Victory Streamer; the National Defense Service Streamer with one Bronze Star; the Korean Service Streamer; the Vietnam Service Streamer; the Korean Service Streamer; the Vietnam Service Streamer with two Silver Stars and one Bronze Star; and the Vietnam Cross of Gallantry Streamer with Palm.

The 3d Marine Division's primary mission is the execution of amphibious assault operations, as well as other operations as directed. The 3d Marine Division is the Marine Corps "Forces In Readiness" in the Pacific. The Division's elements include the Headquarters Battalion, based at Camp Courtney, Okinawa; the Twelfth Marine Regiment and the Combat Engineering Company, both based at Camp Hansen, Okinawa. The Fourth Marine Regiment, the Combat Assault Battalion, and the Force Recon Battalion, all based at Camp Schwab, Okinawa; and the Third Marine Regiment, based at Kaneohe Bay, Hawaii. The Division also includes elements reporting for rotational training cycles from the 1st Marine Division at Camp Pendleton, California, and the 2nd Marine Division at Camp Lejeune, North Carolina, under the Unit Deployment Program.

Dedication

"Dedicated to all Marines and Navy personnel who have served with the 3d Marine Division since it was activated on 16 September 1942."

Veteran Special Stories

3d Marine Division Patch - Caltrap

The 3d Marine Division shoulder patch, worn during World War II, is in scarlet and gold, the official colors of the Marine Corps, and consists of a scarlet triangular shield with a narrow gold line near the out edge.

In the center of the shield is a gold and black caltrap, an ancient military instrument with four metal points so disposed so that any three of them being on the ground the other projects upward, thereby impeding the progress of the enemy's cavalry.

Literally: "Don't step on me!"

Also, the three visible points of the caltrap represent the Division number.

This insignia was authorized in 1943. In 1947, the wearing of unit shoulder patches by all Marine Corps units was discontinued.

The insignia remains the official insignia of the 3d Marine Division

Hand Grenade Hill Engagement
by Dan Bozikis

Thanksgiving Day, 25 November 1943, the 1st Battalion, "A" Company, 9th Marines, 3d Platoon made a ferocious attack on the enemy during the Bougainville campaign battle for Hand Grenade Hill. As the 3rd Platoon was pinned down at the base of the hill, Lieutenant Howell "Moose" Heflin for up after you!"

"No! I'll slide down to you.." Bully exclaimed. I opened fire with my BAR to cover him as he came off the slope. I patched him up and we returned to Heflin.

From the top of the hill, all the Japs had to do was ignite the hand grenades and let them roll down to explode on top of us. As a result, we suffered so many casualties that only 11 of us out of more than 40 were not wounded. So Moose called for mortar fire, but the shelling did no good. The shells would explode at the treetops but would not penetrate the dense cover to reach the enemy underneath.

The one man that was killed on the hill, Don Bertsche of Kentucky, died in my arms in a way that haunted me for months. He had been my assistant BAR man carrying two hundred rounds of ammunition. He was in front and to the left of me in the prone position. He lifted his upper body to fire at one Jap and another one shot him in the heart. The impact lifted him up, threw him backwards into my arms rolling us both down the hill together. He looked up at me and spoke his last words: "Greek, F bleeding like a stuffed duck." To this day I don't know what he meant by that.

The rest of the platoon and I pulled back down the hill as darkness fell on us. Some of us began thinking that Moose wanted to get help and rush the hill.

The next morning, Moose sent me with Jim Hasson, Ed Gill, and Ed Gagye, to see if there were any Japs on the hill because we had heard movement while waited for dawn. It was scary crawling up the hill not knowing when the Japs would open fire on us. When we got to the top of the hill, all we found was a lot of empty fox holes and defense bunkers, but no Japs. They had pulled out. We continued and advance to Hill 1000 where we finally set our defense until being relieved by the army.

Perhaps, A Peacetime Featured Candidate
by Anonymous

Once in a while, betwixt hot wars or hot spots, something arises to jeopardize the honor of the United States, the US Marine Corps, and, maybe the 3d Marine Division, when that something isn't really a battle by battlefield standards. Then, peacetime shouldering must happen.

In July - August 1960, the 1st Battalion, 12th Marines, from Okinawa, arrived by way of amphibious shipping for live-fire field exercises at Camp Fuji, Japan. Indigenous Japanese vowed no US artillery shooting would occur, and they did that at rather stupendous risk of their bodies in the impact area.

Unexpectedly, for a battalion in training, 1/12 suddenly became the cop on the scene in an international "face" situation, perhaps perpetrated by a third nation – as, by the evil empire.

The American ambassador in Tokyo, alerted, became rigorously involved in a training exercise for one battalion of the 3d Division. The Ambassador was precise in stating that artillery shooting will occur on the day that had been advertised by the United States of America. The 3d Division was shouldering the load.

A cool Battalion Commander and a set of Marines who would later make their individual marks in 3d Division and U. S. Marine Corps history stayed the course and set new directions into the night before the day designated for what was international peacetime artillery fire.

The plan was: At daybreak, four Marines would be in the heart of the impact area within 200 meters of the selected artillery impact base point and with clear observation on the site to protect local citizens. Normal safety clearances in training were on the order of 600 meters, minimum. Forget the safety minimums, corrective artillery registration would proceed.

The day arrived to provide vicious weather circumstances, challenging all the technologies of field artillery fire direction—cross winds, near monsoon rains, colossal powder humidity, and fragile vision and survey circumstances.

The special team was in position. The four 3d Division Marines were in far more danger than the perpetrators, the Marines so placed by their volunteer instincts as guts-ball Marines are want to do. Other I/12 Marines, under the gun to provide perfection, were checking it twice and many more times.

The first round from the registering platoon lifted off at 0545 hours into murky daylight, pelting rains and winds swirling. Silence prevailed for 45 seconds, then the radio cracked "right three zero (30), fire for effect" – a near perfect schoolbook solution to an international incident, the solution brought about by 3d Division Marines from across America, thence delivered with a complimentary battery-two for reveille.

For those who may wonder about the troops in danger in the impact area, the four Marines were a version of the fire team – all volunteers. A well proven private first class motor transport driver, a skilled corporal radio operator and communications specialist, a fearless field artillery sergeant scout observer, and their intrepid lieutenant colonel Battalion Commander, the senior Marine on the Camp Fuji scene.

Seven days later, the Battalion scrambled to return to Okinawa by emer-

This is the 3d Platoon just before we hit Bougainville, 1943.
Photo taken on Handgranade Hill. Photo courtesy of Dan Bozikis

gency air transport, to prepare hastily for an international disturbance in some far-away place called Vietnam. One Battery was promptly committed in the area with Battalion Landing Team 3/5, Lieutenant Colonel Kenny Houghton, Commanding. But no element of the Battalion would make land in Vietnam for about five years.

Iwo Jima Then and Now
by Richard "Wash" Washburn

Landed on Iwo Jima on the 21st of Feb. (my birthday) 1945 with "K" Company, 21st Regiment, 3d Division. The first night ashore was cold and wet. The black sand was God-awful loose, with no way to dig in. A 16-inch unexploded shell was lying parallel to the beach. My buddy and I decided this would provide good cover from incoming. We reasoned the chance of a shell hitting the fuse was slim. If it did, it wouldn't matter where we were; we would be killed. We scraped out a shallow basin gathered burning crate wood from a burning ammo dump, layered the hot coals in the basin, covered this with wet sand and were at least warm. We were also protected from shrapnel that banged against our loaded metal breastwork. That night the Japs and our side put on a spectacular fireworks display I was honored but knew it wasn't to celebrate my birthday.

We moved up towards the second airstrip. That night we did not have the comfort of the previous night. Somehow I have erased a day from my memory. I guess that is not uncommon in combat.

I do vividly remember the 24th of Feb. It was my last day on Iwo. We were to take the 2nd airstrip at all costs. We attacked the airstrip. We were about a quarter across the runway when all hell broke loose. All at once, six of us running together were hit. I was the last to be hit. All the rest appeared dead. One had a hole in his back big as a helmet. They hit me in the right shoulder, but I was carrying a machine gun, it took the brunt of the hit, saved my life, but buried parts of the gun and Jap shrapnel into my body. It knocked me backward and slammed me to the cobblestones, my back hurt. I thought my back had been blasted open like I had just seen. Not so. I had landed on my pack of C-rations, a relief, but I knew I had been hit hard. My right arm was useless. I crawled to the edge of the airstrip, removed my pack. It helped me breathe. I dropped my ammo belt, took my canteen, and found I could walk. Started to the rear walking down a Jap trench. Suddenly I saw a Jap under a wrecked airplane wing rise up, and damn if he didn't shoot me through the neck. Lying in the trench I became furious, not at the Jap, but at myself. I could not imagine I had been so stupid, walking in a combat zone waving an aluminum canteen. After a bit, I was able to move so proceeded towards the beach. I got close enough that someone saw me and helped me they jammed me into a landing craft. The trip was very rough and seemed endless. Lying flat on the bottom of the boat with many seasick bleeding marines was not pleasant. We were deposited onto a bouncing barge tied to hospital ship, *USS Solace*, and later hoisted aboard.

I realized I was no longer on the cold, wet sands of Iwo, but on a cot between white sheets. As my eyes took in the lighted surroundings I noticed bottles with tubes running to my arms. The nurse explained the red fluid was whole blood. Some of the first to reach the Pacific War Zone. That fascinated me so I asked what information was on the little label. It listed name of donor, location, and date of donation. "That was my birthday," I yelled! "She donated blood on my birthday, 21 Feb. May I have the ladies name?" She gave me the label and I vouched to call the donor when I reached the States. After stops at two hospitals in the Pacific, I landed in San Francisco where the donor lived. With difficulty I was able to locate her phone number. I called and we talked. It became a heartwarming, emotional conversation. I explained that her blood had saved my life. She was pleased to know her donation had made a difference. We planned to meet to talk. I was moved to another West Coast hospital before we could arrange our get-together. I vowed to call her every year on my birthday. I was transferred to the Naval Hospital at Norman, Oklahoma. I unpacked my toilet bag and found the label was missing. It was a tragic loss; it was my only contact with the lady who gave me back my life. Oh how I wish I could thank her again for her wonderful birthday gift.

I returned to Iwo with my wife Dorothy in March 2000 The trip to Iwo was a lifetime event. As we approached the airstrip, it hit me and I thought of buddies I had lost on that airstrip. It shook me emotionally. We landed, the tail ramp opened and there before us stood an Honor Guard of 400 Marines. What a sight it made me proud to parade between them. It had been over 50 years since I had walked so straight and proud. The Marines had been dispatched from Okinawa to "show" us around the island.

I was not emotionally prepared, so I spent most of my time remembering as I scrubbed my feet feeling the black sand beneath me. Even though I had a couple Marines watching over me, I'm blind, I tripped on a vine and fell, my instincts took over and I rolled to the prone position ready to fire.

We were told the trip would provide closure, in my case it did the opposite, and I'm glad because I never want to forget those that were my comrades.

It was a strange feeling to be back to where a terrible battle had taken place, but is now just a lonely ugly spot in the ocean. The almost total silence was unbelievable. It reminded me of a giant black tomb. The sand is still black, the mountain still visible, but all else is changed. No noise, no thousands of men, no fragments flying, no remains or bloody guts and putrid smells. Nothing left but memories. I left Iwo with a hollow feeling, but renewed memories. Also a big relief that I was alive and well enough to be able to go back.

Rag Doll Marine
by Richard "Wash" Washburn

I was a Marine attached to "K" Co., 21st Reg., 3d Division. It was Nov. '45 and we had retaken the island of Guam. However we were "enjoying" our long over due R&R by making frequent patrols to help reduce the large numbers of Japs that still roamed the island. We had a mail call with many packages from home, all of which contained the usual packages of cookies, all of which were crumbled, and globs of sticky goo that was once icing that took a month or more of the families' sugar ration. I had one package that did not rattle or smell. Opening it, I found my dear Mother had, of all things, sent a rag doll along with a poem that explained that various parts of the doll reminder her of someone of the family and a girlfriend. I admit it reminded me of home. What should a Marine do with a doll while living with a Company of macho jokers? He hides it that's what. Then one day I saw a little girl coming down the path in the tow of a taller girl or lady. I walked over to them and offered the little girl my rag doll. She shied away from me and would not accept the doll until I dropped down to my knees and got to her eye level. She looked up to the older lady and seemed to have gotten the ok, so she took the doll and hugged it.

She smiled at me and walked down the road. I doubted she had ever had a doll before. I wrote to my mother, thanked her for the doll, and told what I had done with it. The thought of the little girl gave me such a warm feeling, I must have relayed this in the letter. Some time later I got orders to report to the "Old Man's" tent. On reporting I was told a man wanted to talk with me. He introduced himself to me as a news reporter. "I want to talk to you about your rag doll." At that, GI Jones, our Major, bellowed, "WHAT THE HELL ARE YOU DOING WITH A RAG DOLL?" Lucky for me the reporter explained the news about the rag doll had somehow reached the news services back in the States. He was sent to hear my story. Which I related. Major Jones listened to every word then walked off not saying a word. I never forgot the smile of the little girl. We left Guam and took part in the battle of Iwo Jima. I was wounded and evacuated to a hospital ship, then to a number of hospitals in the Pacific, then on to more hospitals in the States. Many times while I lay in the hospital, I thought of the Guam girl I had given a doll. I was discharged from the Marines and went home. Here my mother gave me a copy of the news article about giving the doll to the girl. Often over the years I have remembered the shy smile of the little doll girl and it gave me a warm feeling that I had been able to at least do one good thing during the war.

Time flies and it was the year 2000. My wife Dorothy and I decided to go to Guam with the Military Historical Tours. In preparation, I contacted, radio, TV, and newspaper, on Guam hoping I might get help locating my doll lady. No response. I was one of only five of the tour that had landed with the first wave to land on Guam to retake the island from the Japanese. Consequently, I was interviewed, and after the interview I took the opportunity to tell of my search for the Guam Rag Doll Lady. Next day a very nice article appeared in the *Pacific Daily News*. We flew to Iwo and returned for another day on Guam. No response to my search. We came home after a great tour but disappointed I had not found the doll lady. When we arrived home I checked the e-mail and there was a letter from the rag doll lady. What a joy! Her name is Natty Calvo. She did not hear about the news article until we were on our way home. It was a blessing that I had left my e-mail address with the news reporter. Natty

and I have exchanged several e-mails, and talked by phone once. We both want to meet each other and get acquainted with our families but have not been able to arrange this reunion. There is no question the doll incident affected both our lives.

Tenaru River Cruise
by Luther L. Claiborne

On a Sunday trek into the hills of Guadalcanal to visit a native village, I bartered for a Solomon Islands native war club which will always bring back treasured memories. Early Sunday morning, carrying extra food and drink, Willie Weber, one of our division scouts, and I walked for nearly three hours into the foothills through Kunai grass, dense vegetation, and the tropical forest to reach a native village.

We could hear natives singing familiar hymns in a church service being held in an open shelter, long and narrow with no walls, just roof and benches where women were seated on one side and men on the other. Out front, a long split log held many smoking pipes. We wondered, how could they identify them?

Willie had been to the village before on a scouting expedition and knew some of the native boys who had been trained as "police boys" by the plantation owners. With their experience in speaking some pidgin English, and Willie's excellent pidgin English, we were able to make a few trades. I traded a small roll of cloth for a war club and a grass skirt.

At noon, it was time to head back to camp, a half-day away. As we came to the Tenaru River, we decided to make a raft for each of us to float down the river. With our machetes, we cut through the green bamboo which was 6- to 7-inches in diameter. We made the rafts with 7-foot-long bamboo, laced together with vines. I tied my newly-acquired war club and grass skirt with vines to the bamboo raft. While lying flat on our bellies, we dog paddled down the river. As we floated by several native villages high up on the banks, some villagers came to watch us move down the river.

The rivers of Guadalcanal coming out of the high hill country to very gentle sloping land on their way to the ocean take a snaking course, curving back and forth, meandering through the countryside. At one of the bends in the river channel, where storm debris of brush and logs builds up, my raft bumped a big log, together with a mass of debris, to start it rolling over and over down the river. My backpack got tied up with a snag on this large log, forcing me to roll with the log and be trapped under water. Willie came to my rescue by cutting the strap of my pack with his knife so I was able to float free.

As the sun was setting, we had reached the mouth of the river and abandoned our rafts, letting them float out into the ocean. Hiking up the beach and inland several miles, we returned to camp, with stories to relate and bartered items to show – a native Solomon Islands war club that I still treasure today.

Two Unforgettable Marines
by Jay J. Strode

I had the privilege of serving with two special men in the 9th Regiment, during World War II. We were together from Camp Elliot near San Diego, California, to New Zealand, and on to the Pacific Theater. I knew many men who made fine Marines during those years of serving with Com-

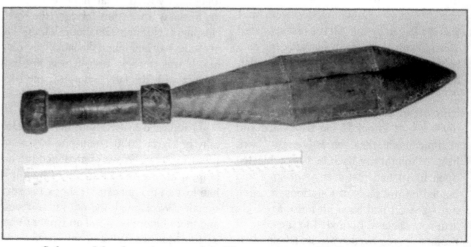

Solomon Islands native war club. Photo courtesy of Luther L. Claiborne

pany A/1/9, but two stand out when I think back over 50 years. The following stories may not be in sequence, but I'll put them down as come to mind.

Before we left the States I was a squad leader in Sgt. Baker's 1st platoon. Lee Gilliam and Otho McDaniel were in my squad as platoon scouts, and worked very well together. Mac was a serious Marine and always ready to go. Gilliam was a lovable character and full of fun. However he fell asleep every time we stopped and seemed always ready for a nap. I'd have to wake him before we marched to another problem. Once the company had stopped, he would usually go back to sleep.

Every day, when the outfit got to camp around 4 p.m., Gilliam was first to the showers. None of us were surprised to see him and a friend come out in a few minutes, all shined up and ready for liberty. No matter how sleepy he might be all day, that Marine was alert as could be then. The following day, it would be the same thing – asleep every chance and sleepy in between problems. This was something we joked about, but once out in the lead he always performed well as a scout. When we went to New Zealand and began training there, Gilliam stayed awake as there wasn't liberty every night. He and Mac proved themselves fine scouts, and always worked very well together. In actual combat we soon learned to appreciate them, for many lives were saved due to their being alert.

While the 9th Regiment was in New Zealand we went on a 35-mile hike that turned into 75 miles. They trucked us out of town, leaving about 7 a.m. I had been on guard duty in the little town by our camp until about 1 or 2 a.m. the night before. About 10 o'clock, during one of our 10-minute breaks, I took both shoes off to cool my feet. The guys commented that was first time they'd ever seen me do so. It was commonly known that anybody with blisters on his feet could ride in a truck provided for that purpose. It followed the Battalion, probably a half or three-quarters of a mile behind "A" company, which was usually in the lead. Along in the middle of the afternoon, Gilliam came to show me how badly his feet were blistered. I told him, "You drop out and ride on that truck." About two hours later when he caught up with me, I asked in surprise, "Thought you dropped out back there."

"I did," he replied, angrily, "but that damned Colonel Smoke was there. When he got done with me, I decided I'd wear

my feet off to the knees before dropping out again." That Marine meant exactly that. When those 75 miles were done, his feet were raw. I mean raw! It was three weeks before they healed so he was able to fall out for another company formation.

A while later, after being on a two- or three-day hike, everyone was about beat. During a 10-minute break, the company was scattered about resting when suddenly we heard a commotion. Two colored men were shooting craps and sounded as if about to come to blows. As the company had no such men, I jumped up to look. There sat Gilliam, all alone, speaking for both men. He seemed unaware that the entire outfit had gathered around to listen. Once again he had boosted our morale. How we all loved that cowboy from Arizona!

The second night we were on Bougainville, Captain Fowler took me and a few men, including Gilliam and a little fellow we all loved, Chick Carithers, out in front of the line. We were stationed on an island of grass 40 feet across, surrounded by swamp, It was a Listening Post, and our job was to watch for any enemy troop movement ahead of the Battalion and to report it. I had the telephone, and was hooked up to Battalion Headquarters and all Company commanders, wherever they might be. Japanese snipers had been firing from several directions since we landed, and were especially active at night. This was our first really spooky situation, so my men were alert and trying to be very quiet.

I had stationed them two to a spot in a circle, one to sleep while the other stood guard. Gilliam had given his .45 automatic pistol to Chick, who was quite a bit younger. When time came to wake his partner, Chick held the weapon as if going to shoot and hit Gilliam on the helmet with the muzzle, Our Scout reared up to exclaim, "What you trying to do, you little S.B., blow my head off." Nobody else made a sound, comical as it was!

Later, on Bougainville, we were on Hill 1000 and made patrols in the area between us and Hill 1200, As usual Gilliam and McDaniel were scouting ahead of us. They were on a trail at the foot of Hill 1200, beside a swamp. There were Jap tracks in the mud, which were still filling with water. Ahead of us was a boulder in the swamp, 20 feet high and 30 or 40 feet across. It was about 60 feet from a rock wall at the foot of a hill. Gilliam stopped and Mac waved me forward. I went to check with Gilliam, who was a few 100 feet ahead of his part-

ner. They changed positions often, always separated so the enemy couldn't shoot both at once.

He said, "Strode, this looks like a great place for an ambush."

Well aware of how dangerous the situation was, we both looked at those filling tracks, and knew enemies were only a short distance ahead. I quickly agreed, "Yes it sure does," but left the decision up to him. At a time like that, scouts were expected to make the call.

"You and Mac cover me," he said, "and I'll go through."

When we were in position, on opposite sides of the trail, and rifles ready, he darted through and stopped in the brush. When we could see his wave, I motioned the platoon to come on, while Mac and I joined Gilliam, That was one of many times when one of those special Marines proved his courage – surely "above and beyond."

During the Guam campaign, we were advancing with our 1st Platoon in the lead. Gilliam and Mac were scouting as usual. They stopped us and called me to the front, There was a small clearing with a little building on our far left. To the right, in front of us, were to black holes in the jungle. Gilliam asked, "What you think, Strode? Looks like gun emplacements to us."

I agreed, so replied, "I'll call for our bazooka and see what he can do." When that Marine and his assistant arrived, they quickly got ready to fire. Before they could, a small tank ran out of one black hole and began shooting at us with a machine gun. Our bazooka knocked his tank out of commission. Immediately another tank came out of the other hole. Our man fired at him and knocked a track off The machine gun on it continued spaying bullets, but fortunately none of us was hit.

Right then, Earl Richmond, our rifle grenade man, fired at the tank and hit the turret track. That put it out of the battle, but the Japanese machine gunner just sat and fired up and down until our bazooka set the tank on fire. Another good job for our two scouts, McDaniel and Gilliam.

While on Guam, on our push south down the far side of the island, we had a native Guamanian for a guide. Captain Fowler sent me and a squad of two men to find a cave that was supposed to be a Japanese headquarters, That teenage boy said he knew where it was, so we took him with us. Mac and Gilliam were scouting ahead so had him along. I was 200 yards or so behind them. We weren't ordered to get into a firefight, just to locate the cave. Suddenly a shot was fired toward us. All of the Marines dove into the brush, as trained to do. The poor boy stopped and didn't move, so the next shot killed him. We all felt really bad as nobody had told him to get down if that happened. Our training saved us, but didn't relieve the guilt, especially on me as I was in command.

McDaniel proved to be a good squad leader when I advanced to platoon guide. He told me at one of the reunions about being called up for the Korean war. He was on duty at the Naval prison in Louisiana when a prisoner escaped and had been picked up. One of the Marines was sent to bring him back, but the man got away again. That time the warden sent Mac after him, saying, "There's a 30 day furlough waiting for you when you come back with that prisoner."

Mac told me, "I got him handcuffed to me and on the way back we went to sleep. Anyway he thought I was, but one eye was keeping watch. The prisoner had one hand out of the cuffs when I slapped the .45 on him and said, 'Put them back on. There's a 30 day furlough waiting when I get you back and I don't care if you're dead or alive.'" Mac grinned as only he could, and added, "You know, Strode, he didn't give me any more trouble."

3d Marine Division Communicators In RVN During Advisory Campaign
by Lawrence H. Roane, Jr.

In the spring of 1962, technicians and radio personnel from Radio Platoon "I," Communications Company (Provisional), HQBN, 3d Marine Division, Camp Hauge, Okinawa, installed and made operational a Naval HF contingency communications network supporting Marine Task Element 79.3.3.6 in the Republic of South Vietnam.

"Contingency Package" was the title bestowed upon this extremely compact and highly mobile comm equipment, which consisted of two transmitter/receiver units with air conditioners, generators, and utilizing a large antenna farm. It had a 100% backup and was designed to be operated 24 hours a day, seven days a week, 365 days a year, and with proper maintenance, no downtime. A five-man team composed of a technician and four radio operators from "I" Comm (Prov) was rotated into Vietnam every 180 days to operate and maintain this equipment. They were known as the "Package Team." This enabled the communicators of Sub Unit #2 Marine Air Base Squadron 16 to have long-range communications capabilities.

From 2 January - 3 July 1964, as a Sergeant, I had the honor and privilege of being the NCOIC of this "Package Team" of communications personnel from the 3d Marine Division.

When I arrived at the Da Nang air base, our area was on the eastern side and at the edge of a 10,000 ft. concrete runway in a small Korean steel corrugated building in close proximity to the helicopter hangar and civilian Air Vietnam terminal. Our living quarters were in the front 2/3 of the building and the operational comm equipment was located in the secured back 1/3 of the building. A large sign stating 1st Comm Prov "Package Team" was prominently displayed over the front entrance. This sign was the brunt of jokes from the occasional CIA pilots and crews who would stop in for a hot cup of coffee and say, "Have you Marines wrapped any packages lately?"

Radio Platoon 1st Communications Company (Provisional) HQBN, 3d Marine Division, Camp Hauge Okinawa July 1964

Being Marines, we always managed an appropriate retort which usually hit a nerve.

The MABS-16 Headquarters was across the airfield on the western side across the highway from a Vietnamese village referred to as "Dog patch." If we wanted to enjoy a good mess hall meal, it involved traveling three-quarters to one mile around the perimeter of the airfield to MABS-16 HQ. If making this trip during dark, it was not uncommon to receive small arms fire from outside the perimeter.

The Secretary of the Navy, Paul H. Nitze, awarded the Navy Unit Commendation Ribbon to all personnel serving with Marine Task Element 79.3.3.6 from 9 April 1962 to 30 November 1964. The Armed Forces Expeditionary Medal was also authorized for service in Vietnam during this time.

Feature Story
by Don E. Spicer

March 1968. My arrival was during the Tet Offensive. We landed about midnight to the receiving area. Not knowing what I should do exactly upon receiving, when suddenly explosions started landing around the area of our departure from the airliner. Someone just grabbed me and screamed to run to the bunkers in the back of the terminal. As I ran, I tripped on a wooden sidewalk and fell flat on my face. Thank God for being clumsy. As I looked up, red metal was flying above my head and in all directions. Someone later told us that several were wounded from the group I was with and two were killed. My watch indicated that only 20 minutes had passed since I landed on South Vietnamese soil and the tragedy occurred.

The next day I was shipped to the 3d Marine Division to decide what unit needs a Forward Air Observer, which was my MOS. Two days later I was on a CH-46 going toward a place called Khe Sanh. The closer we got, the more I could see the ground below, with craters everywhere and then puffs of dark smoke. Landing here was worse than the Da Nang air strip experience two days earlier. People were screaming to move to the trench line as there was more incoming. Wounded were loaded on the chopper that had just landed me here.

Over the next few weeks I learned to live with the rats and spent very little time out of the trench line or bunkers. With less than one year in the Corps, I was still "gung-ho" aggressive. It was very frustrating to be a sitting duck for the beginning of

my tour. Eventually the units were dispersed back to Dong Ha. I was detached from 1/26 to remain with 1/3 for the remainder of my tour. I was then sent to An Hoa, Quang Tri, LZ Stud, and the Rockpile, continually patrolling in the mountainous area on the DMZ.

Each day I lived to survive to the next day. Beyond the sporadic firefights, ambushes, and NVA probes to over run our positions, I had to fight malaria, extremely humid heat, thick vegetation, cool and foggy nights, and loneliness. I had the feeling that I had been in this country for years and would never go home .... Home had become extremely vague and seemed to be a fantasy land where I had once lived but would never return.

By the end of April 1969, I had survived malaria and one Purple Heart, which I received when I received a flesh wound from 82 mortars. My recoup time was spent on the hospital ship USS Sanctuary.

By the first of May, I was back with A/1/3 along Mutter's Ridge. We patrolled down to the old Khe Sanh base, which had been abandoned, destroyed, and left for the overgrowth. So much for its tactical value.

By mid-May we went further north into the DMZ, and I was amazed at the fresh tracked vehicle imprints. I can remember having the eerie feeling that we were being watched. Finding an old rusty helmet helped to increase my stress. Strangely, the design of this find was very similar to the German WW II helmets. I thought it was bizarre. No one debated about what it was doing there. We just kept struggling along, feeling we were under keen observation. By evening, we were back to Mutter's Ridge again, which had been the area of many conflicts with the NVA. There were probes and mortars that night, but no one was hurt. There were a lot of blood trails from NVA soldiers the next morning, but nothing to account for the previous night's conflict.

The next day as we moved down off the mountains toward Cam Lo, it was hot, humid, and unbearable. We were having a lot of cases of heat exhaustion and had to ration our water supplies to minimal intake. We dug in early that day about mid-afternoon waiting for resupply of water, rations, ammo, and 60mm mortars. When the CH-46 choppers arrived, they unloaded supplies and we loaded Marines who were suffering from heat exhaustion.

This was May 19, 1969, Ho Chi Minh's birthday, and the NVA gave a birth-

day surprise in daylight around 2:30 p.m., which caught us with our pants down since not all the fighting holes were complete. Within minutes, 82 mortars were dropping on our position, killing the 3d Platoon's 2nd Lieutenant, his radio operator, and a couple of others. I leaned out of my unfinished hole and started to radio for a medi-vac and air strikes. As I moved from position to position, I took a round in the hip. Then a tremendous explosion erupted to my right, throwing me into the air. When I came down and realized I was wounded in the chest and had multiple wounds throughout all of my extremities. There was blood flowing everywhere. My Company Executive Officer came to my rescue and lifted me up on his shoulders to a fighting hole while a corpsman started applying compresses to all of the major bleeding, especially my mid-section and chest.

I started to drift off, but I kept telling myself to stay awake and the choppers would come soon. I knew I had to fight to stay conscious until I arrived at 3d Med for certain surgery. The choppers did arrive, and I was loaded with all the wounded onto a CH-46. The floor of the chopper was thick with blood. Upon unloading at triage, I was the first to go into surgery and awoke the next day with the knowledge that I had been spared but a long road to recovery was ahead. Ironically, to the left of my bed lay a wounded NVA soldier under the guard of MPs.

In a couple of days, I was sent to the USS Repose, where I almost died because my right lung kept collapsing. It was difficult trying to hang on. I realized that the medical staff feared that I wouldn't make it and tried to distance themselves from me by not engaging in conversation or exchanging friendship, sure that they had done this many times before and had been hurt by the loss of other Marines they had cared for. I was moved to a ward with a lot of empty racks and only two other Marines who looked really bad. After a few days, I was able to make some vocalizations and the staff began to open up to me.

After leaving the Repose, I was transferred to Japan and then to the Philadelphia Naval Hospital by way of Valley Forge Army Hospital. We wounded were stacked three high on stretchers on each side of the bus. I was on a top stretcher. As we started down the street to the hospital entrance, my attention was caught by eggs and tomatoes smashing into the side window. To my surprise, there were 30-40 people with signs protesting US involvement in Vietnam and they blamed us. Lying helpless, I saw that the group looked angry and I feared they would board the bus. The driver and the Marine Guards swiftly moved the bus to the area of our delivery and safety. It was quite a home coming.

On January 1, 1970, I was medically discharged and spent the next years trying to reclaim my life. I am married and have four children. I went back to college, became a licensed architect. I own my own business and look forward to each new day. It took a lot to put all my experiences from the war in perspective. It's something that only those who experienced it with me can understand, that we fought for each other to survive. Some of us came home and others will stay in my memory until we meet again. I can't say that I will ever fully recover from the losses I experienced in Vietnam. Like any traumatic experience, it is with me everyday. But, I have learned that the spirit does heal to a point that allows us to move on with life, if we allow it.

Sea Story: Round Trip
by Walt G. Sandberg

It is Christmas season 1954. 1 am stationed at HQ Co, HQBn, 3d MarDiv, Camp Gifu, Honshu, Japan.

It is mail call the Tuesday before Christmas Day. The mail orderly chucks me a cardboard box, well taped. It is the size of an old-time egg crate, battered but mostly intact. The return address label identifies it as sent by Badger Paper Mills, Inc., Peshtigo, Wisconsin, my hometown. Badger is its major employer. My dad works there. I worked there for the month between my high school graduation in May 1953 until reporting for my enlistment in the Marine Corps, 11 July 1953, at MCRD (Marine Corps Recruit Depot), San Diego.

The folks at Badger have always been very civic-minded, supportive of the town and its citizens. A nice thing they do annually is send a holiday cheer package to any former employee or employee's offspring serving with the military on active duty.

In a Marine Corps squad bay, of course, a package from home attracts immediate and inordinate interest. It is more or less considered communal property, rather than belonging solely to the recipient (although the Marine to whom it is addressed is generally permitted first dibs on its contents). Neither is the recipient permitted to stash it away, to savor it later; to **squander** it. By tradition, packages must be opened at once; there is no shortage of volunteers for the job.

On this occasion, PFC Herbert K.Y.I. Shim, Honolulu, Hawaii, spares me the chore. In moments, he has it open and its contents arrayed on a bunktop. it is an assortment of really good stuff. Lots of pogey bait. Even two packages of Twinkies!

"Hey, what have we here?" says Shim, who is one of the squad bay's most notorious, and aggressive, chowhounds.

Shim is rummaging through the items on the bunk and now grasps two small cans, which he displays at arm's length, slowly rotating them so we have a full view of the labels.

None among us fails to recognize what he holds; we relish them, snack on them often and copiously: Mandarin orange slices, a brand available locally and inexpensively because the processing plant is located not 50 miles from Camp Gifu.

The contents of these two cans we find especially tasty, even after their 10,000-mile round trip to Peshtigo, Wisconsin . . . and back.

Sea Story: Payday Stakes
by Walt G. Sandberg

This story demonstrates the camaraderie that is a normal part of being a Marine:

It is the end of the second week of May 1955. After a year-and-a-half with the 3d Marine Div., stationed at Camp Gifu, Honshu, Japan, I have received orders to transfer to new duty, stateside.

It is a tradition when someone from our outfit ships out to use it as the excuse for a bang-up party. Usually, this is scheduled off base in a secluded backstreet Japanese inn (a ryokan) where we can cut loose without fear of upsetting the populace or gaining the attention of the shore patrol.

When my orders come through, however, we are midway between monthly paydays and everyone is near broke. So we go to the fallback plan we have for such contingencies: we pool our coin, buy as much 3.2 slop chute beer as it will get us, take over an unoccupied room in our barracks, and entertain ourselves with payday stakes poker.

It works this way: Using stick matches, each assigned a value of 5 cents, each player draws as many matches as he wishes. The bookkeeper, a thankless job that usually falls to our company clerk, Cpl. Jerry Amundson, Clear Lake, Iowa, debits this value to the individual's account. At the end of the session, the matches are counted and their value credited to the winners' accounts. At month's end, the night before payday, the accounts are reconciled and the net losers pay off the net winners immediately upon exiting the payline.

We pay nickel-dime, three-raise, quarter-limit poker, so the average individual win or loss during a payday limit cycle is $10 to $15, on rare occasions $25 to $30. This kind of a hit to a payday is not too bad, considering we play dealer's choice, which can result in some weird, wild games with a relatively large pot: "Baseball" – seven card stud where threes and nines are wild and a four draws an extra card; "Betty Hutton" – fives and tens are wild and a queen may be traded for a pick from the hand of the player to the left; "8-Ball" – eights are valued higher than aces, kings and jacks but lower than queens or tens; among others.

This evening, I have a phenomenal run of luck. If I were a horse, I would have won the Kentucky Derby. At the end of the evening, the cache of 3.2 beer having run out, I possess almost all of the matches – $110 worth. Considering my Marine Corps monthly PFC's pay is $108.50, this is truly a bonanza.

But I am shipping out at 0600 tomorrow morning, and I won't be around for the payday reconciliation. Oh, that's the way the cookie crumbles and all that. Still, winning it is a rush.

It is three months later, August 1955. 1 return from weekend liberty to my barracks at USNTC (United States Naval Training Center), Bainbridge, Maryland. The days on the shore at Wildwood, New Jersey, have left me sunburned and tired – we'd stayed overlong carousing through two Joni James shows at a nightclub on the boardwalk.

I shower and hit my bunk. We have an 0600 reveille Monday mornings and, as I've learned from experience, lack of rest will be disastrous in the heat and cloying humidity of a Maryland summer.

I plump the pillow, feel something tucked beneath. It is an envelope. Scrawled on the front in hasty penmanship is: "Sandy. Am at the motel in Havre d' Grace. R.P.D."

R.P.D. is "Rice Paddy Daddy." Buck Sgt. Waterhouse, one of my best buddies from Camp Gifu. He was a demolitions expert attached to our unit. When he wasn't traveling around the division blowing up what needed to be blown up – aircraft wrecks, old ordnance, decrepit buildings – he instructed troops about the proper handling of explosives.

We called him Rice Paddy Daddy or R.P.D. for short – I never learned his real first name – because he took pride in trekking off base whenever he felt the urge without drawing an official liberty card. Instead, he simply struck off across the rice paddy nearest his destination.

I slit the envelope with my thumb, expecting to find a bulky note updating me on his adventures since I'd last seen him at the payday stakes poker party.

There is no note. The envelope holds only currency in assorted denominations – $110 in total.

Quickly, I don my dress uniform, head back out the main gate, hitch a ride into Havre d' Grace, and walk to the motel. I know the place because it is adjacent to a square, single-story, cement block building that houses a nightclub in which, a few weekends back, we had witnessed a group playing some strange new music: Bill Haley and the Comets, suddenly infamous for a raucous composition, "Rock Around the Clock."

The deskman at the motel, when I inquire about Sgt. Waterhouse, says, "Sorry, sir. He checked out at ten this morning."

"Did he say where he is going?"

"No, sir. Sorry."

That was my final contact with Sgt. Waterhouse, although I did toast him several times while making appropriate use of the windfall he left under my pillow that night.

R.P.D., wherever you are, Semper Fi.

Mutter's Ridge
by Michael P. Rodriguez

I was a 19 year old Marine rifleman assigned to Bravo Company, 1st Battalion, 3d Marines. It is September 2, 1968, as Bravo 1/3 awaits at the LZ at the Rockpile for helicopters for the assault on LZ Mack on Mutter's Ridge. The ridge overlooks the Rockpile combat base and Battalion suspects NVA activity on the ridge. I am in the 3d Squad, 3d Platoon, on the point element. I board the second CH-46 Sea Knight helicopter with a fireteam of 3d Squad, one M-60 machine gun team, and half of the Bravo 6 command staff which includes our CO, Capt.

Tuckwiller. Upon reaching Mutter's Ridge, the first helicopter comes under heavy fire as it touches down on LZ Mack and disembarks the first fireteam of 3d squad and the other half of the Bravo 6 command staff, which includes our XO, Lt. Richardson. The NVA open fire with their heavy machine guns on our second descending helicopter as both helicopter door gunners return fire with their 50 cal. machine guns. I felt like a sitting duck, as we haven't touched ground when enemy bullets puncture the fuselage and cause the interior electrical system to short circuit and catch afire. We didn't know it then, but our helicopter pilot had been shot during the enemy fire as the helicopter begins to shudder and drops like a rock.

The Sea Knight crashes hard upon the LZ and begins to roll over its side. The helicopter completely rolls around, which reminded me of tumbling around in a clothes dryer. I knew I was going to die, but the rolling stopped and shaken Marines begin emerging, some crawling, some stumbling, and some that had to be carried. I crawl out of the burning fuselage and examine myself finding both elbows and knees cut and bleeding, but I was alive! Miraculously, no one was killed in the crash. I was stripped of my rifle, pack, and cartridge belt during the tumbling, and I stumble back into the burning wreckage to retrieve my equipment as the others were doing the same before the helicopter exploded from it's fuel and ordnance. The incoming helicopters with the rest of the Company are waved off. We're alone on LZ Mack with the NVA approaching our position. Attack aircraft, helicopter gunships and artillery fire from the Rockpile keeps the NVA at bay all day until late afternoon when we are finally extracted off LZ Mack and returned to the Rockpile. We learned that we had been "written off," but we survived. We will be returning to Mutter's Ridge in the morning.

I was reassigned to the 3d platoon "guns" squad (M-60 machine guns) as a replacement. After completing the capture of LZ Mack and most of Mutter's Ridge, it is now September 11, 1968, and Bravo 1/3 is in its third day of battle for possession of LZ Sierra or Hill 461 from the NVA. I am lying on the crest of the hill as an assistant machine gunner feeding the ammo belt into the M-60 machine gun manned by gunner Larry Hughes. The crest is also manned by 2nd Platoon, and we are supporting fire for 3d Platoon's

sweep of the northern slope of Hill 461 as they encounter the NVA. A friend of mine, Jimmy Upshaw from the 2nd squad, is walking up towards the summit in front of my machine gun position. He is wounded and clutching his bleeding arm. He states that Wayne Christopher of the 3d Squad is lying down the slope and is also wounded. I order the machine gunner to stay put and to cover me. I take with me C.J. Smith, a recent replacement from the 27th Marines, and we go down the slope to bring back the wounded Christopher. We run about 100 meters down the slope, where we find Christopher lying motionless. I check him for signs of life, but he is dead. Wayne Christopher was a well built and stocky guy who weighed around 200 lbs. C.J. Smith is about my build, 140 to 150 lbs. We pick up Christopher's body and carry him back up the steep slope towards the summit. But Chris's dead weight is a hindrance as the NVA spots us and open fire on us on the slope and also on Bravo Company on the summit. We hug the ground as we try to carry Christopher's body up the slope. We manage to get 50-40 meters from the summit, but are unable to advance further due to enemy gunfire and the steepness of the slope. We are stuck on the slope in open view to the enemy who continue their gunfire. We shout for help, but no one comes down to assist us as we are trapped by enemy gunfire. We desperately drag Christopher's body further up the steep slope to no avail, as neither one of us really wanted to leave his body behind but self-preservation was upon our minds now. We continually dragged Christopher as far as we could climb up the slope and out of the NVA's reach so they couldn't retrieve his body. Bravo Company, in the meantime, is returning fire to the NVA to cover our return. We make a dash up the rest of the slope in the face of the NVA gunfire. As I scramble up the slope to the summit to safety, I know that I will be shot in the back at any moment. C.J. and I reach the summit alive in bewilderment! After a while, the shooting subsided and we were able to recover our dead. I see four Marines pulling and struggling with Christopher's body up the slope to the summit. I feel bad enough about abandoning his body but I also felt a little relief that it took more than two men to get him to the top of the hill with no enemy gunfire involved as to what it took C.J. Smith and I to do under enemy gunfire.

Three Stories
by R. John Raspys

A YEN FOR THE GOOD LIFE

Osaka, Japan, was heavily industrialized, regularly bombed during World War II, and thus an unlikely tourist town. But for 9th Marines stationed in nearby Camp Sakai during 1953-55, it provided some unforgettable liberty.

To get off the base, you needed your green military ID card, a U. S. Forces Japan bilingual ID, a liberty card, and a handful of yen.

Right outside the gate was the Sugimoto-cho train station. The surrounding area was strictly off limits. But the MP's never failed to flush out a handful of impatient Marines who were seduced by the siren song of "ojosans" (girls) just outside the station and who decided to slip away into a warren of wooden shacks nearby.

Most of us took the 20-minute train ride to Tennoji, which was a busy rail hub. From there, we would catch a subway train to Namba, the city's famous nightlife district. At first, we were taken aback by the unisex washrooms and by disabled Japanese World War II veterans – till wearing a military cap here and a tunic there – selling the proverbial pencils.

As far as sightseeing, the city had little to offer. The great 16th century Toyotomi Castle was about it. But the entertainment was outstanding everything from Japanese theater to Las Vegas-type all-girl extravaganzas and circus performances. Osaka was home of the famous Bunraku puppet theater, but most Marines had other dolls In mind, And so we invaded dance halls, nightclubs, private clubs, cocktail lounges, Western-style burlesques, erotic baths, and scores of cozy, little "mama san" bars. ("Karaoke" had yet to be invented.)

There were also several theaters showing the latest American movies, with Japanese subtitles. Couple of fancy restaurants, run by White Russian emigres, were high on the list as well.

A PFC made about $105 a month, including overseas pay and uniform allowance. But it went a long way. A large bottle of Asahi beer was equivalent to 20 cents American. Train fare into town – 5 cents.

Hotel for the night – $1.50. And for only $30-$35 a month, you could set up housekeeping with a nice, good-looking "ojosan." She would feed you, wash your clothes, iron your uniform (no civvies were allowed), shine your shoes, and make sure that you got back to camp by 0800. (Overnight liberty was standard.)

To cheer her up, you could pick up a few things from the PX. Nylons, Camay soap, and Max Factor cosmetics were favorites with the local ladies. Or you could take your girlfriend to see a movie on the base, then treat her to a cheeseburger and a strawberry malt. (Back then, it was a treat!)

Dancing at the EM club was also big. Our Japanese band called itself "Alexander's Rag-Time Band,"with a plagiaristic nod to Irving Berlin's famous tune. Their theme song, however, was "Lullaby of Broadway."

"Those were the good old days,"as the cliche goes. But by God, those Osaka days were good. And they were good mainly because we were young – perhaps even in love – and because our lives and our fortunes still lay ahead.

Osaka sidestreet, 1945. They were full of small shops, "mamasan" bars, Pachinko parlors, noodle counters, and tiny 5-6 room family hotels. Kimonos were a common sight. Photo courtesy of R. John Rapsys

-SUKIYAKI BOWL: MARINE VICTORY, ARMY BULLDOG

On a chilly, gray afternoon in Tokyo, the 3d Marine Div. football team met the Army all-stars for a showdown, It was the 1954 Sukiyaki Bowl. The date: Sunday, Dec. 19.

The old Meiji stadium was jammed with some 8,000 fans from all branches of the Armed Forces, including a good number of Army and Air Force dependents. A sprinkling of mostly curious Japanese was also there. Among the crowd were at least 3,000 Marines, who started to converge on Tokyo two days earlier.

From nearby Camp Fuji came 3d Marine tankers, from Camp Gifu came Division HQ troops, from Camp Nara came 4th Marines, from Camp McNair came 12th Marines, and from down south in Camp Sakai, near Osaka, came 9th Marines. Special liberty was granted to all.

This was years before those 135 mph bullet trains, which today zip from Osaka to Tokyo In three hours. Back then, it took us 14 hours to cover the same tracks. We piled aboard an old, coal-fed train at the Osaka terminal. Six cars were reserved for the 9th Marine contingent.

Japanese girls wended their way slowly through the cars, peddling tangerines, steaming soba noodles, and Asahi beer. We had plenty of sandwiches from our galley, but the beer came in handy. Soon half-pints of rotgut Suntory whiskey began to emerge from raincoats and AWOL bags. It was going to be a long ride.

We arrived just before midnight at the Yokohama naval base, where we were quartered in transient barracks for the weekend. Amenities included Navy chow, which lived up to its reputed excellence. ("How do you like your steak and eggs, buddy?")

The next day, Saturday, we took shuttle buses to Tokyo for a full day's sightseeing and shopping. And with 360 yen to the scrip dollar, even a PFC could do a lot of shopping. Most, however, were pursuing other activities in Ginza and elsewhere ...

On the big day, Sunday, we were bused directly to the stadium. Marines scored the first touchdown and were leading at halftime. The 8th Army band and the 3d Marine Div. band played their respective hymns and other rousing tunes, while various drill teams strutted their fancy stuff.

The Army trotted out their mascot, a dressed-up mule. The Marines, naturally, paraded their bulldog, resplendent canine in

Sukiyaki Bowl, Tokyo, December 1954. The scoreboard says it all!.
Photo courtesy of R. John Rapsys

crimson and gold. Except that the bulldog was a she – and she wasn't even a Marine!

She was, in fact, a pedigreed Army bulldog named "Duchess," owned by 1st Lt. James R. Rork, according to a *Leatherneck* magazine revelation decades later.

The Army lieutenant was kind enough to loan the dog and thus solve a last-minute mascot crisis for the Marines. But gratitude was not on the Marines' agenda on the gridiron that afternoons They trounced the Army 27-13.

Great howls of joy went up from the Marines, including dozens of blown-up condoms. It was a shocker at the time. The Army generals growled, their wives hyperventilated, and MPs raced around in futile efforts to apprehend the crafty perpetrators. In one corner, a fight broke out between Army "dogfaces" and Marines. It was expected.

We had about five hours to catch our lumbering train back to Osaka. Once on board, most Marines were to pooped to do anything but sleep.

Forty-six years later, I'm looking at a yellowing sheet of paper, still surprisingly crisp. Special orders for H&S Co. men, 9th Marines, going to the Sukiyaki Bowl: Ron Ahearn, Lyle Ball, Henry Chin, Burt Klein, Virgil Mikolai, Norm Shank, Jerry Stout, Gary Walker ... 32 names in all.

I've never heard from any of them since. But wherever they are, I hope they're as happy and carefree as they were that weekend in Tokyo.

OKINAWA:
HOME, NOT-SO-SWEET HOME

Scuttlebutt had it, in early spring 1955, that 9th Marines were moving permanently to Okinawa. This was not good news. Camp Sakai, with all its modern comforts and superb liberty in nearby Osaka, would be hard to leave behind.

But the day did come. On May 31, we boarded the *USS Calvert* (APA-21) in Kobe and bid a sad "sayonara" to Japan.

However, this was no pleasure cruise: the 9th Marines had to take part in fleet-wide exercises first. We arrived on Okinawa via the scrambling net, aboard a flotilla of LCVP0s, LCMs, and LVTs, among other amphibs. Away from the beach, we were greeted by a swarm of Okinawans, hawking iced beer for an outrageous dollar per can. Nonetheless, they sold it all in a matter of minutes.

And so, Marines once again were on Okinawa, 10 years almost to the day after the fierce World War II battle for the island had ended. Most units of the 3d Marine Div. went back to Japan, but the 9th Marines stayed.

After marching across half the island, we wound up amid rows of Quonset huts, about a five-minute jeep ride north of Koza. This was to be Camp Napunja, headquarters for 9th Marines (Forward).

Things didn't look good. We were stuck with abandoned Army huts. Dust and dirt everywhere. Sinks and commodes were smashed, so we had to rig field showers and heads right away. The weather was hot and muggy, and the huts were virtual mini-ovens. Air conditioning, at least for Marines on "Oki," was light years away.

We slept under mosquito nets, which were a pain in the butt – especially after coming in at 2 am with more than a few beers under your belt. One guy got so entangled he almost hanged himself.

A slop chute with a jukebox was set up in one of the huts. Then a movie theater was rigged in a barn-like superhut. And you could always listen to the radio. (There was no TV.) Or you could go hunt for some Japanese skulls, which were unearthed regularly in the Motobu Peninsula up north and elsewhere.

Prospects for liberty brightened considerably with discovery of Kadena Air Base, some 10 minutes by cab from our main gate. Their movie theater actually had soft Stateside seats, and the Airmen's Club was plush even by officer standards. The club had a live local band every night and comely local dance partners, too. A gigantic jukebox, glowing like a Martian beehive, belted out popular tunes when the band rested. Bill Haley's "Rock Around the Clock" and Perez Prado's "Cherry Pink and Apple-Blossom White" were the top hits.

One day at the club I met Farrell Edwards, an airman at the base and a former Marine, from North Carolina. He pointed out that Marines could eat In the Air Force mess hall: All they had to do Is buy a 25-cent food chit at the door. No problem. We tried it and were hooked on Air Force chow. How can you beat it.

On a typical evening meal, you had a choice of two juices, two soups, two entrees (chicken or pork chops, for instance), all kinds of cooked vegetables plus salads, four types of bread and rolls, a variety of cheese, and two kinds of dessert. Hell, you could have it all. And you could always go back for seconds!

The word spread faster than an Okinawan heat rash. Soon, half the guys in the Air Force mess hall were Marines. Or so It seemed. This was unfailingly true on Thursdays, when cold cuts (to use the polite term) were invariably served at Camp Napunja.

Still, I was glad to get off that island, which later became known as "The Rock." I boarded the *USNS Marine Phoenix* with joy in my heart and 30-day leave papers in my hand.

There is a postscript. While on leave In Chicago, I opened the paper one morning, and there she was – the *Marine Phoenix*. It seems the hapless ship broke in two and sank in a storm, on way to Seattle ... after dropping us off at San Francisco's Treasure Island two weeks earlier. Who says a Marine can't get lucky now and then?

Story
by Dean S. "Doc" Hirst
HM3A/1/9

I believe it was 1957. we had moved from Sukiran, on Okinawa, complete with typhoon-proof barracks and the Rycom Open Mess with that huge salt water clam shell in the entryway to the drafty old wooden barracks of North Camp Fuji, Japan. I was Senior Corpsman with "A" Co., 1st Bn., 9th Marines. Drill, of course, was the order of the day, five days in the field and two days in quarters.

On this particular day, we were working with a demolition section from Engineers who were giving us demonstrations on the use of C-4 and shaped charges. Since I was not directly involved, I was having a smoke and talking with a couple of my Platoon Sergeants about a hundred feet away. We would take a look from time to time.

The Sergeant giving the demo was good. Going by the book, he built a cone with a depression in the center and was working with only one hand over the top at a time, in this case, his right one. He was setting the charge, wiring the cap, and going about his business. He was using quarter-pound blocks of C-4. When I heard the explosion, I turned and begin running immediately toward the site even before I heard the cry, "Corpsman." As I turned to-

Camp Sakai, Osaka, Japan. View from HQ building. Photo courtesy of R. John Rapsys

ward the explosion and began running, I heard something hit my helmet and a fine mist struck my face. Looking down, I saw two fingers lying on the ground. I got to the scene as quickly as I could and began administering First Aid. Most of his right hand was gone, with only his little finger hanging by a thread of skin. As I worked to staunch the flow of blood I requested the Company CO to contact the Bn. Aid Station, ask for a chopper, and instructions from the doctor. I gave the Sergeant a shot of morphine and monitored him for signs of shock as I applied a tourniquet and battle dressing. The chopper was dispatched immediately with instructions from the doctor to by-pass Bn. and Regimental Aid, and Helivac him directly to the Naval Hospital at Yokosuka. The chopper arrived quickly. We loaded my patient inside and strapped us both in with safety belts since it was an old Korean-era chopper where the pilot and co-pilot sat on a bench-like platform high above the troop bay and there was no door. I covered him with a blanket and everything I could find to avoid the possibility of him going into shock. I asked him if he wanted a smoke, thinking it would occupy his mind somewhat and help to calm him down. As we lit up, the pilot immediately begin screaming at us to put out the cigarettes, I just shook my head, No! The Sergeant. was beside himself with anger at the foolhardy mistake he thought he had made which was to cost him his hand.

Medically he was stabilized and as I administered another syrette of morphine, my mind raced with thoughts of what I could say to allay his fears of what was to come. I knew that his greatest problem now was going to be psychological. He said, "What do you think Doc?" I decided to be perhaps brutally frank with him. I said, "Sarge, sometimes no matter how well trained we are, or how good we are, or how much experience we have, things just turn to shit. You were working with old C-4. Don't blame yourself. Maybe it was just unstable. There are a hundred different reasons why it could have gone off and maybe none of them had anything to do with what you did or how you handled the stuff. I've done everything I can do for you, you're alive, and that's the main thing. At Yokosuka you'll get the best medical attention available anywhere in the world. The toughest part for you now will be dealing with it mentally. But I want you to remember this: from now on they're going to be calling you 'Lefty.' You're a Marine and you can deal with it!"

At first I thought perhaps I'd been too hard on him. He looked at me kind of funny-like and suddenly his face lit up with a big smile. "By God Doc, you're right. I am alive. Thanks for what you've done. You're OK with me!"

It was forever-ago, in the golden days of my youth, but I think about that incident so many years ago, particularly as I grow older. I don't remember his name, but I wonder from time to time how he made out, where he is, and how and what he is doing with his life. I never heard anything further about his condition. We are with you, in War and Peace. We are "Family." Semper Fi.

Story
by Charles W. Lease

It has been 34 years since returning from South Vietnam. Repressing all memories and being in denial all these years has done irreversible damage. These past 34 years can be associated with what I had to do in South Vietnam. I have tried to take full responsibility for my life since returning without success. There was not one single day I did not live in constant fear. I was more fearful of not coming back a whole man than of being killed. Many of our orders were given by the politicians. Reflecting back, it is no wonder that some people take matters into their own hands. I don't agree we lost anything in helping the South Vietnamese, except our innocence and youth. If we would have known for sure who the enemy was, we would not have been so scared. There were too many innocent people injured, maimed, or killed. In and around Da Nang there were secure and unsecured areas. We would take a hill and give it back. One day it would be secure and the next day hostile. In other words, someone might walk right into the enemy thinking it was a secure area. When on patrol, there was always the fear of booby-traps and sniper fire. There were a lot of hit and run tactics. We would take on fire just long enough to injure or kill one or more. Then 15 minutes later we would be hit again, never being fully prepared to how or when. The NVA would rather disable than kill because it took more people out of action. This is how they kept the war going as long as they did. When the 1st. Btn. 3d Marines were assigned to take over Khe Sanh in August of 1966, there was only half an airstrip built and trees surrounding the whole area. We had to clear the area and set up perimeter. We made constant

patrols up and down the surrounding hills preventing the NVA from coming across the DMZ from the North. We lost a lot of good men during these operations. We thought we were doing a good job, until the Tet Offensive in 1968 when we learned the NVA were coming South through underground tunnels and through Cambodia. All our patrols did was slow down the NVA without effectively stopping them. We were at such a remote area that you can tell by my picture that we allowed our hair to grow uncut and continue to wear the same uniform for 6 months or more. Sometimes we would go 2-3 days without food. During the monsoon season, we would never dry out for months on end. We suffered jungle rot and put up with leeches, elephant grass, and bamboo snakes. We were without comfort or supplies until the time I left in June 1967. We would wash in freezing cold streams running down the mountains, without soap. We would rinse out our clothes in the streams and put them back on, also without soap. When we were relieved in June 1967 and returned to Da Nang, no one could believe how awful we looked and smelled. Everyone just stared at us with open mouths. I survived by my instincts and judgement, sometimes against orders. I lived and died in South Vietnam many times over and am grateful I am alive today to tell my story, I am not shameful for what I did while I was in South Vietnam and do not regret it. It is just a shame that so many people had to suffer and die. Life goes on and I pray that there will be no more Vietnams.

I went to South Vietnam when I was 18 and left feeling 28. 1 lost a lot of years because of the war from May, 1966 to June 1967.

Semper Fi,
Charles Wilson Lease, Jr., Corporal

Stories
by Michael R. Ryan
USS MOUNT VERNON

Month was January 1943. We left Camp Pendleton on trucks. A few hours later,awe arrived at San Diego docks in pouring rain in a complete blackout. My name: Pvt. Mike Ryan, Co. "E", 2nd Bn., 9th Marines. *Mount Vernon* was to be our home for two weeks. As we left the harbor, land swells greeted us, everyone became seasick. The trip was to be zig zag across the pacific without naval escort. The days where spent doing exercise, life boat drills.

I do not remember having contact with Navy personnel.

The *Mount Vernon* was a large ship dating back to World War I. It had been the luxury liner *George Washington* that brought President Wilson to the world war peace talks in France. I was able to see evidence of luxury in the grand staircase and more.

I remember most vividly the blackouts, cramped quarters. Lighting was not possible, you could not see the person next to you. We spent the nights hot and measurable. The *Mount Vernon* was my first experience aboard a naval ship. We did not know our destination was Auckland, New Zealand. I would sail on many more troop ships, but the *Mount Vernon* experience is still a vivid memory.

New Zealand 1943

E Co. 2nd Bn., 9th Reg., spent night and day training for eventual combat. We had five mile runs in morning (and 60-mile hikes with full pack). Captain Ptak could be very proud of troops under his command. Our base was an old New Zealand Army camp.

We did have time for liberty in Auckland and Papakura. My favorite stop was Moma Lo Cosa's restaurant. She treated me as one of her family, feeding me steak and eggs and helping me in many ways. People of New Zealand were very hospitable to the men in green. We had company dances locally also had a wedding, Corp. Roberts, who had a baby later. Time in New Zealand was spent molding the finest outfit in the Corps. We sailed from New Zealand to Guadalcanal for additional training preparing for landing on Bougainville, BSI, in Nov. 43.

Escaped Jap Raid On Hospital

E Co., 2nd Bn., 9th Marines, had immediate contact with enemy on beach. Moved inland where we received casualties. Moving up to Fonte Ridge, where we were under fire from mortars, artillery and gun fire. I was wounded and found myself in a hospital on the beach. Naturally, when I woke up the next morning in the hospital I was still dopey. People were moving in every direction and I was still laying on a cot with no clothes on. I was the only one left in the hospital tent. When I realized it was really Japs, I got up and wrapped a blanket around myself and ran out of the tent. I had no clothes or weapon as they had been taken from me the night before. Caught in crossfire, I ran through our lines

War Dogs

I walked post with sentry dogs in late 1944 and 1945 at Mare Island, California. Many of the dogs had seen combat in South Pacific, I was transferred to Camp Lejeune, North Carolina, for war dog detraining. We worked with dogs with hopes of being able to return them to their original owners. If this wasn't possible they would have to be destroyed. Late 1946, the kennel at Camp Lejeune was closed, ending proud history of war dogs.

Mare Island, California. Photos courtesy of Michael R. Ryan

Von

Dog kennels at Camp Lejeune

to safety. Evacuated on a stretcher to beach. Given last rites by chaplain because of the ongoing situation. A few hours later was evacuated to hospital ship, destination Hawaii.

Letter Home

Dear Mom and Dad,

This letter was written a short time before I went into battle just in case I did not return. If you receive this letter please don't take it too hard. You'll know I've gone to a place where earthly troubles and worries are no longer present.

I probably could have been doing a much safer job in this war. Maybe not. At any rat at this time I am not sorry about my choice as I am in an outfit which truly intends that the United States and liberty should live together, forever. Since I have been in the Marine Corps the fact has come home to me that we Americans can do without a lot of things but freedom never. It

would be like slow starvation. I've known what it is like to take all your orders from other person. To go where you want only on a pass and even then to specified areas in a specified amount of time. To go nearly mad in a military camp and life when it is against all the principles of the average American's way of life. But don't get me wrong, in America's case she has against her will been forced to regiment and control her men to fight down a wave of tyranny which threatens her very life. I know what I've gone through is a part of that big job which every man and woman must see through. This war forces America to subject her people to being dictated and mobilized for a comparatively short time so that they will not be enslaved forever. When you think of me I don't want you to remember me sadly but with pride and say "He was a good and true American."

I know in my time I have occasionally been thoughtless and inconsiderate of you the two persons I loved best and probably hurt most. I know you have forgiven me and understand that unfortunately I was quick tempered and little things bothered me. I would flare up in a rage and almost immediately I would calm down feeling very guilty and sorry for whatever wrong or hurt I had done you. These are the only things in my life that I'm really sorry for.

Give my love to the family especially Grandma who has done everything she could for me all through her gracious life. Tell Marv who was more like a brother to me than a friend I'm sorry I let him down, but I know he'll carry on for both of us.

"Au Revoir"
All my love,
Your son

P.S. Give my "Sax" to Bobby if he wants to take it up.

Tales of My Youth
by Francis E. Hall
A NIGHT IN THE JUNGLE

It is dusk on a hot December evening in 1943, and we are settling down for the night in our foxhole. We are settling down because once it is dark, we do not light a match, we do not talk above a whisper, and we positively do not leave our foxholes. Any one walking around after dark gets shot because he will be Japanese. They get very brave at night and try to infiltrate our lines and quietly cut a few throats. This evening, I'm very happy we have that rule.

We are in a foxhole because we took this piece of land away from the Japanese a few days ago, which makes them very unhappy and they wish to take it back. If you see this piece of land, you will wonder why any one wants it because it is a swamp full of mosquitos, other pesky creatures, and most of all mud. This does not, however, deter the Seabees who are busy building an airstrip inside our lines. In six weeks, starting with a swamp, they have B-24 Navy bombers landing and taking off. It is our job to land on the beach, push inland to form a semi-circle about 10 miles deep, then make sure the Japanese keep off the Seabees backs. This we do. The day we come off the front lines to leave the island, we cannot believe what we see – a miracle, a gigantic airstrip built on crushed coral piled about 6 or 8 feet above the level of the swamp.

Our foxhole is not really a foxhole, it is an "acting" foxhole. Since we are in a swamp, we cannot dig down, we must build up. We outline what would be our foxhole and use tree branches and mud to build a little log cabin with walls about a foot and a half to two feet high. Then we stretch our shelter halves over the top to keep out the rain. It does a pretty good job keeping out the rain, but I am not so sure it will keep out the shrapnel if the Japs attack with their mortars.

About dawn this morning we wake with a shake – the ground is moving around and the trees are swaying – we decide it must be an earthquake. Now we have a problem. Do we stay in our foxhole and maybe have a tree fall on our roof and bury us, or do we jump out and maybe get shot by a Jap prowling around? The shaking stops before we can make up our minds. A few trees do fall, but not on us. They are already weakened by all the mortar firing when we take over. As the daylight gets brighter, and we can see across to the mountains about 10 miles away, we see the biggest one has smoke coming out of it. We get a little spooked, what with the jungle, the earthquake, and now a volcano. All we need is King Kong to show up.

Most of the Japanese are on the other side of those mountains and they have a big problem trying to get their artillery and other heavy equipment onto our side of the island. In fact, for three of four days, we have a forward observer from the 12th Marines, our artillery regiment, way up a tall banyan tree right near our foxhole. He has a pair of field glasses and is watching some Japs about seven miles away carrying a big artillery gun through a mountain pass on their backs. The gun is broken down into several pieces. We hear him on his field telephone reporting their progress. Finally, on the third day we hear him say, "They are digging in and assembling the gun,"and he gives their map coordinates.

The next day, just as the Japs are about ready to load the gun and start firing, our guy in the tree says, "fire one." Then, "fire two." After he sees where his 155mm shells land, he gives new coordinates, then hollers, "fire for effect." We hear the whomp, whomp of about 10 shells exploding, then he cheers and reports they blew up the gun. We all cheer and when he climbs down, we tell him we like the way he waits until the Japs do all that work before he destroys the gun. We invite him to come back any time.

Now the reason most of the Japanese are on the other side of the island is because just before we land, they send about two divisions out of the four that were in this swamp over to Choiseul Island in response to a feint by Admiral "Bull" Halsey. He lands a battalion (about 1000) of Marine paratroopers on Choiseul Island which is nearby, and has few Japanese defenders.

The paratroopers dash in, make a lot of noise, shoot up the Jap camps, and generally make a nuisance of themselves. Then they leave. The Japanese believe this is our real target and send a couple of divisions over from Bougainville to help out. Since they have troops all over Bougainville, they pull their divisions out of the least desirable part of the island – the Empress Augusta Bay swamp area, figuring if we do invade Bougainville, we will never invade the swamp.

Bougainville is the northernmost of the Solomon Islands, about 500 miles northwest of Guadalcanal. It is about 200 miles long by about 50 miles wide with a chain of mountains running lengthwise. If we build an airfield here, our bombers can reach into many Japanese strongholds and can have fighter planes along to help. They can support MacArthur over in New Guinea and also hit north to Rabaul in New Britain and Kaviang in New Ireland.

So the Japanese have about 40,000 troops on Bougainville to make sure we do not proceed any farther. It seems they do not wish us to build any more airfields. We have the 3d Marine Division – about 20,000 – not counting a battalion of Seabees who can also fight when they have to.

As soon as the Jap troops land on Choiseul, Halsey moves the Navy in to make sure they stay there. Then we land on Bougainville. First the Raiders land on a small island which is only a half a mile or so off the coast. After a severe battle, they secure the island, and the main force, the 3d and 9th Marine Regiments lands on Bougainville. There is another battle, and then the troops start moving inland and also in both directions along the beach to expand the beachhead.

We (the 21st Marines) do not land until later. It is November 11, 1943. We come up from Guadalcanal in old four-stack destroyers. Ours is the *John Walker*. Like some of our rations, it is made for World War I. How we go from the beach to our foxhole is another story.

Earlier today, while we are out on patrol, a tree falls down and lands on top of our foxhole. When we return, we can not find our foxhole and at first we are upset, but quickly change our minds. It does not hurt our walls, and since we can still see out the front, we are happy, because we are now well camouflaged.

Every day we go out on a five- or six-man reconnaissance patrol to cover the jungle right in front of our position to make sure the Japanese are not massing for a surprise attack. Our Colonel does not like surprises.

Since I am a first scout, I lead the way while we look for Japs. We hike out two or three miles in one direction, take a left turn for another couple of miles, then left again to return. We make a big triangle using a compass and make notes as to where we locate Japanese. We do not attack, we reconnoiter. We come across small groups at times, but they do not see us. I hear other patrols are ambushed, but we are lucky; we always see them before they spot us.

This morning, after we recover from our earthquake, we wash up a little out of our steel helmets, have a cup of "Joe" and some C rations, we take off for our patrol. Today, Mike, our Sergeant, tells us we must hike three miles out toward the mountains on a compass azimuth of 95 degrees (east), then turn left for two miles at 350 degrees. then left again at 225 degrees. We each have a compass, so in case we get in a firefight and get separated, we can find our way back. As usual, we are looking for any large groups of Japs to see if they are gathering for a surprise attack.

We climb through the barbed wire and go down the hill and walk in single file through the jungle. Louie the Lip is second scout, so he's about 5 yards behind me. Behind him is Mike, then Tony with his BAR, and "Gunner" Budell brings up the rear, all about the same distance apart. All we have to do is stay close enough to see the guy in front, and far enough so we do not get hit by the same Nambu machine gun or grenade.

I line up my compass for 95 degrees and draw a bead on a tall tree about 100 yards away and start heading toward it. There is a patch of thick underbrush about 20 feet high between me and the tree, so I have to very quietly ease my way through and around wait-a-minute vines, small trees, bamboo and all kinds of bushes, keeping an eye on where I last see the tree. Meanwhile, I watch for possible ambush sites. It will be a lot easier to follow a trail and the other guys let me know this after our first patrol. But after they hear our buddies in E Company and G Company get an shot up when they follow the trails, they

do not complain. I see my job as to find out where the Japs are and not let them see us so we get back alive.

So we never follow a trail. The Japs love to wait along side of trails wherever there is a sharp bend, a small hill to climb, or a little stream to cross – any kind of natural barrier which will distract us while we walk around it – so they can surprise us while we are not looking.

I walk silently, keeping about 10 to 20 yards away from any trail. Nobody in the patrol says anything. We use hand signals. When I reach the big tree, I take out my compass and do the same thing again. Mike double checks with his. He delegates Gunner to count paces so we have an idea when we go three miles. Now the jungle is pretty thick, and what with weaving around trees and bushes and over dead tree logs, it is not easy to keep track of our direction or the distance we travel.

I have my machete in my left hand, and a Browning Automatic Rifle (BAR) in my right. I am supposed to carry an M-1 rifle, but I soon learn that what with being out in front and all, having an automatic weapon that can get off 20 rounds in a hurry is much better insurance against a surprise ambush than an 8-shot semi-automatic M-1. So after we land in combat, I pick up the nearest BAR that is no longer needed by the original owner. One problem that tends to discourage such trade ins, is the BAR weighs 18 pounds, while the M-1 weighs about 9 pounds. Except for the BAR, today we are traveling light. All I have with me is my cartridge belt with two canteens of water and a First Aid kit, a bandolier with six magazines of ammunition, and a couple of grenades. Oh yes, I also have a D ration in my pocket. It looks sort of like a chocolate bar, but it win never melt. It is not exactly homemade chocolate and does not taste very good, but I survive on it.

After about two hours, we reach the three-mile point and we take 10. Mike and I very quietly discuss the new 350-degree direction. We no sooner start forward when we come to a stream and I see what might be a good spot for an ambush about 30 yards upstream. On our side a path meets the stream and a big tree is laying in the water, blocking the way. The path continues on the other side, and passes right by a little hill covered with very dense underbrush.

I motion for our guys to hold up, and Louie and I go downstream so we can cross out of sight of anybody who might be wait-

ing for us at the log. We make a big circle and come up beside the path as it continues toward the mountains. Sure enough, we hear a low murmur and as we sneak a little closer, we see two Japs peering over a mound watching the tree trunk in the stream, while about 15 more are lounging around eating their fish heads on the reverse side of the little hill, and only about 5 feet off the path We can not be sure of the exact number because of the density of the bushes, but 15 is enough for us. We know they do not plan an attack on our front lines today, they just want to pick off a patrol or two.

Louie and I very cautiously sneak away and rejoin the rest of the guys. We explain what we see and Mike marks the spot on his map. We go around the ambush and continue on our course. Nothing much happens during the rest of the patrol, but in a couple of places we spot evidence of recent Japanese occupation by 40 or 50 soldiers. Today we can be sure they do not plan a big attack because for a big attack they will need at least a division and a couple of days or so to get organized. Our patrols keep them off balance.

After we leave the island and the Americal Division of the US Army takes over, we find out later, their patrols do not do their job. They walk out only 100 yards or so into the jungle until they are out of sight of the front lines, then sit down and hang around all day. When they come back later, they report they see no enemy. After a few days of this, the Japanese catch on. They bring in a couple of divisions from over the mountains, get organized, and catch the Army by surprise at dawn and overrun our old foxholes. The Navy has to call in some Marine reserves to protect the airfield and take back the lost ground.

So in the day time, we stalk the Japanese. At night, they stalk us. We have what we call a double apron barbed wire fence zig-zagging along our front line.

The land drops off about 30 feet or so in front of the barbed wire, so to surprise us, the Japs must climb a steep hill, then get across the wire. It is called double apron because, if you look at it from the end, it is shaped like a pup tent. And it zig-zags so we can have machine guns aimed lengthwise down the zig in one direction, and up the zag in the other. We are prepared for a night attack, but can be surprised by one man.

The Japanese try to sneak up on us, but they run into the barbed wire. We tie empty C ration cans containing a few pebbles on the wire, so when the Jap touches the wire, we hear him. Then the Japs shake the wire to try to panic us into firing our machine guns so they can spot them and call in their mortars. We do not bite. Not even when they holler insults about Babe Ruth. We toss a few hand grenades and that usually quiets them down. Every night they play these games, so by dawn we are more than somewhat annoyed and cannot wait to get at them.

Anyway, as I mention, it is dusk and we have stopped talking. I have the first shift of guard duty for our team in our foxhole so I am in the front looking out through the firing slit at the double apron barbed wire about 10 feet in front of us, when I see this guy walk straight toward our foxhole and bark his shins against the tree trunk that now covers the front of our hole. He mutters something low and as he turns, I see his wrap around leggings – Japanese. I cannot understand how he gets through the barbed wire without us hearing him.

He is so close to the edge of our foxhole, I can reach out and grab his legs, but because of the roof of our foxhole and the tree, I can not see anything above his knees. All I can picture is him holding a grenade in his hand waiting to throw it into somebody's foxhole. I motion to Louie the Lip and Tony Frate, who are laying down behind me watching this scene, to be quiet while the Jap leaves. We do not hear another sound so we can not figure where he goes or where he comes from. How does he get through the barbed wire? Maybe he is on our side, a Marine or maybe a lost dogface who stumbles into our lines from the rear, but then, there are those leggings.

I spend the rest of my shift imagining I see a whole platoon of Japs marching right up a coconut tree out in front of our lines. I cannot wait for dawn so I can go out on another relaxing patrol.

A DAY IN THE JUNGLE

Every time I ask myself, what am I doing strolling through the jungle carrying a rifle and hunting for Japs, a little voice in my head asks, "Do you not rush over to 299 Broadway in New York City to sign up soon after the Japanese bomb Pearl Harbor?" I always answer yes, but it is all Red Meany's and Goldie's fault. They decide they want to join the Marines and talk me into going with them. They both fail the physical, but I do not, and I wind up a Marine. Red is now in the Air Corps learning how to fly a plane, and Goldie is in the Seabees eating all that good chow, while I am looking for Japanese behind every bush.

So here I am, a first scout, walking about 10 feet in front of Louie the Lip who is a second scout. He is about 10 feet out in front of the rest of our squad who form a skirmish line behind us. (A skirmish line means the men are walking side by side instead of one behind the other.) Over to our left is the 2nd Squad with the Beaver leading as their first scout. And to the left of them is the 3d Squad. To their left is the 2nd Platoon, then the 3d Platoon, all in the same formation.

Our whole 2nd Battalion is on a skirmish line with our F Company on the right and G Company on our left. E Company is behind us ready to plug up any holes if and when the Japs open up. We know there are several companies of Japs dug in just ahead of us. These are what are left of a battalion or more after our artillery work them over this morning. Now we must find them and root them out of their foxholes. The problem is, what with the dense woods we walk through and the skill of the Japanese at camouflage, we cannot spot them until they shoot at us. This is very spooky.

The whole skirmish line, with scouts out in front, walks forward until the Japs open up. Then everybody hits the deck, in this case the mud, until the guys nearest to the shooting spot the Japs and wipe them out. As I walk along, I can barely see Louie behind me, but can see no one else – we stay far enough apart so one mortar or grenade does not get more than one of us. I hear much crashing through the bushes, however, because this is no time to be subtle. We are attacking, and the Japs know it and are very determined to bump us all off.

Somehow, I get the feeling that I am playing Russian roulette, because they get the first shot and we do not know where they are or who they will shoot at. I cannot help wishing I am somewhere else. But today, I am lucky that I am not somewhere else. I do not walk into any Jap foxholes.

The Beaver over on my left is not so lucky, but when they shoot at him, they miss. We hear a Nambu open up, then some grenades. Everybody hits the deck, and I hear the Beaver shout, "They are in the roots of that banyan tree." Then I hear Claude Lomars (who always chants, "the fish you eat today slept last night in Mobile Bay") swearing a blue streak at Leal, the Indian, in his Alabama drawl, then a loud bang. It seems Leal tosses a grenade at the Japs because he is closest, but it hits some branches and bounces back right beside Claude. Somehow, Claude escapes getting hit by squishing himself deeper into the mud, but it takes him a while to forgive Leal. Now the 2nd Squad gets serious and wipes out the machine gun nest with their Browning Automatic Rifles (BARs). We all get up and continue our attack.

All at once, I see a tank come out of nowhere from behind us and immediately get bogged down. A Japanese officer comes running up to the front of the tank and starts to slash at the it with his sword. We stand there with our mouths open as he tries to slay the tank with his saber. Some more Japs come running up, but they have a magnetic anti-tank mine which they try to stick on the side of the tank to blow a hole in it. We open fire and finish them off. The tank commander comes out and thanks us, then calls for a tow.

Somehow I do not think these tanks are made for this swamp. Later, I see why this Jap thinks he can cut open our tank; even though our tanks are so old they must be left over from World War I, Japanese tanks are like sardine cans on tracks. The metal on the sides is not much stronger than stiff canvas.

We continue on. There is much noise of machine guns, rifles, grenades and hollering coming from our left, then all is quiet. G Company runs into the Jap stronghold and, after a couple of hours, wipes it out. They pass the word, the battle is over, and we get orders to dig in for the night.

Our sergeant, Mike, grabs Louie, Gunner, Tony, and me, and says we must look around out front of our lines. Now, after all the shooting and shouting we just do, we are a bit edgy about walking down a trail toward the river. We walk a little ways, then hear running water. Mike says that's our goal, to see if there are any Japs between our line and the river, which turns out to be the Piva River. We spot a Jap rifle leaning against a tree and everybody wants to pick it up as a souvenir.

Our training film about booby traps comes to mind where it shows how tho; Japanese love to leave something around for us and booby trap it with a grenade. So Louie gingerly ties a string around the barrel, then we get about 20 feet away, hit the deck and pull the string. Nothing happens. It seems they are in a hurry today and do not have time to booby trap this one. So Louie has a souvenir. We look over the river, which is really a creek, about three feet deep and some 30 feet wide, and seeing no other signs of Japanese, we go back to our lines where we dig our three-man foxholes for the night. Actually, we dig the mud around the foxhole and pile up little walls around us.

We find out later that we just fought the battle of the Coconut Grove and finished off most of the remains of the two Divisions in this Empress Augusta Bay area. The 3d Marines do most of the hard fighting right after they land. Now we work over a couple of battalions. We find out a little later there are still enough Japs left to give our first battalion a tough fight on Hellzapoppin Ridge.

Tonight turns out to be the spookiest night I ever have. Our battalion forms a big circle in the jungle, like pioneers circling their wagon train when they stop for the night as they cross the prairie. Everybody is on the front line in three-man foxholes. We take turns keeping watch but no one sleeps. We can see nothing, we hear all kinds of strange sounds, birds, bugs, and swear it is the Japanese signaling to each other. It is pitch black; there is no moon tonight, and we are sure every sound is a Jap sneaking up to cut our throats. This makes the guys edgy, so all along the line people are opening up with rifles, BARs, and even machine guns.

Every time someone opens up, we think the Japs are attacking. One section spooks the next and around and around it goes. We spend the whole night like this, shooting at every sound. If we are not Marines, I would say we are scared silly. But of course we are, so we are not. I am sure I see a whole platoon of Japs marching up and down in front of my foxhole. It seems every spooky movie I ever see becomes real tonight. I swear if I ever get out of this, I will never go see another one.

Finally, when we think the night will never end, it does. The sun decides we've had enough and comes up. We all decide we have enough about 10:00 last night. There is not a Jap body in sight, so what with some 1000 guys shooting at shadows all night, that is all it is – shadows. All the guys are very angry and can't wait to find some Japs.

We find out later that every unit goes through something like this their first night in combat in the jungle. We never do that again, but later, on other nights, we hear sounds of much shooting in the distance, and shake our heads in scorn and say,

"Boots." We are now truly salty. But the nights remain spooky until we leave this island.

No Weapons
by James E. Gilley

After an eight-week boot camp was completed. 1 arrived at Camp Lejeune via bus with a poorly mimeographed order to report to F Co., 2nd Bn., 3d Marines. Requesting information, a Marine pointed to company in full gear marching and said, "That's them." I ran up to the head of the company and told the 1st Sergeant about my orders and his remark was, "Fall in back." We boarded a train and proceeded to San Diego with me playing catch as catch can for sleeping and eating accommodations. Same thing applied aboard the *Lurline*, which headed for Lord knows where. The scuttlebutt ranged from Australia to Guadalcanal, with the latter as an almost sure bet. The bunks were so close that you had to sleep on your stomach or back. Your choice, mate! I sure didn't know where or how but I had no plans to fight with my bare hands. No rifle, helmet, or any equipment and the sergeant had a novel suggestion "steal them."

After a few days, the *Lurline* dropped anchor in a beautiful harbor, which they informed us was American Samoa. No dock was available. Oh, yes, I went down the rope ladder into a Higgins boat with full equipment and no official help from the US Marines. Greeted on the beach by a small native boy with, "Ai Ki Melanie," which I found out a couple of days later means, "Eat shit Marine." You know, I gave that kid a candy bar for his cheerful-smiling welcome. Obviously, the handiwork of some Marine, probably a member of the 8th Marines stationed on the island. Nice to know you are loved and appreciated.

The outfit proceeded to walk around the island dropping off various units at different locations with my squad to be left to "guard a beach" near Leone. Not my idea of fighting the war. After about three weeks, the word was passed indicating they wanted volunteers for the Raiders. Various members seemed to think this was tantamount to suicide. I walked to Pago, and contacted LTC Bean, or Beans, who was interviewing applicants. He dismissed me stating I had only about three months in the Corps and he wanted men who had a year or more. Second day, I appeared at his tent and received the same statement. On the third day, he smiled, and said, "Sit down." After ques-

tions about my academic record, and various sports, he pointed to the harbor and said, "Can you swim across?" I replied, "If it can be done, I can do it," and he said, "You are my type of Marine." I did not even return to the squad for my personal gear, the Colonel informed me they would bring it to the Raider camp and I should proceed directly to a truck with a couple of other volunteers. Later, I saw a few guys from F Company who were still of the opinion I was "crazy."

Company A, 3d Platoon, was home. The Raiders had no heavy weapons and an air-cooled 30 in addition to a 60mm mortar was the big stuff. You cannot get a water-cooled machine gun or 80mm. mortar on a sub. More emphasis was placed on individual actions and responsibility. In fact, I was caught in a storm in a native village and decided to just spend the night and wait for things to "clear." The headman could speak English and asked what I planned to do after the war. I said, "Go to college, get a job, etc." He said, "Then what?" I answered, Probably retire." His reply, "Come back here when you leave the Marines, and you can retire without going through the other stuff." I did visit a great many years later.

I was not aboard any sub, but on one of the old destroyers (*USS Sands*) which had been painted camouflage green and two of the stacks removed. As a rule we would have a company or less on each. Moving from Samoa, my company or parts of it checked some islands in the Espiritu Santos group. The island which had the "sky divers" was interesting, with the small black natives with rotten teeth and hair with a crown of blond or red. To prove their manhood, they would jump from a tall tree with the ankles attached to vines to stop the fall about four to six feet from the ground. The forerunner of the bungee jumpers! At the canal, we were not used in any combat role since the battle was winding down.

We landed on the Russell Islands, north of the canal, and I heard the destroyer captain tell our company commander, " take you in so close that you can walk on the beach." He did, and I could hear the bottom of the "can" scrape the coral. The Japanese were nice enough to withdraw with a little air action. About the middle of March, Matthews, a buddy of mine, decided he wanted to obtain some fresh fish. He was sick of the C rations and Spam. His plan was to use a rubber boat at dusk. I told him that this was not a good idea in view of a recent strafing attack, but he insisted no planes would come in at this time of day. He would use grenades, which I also questioned. A hard head if I ever saw one, and he proceeded to go on his own with me watching from the shore. He drifted about 300 yards out, and I noted a tank lighter coming from the direction of the canal. Colonel Liversedge, who the men referred to as Harry the Horse, was very visible standing near the coxswain on the lighter. Matthews also saw the Colonel and attempted to paddle frantically back to the beach and waving the Colonel's lighter away at the same time. No soap! The lighter picked him up, and I could hear some the comments. Boy, did he get "chewed out."

Quite a few of us picked up tropical ailments, and I ended up in the hospital.

Return To Iwo Jima February 15-22, 1998
by Conrad Fowler,
CO, A/1/9, 1942-1945

Departure, Korean Asiana Airlines, Los Angeles, 11:50 p.m. Sunday, Feb. 15. Arrived Seou,l 6:22 a.m. (still dark), Tuesday, Feb. 17. Having crossed the International Date Line, we had no Monday.

On to the Pacific Hotel, Naha City, Okinawa, 90-minute flight, arriving at about 10 a.m. The Asiana plane, pilots, and flight attendants were topnotch in all respects, and the food was good all the way.

Colonel Warren Wiedhahn, USMC (Ret.), President, Military Historical Tours, had outstanding plans for our group of 70. Each day was filled with activities and events of great interest. Members of the Marine Expeditionary Force on Okinawa were our host, and it was a great reception they gave us. As members of the World War II generation, we were given credit and appreciation for the greatness of the Marine Corps today.

Members of the tour will long remember the hospitality and thoughtfulness of our host. Lt. Gen. Frank Libotti, CG III MEF/Commander, Marine Corps Bases, Japan, and members of his staff attended each of our special dinners.

Thursday night, the 53rd Anniversary Iwo Jima-Okinawa Commemorative Dinner; Lt. Gen. Libotti, presided and Lt. Gen. Al Bowser (Ret.), 3d Mar. Div., was principal speaker.

Friday night dinner was hosted by the International Community of Okinawa Prefecture. American Consul General Robert S. Luke gave a welcome address. A response was given by Maj. Gen. James L. Day, USMC (Ret.) Congressional Medal of Honor, Okinawa. School children provided entertainment with dances and music.

Thursday and Friday, we visited many points of interest. The Battle of Okinawa began March 26, 1945. It raged for 90 days. More than 12,500 Americans and 244,000 Japanese were killed. Today, Okinawa, with a Florida-like climate, is a Mecca for tourists from throughout the world.

Saturday, 53 years and two days after D-Day 1945, we went to Iwo Jima. An eight-hour visit had been arranged. A flight on Friday had flown to Iwo with several vans, tents and other equipment for our use. We flew in an Air Force C-141 plane; about an hour flight.

The thoughts and conversation of many of us were of 53 years ago. Iwo Jima, called the Gateway to Final Victory by Marine author Raymond Henri, was the first landing by American forces on Japanese soil. The goals leading to the invasion were to decrease the loss of airmen and air craft, increase the effectiveness of the air bombardment of Japan then underway, and have an advanced base for the invasion of Japan.

The Japanese anticipated landings on Iwo and had constructed secure underground areas for the defenders to protect them from our intensive air strikes and naval gun fire preparatory for and in support of the landing. When these fires lifted to permit Marines to land, the Japanese moved through tunnels and trenches to occupy their strongly constructed and numerous combat positions. Thus the stage was set for one of the most intensive battles in the history of the Corps.

Eighty-five thousand combatants (62,000 Marines and 23,000 Japanese) on an island eight-and-one-half square miles in area. Commandant Krulak has said Iwo is the only battle in the history of the Corps in which Marine casualties exceeded those of the enemy; Marines 6,800+ KIA and over 21,000 wounded; Japanese had 21,000+ KIA and 1,000+ wounded or captured.

Under terms of the treaty signed to end the war, Japan is permitted to have a military with defense capability but no offensive capability. Today Iwo Jima serves as a base for the training of Japanese fighter pilots. A concrete runway with barracks and hangers is located in the area of their WWII second runway. Today, east of this runway, a golf course that looks quite playable has been added. Yes, the island still consists of coarse, shifting, soft black sand but there are shrubs, and vines, not present in 1945. Defensive positions constructed of steel reinforce concrete walls; some, three feet thick, can be seen overlooking the beaches; many of them damaged by direct hits.

We were greeted by our advance party from Okinawa. The first order of business was a joint memorial service. About 100 Japanese were present. A tent with chairs had been provided. The service was held near memorials: one Japanese and one American. It is my understanding that there were a few Iwo veterans among the Japanese, but most were kin to Japanese who had been killed.

It is important to the Japanese to protect Iwo Jima as the resting place of the spirit of Japanese killed in 1945. Commercial aircraft are not permitted to land. At different locations, particularly entrances to underground ways, small shrines had been constructed. The Japanese placed food, water, and flowers in small quantities at the shrines.

In 1945, the Japanese soldiers were under orders to kill all the Marines they could before dying for the Emperor. For the first time I heard that the 1000+ Japanese who made it back to Japan, up until 12 years ago, would not acknowledge that they had been on Iwo. They had disobeyed orders. They had not died for the Emperor.

After the Memorial Service we visited, by van, locations of interest.

From Mt. Suribachi, one had a complete view of all the island except the north end, a great advantage for the defenders. A white monument, with a large Marine emblem on each side and with appropriate bronze plaques, memorializes the raising of Old Glory at that spot on 23 February 1945 when six members of 2nd Battalion, 28th Regiment, 5th Division, made history that will live forever.

At the north end, we visited the underground headquarters of the Japanese commander. The passageways were extensive and well constructed. We visited hills 362A, B, and C, Cushman's Pocket and other memorable terrain features.

I walked over that portion of the island over which A/1/9 had moved before I received a disabling wound. Then and now I am impressed that we won because of the courage, bravery, and determination of young well-trained Marines who were well led by young NCOs and young officers. Tactics using flame throwers, pole charges, satchel charges, hand to hand combat, and with great support from tanks, artillery, and combat engineers were adequately effective. To which should be added, "Never have Marines been served by a more courageous, dedicated, and capable group of corpsmen and medical officers."

Two Personal Experiences
One Salty Sgt. Major

Retired Marine Sgt. Maj. Bill "Cactus Jack" DeLoach has lived on Okinawa since 1973. We had not met but we have exchanged letters for several years. I invited him to be my guest for the Friday night dinner. I called him Thursday, "Cactus Jack, how will I recognize you when you get to the Pacific Hotel?" He said, "I am 6' 6" tall, 76 years old, and weigh 250 pounds, have red hair, and a crew cut." He could have added, "I am one salty Sgt. Major." Great to be with him!

Surprised and Delighted

Marine Lance Corporal Justin Stodghill, Granada, MS, age 21, wearing kilts, entertained us by playing a bagpipe. He had heard that I would attend an Iowa Jima Veterans Reunion in Mobile, Alabama, Thursday after my return home on Tuesday. His father, a minister, though not an Iwo vet, was Chaplain for the Mississippi Chapter and was to attend the reunion. Justin wanted to surprise his father. He handed me a tube of Iwo black sand, a letter to his father and we had our picture taken. His father was both surprised and delighted.

Not All Marines Were Treated Like Heros
by Robert M. Palmer

The other evening I was watching the news on TV with my grandson Tim. The topic of this news story was the Vietnam veterans who were holding a demonstration at the Vietnam Memorial in Washington, DC.

This demonstration was in protest of the way Vietnam veterans were being treated by the U.S. government and by the people in general upon their return home from Vietnam. They felt that they were being treated as criminals instead of war heroes, which they felt they were after fighting for their country.

My grandson turned to me and asked, "Were you in the second World War? How come the Vietnam veterans weren't treated like war heroes like the Marines were when you came home from the war?"

All I could say was, "Not all Marines were treated like war heroes when they came home from the South Pacific."

I enlisted in the Marine Corps in 1942, when I was 17 years old. Within four months, I was in combat on Guadalcanal, and over the next three years, I was in combat on Bougainville, Guam, Vella LaVella, Munda, and Iwo Jima. As the action on Iwo Jima was coming to an end, I returned with the rest of my unit to the island of Guam.

Upon arrival on Guam, myself and 14 other men from my unit were selected as guards to transport approximately 60 Japanese prisoners to a prisoner of war camp in Hawaii. These prisoners were captured by part of the 3d Marine Division (3d Marines) that stayed on Guam when the rest of the division went to Iwo Jima.

We had no problem transporting these prisoners to Hawaii, where we turned them over to the prison camp personnel.

We were then given orders for transportation back to the United States. Upon arrival in the US, the 15 of us came down the gangplank and were directed to board two trucks which were standing on the dock. Two marines from unit in San Francisco climbed on the back of each truck. The Marines had loaded carbine rifles.

We were taken to a large barracks that had been part of the World's Fair complex on Treasure Island.

We spent the night in this barracks, still under guard by those Marines. In the morning, we were taken to the train station, still under guard.

The train took us to the Marine corps Recruit Training Center in San Diego, California. We were put into a barracks on the far end of the base, which was enclosed by a 12-foot-high fence, which had other Marines walking guard around the compound. Those Marines also had loaded carbines.

For 14 days, we were kept at this compound. Everything we had, including clothing, was taken from us. We were deloused, fumigated, showered, and processed for new duty stations. We were issued complete sets of new uniforms, and our transfer papers were prepared, along with a full updated record of our pay records over the three years we were overseas. Some of us had not had a regular pay day for almost three years.

The only reason we were given for this 14-day confinement was that the US government felt that after our experiences in the South Pacific, that we were unfit to associate with human beings and needed time to be indoctrinated back into civilization.

After these 14 days of confinement, those Marines who lived on the west coast were given their leave papers, orders, and back pay, and released to go home. The rest of us were agin put onto a train which was headed back east.

In Kansas City, as I got off the train with five other Marines, I was given leave papers, transfer orders, and back pay, and released to head for my home in Minnesota.

So, Tim, you see that not all Marines returning home from overseas were treated as war heroes when they returned to the US.

STORY
by Cecil Matheney
F-2, 21st Marines
Jackson, MS

On my third day on Iwo, February 23, We started an advance early in the morning, near the #2 airfield. Shortly after the attack started, we received bearing incoming shells. One of our tanks had a track blown off and was disabled. The artillery was so heavy that I ran to get under the tank. When I dove under the rear of the tank, there was not enough clearance for my BAR and me, which carried my extra magazines for the BAR, so I ripped the harness, but finally I was able to get under the tank, along with my foxhole buddy. We started digging and finally shoveled enough dirt around the tracks, the front and rear, that we were able to sit upright under the tank. At that point, it was the only time that I felt safe the entire time I was on Iwo Jima.

I said to myself, I believe I'll stay here until they secure the island. We spent that day and night under the tank, but the next morning while talking to my buddy, I heard this gruff voice of my 1st Sgt. Raeford Scott. He said, "Is that you, Matheney?"

"Yes," I said.

"Get you're a## out of there! I have had you listed as M.I.A. since yesterday! "

My foxhole buddy (Myers), from Kentucky, was later wounded and sent off the island to a hospital ship. He was later returned to the island, and was killed before the end of the campaign. Raeford Scott, from Texas, made a career of the Marine Corps. He is now retired, living in Ocean, CA.

V Battalion, 3d Marines, Respond to the Philippine Coup of 1989

By Major Leonard J. DeFrancisci, USMCR

During 1st Battalion, 3d Marines' (1/3) deployment to Okinawa, Alpha Company boarded the *USS Tuscaloosa* (LST-I 187) on November 30, 1989, in preparation for a two-month cruise. That evening, just after midnight, a military coup began in Manila, as a contingent of 200 Philippine Marines and Scout Rangers took up positions near Fort Bonifacio, located outside of Manila. Shortly afterwards, other targets were struck throughout the Manila area, including the international airport and two TV stations as well as the Presidential Palace, location of President Corazon Aquino. The attack was well planned and well orchestrated by a rebel force comprised of approximately 2,000 disgruntled members of the Army, Air Force, Navy, and Marines. Unhappy with her leadership, the rebel military members vowed to "fight to the death" to oust Aquino.

As the situation in the Philippines deteriorated, the *USS Tuscaloosa* steamed full speed towards Manila Bay. Charlie Company 1/3 boarded the *USS Saint Louis* (LKA116) at Okinawa, which joined the *USS Tuscaloosa*. The *USS San Bernadino* (LST-I 189) and the *USS Olendorf* (DD-972) also joined these ships to form a makeshift Amphibious Ready Group (ARG). In late November, to conduct training maneuvers, Bravo Company 1/3 had sailed to the Philippines aboard the *USS Dubuque* (LPD-7) and off-loaded at Subic Bay Naval Station two days prior to the coup. Shortly after the Marines debarked, the *USS Dubuque* joined the ARG currently in a Modified Location (ModLoc) assignment off the coast of Manila to round off CTG 76.4 as the flagship. To utilize the LPD's better landing capability, Charlie Company was cross-decked from the *USS Saint Louis* to the *USS Dubuque*.

Although outgunned, the rebels repeatedly outwitted the loyalist forces and appeared to have the upper hand. The Presidential Palace had been bombed and strafed by rebel T-28 aircraft, which are vintage World War II prop-driven trainers. At this point, President Aquino personally requested US

assistance. While aboard Air Force One en route to the Malta Summit, President Bush gave the "green light" to allow F-4 Phantom flyovers. Although Aquino wanted the US planes to engage rebel forces, President Bush's orders were for the F-4s to show "extreme hostile intent." This came in the form of low-level fly-bys using the shock effect from sonic booms. This action was decisive for two reasons. First, no rebel aircraft took to the sky afterwards, which provided an advantage to the loyalist forces and secondly, it showed that the US was in full support of Aquino.

In response to the US support to the Aquino government, anti-American demonstrations took place in front of the American Embassy at approximately 1400 on December 2. In addition, intelligence reports indicated that an attack on the American Embassy was a possibility. One platoon from Bravo Company 1/3, commanded by 1st Lieutenant Mike Plue, deployed to the American Embassy as reinforcements. This platoon of 38 Marines relieved Embassy Marines currently providing security for the Seafront Compound during the evacuation of Americans from the Makati Subdivisions. In case the situa-

1st Platoon, "A" Company, 1st Battalion, 3d Marines on maneuvers. Green Beach, Philippines. December 1989. Photo courtesy of Leonard J. DeFrancisci

Launching AAV's off the USS Tuscaloosa (LST-1187) "A" Company, 1st Battalion, 3d Marines. December 1989. Photo courtesy of Leonard J. DeFrancisci

tion ftn-ther deteriorated, Alpha Company prepared for a Non-combatant Evacuation Operation (NEO) of American civilians in the Makati Subdivisions. The rest of Bravo Company remained on the flight line at Subic Bay Naval Station as a helicopter-borne reaction force. Charlie Company prepared for a helicopter-borne insertion into the Makati area if required. Since August, while deployed in Okinawa, 1/3 had received intensive Special Operations Capable (SOC) training, which prepared the Battalion for rapid response planning and special missions such as NEOs.

With American might clearly on her side, Aquino and the loyalist forces gained momentum. However, on December 2, the rebels still held positions in the Makati area, where they were able to shield themselves with civilians and blend in with the local population. At the Inter-Continental Hotel, it was reported that the rebels had hostages, to include foreign nationals. Lt. Colonel Stevens, 1/3 Battalion Commander, attended a briefing at a warehouse where Special Operations Forces were also preparing for a hostage rescue. During this briefing, plans for further military actions were developed; however, by December 3, the fighting had turned to sporadic firefights, mostly in metro Manila. A few days later, by December 7, the coup was crushed and the Philippines was essentially back to normal.

About the author: Leonard DeFrancisci was the lst Platoon Commander for Alpha Company, 1st Battalion, 3d Marines, during the Philippine Coup of 1989.

Two Letters
by James F. Davis

The following is a letter I sent to the family of a close friend of mine, Bernard Brende, and his sister's response to my letter. Bernard lost his life in the invasion of Guam. At his family's request, I attempted to step back in time to the 1944 invasion.

Dear Kathryn and Family,

About 56 years ago while serving in the US Marines in the Central and South Pacific, my best friend asked me to write to his sister back in the USA. This is an attempt to write the letter he requested. I will try to step back in time and try to relay my thoughts as closely as I can to my thoughts and feelings at that time.

We have been very busy living the life of a Marine in the area of Guadalcanal, Bougainville, and Guam and trying to re-

member what it's like back home longing to see the faces and hear the voices of family and hometown friends. Bernard and I are both in HDQ. Company, 1st Battalion 3d Marine Division. We (all of us) are fighting a war that we are not sure will ever end and an enemy that will never give up; so we don't know if or if we ever will return home. We can temporarily escape the fears of war, terrific daily heat and the every afternoon drenching rain fall.

So it is especially nice to have a special friend to talk to and confide in about our common feelings, fears, and fond memories of home and the people there – especially family members. We both know that it would be very difficult to face – tonight – tomorrow, and the next landing on some enemy held remote island with this fond memory and the hope to return home, some day.

In discussing our family life growing up, we discovered there were many similarities – the strictness and discipline of our two families and the importance of God, church, and our own belief in God and his son and our savior Jesus Christ.

We discussed mutual feelings that we had been "over churched" in our years at home, and how we might change that pattern when we were able to do so. As we approached and experienced the horrors of war we felt that that attitude may have been a mistake. In fact we were sure of it. As we looked around we found that God had left us, only we had strayed from him. We could attest to the comfort God brings in the times of trouble.

As we boarded ships and headed into open sea, we were wondering where we were going and what our future might be. We had heard that we might be headed for the island of Guam, since the 2nd Marine Division had already landed in Saipan It looked very much like we would be needed to also land on Saipan and help retake that island. This uncertainty to keep floating back and forth from the Marianas Islands to the Marshall Islands and back again for the entire month. When it was decided that we would land on Guam, we packed our gear and planned to disembark the next morning. Bernard & I discussed the coming landing. We hoped and prayed that we would get through one more peril that might be ahead for us. For several days, my friend (Bernard) mentioned to me a strong feeling that he would not make it through this landing and battles that

would follow. I assured him that we all had the same fears late in the evening on the day before disembarking, Bernard and I were notified by our Commanding Officer that we had been reassigned to different landing crafts. The reassignment meant that I would be going to shore in the boat Bernard had been assigned to and he to my original boat. We planned to meet on shore as soon as we could.

Kathryn, you know the rest – the rest being that the boat Bernard was assigned to in my place which took a direct hit and was blown out of the water. My best friend had taken my place on a landing craft that didn't make it to shore.

In remembering this experience I am always reminded that a person named Jesus Christ also took my place on a cross many years ago. I know as Bernard knew the acceptance of Christ. So you see Kathryn I know that there will be a reunion in a place where there will be no more sorrow; pain, or death.

I believe, as you do, that we will all meet in this place in God's time. Kathryn, I'm sorry it took me 50 + years to have the courage to write this letter that perhaps should have been written years ago.

Sincerely,
James F. Davis

Dear Friend Jim,

My first wish is to thank you for the letter you sent with your reflections about brother Bernard. I appreciated how you attempted to write it as if you were way back there living the life with Bernard. It is a letter I shall keep with an the other things about him. Thank you so much!

And you DO have a picture of me! I was so startled to see what it was because I did not think it could possibly be of me, but perhaps of some other relative or girl Bernard was writing to. He was always asking for more pictures. I guess I was about 20 when that picture was taken and that is a long time ago!

My son Dan has been at work getting information that is available on the Internet. He got a thorough printout of the USS Elmore and everything about it. He also asked if anyone who had been on it was checking in and he would like to connect with them. A man named John Ferrill LCDR USN (Ret.) responded. He wanted Bernard's name and identification and he would check what he could because he had served on the Elmore from '44-'45, which covered Bernard's time. Here is a quote from his response after he got Bernard's name: "I was in one of the boats that was hit in the Guam landing. Three of my crew were hit besides myself. Also several of the Marines were also hit, a couple very seriously as I recall. Perhaps your uncle was one of the ones that was hit and subsequently died in the sickbay (hospital). I never did know their names. I will get together the addresses of the Marine Corps and Naval sources who can probably be helpful in providing the information you seek."

Then, Dan also found a place where they provide videos of the battles of the Second World War. Dan ordered the one about Guam. We have seen it now and it is an amazing experience to watch this and realize you and Bernard were actually there at that time, someplace in that turmoil. First, on the video is a diagram of Guam and a long discussion of the actual battle plan and the details to be carried out. You would be fascinated with that.

Our video was damaged when it came but we were able to play it anyway. They are sending us another one. If you are interested in this damaged one, I would be glad to send it to you when our new one comes

I am so sorry to realize you have had such trouble with your eyes. That means your dear wife is being your eyes at necessary times. She will no doubt read this to you. Are you able to drive with use of your one eye? I hope so.

Also I think it would be great if you wrote down your memories for your family. I don't think we who are indebted to you for what you did can know too much about what you went through.

I have a younger brother who was in the Korean War and when the 50th Anniversary of that one was just talked about, I realized I didn't know much about what Herb had gone through! I called him up and we had a long conversation just like I had with you but with more details. I need to talk to him more about that and he was very willing and even anxious to talk about it.

God bless you and Idella and your family and I am so thankful you have come into our fives with all this wonderful connection of a brother so long gone – but not forgotten! Now I can say to my children that "Your uncle lives because others who knew him say he lived too!!!"

Stories
by Grant J. Limegrover
written by Rex Gregor

This is the hidden story about the 3d Marine Division in the first days of combat during World War II.

The 3d Special Weapons Bn., 3d Platoon, 3d Marine Division should have been credited as being the first unit of the 3d Marine Division to participate in combat; was the first to suffer casualties; was the first to shoot down enemy planes; and the first to ride an LSTs into combat!

I wouldn't be surprised if the history books of the 3d Marine Division would turn their face towards the records of General Douglas MacArthur and here they might find some interesting facts.

In early January of 1943 it became very evident that the 1st Marine Division had made its mark in history and now it was the 3d Marine Division's turn to become the gung-ho brother in combat.

As we moved from New Zealand to Guadalcanal, the rumors begin to float around that General Douglas MacArthur was making his own move to take charge in the South Pacific. Among our troops, there was a fear that he and his public relations efforts would be turned against the Marines. There was a strong feeling among the Marines that General MacArthur had abandoned his troops in the Philippines in the early part of the war. There was a feeling among many Marines that the General had NOT received orders from the Commander-in-Chief (President Roosevelt) until after he had left his Command without proper authority. I have no way of proving this might be a fact, but I do know that Marine rumors almost always turn out to be fact. I also do know that on or about September 15, 1943, portions our Battalion changed its address from 3d Special Weapons Battalion to 1st Provisional Task Force for no other apparent reason than that General MacArthur had ordered it.

My diary shows that on September 23, 1943, Major Donald Schmuck was assigned to the 1st Provisional Task Force as Commander and 1st Lieutenant Grant Limegrover and his entire platoon was transferred to the 1st Provisional Task Force. We were no longer a part of the 3d Marine Division and our command was transferred from the 3d Marine Division to General MacArthur, who was stationed in New Caledonia several hundred miles away with little or no radio communications. I

was transferred from the 3d Marine Headquarters Company to the 3d Platoon of the 1st Provisional Task Force as the only medical personnel in this hastily assembled expeditionary task force. I kept a personal diary during my entire service in the Marine Corps as a Pharmacist's Mate 2/c. After I was discharged I rewrote my diary, updating the events as I remembered them. My records show this portion of my diary was completed in October 1946 and this portion of my diary was copied without further editing.

1. On or about Sept 23, 1943 Major Donald Schmuck was assigned as the Provisional Task Force Commander of a small expeditionary force with the orders to establish an advanced base on the Japanese held Island of Vella LaVella in preparation for the Choiseul raid and the subsequent invasion of Bougainville. The hastily assembled Task Force was put together by personnel without the knowledge or input from the Provisional Task Force Commander – Major Schmuck. It was necessary to launch this amphibious operation without proper enemy intelligence, reconnaissance, or a fully equipped expeditionary force. The Provisional Task Force consisted of two (pick-up) rifle squads who had no previous training as a fighting unit, and an AA Platoon commanded by 1st Lieutenant Grant Limegrover, a motor transport section, and other supporting elements. The entire medical support team for this combat force consisted of one Hospital Corpsman, Rex H. Gregor, Phm. 2/c, assigned to the AA Platoon commanded by Lieutenant Grant Limegrover.

2. The amphibious task force consisted of two LSTs with one destroyer and two APDs as escorts. The LSTs were new to military invasion and little was known of their capabilities. The Navy Commanders recognized the "slot" as a deadly dangerous place and wanted the troops off their LSTs as soon as possible. The result was the LSTs landed at the wrong beaches and Major Schmuck had to land his troops without knowledge of the existing terrain, and, as later records show, the landing was made about 500 yards down the beach from an armed work battalion of Japanese soldiers.

The enemy battalion consisted of approximately 1,200 armed workmen. It is apparent the Japanese had planned on building a defensive air strip at some where's near Ruravai. (According to Admiral Morresy's report on the "History of the South Pacific") the Japanese Commander evacuated his troops to Kolobangaro in face of a murderous attack by a division of enemy troops. The task force commanded by Lieutenant Limegrover put up such a barrage of fire power that the Japanese Commander thought the landing force was a division of Marines and thus evacuated his troops.

3. Immediately upon landing the Task Force was bitterly attack by enemy dive bombers and fighter planes. In spite of the fact that Lieutenant Limegrover's AA platoon shot down five enemy fighter planes; one of the gun crews and one LST were destroyed. Against overwhelming odds the task force under the Command of Major Schmuck continued to give effective battle to the enemy. Without regard for his own personal safety and with resolute courage Major Schmuck's leadership turned the tide of the battle to victory.

4. During the night of September 25, the Japanese bombed the landing beach almost continuously. In the early morning hours of September 26, Major Schmuck obtained the use of a salvaged LCVP and reconnoitered the beach areas. Again under bitter attack by the enemy, Major Schmuck, without regard to his own personal safety established effective gun locations which prevented greater causalities and effectively opposed the enemy attacks. Because our landing group did not have proper radio communications, our Communication Corporal (John Kennedy) swam to a downed Japanese aircraft and removed the radio equipment and thus was able to establish communications with our unit in Guadalcanal. It was through his knowledge and his expertise, along with his personal bravery, that he was able to effectively contribute to the success our landing.

The adversity of this Task Force operation was compounded by some apparent confusion within the High Command. General MacArthur had abandoned his troops in the Philippines in the early part of the war, (according to some authorities) believed his orders to leave the Philippines was not issued by the Commander-in-Chief (President Roosevelt) until sometime after his escape. Some believe he left his command without proper orders to do so. According to some authorities, General MacArthur sought to become the Commander-in-Chief of the entire South Pacific operation; however, the Marines were placed under the command of General Alexander Vandegrift while William (Bull) Halsey became the over all Commander of

the South Pacific Forces. It seems apparent that there was some internal political bickering within the elements of the High Command right up to the time the Provisional Task Force made the invasion of Vella LaVella. This task force was made up entirely of 3d Marine Division personnel yet it was placed under the Command of the 1st Amphibious Force which was located in New Caledonia, several hundred miles away and without direct communications with its command. Although we have never been able to confirm that the 1st Provisional Task Force was transferred to General MacArthur's command, at least we became a lost unit according to the records. (This mix-up may also explain why the bureaucrat F.P. Anthony insisted the Marine Corps had no record of units of the 3d Marine Division serving on Vella LaVella even though all Marines were advised that our mailing address had been changed to 1st Provisional Task Force.)

It was obvious we were involved in a mixed-up mess. After the war and during a visit with BGEN Donald M. Schmuck, USMC (Ret), Triangle S Ranch, 105 Little Fork Road, Buffalo, Wyoming 82834, in October 1994. General Schmuck told me about his experiences on Vella Lavella. This confirmed the fact that Major Schmuck had been assigned as the officer in charge of the Provisional Task Force and without his knowledge that his unit had been transferred to the Command in New Caledonia. He had no communications with this command, I can personally confirm that our mail address was changed to the 1st Provisional Task Force. In this same visit with General Schmuck he seemed concerned that I did not receive The Congressional Medal of Honor. He told me that he was surprised that it had not been awarded. He later told me that it was possible that during the chain of command it could have been down-graded. I must assume that the Medical Officer in the Division staff had killed the recommendation. (See my report about this in another part of this report. I do not remember the doctors name. I think it was Dr. Winthrop - but I cannot be sure.)

In pursuing the facts in this task force operation, we have been involved in numerous obstacles, not the least is a military regulation that states awards of merit must be approved within three years from the date of the action. This connected with the inflexible attitude of such lower echelon bureaucrats such as F.P. Anthony who insisted that the Marine Corps and no record of Major

Schmuck's service in the P Marine Division. Certainly Major Schmuck's bravery and leadership would equal or exceed service defined as "beyond the call of duty. The disappointing fact is that we have never been able to get by the lower echelon's of the military bureaucracy to have our request heard. Maybe, just maybe, we might be able to have our story heard and that Major Schmuck will receive the recognition he deserves!

Semper Fidelis
Rex H. Gregor

Statement:
REX H. GREGOR
638-15-24
C 05 404 577

During my service in the US Navy, I kept a diary with most entries entered daily from January 5, 1942, until December 25, 1943. These entries (I am reporting here) cover the period from September 25, 1943, to December 24,1993. Some portions of the diary were written several days after combat days, but all entries are based upon notes I kept and by my best memory of the events as they occurred at the time.

At the time I joined the United States Navy (January 10, 1942) my Mother purchased a diary and urged that I make daily entries during the time I was in the service. She was anxious that I would write her weekly and thus I made daily entries in my diary. Although there were times when I was unable to make entries due to combat conditions but I was able to make entries when time and conditions permitted. I made no further entries after January 10, 1956. This report is copied from these entries; however, I must state that some portions of my diary are personal in nature and thus I have omitted these particular items.

I wish to make the following statements as a part of my record:

Upon completion of Basic Training and Hospital Corps School, I was assigned to the *USS Vixen* (Commander-in-Chief's flagship of the Atlantic Fleet) While aboard the *USS Vixen* I applied for and was granted special training for independent duty. Subsequently I was promoted to Pharmacist's Mate 2/c and transferred to the Marine Corps as a Pharmacist's Mate.

In the Marine Corps I served at the following stations - - New River, NC; San Diego, CA; British Western Samoa; New Caledonia; New Zealand; Guadalcanal; Vella Lavella; Bougainville; and Officers Training School, Ursinus College, Collegeville, Pa.

MY DIARY:

On September 25, 1943 the 3rd Platoon Battery A, 3rd Special Weapons Bn., landed on the enemy held island of Vella LaVella.

The day was clear and the sun shone brightly as the LSTs pushed their bows up on the beach. Almost immediately and without warning, three Japanese dive bombers roared out of the sun diving down towards the two ships that were fully loaded with men and equipment. One of the dive bombers peeled out of the formation and headed towards LST #167 (the one I was on). We had landed about one-half mile down the beach from the other LST – there was a small peninsula jutting out between us. I could plainly see the three dive bombers screaming down towards their targets. The bomb-bay doors were open and the pilots' faces seemed to be tense.

On LST #167, all guns were trained on the diving planes. The 40 millimeter antiaircraft guns were firing too high and their tracer shells were missing the target. There was one Navy gunner, a member of the ship's company, firing a 50 caliber machine gun. He was right on target, and I could see his tracer shells going in right behind the propeller. I saw the pilot dipping his right wing of the plane sharply to the starboard and he then released his bombs. They fell short of the target and exploded harmlessly on the beach. As the plane turned starboard I could see the tracer shells of the of the 50 caliber tear into the cockpit of the plane. The pilot slumped forward and the aircraft plunged into the jungle just beyond the bow of the LST.

On the topside of the LST, PFC James Lashley, a member of a gun crew, took aim at one of the diving planes. Just as he was ready to fire, two members of his crew fell dead at his side. Without flinching, this young marine faced a barrage of bullets and fired his gun. The second shot tore through the propeller and the plane burst into a ball of fire. Immediately he turned his weapon on the second plane. When he fired, a trail of black smoke poured from the plane and it too burst into flames. Both of the dive bombers had managed to release their bombs before plunging into the sea. The bombs crashed into the ship tearing gaping holes in the deck and superstructure and igniting huge fires. One of bombs landed near PFC Lashley's gun, taking his life. No braver man ever lived.

On the main deck of the LST #167, I heard the bombs explode and shortly black smoke billowed above the jungle on the far side of the peninsula. Realizing they might be in deep trouble, I raced across the peninsula (infested with Japs). When I arrived, most of the personnel were off the ship. There were dead and wounded lying all around.

I located some litter bearers and instructed them to move all the wounded to the jungle's edge which would offer some protection in case there was another air attack. I was told that none of the medical supplies or equipment had been unloaded All of my medical supplies were still aboard this flaming vessel.

The Marine and Navy personnel were working desperately to save equipment and unload supplies as the ship burned furiously. With the exception of my First Aid kit, all my medical supplies were aboard the ship and I had to have them if I were to going to care for the wounded. The loading hatch to the ship was open and the bow was pushed up on the sandy beach. As I dashed up the ramp into the main hold of the ship, I was stopped by the flames and heat from a bunch of gasoline drums that were burning furiously. I remembered from my inspection tour the day before that there was a ladder on either side of the bulkhead in the forward part of the ship that led to the main deck.

Once on the main deck I headed towards the fantail of the ship where I knew there was another ladder leading to the ship's hold in which the jeep ambulance was parked with our medical supplies. As I approached the superstructure of the ship's bridge I was confronted by roaring flames, black smoke, and exploding ammunition. I put my head down and made a mad dash through the flames and smoke towards the fantail of the ship. The exploding ammunition that surrounded me, scared me; but somehow I made it though this pit of burning hell.

As I made my way down the passageway to the ladder that led to the ship's hold, it was dark and as I opened the hatchway to climb down the ladder that led to the ship's hold, it was pitch black. The ship's engines were dead and there was no electricity. I figured there had to be some flashlights in the sickbay and sure enough I found two of them. With the aid of the flashlights I climbed down into the hold and located my jeep ambulance and the supplies almost directly below the ladder. Besides the ambulance there were several other jeeps and trucks jammed into the area. I turned on the headlights of several of them lighting up the entire area.

Most of the medical supplies were packed according to GI instructions in knapsacks, and it was not difficult carry them topside. When I reached the main deck, I waved and attracted the attention of some marines on shore and tossed the knapsacks over the side into the water. I hollered down and told them to take them ashore.

After three or so trips, I had rescued all the knapsacks. There was one large wooden trunk left that contained blood plasma and miscellaneous supplies and equipment. It was too heavy to carry and too big to get up the ladder. I found some ammo cases in one of the trucks and I emptied them. I transferred the blood plasma to these empty cases and took them topside.

I am not quite sure for what good reason, but I made another trip to the hold of the ship to turn off of the headlights of the trucks and jeeps! By this time the quarter deck and the forward part of the main deck were completely on fire. The only way I could get off the LST was to jump over the side. I found a "line" (rope) coiled on the fantail. I looped it around the ship's railing and scrambled down into the water and made way ashore. One of the litter bearers was waiting for me and he said, "Doc, you gotta hurry. There's lots of guys hurt and some real bad." I asked him to locate Corporal Bill Kennedy, the radio man, and have him contact an evacuation ship. At the treatment area I found about 20 dead or wounded. One of the wounded had his leg nearly blown off. Someone had tied a tourniquet on it, but he was still bleeding profusely and I determined he had lost considerable blood. I had to stop the bleeding. His foot had been severed and nearly half of it was missing. The ankle was crushed to a pulp. About four inches above the ankle, a bone about two inches in length jutted out through the torn flesh. When I took hold of it the bone moved readily and I figured it had been completely broken. I probed to find the artery as I wanted to clamp a hemostat on it to stop the bleeding; but, I was unable to locate it. I took a pair of tissue scissors and cut the torn pulpy flesh until I located the artery. I clamped it with a hemostat. There was only a half circle of flesh that held what was left of the ankle. I wanted to put a compress bandage on the stub of his leg. I took my tissue scissors and carefully cut away the remaining flesh. I cleaned the wound the best I could, and clamped the bleeding points with hemostats then sprinkled it with sulfanilamide powder and tightly bandaged the stub with a compress bandage. I mixed a bottle of blood plasma but had difficulty locating a suitable vein in this arm to administer it. I finally got the needle inserted and got the flow properly adjusted. I gave him a shot of morphine tartrate and tagged him for immediate evacuation.

There were seven more marines and three sailors who were wounded and brought to my treatment area. Four were serious, and I treated them the best I could, and tagged them for immediate evacuation. Six others had minor injuries which I examined and treated. I then arranged for an escort and sent them to the Command Post with instructions that if necessary they should report for duty. I later learned that all six decided to directly report for duty.

Four marines were dead when they arrived at the treatment area. I identified them by their dog tags and completed a death tag and marked it for evacuation. The last of the dead and wounded were being evacuated when I heard some bombs exploding about 500 yards up the beach. A few minutes later a messenger came running to tell me that a marine had been hurt by a bomb explosion "He's hurt bad," the messenger said. "They are bringing him over here."

The wounded was Private James E. Edwards, a member of a gun crew. Private Edwards had multiple shrapnel wounds and the major portion of his buttocks had been torn away. He was in a state of shock and his complexion was an ashen gray. I had treated him for a sprained finger at the sickbay on Guadalcanal, and knew him quite well. When he saw me he said, "Doc, I hurt real bad all over," then he closed his eyes and groaned. As I started to examine him, he opened his eyes and in a pleading voice that was just barely above a whisper he said, "Doc, say a prayer for me, please." I hesitated for a moment then took his hand and held it in both of mine. "Oh Lord," I prayed, "give us strength in this hour of need. Grant that we may find peace and comfort in your name. Reach out and touch Jim Edwards and let your will be done, Amen." Private Edwards opened his eyes and he weakly smiled. I knew he had probably lost a lot of blood and I went to get a bottle of plasma. As I was mixing the liquid with the dry powder, I heard him groan and he cried out, "Oh Lord please let me die." It took me no more than three minutes to mix the plasma and ready it for ad-

ministration. When I kneeled beside Private Edwards, his eyes were glassy and he was staring straight ahead. I picked up his arm – it was limp. I tried desperately to find his pulse, but there was nothing. I placed my hand on his chest. He was not breathing. Private Edwards was dead. Just then I heard some guns firing and I saw a Japanese Zero diving towards some ships off shore. I grabbed my carbine and in a moment of bitter anger I fired at the plane until the chamber of the rifle was empty. I threw the gun on the ground and sat down with my head bent forward holding it in my hands. My eyes were dry and burning. I felt a choking sob in my throat. I trembled all over and broke into uncontrollable sobbing. I don't know how long I sat there, three or more minutes maybe, when I heard voices. The litter bearing were returning to the treatment area. I regained my composure and stood up.

"What happened?" one of them asked.

"It's Edwards," I said, "he's dead."

One of the marine litter bearers walked over and stood looking at him. Finally he said, "That's too bad. He was a nice guy."

The beach area was strafed and bombed repeatedly and the support ships off shore were dive bombed a number of times. Although I saw a great number of individuals perform acts of bravery, it was hard to understand why some gave their lives and others did not.

PFC Lashley and Private Edwards, with complete disregard for their own personal safety, performed their duties without once turning from danger. For these acts of bravery they gave their of lives and others did not.

Private First Class Clarence Giarrusso (who after the war became Supt. of Police in New Orleans) time and time again, with super human courage and devotion, he performed beyond the call of duty, and he lived.

Corporal Kenneth McIntyre reacted with courage, skillful judgment, and uncommon bravery that contributed materially to the prevention of greater casualties. He lived.

First Lieutenant Grant J. Limegrover, a 23-year-old officer, assumed the heavy burden of commanding officer, and under conditions that would challenge the training and professional experience of an older and more mature officer, he reacted in the highest tradition of combat leadership. His bravery inspired all those who served with him.

The common denominator was that Lashley, Edwards, Shafer, Nay, Peacock, and Owens gave their lives and the rest of us did not. The mysterious factor that existed and remains unsolved is a series of events that occurred before and during our landing at Vella. The question that remains unanswered is whether these events were simply a bizarre pattern of coincidences or whether some supernatural power uniquely planned and guided them?

Because, while on Guadalcanal I received what I personally considered a despicable and demeaning assignment as "latrine inspector," I sought an outlet for my frustrations with a friend at the mobile hospital emergency treatment center. It was through this friend I met Dr. Truscott, who spent endless hours training and teaching us advanced techniques in First Aid, including emergency surgery. By his patient and thorough instruction I became uniquely qualified to meet the challenge of a Hospital Corpsman in combat. I became proficient in making preliminary diagnosis. I learned how to control bleeding, administer blood plasma and a multitude of emergency first aide treatment techniques. Could this have been some sort of subconscious mental telepathy that brought us together?

On the way to Vella LaVella, aboard the LST, I decided to investigate the ship. I searched every foot if it and I learned where all the escape hatches and ladders were. I did this for no compelling reason other than to pass the time. Thus, when it became necessary to re-board the ship to rescue medical supplies I was familiar with all the passageways, escape hatches, and below deck ladders. Without this knowledge it is very doubtful if I would have ever been able to reach the ambulance and my medical supplies. Once again was this a mere coincidence or was it an extrasensory phenomena of clairvoyance or precognition in being able to subconsciously perceive events and prepare for them?

To me the most mysterious of all the events was locating the flashlights. As I opened the hatchway to make my way down the ladder to the ship's hold, where the jeep ambulance was located, it was pitch black. It is true I knew from experience that flashlights were standard equipment in every Navy sickbay; however, I had only a general idea where the sickbay was located. I had never been inside a sickbay on an LST and I was not familiar with the location of any of the supplies or equipment It seemed that I knew exactly where to go. I entered the sickbay hatchway door and without hesitation I opened the correct cabinet drawer and retrieved the flashlights. Again was this a case of extrasensory perception or some strange and unexplained psychic detection?

When I arrived in the ship's hold with flashlights in hand and had located my jeep ambulance, the light was inadequate. It seemed like the solution to this troublesome problem had been implanted in my subconscious mind and was released when the time came and I turned on the headlights of the several nearby jeeps and trucks giving me adequate light. This remarkably simple solution surfaced without thinking! Did each of each of these events surface as a mere coincidence? Or did some outside supernatural power, plan execute them through some form of mental telepathy?

In the days following our initial landing, we were attacked bitterly by enemy aircraft on a number of occasions. For the most part, their bombing raids were inaccurate. Gradually our Navy and Air Force put more and more pressure on the enemy, attacking their key bases and engaging their naval task forces, and it became apparent that we were beginning to dominate the fighting.

The Navy and Marine air wings, with the help of some New Zealand pilots, for the most part, controlled the skies over the "slot" and few enemy dive bombers and fighters got through daylight hours. This, however, did not prevent the enemy from attacking with a ferocious determination and we had a ringside seat for some of the most vicious dog fights in the South Pacific. For two weeks after we landed on Vella, the sky over the Kolobangaro Straits became a hornet's nest of angry fighter planes from both sides, diving, turning, twisting, and attacking each other in the morning sun.

The environment on Vella LaVella consisted of a muddy slimy swamp that was infested with alligators, snakes, lizards, bats, black gnats, mosquitoes, and enemy soldiers. It rained nearly every day and the troops were consistently wet either from the rain or sleeping in waterlogged foxholes. Most developed a skin infection which we called "jungle rot." The skin became raw and infected, mostly on the legs, feet and back. Frequently pustules would develop and the areas, even if bandaged, would constantly be covered with black gnats. At one time or another, every man in the outfit had jungle rot. Some were more susceptible

then others, and the pain and misery it caused was worse then the nightly bombings and strafing from the enemy planes. To add to the misery and discomfort, dysentery was a common occurrence and there was little I could do to treat it.

In spite of the heavy concentration of enemy bombardments, which occurred nearly every night, the men learned to accept them with little more than a necessary inconvenience. Our orders were to hold fire at night to prevent giving our gun positions away.

The US Navy was wreaking havoc on the Japanese troop transports and supply ships, and they no longer could afford to gamble sending their large ships down the slot. Instead they turned to barges and increased their number tenfold. The barges would travel by night and hide along the jungle during the day. The destroyers and big ships in our Navy seemed to pay little attention to the barges, and they increased daily. Some even got so brave as to travel by day, and we could see them hugging close to the shore along and near Kolombangaro, which was seven miles across the strait from our gun positions, and we were helpless to do anything about it. Some of our guys got so frustrated they would sometimes point their carbines in the direction of the barges and fire.

After a month on Vella LaVella, we received orders to return to Guadalcanal for reassignment. When we returned to the 3rd Special Weapons Battalion Headquarters, we were welcomed with open arms. Our combat experiences had preceded us and our reception was like a giant family reunion. The mess tent was filled with bananas, pineapple, heart of palm salad, papaya, limes, and fresh fish. We were even served a large steak. A more than adequate supply of gook gin was readily available, and the party ran late into the night. The next day I was kept busy making reports, updating medical records, and being interviewed by both Marine combat officers and medical doctors. The questions were endless. The questions went on until I complained to Gunner Wilkie that I had enough.

The following day a Marine Captain from Division Command arrived at Battalion Headquarters and requested to see me. "Arrangements have been made for combat reporters and photographers to interview you. You are news," he said with a big smile. "It is isn't often that a hospital corpsman will amputate a leg in the heat battle while being strafed and bombed. It's a news story and they want to write about

it." I protested. I was of no avail, and write about it they did. Associated Press released the story and nearly every major newspaper in the country – even in England. My picture was printed in many newspapers and thousands of people wrote me. Hundreds of young girls wrote me, and I even got several proposals of marriage.

Three days after the interviews, Gunner Wilkie told me that I had orders to report to a Navy officer at the Commanding Generals Headquarters. The Gunner got me a new set of dress "tans" and a pair of dress shoes. The gunner had my shoes polished and I got a GI haircut. The Gunner inspected me from top to bottom and sent me on my way. The Navy Officer was a young Lt. Commander, that I would judge was in his middle thirties, He had a quick smile. I sensed he might be a reserve officer by his informal attitude. When I entered his tent he greeted me with a warm smile and a firm handshake. He invited me to sit down and started our conversation with small talk and chit chat. He asked me where I was from and about my family. He asked me where I went to school and when he learned I had played football, basketball and baseball in high school his conversation sparkled with enthusiasm. We talked about the University of Minnesota football and Bernie Bierman and his Golden Gophers. Gradually the conversation changed to Vella LaVella and my experience in combat. He questioned me at length about the landing operation and my part in it. Finally he said, "Gregor, I want you to know that Lieutenant Limegrover, your Commanding Officer, has recommended you for a medal." He handed me a typewritten report that read in part as follows: "It is my recommendation that an appropriate award be given Pharmacist's Mate Second Class Rex H. Gregor, U. S. Naval Reserve, who was the only one present to administer medical aid to the casualties, for his outstanding coolness in action, his daring in returning to the burning LST for blood plasma for vital transfusions; his evacuating of the wounded and competence in rendering them first aid; his securing of assistants from the troops and instructing them in first aid." When I had finished reading, he said. "The Battalion Commander has concluded that your conspicuous gallantry and actions without regard to your own personal safety were beyond the call of duty and after a through investigation I whole heartedly agree. You are being recommended for the Congressional Medal of Honor. Congratulations!"

I decided not to discuss the recommendation with my fellow hospital corpsmen. I did tell Gunner Wilkie, and I made a special call on Lieutenant Limegrover to thank him for his confidence in me. It was five days later that Gunner Wilkie sent a messenger that I should report to his tent. The Gunner handed me a set of orders that stated that I should report to Special Troops Medical Detachment at Division Headquarters The Pharmacist's Mate at the Headquarters was a guy by the name of Brownie. I had met Brownie in New Caledonia and our paths had crossed several times since then. "The Commander is expecting you," Brownie told me.

The Commander was sitting at a field desk writing what appeared to be a letter. "Sit down," he said in a brusque voice as he pointed to a folding canvas backed chair. The Commander continued his writing, and I must have sat there for at least six or seven minutes before he turned and looked at me. As I sat waiting I looked around his tent. On the far side next to his field desk were a couple of wooden trunks.. Setting on top of one of them was a case of 8-oz. bottles of GI Brandy for medicinal purposes. Sitting on the ground next to one of the trunks were two gallon tins of 100 proof pure gram medicinal alcohol. On one corner of his desk was a small woven basket filled with fresh limes. Next to it was a glass mug filled with a light amber colored liquid and a half empty bottle of brandy. In a trash box next to his desk were several empty brandy bottles. The consumption of alcoholic beverages in combat areas was common and in one way or another it was seldom in short supply. While the commissioned officers drank GI issue brandy and medicinal alcohol, the enlisted men drank "gook gin!"

Anybody who drinks at ten o'clock in the morning has to have a have a problem, I thought to myself. Suddenly the Commander dropped his pen, took a drink from the mug, turned and looked at me and then stood up. In accordance with military courtesy I started to stand up.

"Sit down," he said rather sharply and he paced around the tent. "Your name Gregor?" he asked. Without waiting for me to answer, he said, "So you are the self appointed Division Surgeon."

"I don't understand Sir."

"You amputated a leg," he shot back.

"Well not exactly," I replied. " I was trying to stop the bleeding and I ... "

"I read your report," the Commander interrupted. "I know what you did. If you

were in the States you would be prosecuted for performing surgery without a license."

"Dr. Truscott told me that I did exactly right," I protested.

"I did not ask for your opinion. You are lucky I don't have you court martialed," he growled. He pointed his finger at me and in a loud voice he said, "If you think for one minute I am going to approve awarding you a medal for performing unauthorized surgery you are sadly mistaken. If you get an award for amputating a leg then every knife happy corpsman in the Navy will be striking for a medal."

I could smell liquor on his breath and I became angry. I snapped to attention.

He said, "Dismissed."

It is my personal belief this doctor was personally responsible for killing this recommendation. I was not so much concerned about fact that he threatened to stop the action as I was about the fact that he chewed me out for doing what I considered was necessary to save this man's life. In a later conversation with Dr. Truscott he encouraged me to "forget about it." He said, "you did right and that is the important thing." I did not keep a record of this doctor's name but I believe it to be a Doctor Winthrop – I cannot be positive but his name should be found in the records of the 3d Marine Division's roster.

Headquarters, 3d Marine Division, Fleet Marine Force, In The Field.

October , 1943

The Commanding General, 3d Marine Division, Fleet Marine Force, takes pleasure in COMMENDING

3d PLATOON, BATTERY A, 3d SPECIAL WEAPONS BATTALION, 3d MARINE DIVISION for meritorious service as set forth in the following

CITATION:

"The Marines and sailors attached to an antiaircraft platoon of a Special Weapons Battalion, during operations against Japanese forces on Vella LaVella, British Solomon Islands, on September 25, 1943, displayed outstanding courage under enemy fire. When the beachhead at which the weapons of their platoon were enplaced was attacked by Japanese planes, the men of the platoon fought bravely under heavy aerial strafing and bombardment, despite the fact that bombing hits were made on two of the guns and inflicted casualties on the crews. As the result of the personal brav-

ery and skill of all hands, the platoon destroyed four enemy aircraft, and continued to give effective battle to the enemy even after it had sustained heavy casualties. The conduct of the men of this platoon was in keeping with the highest traditions of the United States naval service."

Major General A.H. Turnage, 3d Marine Corps Commanding.

Copy from files of Major D.M. Schmuck, USMC, Provisional Task Force Commander, Vella LaVella, 1943.

CITATION
DONALD M. SCHMUCK
Brigadier General,
U. S. Marine Corps Retired

Headquarters, 3d Marine Division, Fleet Marine Force, In the Field.

March, 10, 1944.

The Commanding General, 3d Marine Division, Fleet Marine Force, takes pleasure in COMMENDING

FIRST LIEUTENANT GRANT J. LIMEGROVER, US MARINE CORPS RESERVE, for meritorious service set forth in the following

CITATION:

"As leader of an anti-aircraft platoon of a special weapons battalions during operations against

Japanese forces in the Vella LaVella area, British Solomon Islands, on November 25, 1943, you displayed outstanding courage under enemy fire. When the beachhead at which your weapons were stationed was attacked by Japanese planes, the platoon under your command fought bravely under heavy aerial strafing and bombardment, despite the fact that bombing hits were made on two of the guns. As the result of your exceptional leadership and example of personal bravery, your platoon destroyed four enemy aircraft during the engagement, and continued to give effective battle to the enemy even after it had sustained heavy casualties. Your conduct was in keeping with the highest traditions of the United States naval service."

A.H. Turnage
Major General, US Marine Corps, Commanding.
Temporary Citation

CITATION
SOUTH PACIFIC FORCE

Of the United States Pacific Fleet
Headquarters of the Commander

In the name of the President of the United States, the Commander South Pacific Area and South Pacific Force takes pleasure in awarding the SILVER STAR MEDAL to

REX H. GREGOR, PHARMACIST'S MATE SECOND CLASS, UNITED STATES NAVAL RESERVE for service as set forth in the following

CITATION:

"For conspicuous gallantry and intrepidity in action against the enemy while serving with a Marine special weapons battalion in the South Pacific area on September 25, 1943. GREGOR was the only medical personnel present to administer medical aid to the wounded resulting from an air attack as a landing was being made on an enemy held island. While under fire, he displayed the utmost coolness in caring for the wounded and, without regard for his personal safety, he returned to a burning landing ship to obtain blood plasma required for vital transfusions. His courageous conduct was in keeping with the highest traditions of the United States Naval Service."

W.F. HALSEY,
Admiral, U.S. Navy.
Temporary Citation

3d PLATOON, BATTERY A, 3d SPECIAL WEAPONS BATTALION, 3d MARINE DIVISION, Roster

First Lieutenant
Limegrover, Grant J.

Sergeants
Cyga, Walter W.
Davis, Richard F.
Grandstaff, Marvin E.
Grandstaff, Melvin J.
Hanson, Harold G.

Corporals
Bryant, Carl A.
Giffin, Riley Jr.
Kennedy, John W.
Kilmartin, Daniel J.
McIntyre, Kenneth A.
Reeder, Howard E.
Shafer, Howard E.
Tuttle, Willaim G.

Private First Class
Barnhill, John R.
Beck, Don R.
Cline, Marshall E. Jr.
Creech, Harmon
Dannels, Jack R.
Duhon, William L.
Edwards, James E.
Esquivil, Fred P.
Frank, Wendell H.
Gassner, Albert C.
Gassner, Richard
Haas, Eugene B.
Harris, Thomas A.
Jones, Raymond E.
Kellenberger, Kay
Kidwell, Erbie L.
King, Daniel T.
Lashley, James M.
Manus, Herman G.
McCool, Joseph B.
McCarthy, Patrick E.
Moon, Robert F.
Nay, Roley Jr.
Nordlund, Urho W.
Oubre, Raymond
Queen, Delmar G.
Richardson, Robert S.
Rizzo, Peter
Rogers, Thomas G. Jr.
Rumfelt, William G.
Schmitt, Robert L.
Schmittou, James B.
Setzer, Carl E.
Speer, Willard H.
Stepp, Lawrence D.
Strickland, Melvin D.
Sullivan, John L.
Sullivan, William H.
Taber, Lester
Giarrusso, Clarence B.
Owens, William G.

Privates
Cottingham, Douglas P.
Daniels, Donald A.
Denton, Clarence F.
Floyd, John R.
Jett, John Harvey
Leath, Truman O.
Owens, Robert E.
Peacock, Gilbert H. Jr.
Petty, Thomas G.
Rowe, James N.
Silz, Joseph J.
Simon, Jimmy
Vulgamore, Vic

Pharmacist's Mate Second Class
Gregor, Rex H.

Corpsman Amputates Marine's Leg During Jap Bombing Attack
by Sgt. Winthrop A. Cady of Salt Lake City, a Marine Corps combat correspondent published in the *Sun Star* Washington, DC, January 2, 1944

SOMEWHERE IN THE SOUTH PACIFIC (Delayed) – A Navy hospital corpsman, Rex H. Gregor of Rochester, Minn., who never had seen such an operation, amputated a wounded marine's leg during a bombing raid.

Gregor, a Pharmacist's Mate second class, went aboard a flaming craft, braving Japanese bombs and exploding ammunition, to rescue medical equipment. Later, he exposed himself to Jap bombs to stay with two of his patients he could not get to shelter.

"In a month of action on Vella LaVella in the Central Solomons I saw many heroic deeds, but none to compare with Gregor's actions," said First Lt. Grant J. Limegrover, 23, of Wilikinsburg, Pa., who was in charge of the marine detachment with which Gregor was serving.

While their big landing barges still were being unloaded on the beach, three Jap dive bombers came over Lt. Limegrover's men, an anti-aircraft unit, shot down two of the planes, but the third scored a direct hit on the craft.

Gregor dashed to the vessel and with a party of volunteers boarded the flaming craft to bring off 14 wounded men.

"We started to carry the wounded off, but as we neared the ramp with them, ammunition there began to go off and we were forced to get them over the side to a crew in the water," he said. "When I began treating the wounded. I found most of my medical supplies still were on the burning craft so I went back and got some blood plasma and all the other supplies I could carry."

"One of the boys had a leg almost blown off," Gregor continued. "There wasn't a doctor there and he had to have immediate treatment. I called for an ambulance, gave him a sedative removed the remainder of his leg the best I could with equipment available, put clamps on the arteries, gave him some blood plasma and sent him to a field hospital."

Lt. Limegrover said the physician informed him the victim had a good chance to recover, thanks to Gregor's speedy work.

Warrior Without a Gun

When bombs come crashing down ... when shells scream and whine on the world's battlefields ... when the fighting is the thickest and the hardest – then you will always find a "warrior without a gun." In the Army he is the Medical Corps soldier, in the Navy, the hospital corpsman.

He has no weapons yet he walks in the wake of fighting soldiers, caring for their wounds as they fall. On the islands of the Pacific, Jap snipers have planted themselves above the marines and soldiers fallen in battle – to pick off medical corpsmen. Yet these warriors have gone into the fray, their armbands signifying their mission of mercy; they have gone into the face of death without weapons.

One of these men was Pharmacist's Mate, Second Class, USN.R., Rex H. Gregor. Twenty-one years old, he hailed from Rochester, Minnesota. From the moment he entered the Pacific combat zone, he impressed his superior officers as the kind. of "medic" to whom the word fear had no meaning. Some of them kidded Rex about this lack of fear, remarking "The way Rex has it figured, his job is to save the lives of others. So nothing can happen to him!"

Said First Lieutenant Grant J. Limegrover 23, of Wilkinsburg, Pennsylvania, who was in charge of the Marine detachment with whom Rex was serving. "In a month of action on Vella LaVella, I saw many heroic deeds, but none to compare with Gregor's actions."

On the opening day of the landing at Vella LaVella, Rex was right there in the front lines. The landing barges have not yet unloaded all of the troops. Suddenly, three Jap divebombers swept down on these seemingly defenseless ships. As the first two enemy plants roared down, they went right smack into a hail of anti-aircraft fire and continued their dive right into the sea. But the third Jap plane found its mark and soon one of the landing ships was a mass of flames.

Witnessing this attack on shore was Hospital Corpsman Rex Gregor. While men streamed from the blazing ship, Rex had but one thought. He had to get back to the landing ship. For an it were all the medical supplies he might be able to get his hands on for a long time to come. He couldn't let it go up in smoke. He just couldn't.

And so reversing the usual trend, Rex Gregor headed for what should have been certain death, boarding a vessel ablaze from stem to stern. Weaving between the long tongues of flame, shuddering each time live ammunition exploded from the heat, he reached his valued cache of supplies. At last, weighed down with medical supplies and invaluable blood plasma, he came out of the ship unhurt, miraculously alive.

But once he came to shore, he could not even sit down to rest from his hair-raising experiences. Another Jap air raid began. Rex swung into the task of saving wounded marines from the angry enemy bombs that were now bursting all along the beachhead.

One of the boys had a leg almost blown off. The marine's face was a picture of extreme pain and Rex knew something would have to be done and done quickly. He scoured his section of the beachhead and couldn't locate a doctor – all of them were in more advanced positions.

So Rex Gregor was placed in a dilemma. The wounded Marine needed immediate leg amputation. An unprofessional job could result in the man's death. No operation at all would mean a painful demise. He had to make a decision and make one quickly.

With a prayer in his heart, he called for an ambulance and gave the marine a sedative. He was going to perform the operation himself. His mind was a whirling dervish of pictures – mental pictures of all that he had ever learned in his Navy training, pictures of textbook pages he had studied during free moments aboard ship – pictures and pictures and now – the real thing.

Though his heart pounded nervously, his brain and fingers became cold, thinking mechanisms. The operation had to be successful.

He sterilized all of the instruments he had salvaged from the blazing landing ship. Then he proceeded to the task at hand. As assistants he had a few of his fellow hospital corpsman. For tense, agonizing minutes, he worked, put clamps on the wounded soldier's arteries and worked his scalpel.

Then, the operation over, Rex Gregor sat down for a much deserved rest. But he could not rest until word came back from the field hospital that doctors had examined the amputation and reported it a success, This inexperienced navy man had performed a delicate operation with great skill.

In the days that followed, Rex proved himself a hero time and time and time again. During the heaviest air raids, he could be daring the fates as he dashed about from foxhole to foxhole giving aid and comfort to wounded men. Yes – Rex and his kind are truly great warriors – warriors without weapons.

Memo From Brigadier General Donald M. Schmuck, USMC (RET) Triangle S Ranch Buffalo, Wyoming 62834 3 October 1994

From: Brigadier General Donald M. Schmuck, USMC (Ret)

To: General Carl E. Mundy, USMC

Subj:Vella LaVella, Solomon Islands, September, 1943

1. I have perused with keen interest the series of HQMC monographs covering Marine combat operations in the Pacific 50 years ago. These excellent studies, however, served to reinforce an impression reached by me earlier that the official records and historical accounts of one small bloody, but successful, Marine engagement in the Central Solomons are apparently incomplete. That operation was the landing of a provisional task force an Vella LaVella, September 25, 1943. In paragraph 4 of this letter, I will propose to correct this oversight.

2. In March of this year, correspondence with former Navy Corpsman Rex Gregor and retired Major Grant Limegrover convinced me that it was high time to bring this matter to the personal attention of the Commandant of the Marine Corps. Enclosure 1 is a copy of that correspondence. The remaining enclosures attached herein are directly related to the Vella LaVella action and cover the recent efforts by the Marines of a small unit of the task force (3d Platoon, Battery A, 3d Special Weapons Battalion, 3d Marine Division) to locate a unit commendation which they were informed was signed by General Turnaget but presumably not delivered because their outfit was disbanded shortly after the Bougainville operation. This commendation was one of two which I wrote for the general's signature on Guadalcanal just prior to our landing on Bougainville. The commendation for the platoon leader, 1st Lt. Grant Limegrover, was delivered (Encl 2) – but not the one for the platoon, which I considered equally important. Fortunately, I have the original platoon commendation (Encl 3) which I indicated in my letter to Lt. Limegrover, dated Feb. 16, 1944, (Encl 4) had been signed by General Turnage. I

will make this copy available to these deserving Marines who have waited half a century for this recognition. With regard to Navy Corpsman Gregor's recommendation for the Medal of Honor, I can only presume that this was downgraded during review along the upper chain of command to the Silver Star ultimately awarded by Admiral Halsey (Encl 3).

3. I must report that when the platoon leader, now Major Grant Limegrover, USMCR (Ret), contacted the Military Awards Branch of the Human Resources Division at HQMC on this matter, the head of that branch, F.P. Anthony, wrote that they could not discover any pertinent records, and then further announced, by direction of the Commandant of the Marine Corps, that: "A review of the records fails to reveal any record of Major Donald Schmuck." It is an understatement to say that I am chagrined personally to discover that I am expunged from the records of an important HQMC staff division, after a proud lifetime in the Corps, several wars and numerous combat honors. (see Encl. 6)

4. As the commanding officer and senior survivor of the landing in Vella LaVella, September 25, 1943, 1 have long since concluded that I should endeavor to fill out the hazy records of that particular operation. To assist in this work, I will hope to call on the Historical Branch to unearth such records as may exist, and the Navy to identify the command afloat and the identity of the troop-carrying APD's and LSTs (several of which were destroyed or damaged during the action at Ruravai beach the morning of the initial landing and later when other troop elements, such as the Paramarines, were also attacked on their arrival.)

5. Although the small provisional force under my command (two put-together rifle companies, an AA platoon, a motor transport section, and various supporting elements) landed at Ruravai, Vella LaVella – on the wrong beach – at dawn after a night run from Guadalcanal, then still under nightly bombing, with orders to clear out any enemy and establish an advance base for the Choiseul raid and later Bougainville assault – and should have been a minor event in the overall picture – the Japanese reaction to this landing in their area was major in every sense – they attacked with large formations of low-flying bombers, we suffered 32 KIA and 58 WIA, and our amphibious fleet had several ships destroyed or heavily damaged. My AA unit – 3d Plat,

Batt A, 3d SW Bn, 3d Mar Div – fighting under constant enemy air attack, and suffering losses of men and equipment, was officially credited with shooting down four enemy planes. Even when reenforced several days later by an Army 90mm AA battery from New Georgia, the enemy was able to avoid friendly air cover and attack the landing of our Paramarines with substantial losses of unit materiel and some casualties. In terms of combat results and American bloodshed, therefore, this operation obviously deserves an honored position in Marine Corps history, even if it lacked the media attention given to other better known adventures of the time.

6. In attempting to assemble a factual account on this hectic long-ago chapter in World War II history, I anticipate numerous obstacles: 50 years of fading memory, the lack of an after action report, no muster roll or troop list, missing operation order, as well as the one hazy air photo available, or the hand written report of Australian coast watcher on the island. The most important record in my possession is a faded notebook in which I made daily entries on the action – frequently while under enemy attack. These notes contain, as well, my observations of a naval battle fought between our beach and Kolombangara in the Vella Gulf in which ships were lost on both sides. Although not as large as the Vella Gulf battle in August of that year, we on Vella LaVella at the time did not know it as we huddled in our holes on the beach with rifles, fixed bayonets, machine guns, and grenades, ready to repel the enemy. The next morning when I reconnoitered the sea to our front in a salvaged LCVP, we found the area littered with wreckage, unexploded torpedoes, and bodies – some in parachutes – but no identifiable friendlies were found.

7. I am convinced that a proper account of this operation could be a text book example of how the war was some times waged during the early days in the South Pacific – of a hastily contrived amphibious operation launched without proper enemy intelligence or reconnaissance, with a confusing chain of command (they neglected to inform me that the 1st Amphibious Corps on New Caledonia was in charge – not the 3d Marine Division on Guadalcanal), with inadequate medical personnel, communications, antiaircraft capabilities, as well as little if any air and naval cover. The young Navy Captain in command of the amphibious task force knew even less than I did

about the situation except that the "Slot" was a deadly dangerous place for his group of slow moving vessels, and he wanted me and my troops off his ships ASAP! I can never forget the gut-wrenching experience of standing there on the open bridge with the captain at dawn midst those enemy held islands, I in full Marine combat gear armed to the teeth, he in gold braid and starched khaki, both of us searching desperately for a beach suitable for landing on that dense jungle shore – and me steadfastly insisting that it was his responsibility to say "land the landing force" as well as where and when – just as I had been instructed in Basic School. History should record that the Marines did land and that although the enemy gave them a warm welcome, we got the job done.

SEMPER FIDELIS

DONALD M. SCHMUCK
Brigadier General, U. S. Marine Corps Retired

Enclosures:

(1) a. Ltr from Rex Gregor.
b. Reply by BGen Schmuck.
c. Ltr from Maj Limegrover.
(2) Commendation for Limegrover.
/s/MG Turnage
(3) Commendation for 3d Plat
A Bat, 3d SW Bn, 3d Mar Div
(4) Maj Schmuck ltr to Lt Limegrover dtd Feb 16, 1944
(5) Citation Silver Star to
Rex Gregor /s/ Adm Halsey
6) Ltr from Hd Military Awards Branch to Maj Limegrover dtd 18 May,1993

AN INCREDIBLE JOURNEY
On December 24, 19431 after 100 consecutive days in combat on the Islands of Guadalcanal, Vella LaVella and Bougainville in the South Pacific a messenger came to my First kid Station (I was a medical corpsman in the Marine Corps) with a request that I report to the Command Post at Division Headquarters immediately. When I reached the Command Post I was told that Admiral Halsey wished to see me. In a few minutes a Marine Major came out and told me that the Admiral was in conference with General Turnage, the 3d Marine Division Commandant but he wanted me to have this ... and he handed me a sheet of paper. It read, "Upon receipt of these

orders and when directed by proper a u - thority you will proceed via first available transport on to the US Naval Station in San Francisco, California for further assignment to Officers Training School." These orders were a complete and total surprise and as I stood there in shock – hardly believing what I read, the officer said, "There are some ships out in the bay and it I were you I would got my butt on one as soon as I could. Good luck." I later learned my Commanding Officer Grant Limegrover had recommended me for the medals I received and for selection to Officers Training.

That night as I stood on the deck of the ship going down the "slot" to Guadalcanal where I would obtain transportation to the States, I promised myself that someday I would return.

Through the years I have harbored a strong desire to retrace my war time steps in the South Pacific and this past February it became a reality. Arlene had agreed to go with me and we had worked on our plans for more than two years. It was our plan to travel to Upolu (British Western Samoa), New Zealand, Australia, Now Caledonia, Guadalcanal, Vella LaVella, Bougainville, and Fiji. I had made the initial invasions on Vella LaVella and Bougainville and both of these islands were high on my priority list. In January we were advised that the State Department had restricted travel to Bougainville due to native unrest and fighting on that island. Reluctantly we scrubbed Bougainville from our travel destinations.

Pearl Harbor was the first leg of ur journey. It was proper that we start our trip here as this was where it had all started. Arlene had a friend who was killed during that infamous attack and we paid our respects to him and the thousands who lost their lives on that Sunday morning more than fifty years ago.

The second leg of our journey was a 11-1/2 hour flight to Melbourne, Australia, where we were met at the airport by Jeanette Adams and her parents Don and Pauline Hutt. Jeanette and Leo Adams own a travel agency and are friends of Ruth and Mel. An instant bond of friendship developed, and we were guests of Don and Pauline in their home. Don and Pauline took us on a tour of Victoria (a province in Australia). This truly was one of the most fantastic experiences of our lives. The Hutts spared nothing in making this portion of our trip most enjoyable. We were mesmerized by the friendliness of the people, the beauty of their country, and the hospitality of the Hutts..

We stayed three nights at the Haven Motor Lodge in Bright, Australia, a wellknown resort area. Betty and Dennis Burt, owners of the motel, arranged for a bus to tour the sights. The area is known for it's beautiful flower gardens and we were given private tours of many of these. On our last night Dennis and Betty gave a barbecue in our honor, and the next morning when we checked out of the motel they refused to accept pay stating simply that we were their personal guests.

While in Australia we had an opportunity to meet and visit with Desmond Sidington. Desmond was a Private in the Australian Army and served with the 15th Brigade of the 57/60th Infantry Battalion which was attached to the 3d Marine Division on Bougainville. Desmond's outfit landed on Cape Torokino on the 14th of November, 1943. Their unit was split and for a couple of weeks they were without medical personnel. Desmond, along with several of his comrades, had come to my First Aid Station for sick call – mostly to pick up that little yellow tablet we took to prevent malaria attacks. we had a great visit. It was almost unbelievable that our paths should cross after 50 years.

On our return to Melbourne we spent a night at a sheep ranch. In Australia and New Zealand, they have what is known as "farm stays, beach stays, and home stays." This is where you stay with a family in their home, live and eat with them. I mention this experience in our journey only to tell you that once again our stay was at no charge.. We were "guests" and our hosts refused to accept pay.

After a bon-voyage party given by Jeanette and Leo Adams, we flew to Cairns, Australia where we visited the Great Barrier Reef and the rainforest. The beauty of the land and the friendliness of the people made a deep and lasting impression. We found this to be one of the great wonders of the world.

Jeanette and Leo had worked hard to make reservations and complete travel arrangements; however, due to the primitive conditions on Vella LaVella, they were not able to make arrangements for this leg of our journey. There was no scheduled public transportation to Vella and the best we could hope for, should we be able to find a bush pilot or a private boat to take us there, was to stay with some native plantation owner, and if this were possible we needed to take our own provisions with us.

Our flight to Guadalcanal had been

confirmed along with reservations at the Honiara Hotel. Honiara, Guadalcanal, has developed into a semi-modern metropolitan area with two major hotels, a Rotary Club, and a travel agency. There are taxis and Avis has a rental car service. We were told that the best we could do would be to contact the Guadalcanal Travel Service after we arrived and they would see what they could do to get us to Vella LaVella. They would not even attempt to make any arrangements until after we arrived and the only information we could get in regard to cost was that "it depends."

Do you believe in miracles? We do! At the airport in Cairns, while we were awaiting our flight to Guadalcanal, I was depressed. After two years of planning we had to scrub our trip to Bougainville. I had participated in the initial invasion of that island and spent more than 60 days of front line combat in some of the bitterest and most costly fighting of the war, and now at the last minute I had no assurance that we could even get to Vella LaVella where my outfit was also the initial landing force against an enemy that outnumbered us more than ten to one, and whom, incidentally, we defeated.

As I sat there discouraged and depressed, a well-dressed gentlemen sat down beside me. He introduced himself as Jurgen Vetter, a contractor and land developer from Cairns. He was on his way to Guadalcanal on a business trip. In the conversation that followed, I told him of my desire to get to Vella LaVella.

"You want to get to Vella LaVella?" he asked. "No problem, I will make the arrangements for you. When you get to Honiara check into your hotel and don't leave until you hear from me." About an hour after we checked into our hotel Jurgen arrived. "Arrangements are all made," he announced. "You will fly to Vella the day after tomorrow on the SDA airlines." The SDA airlines, we were told, was the Seventh Day Adventist Church missionary plane. My dream of returning to Vella LaVella was going to become a reality. Jurgen said he would like us to meet some friends of his, Janita and Rodger Radford. The Radfords own a very successful boat manufacturing business on Guadalcanal.

Shortly after the war Janita's parents (Australians) purchased the island of Liapari, a small island located no more than 500 feet off the southern tip of Vella LaVella and just a few miles from the old Marine air base on Vella. During the war the Navy had built docking facilities on Liapari – the bay between Vella and Liapari is a naturally protected lagoon.

The Radfords had built a resort on the island of Liapari, complete with modern bungalows. Among other things the resort was used as a religious retreat for the Japanese. Many Japanese believe that in order to go to Heaven, the relatives must return to the place of death, hold a religious ceremony which releases the spirit so it can ascend into Heaven. Thousands upon thousands of Japanese were killed in the Kolombangaro straits adjacent to Vella LaVella, and for many years the resort on Liapari prospered like no other. In addition Janita's husband, who is an engineer, started a boat works on Liapari and it too grew and prospered. Some years later the Radfords moved their boat works to Honiara, Guadalcanal which had become the industrial trade center of the Solomon Islands. They, however; maintained the resort on Liapari and had natives care for it.

From the moment we met the Radfords an instant friendship evolved and Janita invited us to stay at their resort. Liapari is about a 15 minute boat ride from the airstrip on Vella, and Janita arranged to have boat a pick us up at the airstrip. Incidentally the airstrip on Vella was the flight base for Pappy Boyington and the Black Sheep of World War II fame. Just a few miles away is "Kennedy Island" where Lt. John F. Kennedy's PT Boat 109 was sunk.

The pilot of the twin-engine six-passenger plane was a young man from Toronto, Canada. He was going to school in Gary, Indiana, studying to become a Seventh Day Adventist missionary. He was a skilled pilot and landed that plane on a dime on those short runways carved out of the jungle. We landed at four other islands before we reached Vella - New Georgia, Munda, Gizo, and Kolombangaro.

Arlene was deeply impressed with the beauty of the Coral Sea.

When our aircraft landed at Vella, there was a large group of natives standing along the runway. As I was helping the pilot unload our luggage I asked him if he always had that big a crowd to meet him. "No", he replied, "they are here to meet you."

Some young native boys gathered our luggage and carried it across the airstrip to the waiting boat. Some of the more aggressive would come up and shake our hands and welcome us to their island. A few of the more timid would ease up close to us then gently reach out and touch us.

Before we left Guadalcanal, Janita had told us that Rodger used to have a native work for him by the name of Vivian Maeke. "Mikey" had served in the Australian Army during the war as a Coastal Watcher on Vella LaVella. Coastal Watcher was another name for spy. Janita told us she would try to contact Mikey (they had radio contact with Liapari) and maybe he could help us find the exact spot where our Marine Platoon had landed.

At Liapari we were met by a group of natives including two native women, Grace and Oelena. Grace and Oelena were caretakers of the bungalows on Liapari and they dedicated themselves to make our stay as comfortable as possible. They anticipated our every possible need and took care of us like we were royalty.

Shortly after we were settled in our bungalow, Mikey arrived. He stood looking at me for a moment then said, "I know you."

When our Marine unit invaded Vella LaVella, our unit consisted of a Platoon of 70 men. We landed at a place called Ruruvai. Unknown to us at the time there was a battalion of Japanese soldiers about 500 yards up the beach. A battalion is approximately 1,200 troops.

The Japanese had conscripted somewhere near three or four hundred natives and used them as a work party. They paid them in paper money which they had printed for that purpose. The money was useless to the natives because there was nothing they could spend it on and no place to spend it.

Mikey, through his intelligence sources, was anticipating our arrival. When he realized where our landing site was, he knew our unit would be in deep trouble, for a platoon of 70 men would hardly be a match for a battalion of 1,200 enemy soldiers. Placing his life on the line, Mikey infiltrated the Japanese camp and started a rumor among the natives that the Marines had landed at Ruruavi with a division of troops – a division is 18,000 troops. Apparently the rumor reached the Japanese Commander and he believed it because that night he evacuated his troops to Kolombangaro an island seven miles across the straits from Vella.

Admiral Morrissey, in his *History of The South Pacific War*, wrote that "The Japs in their official report of the action had written that they evacuated their troops in face of a murderous attack by a 'Division of Enemy Soldiers.'"

Two days after we had landed, Mikey came to my First Aid Station. He had injured his arm and it was infected. I treated it for him and we subsequently became friends. Now, 50 years later, we stood face to face in an emotional reunion.

Mikey and I talked until late in the evening, and from that moment on he was our constant companion. He would be with us when we got up in the morning and stay with us until we went to bed at night. He walked for more than an hour through the jungle trails to and from Sambora Village, where he lived, each night and morning.

I was anxious to visit the exact spot where we had landed, and Mikey agreed to arrange for a motorized canoe and volunteered to escort us there. (See map of Vella LaVella) It was a 1-3/4-hour trip each way.

We were to leave the next morning at 8:00 AM; however, before we got started it rained – a typical tropical downpour. It was nearly 10 o'clock before it quit. As we were getting ready to board the canoe Mikey advised us that they did not have enough "petrol" to make the trip and it would be necessary to go across the bay to get some. I suggested to Mikey that he and the canoe driver, a native by the name of Wally Wukaloo, get the petrol then stop and pick us up on the way back. However, Mikey insisted we go with them. It was only a short trip across the bay to a warehouse where some natives were loading copra on a barge. As soon as we landed, a large group of natives crowded around our canoe and stood on the beach. Several young native boys helped us out of the canoe and guided us up on the beach where this crowd of people stood. Several of them came up and shook our hands and welcomed us to their island. I suddenly noticed this native who had on a bright orange T-shirt – he was pushing his way through the crowd and walking with a bad limp. He came up to me and threw his arms around me and hugged me. "You saved my life," he said. "I would not be able to walk if it weren't for you." I had nearly forgotten the incident he was talking about, and frankly I had never considered it a life saving effort. About two weeks after we had landed some natives had brought this eight-year-old boy to my First Aid Station. He had apparently stepped on a Japanese land mine or possibly accidentally detonated an unexploded shell. At any rate, the calf of his leg and his foot was badly mangled. I cleaned his wounds and sprinkled them with sulfanilamide powder and bandaged his leg with splints. Later, when the 77th Seabee Battalion landed to build the airstrip at Pusisama, I took him down to their camp and the doctor with the Seabees (Dr. J.J. Korn) treated and cared for his leg. When we parted, Leashe Magila had tears in his eyes and he gripped my hand so hard I thought he was going to crush it. Although Mikey did not tell me, I think he arranged for us to meet. For both Arlene and I this was a very emotional experience. Incidentally Leashe had walked for more than two hours through the rain and jungle to be there to meet us.

It was nearly noon before we finally got the petrol and were on our way to Ruruvai. (See map.) We were traveling in a native dugout canoe that was about 12- or 14- feet-long with a five horse motor. There were no seats in the canoe. We had to sit in the bottom with our legs stretched out in front of us. Not exactly a very comfortable position to be riding for 1-3/4 hours. It was not until we were about one mile offshore heading for Ruruvai that I realized there were no life jackets or oars in the canoe. Would you believe that just about then the motor sputtered and nearly stopped, but Wally got it going again. In fact, it did this several times on the way up and back but each time Wally got it going. Needless to say we held our breath.

I had told Mikey that as soon as we reached Ruruvai and we touched shore, I wanted to go straight to the spot where I had dug my foxhole that first night. As we headed into shore, I recognized the spot where we landed nearly 50 years ago and the thoughts of our experience flashed back in my memory. As we reached the beach a group of natives were waiting for us, as they were every place we went. Some native boys helped us from the canoe and before I had a chance to head towards the jungle Mikey took Arlene and I by the arm and led us down the beach about 25 feet. There in the undergrowth was a monument about 3-1/2- to 4- feet high. There was a copper plate on two sides of the monument. It was very difficult to read the embossed words, as the copper was badly tarnished and the monument showed its age from the savage treatment of the tropical environment. We were able to decipher most of the words. It read .....

"On 25 September 1943 the 3d Platoon, 3rd Special weapons Battalion landed here and brought freedom to our island."

Below this was listed the names of the Marines in the 3d Platoon who were killed. On the other side were the names of the Navy Personnel that were killed. It gave the numbers of the LSTs but I could not

make them out. Mikey told me the monument was placed there by "his people." He also told me that we were the first Americans to see the monument. He couldn't remember exactly when it was placed (he helped put it there) .... he thought it was about 1949 or 1950. Both Arlene and I were deeply touched and the memories of that day flashed before me. I was deeply moved. "A few good men" .... the 70 men of the 3d Platoon, 3d Special Weapons Battalion, 3d Marine Division, without regard for their own lives, fought bravely and left their mark in history.

I found the place where I had placed my First Aid Station and where Lt. Grant Limegrover had his command post. Much to my chagrin I could not find my fox hole – not even a slight depression in the ground.

The invasion of Vella LaVella was made on two LSTs escorted by several destroyers. At this stage of the war the Japanese had air superiority; in fact, we had no air coverage at all and the Japanese attack us like sitting ducks.

When we loaded the LSTs at Guadalcanal, I was assigned to LST #2. In a combat situation, my jeep ambulance and medical supplies were loaded first as they came off the ship last – combat equipment came off first to engage the enemy. Just as we were getting ready to leave, my Commanding officer, Grant Limegrover, asked me which LST I was on. When I told him LST #2, he said, "No way. I want you on LST #1 with me. In case we have conflict with the enemy I want to be able to communicate with you." We decided that the two litter bearers would be billeted on LST #2, and immediately upon landing they would bring the jeep ambulance and medical supplies to me.

Our landing sites were in two small lagoons on either side of a peninsula that jutted out in the ocean at a place called Ruruvai. Our battle plan was to form a pincer movement and take the peninsula, then dig in our gun positions. Our orders were that all personnel, equipment and supplies were to be unloaded and the ships back at sea within 20 minutes of touching shore. From that point on we were told we would be on our own, and it would be at least two weeks before any reinforcements would reach us.

Immediately upon touching shore, a formation of Japanese dive bombers appeared. The first wave consisted of three planes. The lead plane peeled out of formation and dove at the LST I was on. We

shot the plane down and it crashed in the jungle. His bomb missed our ship and exploded just off the starboard bow. The other two planes dove at LST #2. Both of these planes were shot down. One crashed in the ocean and the other in the jungle; however, both pilots managed to release their bombs and they struck the ship just forward of the bridge.

I saw a huge cloud of black smoke rise above the jungle, and I knew the ship had been hit and there was no doubt some causalities. In spite of the fact that there might be Jap snipers along the jungle trail, I raced across the peninsula. When I reached LST #2, they were bringing the killed and wounded off the ship. I found a depressed area along the jungle's edge that offered some protection from the second wave of enemy planes that were now bombing and strafing the beach. I instructed the litter bearers to gather the wounded there and asked where my jeep ambulance and medical supplies were. I was told they were still aboard the LST. There was no way I could treat the wounded without my medical supplies, and I desperately needed the blood plasma. I had to return to the LST in an attempt to get them.

I raced up the gang plank of the LST into the hold of the ship. About one-third the way into the ship's hold, I was confronted by an inferno of burning gasoline drums and I could go no further. At the forward bow of the ship there was a ladder to the main deck. I climbed the ladder and headed towards the fantail where I knew there was another ladder that led down into the back compartment of the ship where my jeep ambulance was located. One of the bombs had apparently struck just forward of the bridge, and the heat and flames from some gasoline drums stored there was causing the ammunition in the main magazine to explode. I put my head down and raced through this blazing inferno of hell and I came through with nary a scratch.

I climbed down the ladder into the back compartment of the ships hold to my jeep ambulance. It was dark and smoky, and I could not see. The ship's engines were dead and there was no electricity. I cannot account for the next actions that occurred other than to say it was a miracle. I knew that on every Navy ship there was a sickbay and that part of the standard equipment was flashlights. I had never been in an LST's sickbay in my life, and I only had a faint idea where it might be located. I climbed back up the ladder and the first hatchway I came to, I opened and it was the sickbay. Inside there were shelves and drawers .... the first drawer I opened had two flashlights. I found my jeep ambulance but I had difficulty carrying the flashlight along with an armful of medical supplies at the same time. A thought suddenly occurred to me. I pulled on the headlights of the jeep ambulance as well as all the other vehicles parked in the hold. It lit up the whole place, and I carried my medical supplies and equipment topside. There were a couple of Marines and a native on shore and I hollered to them. I threw my supplies over the side. They fished them out of the water and took them ashore. My last trip was with blood plasma. By this time the fire by the bridge was burning completely out of control, and the only way I could get off the ship was to go over the side. There was a line (rope) coiled next to the ship's rail. I tied it to the rail so I could scramble over the side. Just as I started to go over the side I suddenly remembered I had not turned the lights off on the jeep and trucks. Would you

believe that I went back down into the hold of the ship and turned them off. To this day I cannot give a good answer as to what led me to do this. Wave after wave of Jap dive bombers and fighter planes were still bombing and strafing us. The ship was on fire and burning furiously. The main ammunition magazine was minutes away from exploding, and here I am going back down into the hold of the ship to turn off the lights on my jeep ambulance and the other vehicles.

I had told Mikey that I wanted to visit the place where LST #2 landed, as I wanted to take pictures of the spot where I treated the wounded. As we walked across the peninsula that jutted out between the two landing spots, it seemed that we were walking forever. I said to Arlene, "I don't remember it being this far." To Mikey I said, "Are you sure we are on the right trail?" Mikey insisted we were, and Arlene scolded me saying, "Fifty years ago you were a 25-year-old boy and today you are a 70-year-old man. Just be patient."

There was no question we were in the right spot when we reached the sandy beach where the LST landed. The vision of the place was so deeply burned in my memory that I shall never forget it. I was, however, puzzled by the small stream of water that flowed out of the jungle. Mikey explained that we were there during the rainy season and if I came back in September there would be no stream.

I wanted to cross the stream to take pictures of the place where I had gathered the wounded. It was a place just inside the jungle's edge that was slightly depressed and offered some protection from the bombing and strafing. Like magic, the natives produced a small canoe and they helped me into it. On the other side of the stream there was an elderly man waiting for me. He only spoke "pidgin" and as he approached me, he said, "You Marine?"

"Yes," I replied.

"Airplane boom boom ship," he said. Then looking at me for a moment, he said, "I help you."

When I went back aboard the LST to get my medical supplies I had to throw them over the side. Two marines and a native fished them out of the water. Later this same native used his machete to cut sticks to hang the bottles of blood plasma. It was almost unbelievable that this same native should be there 50 years later. He wanted very badly for us to visit his village, Lambu Lambu. It was too late in the day to make the trip – a two-hour walk through the jungle trails. Reluctantly we had to disappoint him. In all the excitement I forgot to write down his name. Mikey agreed to get it and send it to me.

Mikey told me that three of the planes we shot down crashed in the ocean and two crashed in the jungle. He told me that those that crashed in the jungle were still there. I wanted very badly to get to at least one of them to take pictures and get a piece of the wing or fuselage, but Mikey would not let us. He said the jungle was too dense and it was a very difficult walk to get to them.

That night the natives had a barbecue on Liapari and we were the guests of honor, an experience that will live with us the rest of our lives.

From the Solomons we flew to New Zealand. In Auckland, we were met at the airport at 1:00 in the morning by Rob and Theresa Hood. Rob is a friend and pen pal of Grant Limegrover, and they surprised us by meeting us at the airport. Rob and Theresa opened their arms to us with a warm and friendly welcome. The next day Rob drove us to the Marine base where I had trained, and their hospitality was unexcelled. I enjoyed revisiting all the old spots where I spent my hours of liberty in Auckland. Theresa's twin sister Joan and her husband Keith joined in making our visit unforgettable, and we stayed at their home overnight. There are no words in the

English language to describe the warmth of their hospitality.

Jeanette Adams had made arrangements for us to have a "farm stay" while in New Zealand. Les Brownlee drove to Auckland and picked us up. Judy, his wife, and their teenage children, Melissa, Fluer, and James, opened their home to us and for three days they surrounded us with warm hospitality, good food, new sights, and a warm and loving friendship. In New Zealand, farm stays are a commercial venture. When it came time for us to leave and I was going to pay Les the agreed upon amount he said, "I cannot accept money from you. You have become our friends and we do not accept money from friends." The impact of this gesture left us speechless.

Our trip to Upolu (British Western Samoa) was the only disappointing part of our trip. When I trained for jungle warfare on this island it would be fair to say that it was then the closest place to Utopia in the world. The beauty of the island, the friendliness of the people, was unexcelled. Although there are still pockets of beauty and some of the friendliness and hospitality of the natives still exists, the port of entry, Apia, has turned into a garbage pit of humanity where greed and poverty is rampant. The visit to Robert Louis Stevenson's home and a meeting with the Reverend Maufafoa, son of a friend I made while there in early 1943, saved this portion of our trip from being a disaster.

On Fiji we stayed at the Fijian Resort. We arrived at night and left two nights later and did not get to see much of the island. The resort was spectacular, the weather perfect, the food excellent, the service great, and the people friendly. We can highly recommend this for a South Pacific vacation.

The next leg of our journey took us to the island of Maui in Hawaii for a few days of R & R (rest and relaxation). Upon arrival I wanted to rent a car. While I was making the arrangements, Arlene was guarding our luggage. She started a conversation with another lady who was doing the same. The lady asked where we had been and when Arlene mentioned Vella LaVella, the lady said, "My husband was stationed there during the war. We are going to have to get these two guys together." It turned out to be Ned Corman. Ned flew wing with Pappy Boyington of the Black Sheep. I had met Ned once or twice while on Vella but I had gotten to be friends with Pappy. We had dinner and breakfast together, visited and told sea stories for hours on end.

To have our paths cross after 50 years was nothing short of a miracle.

We spent three days in Los Angeles at the home of my cousin Betty Jean O'Connor. My niece Gloria Matoba met us at the airport and we had a long visit and a lovely dinner with her family. It was great spending some time with my sister Betty. On Sunday our niece Vicki Hanson hosted a family reunion. Many family members I had not seen in years were there. This was a very enjoyable way to end our travels. We finished our trip by having dinner with Sgt. Richard (Dick) Davis and his lovely wife Harriet. Dick was one of the great guys in our old Marine outfit. We also squeezed in a breakfast meeting with former neighbors Mel and Pat Sargeant.

I cannot complete this report without paying a special tribute to Arlene. Through all the primitive conditions, the rain, the hot steamy jungles, the dugout canoe, the lizards that crawled on our cots at night, the screaming night birds, and the ever present mosquitoes, she was at my side. When the emotion of the memories touched me deeply, like when I stood at the spot where Jim Edwards died while I was getting ready to give him blood plasma, she was ready with words of comfort and encouragement. When I stood beside the monument that honored our outfit, her words instilled in me a feeling of pride. This indeed is true love.

On September 25, 1993, the 3rd Platoon, 3rd Special Weapons Battalion held its first reunion on the 50th Anniversary of our invasion of Vella LaVella. Seventeen of the 21 surviving members of that platoon were able to attend.

As a result of their personal bravery and valiant devotion to duty, the 3d Platoon was awarded a Unit Commendation for action on Vella LaVella. Due to heavy causalities in the 3d Marine Division on Bougainville, the 3d Special Weapons Battalion was disbanded and absorbed into other units before the Commendation was officially presented. The official presentation was made at our reunion 50 years later.

Mikey, the native Coastal Watcher, was our guest of honor. His trip was made possible by Mr. Charles W. Oswald, Chairman of the Board of National Computer Systems. Charley is a long time friend of mine and an ex-marine.

Mikey spent two weeks with us in our home. We crowded in all the activities possible, including the Mall of America. Mikey, who had never been away from the Solomon Islands, was overwhelmed by what he saw.

During the last week in August Don and Pauline Hutt, our new found friends from Australia, arrived and we had a very enjoyable two weeks together. We are looking forward to a visit from Janita and Rodger Radford in January. It is also our hope that our friends in New Zealand will soon visit us.

It truly was in incredible journey, and we are happy to share it with you. we hope that each of you will have a very Merry Christmas and a New Year that is complete with love, joy, and happiness.

Our Love and Best Wishes,
Rex & Arlene

USS Leonard F. Mason
Newspaper article

The USS Leonard F. Mason was commissioned on June 28, 1946, with Cmdr. S.D.B. Merrill in command.

Following shakedown in the Caribbean, the destroyer joined Des. Div. 32 in the Pacific Ocean Jan. 22, 1947. From 1947 to 1950, the ship completed two cruises in the western Pacific as well as stateside operations. During the early stages of the Korean War, she steamed for the Pacific Nov. 13, 1950 and joined in anti-submarine exercises. On May 16, she joined TF 85 at the siege of Wonsan to fire in the continuous shere bombardment which inflicted heavy damage on enemy bridges, tunnels, and troop concentrations. Departing Wonsan July 23, she steamed for San Diego, arriving Aug. 8, 1951.

After an overhaul, the Mason sailed Feb. 23, 1952 to the Orient and again operated in Wonsan Harbor and along the eastern coast of Korea. Departing Yokosuka Sept. 13, the Mason arrived in Long Beach, Calif., on Sept. 27, and remained there until May 16, 1953 when she again went to Far East. Arriving in Korean waters June 9, she joined TG 70.1 for escort and bombardment action with the battleship New Jersey off Wonsan and in the Yellow Sea.

After the close Korean hostilities the Mason departed Yokosuka Nov. 20, for Long Beach, arrived Dec. 8 and was recalled for peacetime duty. Between 1954 and 1960, the Mason made three more west Pacific cruises.

From May 1960 to May 1962 the Mason was homeported at Yokosuka for anti-submarine patrols and other peacekeeping missions. For the next two years the Mason operated with various task groups of the Seventh Fleet, conducting gunfire support missions off the coast of Vietnam, and serving in the Gemini Recovery Force. On March 17, 1966, when Gemini VIII splashed down southeast of Okinawa, the Mason had astronauts David Scott, Neil Armstrong and their capsule aboard within three hours and was headed for Okinawa.

The Mason received three battle stars for Korean service, and was decommissioned in November 1976. The ship was sold and is now in service with the Taiwanese Navy.

On Golden Pond
by Alan P. Loper
On Golden Pond
The place to be
Serenity and goodness
Surround you and me.
On Golden Pond
Hear the Loons, as they sing
When sweetness and loving,
To all, they bring.

The shimmering of the pond,
The wind through the trees,
God smiles down
On all that He sees.

On Golden Pond
That is the place
To be restful and quiet
and out of the race.

We'll all have the memories
With the wave of our wand,
The wonderful magic of,
On Golden Pond.

To you my comrades,
The joy that you bring,
Thank you and thank you
With joy I will sing

The Gunnery Sergeant Alan P. Loper, Third Marine Association, Wisconsin Chapter will be committed to continue his patriotism, his dedication.
With fondness to all of you.
Semper Fi
Annette Loper

4 Stories
by Gerald F. Merna, 1st Lt., USMC (Ret)
A Vietnam Remembrance
In 1966 I was the Marine Corps escort officer for Roy and Dale when they made a

"handshake visit""to the 3d Marine Division in Vietnam.

What a thrill for me! I'd grown up watching their movies, as well as Tom Mix, Hoot Gibson and Hopalong Cassidy. And, here I had Roy and Dale in person! The only thing that could have improved on that would have been to see Trigger trailing along.

It was a cold, rainy night when they arrived but it didn't seem to faze them one bit. They were decked out in their finest Western garb, six-shooters and all. (Maybe we could have used their help on a few patrols. At the very least, they would have shot the guns out of some of the VC's hands like they always did in their movies.)

I took them around to individual "hutches" to meet the two, three or four Marines that might be huddled in them. Roy and Dale would shake the hand of every Marine they met. Then they'd sit down and tell us all about their adopted children – how and why they adopted them, and how much they loved and missed them. They also made it clear they were thrilled to be visiting with us.

I took a lot of other "stars" around during my tour in 1966 to 1967. They included Robert Stack, Robert Mitchum, Henry Fonda, Wendell Corey and Floyd Patterson. Though all of them were very nice, Roy and Dale stood head and shoulders above all of them in the impression they made on us. As cold as it was, they *exhaled* warmth, friendliness and love. They literally mesmerized us with their presence and their genuine concern and feelings for their fellow man.

I had the pleasure and privilege to hear many of their stories as we went from hut to hut, since they knew they had to shorten their time in some of them in order to make as many visits to Marines as they could.

World War II and Korea had their big USO shows (I was also in Korea) but Vietnam ushered in a whole new era of handshake visits by stars such as Roy and Dale. I will never forget that cold, wet night – seeing two magnificent people ignoring their own discomfort and needs to try and cheer up and brighten the day (night) of a bunch of Marines they were meeting for the first time, and would probably never see again.

I know Roy is "riding into the sunset," as the famous song reminds us. But Roy and Dale will always ride into the memory of the United States Marines they so generously shared their time with, during some very tough times.

Phu Bai, Vietnam: August 1967: L to R: First Lieutenant Gerald F. Merna and Wendell Corey, Actor boarding helicopter to visit troops. Photo courtesy of Gerald F. Merna

July 1967: Center: Floyd Patterson, World Heavyweight Champion 1956-1959 and 1960-1962, visits the 3rd Marine Division. Photo courtesy of Gerald F. Merna

Phu Bai, Vietnam: August 1967: Actor Wendell Corey with members of Third Marine Division Reconnaissance Patrol. Photo courtesy of Gerald F. Merna

A Potentially Deadly "Night Dancing Party"

In the Old Testament, Noah was chosen by God to build an ark to save his family and a pair of every animal from the Flood. While there was no Noah or flood, God was certainly protecting other "pairs" of 3d Marine Division Marines in a similar way on January 7, 1967, in Vietnam.

Major General Wood B. Kyle, the Division's Commander, received some rather unusual invitations from Colonel Ngo Quang Truong, Commander of the Ist Infantry Division, 11th Tactical Region, Army of the Republic of Vietnam (ARVN). The Colonel was inviting pairs of Marine Corps officers of the 3d Marine Division to attend a "Night Dancing Party."

The party would be at what was, prior to the war, a pretty nice hotel in the historic Vietnamese City of Hue, regarded as Vietnam's most beautiful city and once the imperial capital of Vietnam. (Ironically, one year later, January 1968, the Tet Offensive took place. The fierce fighting during that battle seriously destroyed much of that city, including its imperial palace).

Individual written invitations were provided for at least two officers of each rank, i.e., two Lieutenants, two Captains, two Majors, two Lieutenant Colonels and two Colonels. I say "at least" two, since while that adds up to 10 officers, I recall a slightly larger group of maybe 15 in all. Perhaps the Division padded it with a few "extras" for their own reasons. Perhaps because I was on the General's staff at that time, I was one of the Lieutenants selected. (Shown below is the actual invitation I received, written in Vietnamese, which has been in my files all these years.)

Needless to say, there was no Marine then serving in Phu Bai, Vietnam, only miles from Dong Ha and the Demilitarized Zone (DMZ) separating North and South Vietnam, that had any neckties; the only "jackets" we had were flak jackets (armored vests). I did not RSVP to this invitation either, though presumably someone did when they were initially proffered. The invitations were rank generic, and not name specific, e.g., LIEUTENANT, CAPTAIN, MAJOR, LIEUTENANT COLONEL and COLONEL, almost like Noah's general designation for two animals of each description.

I can't recall the names of others in this group selected to attend this party. And we were all rather puzzled what it was all about, until someone said it was a "goodwill'" visit of Americans with Vietnamese counterparts.

We put on our best utilities, and each of us wore our sidearm. Together with a small security force the division provided who were appropriately armed, we boarded our "buses," which consisted of several motor pool trucks. We arrived in the City of Hue around 1730 and located the Huong-Giang Hotel that overlooked the River of Perfumes (shortened to Perfume River) that divided the City. From the outside the hotel appeared to be an attractive building, though showing some of the neglect caused by the war that had been raging for many years. Entering the hotel, we were greeted by a Vietnamese officer and assigned individual rooms. Here's where any semblance of a normal hotel quickly evaporated and reminded us where we were.

While there was running water, it was all cold water. There was no heat in the entire building, and the room was damp and cold. And this was January! Even though we would spend very little time in it, there was a fairly comfortable bed, much better than our sleeping bags in our hootches back at Phu Bai. Overall, it was an unexpected and pleasant change from the mud and rain and other uncomfortable conditions we temporarily left behind.

We had a chance to relax and clean up a little, and at the appointed hour of 2100, still wearing our sidearm, walked into a large ballroom on the third floor. Upon entering the room it was obvious the party was already underway. We saw a fairly large group of Vietnamese men and women; the Officers smartly dressed in uniforms we were not accustomed to seeing them in. Their ladies were also nicely dressed, a few in "western" clothing but most of them in ao dais, a dress Vietnamese women traditionally wore that consisted of a long tunic split on the sides and worn over loose trousers.

We were affably welcomed, and invited to help ourselves to the wine and buffet that had been set up. We didn't need to be told twice, and while I can't remember exactly what food was available (even today I pay little heed to buffets) I remember being thrilled upon seeing the dessert table. It was full of French pastries and other delicacies. I never expected to see such treats again until I got home. Any one who knows me also knows the priority I place on good bread, and almost any kind of pastry or other desserts, with meat and potatoes coming in a poor second! So I picked at whatever real food was there, but satisfied my appetite on the bread and dessert. My fellow officers seemed to enjoy the entire buffet.

It was from this point on that things seemed to take a turn for the worse. There was very little mingling – they were on one side of the room and we were on the other, like bashful boys and girls at a prom. Music was playing both Vietnamese and American music, and several Vietnamese couples were dancing. Two or three of our men, attempting to "break the ice," walked across the room to ask some of the ladies who appeared to be by themselves if they

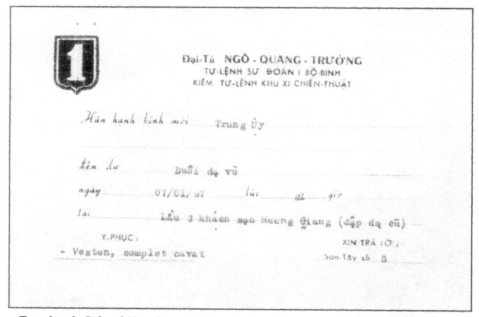

Translated: Colonel Ngo-Quang-Truong Invites Lieutenant to attend a night dancing party that will be held at 07 January 1967 at 2100 at Houng-Giang Hotel (on 3rd floor)

would like to dance. Almost rudely and even discourteously, they were snubbed, ignored or otherwise turned down. It quickly became apparent that we were invited for food and drink, but not to socialize with their ladies. The men only wanted to *dance* with them, not marry them, and were only trying to be friendly in the first place! I remember wondering why in the world they even invited us?

It didn't take long for our senior officer to let us know it was time to "say goodnight, Gracie" (the line George Burns always used on TV to Gracie Allen when he wanted her to break off her renowned yakking and leave with him.) None of us were upset with this decision.

We returned to our rooms, and it seemed like I had just got into the sack when there was a knock on my door and one of our group quietly told me to saddle up, and that we would be leaving in 10 minutes. Not really undressed since I still had my pants and socks on, all I had to do was add my utility top put on my boots, strap on my .45 pistol and proceed to the lobby. Then we got back in our trucks, and left the hotel and Hue between 1:00 and 1:30 a.m. to return to Phu Bai.

The decision to leave very early literally turned out to be a life-saver. The Viet Cong either knew that 3d Marine Division and ARVN officers were staying at this hotel on this night, or, they coincidentally planned an attack on this hotel. Either way, an attack was about to be made on the hotel.

Sometime before dawn and not long after we left, several Viet Cong "sappers" (VC or NVA commandos particularly trained in infiltration and demolition), swam up the Perfume River toward our hotel. Almost naked except for explosives strapped to their bodies, they succeeded in placing their deadly explosives around the hotel. Shortly after accomplishing this, violent explosives wrecked havoc on the hotel. I do not know how many, if any, ARVN officers or their guests, or possibly others staying in the hotel, were wounded or killed. I do know there were no 3d Marine Division Officers injured. It was reported that at least one of the sappers was captured.

So the next time I'm invited to any "night dancing parties," I will consider it "hazardous duty," keep my clothes on after the party, expect anything, and leave early like George Burns always wanted his beloved Gracie to do!

The Trials and Travails of a Mustang Lieutenant

The term "90-day wonder" came into vogue during World War II when a service member completed some fast-paced Officer Candidate School (OCS) and became a commissioned officer after about 90 days in the service. (The Corps takes longer than that for boot camp!). Well I must have been an especially slow learner, because I was an 18-year wonder.

In 1966 the Corps selected over a thousand senior staff noncommissioned officers (SNCOs) for the officer corps. Vietnam was raging, and cannon fodder was sorely needed. Most of us headed for Vietnam within a month or less of the date we were commissioned. I was part of a brief ceremony with several other now former SNCOs at Headquarters Marine Corps in Arlington, VA. The brief ceremony consisted of taking the oath of office while my wife and a two-star General each pinned a gold bar on my shirt collars. I missed the stripes I wore on my sleeves for so many years. I could see them, but not those tiny little bars. But this was quite a thrill nonetheless, and pretty heady stuff after 18 years of enlisted service. Several of my buddies were lined up outside waiting to give the traditional "first salute" so they could get the traditional dollar. While I did pass out a few of those, my wife got the first one, and it was a two dollar bill that she still carries in her wallet today!

Nor were any of us sent to OCS, Basic School, or any other so-called "charm school" to learn the finer points of being a Marine Corps Officer. While it was fun, and very interesting, it was also pure trial and error. I think it took me forever to learn the proper position for wearing the new insignia, and more than once was told I had them on wrong. To begin with, this "promotion" from Master Sergeant E-8 (I was later promoted to Master Gunnery Sergeant E-9 while an officer) to a mere Second Lieutenant was seriously questioned by a lot of my colleagues at the time. "Why," they asked, "would you do such a thing?" My reply was always, "The last time I checked, you have to make Second Lieutenant before you make Colonel!" I wish now that I could foresee then for those doubters how many doors that special opportunity opened for me, even as a mere lieutenant after I retired. As Marines know, when you become an officer and a gentleman by coming up through the enlisted ranks, you are referred to as a Mustang.

In 1952 I volunteered for service in Korea while a Staff Sergeant on recruiting duty in New York/New Jersey. The Officer-in-Charge then was Lt. Col. Lou Wilson, a Medal of Honor winner and future Marine Commandant. Several times my request was refused, being told the Corps had a long waiting list of volunteers. Learning my younger brother, Jim, had his orders for Korea, I earnestly appealed to Col. Wilson to help me get there too. Though he probably thought I was nuts, he came through for me, and in two weeks I had my orders! (A third Marine brother, Richard, would serve there after Jim and I left). In Korea (1952-1953) I made Technical Sergeant (E-

Lt. Col. Leo Donahue, USMC, Division Adjutant, 3d Marine Division, Vietnam, August 1966. Photo courtesy of Gerald F. Merna

6) while serving as a Section Leader of an ATA Platoon of Weapons-1-5, 1st Marine Division. Almost eight months later I was a platoon sergeant with E-2-5 on Outpost Vegas.

Thirteen years later, on August 24, 1966, less than 60 days after being commissioned, I found myself with the 3d Marine Division in Vietnam as a brand new, 36-year old 2nd Lieutenant. Stepping off an airplane in Da Nang, Vietnam, I was completely surprised to be greeted by two field grade officers. One was Lt. Col. Leo Donahue, whom I worked with at Headquarters Marine Corps (when he was a Major) just before I was commissioned; he was Adjutant of the 3d Marine Division. With him was Major Wayne Massey, the Assistant Division Adjutant. In addition to being surprised, I was impressed that they had come to personally welcome a modest Second Lieutenant, until I learned why.

I mentioned to both officers that I *expected* to be assigned to the lst Bn, 4th Marines to work for another officer I also served with at HQMC. He had requested and was expecting me to be assigned to his unit. Imagine my chagrin when Col. Donahue informed me that he was going home soon, that Major Massey would replace him as Adjutant, and I was to be the Asst. Division Adjutant. Though pleased with the confidence they were placing in me, I must have also telegraphed my disappointment. If I had any doubt I was losing ground for my preference, all doubt was removed midway through my second attempt asking to go to the 4th, Marines, Col. Donahue abruptly ended the dialogue. With a half smile, he said, "Nothing has changed, *Lieutenant* Merna. I'll still call you *Jerry* and you can call me *Colonel*. We've been *expecting you* and you are *going* to be the Assistant Adjutant!"

With a salute and a hasty "aye, aye, Sir," I became the Asst. Division Adjutant. Several months later, I became the Division Awards Officer. So much for the 4th Marines! Who knows, perhaps they saved my life that year! Upon reflection, that year in Vietnam, while far from enjoyable, turned out to be a very interesting and memorable one.

Upon returning to the U S in September 1967, 1 spent the following year as Adjutant and Casualty Notification Officer at the Marine Air Reserve Training Detachment (MARTD), Andrews Air Force Base. I was blessed with yet another fine commanding officer, Lt. Col. Ed Rutty, a former

Blue Angel pilot, now deceased. Despite the strong possibility of making Captain in less than six months (my peers all did), the unpleasantness of the casualty notification duty, and the even stronger possibility of another Vietnam tour as a Captain, I acceded to my family's desires and retired. I never looked back and never regretted the decision. I loved my 22 years as a United States Marine, and it was time to devote myself to the family I also loved.

Postscript: A few years after Lt. Col. Donahue and I were both retired, I was able to achieve some small and equally satisfying measure of retribution for that day we first met in Danang. I was the Executive Assistant to the Postmaster General and Donahue was the Executive Director of a DC-based trade association. I don't know how he found me, but he did, and called one day out of nowhere. He said he was very pleased to learn of the position I then held, and volunteered that his association was having serious mailing problems. He wondered if I could "send someone over to help him out." My response came quickly as if I had talked to him the day before. With tongue-in cheek I answered: "Nothing has changed, *Mr. Executive Director*. I will still call you *Leo*, and you can call me *Mr. Merna!*" He instantly understood and remembered that day, and we both had a good and long laugh. I of course helped him out But the moment was delightful!

Semper Fidelis.

A Great Marine Corps General Died In Vietnam Major General Bruno A. Hochmuth, 1911-1967

As a new Mustang 2nd Lieutenant in Vietnam, I had the privilege and unusual opportunity to work closely with two Commanding Generals of the 3d Marine Division. These were Major General Wood B. Kyle from my arrival on 24 August 1966, until he was relieved in a change-of-command ceremony I witnessed on 18 March 1967 by the then Commanding General of III MAF Lieutenant General Lewis W. Walt. On that day General Waft installed Major General Bruno A. Hochmuth as the new Division Commander. I worked for him until my tour ended on 1 September 1967. By the nature of my assignment as the Division's Assistant Adjutant, and even more so as the Division Awards Officer, I was required to meet often with these Division Commanders and Chief of Staff,

Colonel A.D. Cereghino. While I also have positive memories of working for General Kyle and admired his leadership style, I developed an even closer working relationship with General Hochmuth, to whom I dedicate this writing.

In 1996-1997 the 3d Marine Division's Headquarters was based at Phu Bai, about 4-5 miles south of Hue, 35 miles north of Dong Ha, and about 50 miles north of the buffer zone, called both the demarcation line and demilitarized zone (DMZ), which divided North and South Vietnam. In Phu Bai, I especially remember the heavy, sticky mud that made it very difficult not only for vehicles, but also for walking. Vietnam is typically tropical with two main seasons: hot and dry, and hot and wet. The wet season generally begins in mid-April and lasts until mid-October. The rain begins in September and lasts through January.

Marines were entrenched along this DMZ to engage the enemy, stop their infiltration by clearing out guerrilla forces' basic facilities, services and supplies, such as water, rice, and sometimes ammunition, in the villages and hamlets stretching the length of the coastline. Eliminating their long-established infrastructure within each village and hamlet was as important as defeating them in the field. Unlike most other wars, there were really no front lines in Vietnam and no rear areas. The jungles and swamps belonged to whoever occupied them at any given time. I was regularly assigned to nightly patrols as a platoon leader of a Provisional Platoon around our CP perimeter with a force that was responsible for assuring the command's security. I also went on counter-intelligence patrols to nearby hamlets to inspect for enemy infiltration efforts, and to search for their hidden supplies or other provisions.

But my primary duties were assisting the Division's chief administrator, the Adjutant, with the myriad duties involved in supporting a Marine Division in a combat environment. Some of these included casualty reporting, graves registration, troop replacements, discharge boards, and the ultra morale booster, mail services. Ultimately, as the result of the division's increased combat activities that resulted in a very heavy load of award recommendations, I became fully involved with establishing an all-important award processing program for the division. It was here that I became much more involved with not only the Chief of Staff, but also General Hochmuth. I was an advisor to them, and a voting member of the Division Awards Board. I spent a lot of time on choppers visiting forward area units to find and interview witnesses for the highest level awards, and to assist unit personnel in preparing appropriate award recommendations.

General Hochmuth, who was very easy to work with, was an *extraordinary* human being and Marine. This tall Texan was then 56 years old (20 years older than me), was a graduate of Texas A&M, and had already been a Marine for some 30+ years. He had extensive combat experience in World War II where he won two Silver Star Medals. He was quietly religious and well respected by those who knew him. He didn't curse, smoke or drink, and did not have a lot of tolerance for anyone who did, *especially* if done to extremes. But he was also very understanding of the war situation and the times, and was therefore not overzealous about anything, except the well being of his Marines. He would often invite a small group of officers of various ranks to dine with him in his quarters, such as they were in those rainy mud flats, It was his personal way to get to know his officers better, away from their responsibilities. He also used these opportunities to let us know where he stood on a lot of matters, hoping we would in turn pass that information down the chain of command. He not only inquired as to how we were doing, but also wanted to know about our families. He would even ask if we were writing to our wives, children, parents, and others.

One of the more interesting additional assignments Gen. Hochmuth tasked me with was to be the escort officer for celebrities or dignitaries visiting the Division. These visits were informal, one-on-one, non-staged visits by stars that wanted to go out among the troops to meet them. This was unlike some of the more formal USO-type visits of stars where there were either large clubs or stages erected for stars such as Bob Hope, Anita Bryant, Marilyn Monroe and others. Since we were so close to the DMZ there weren't any large enough clubs or stages in the areas occupied by the 3d Marine Division. Clubs were available much further south at primarily Army or Air Force bases in Saigon, Tan Son Nhut, Cam Ranh Bay, Da Nang and Chu Lai.

Some of the famous Hollywood stars I had the privilege of escorting around the Division for "handshake" visits to troops in the field, in their hutches and tents: Henry Fonda, Robert Mitchum, Robert Stack, Roy Rogers and Dale Evans, and Wendell Corey. Also a very popular sports figure of that era was Floyd Patterson, the 1952 Olympics middleweight boxing gold medallist who later held the world heavyweight title from 1956 to 1959, and again from 1960 to 1962. Although Patterson was by far the favorite of the troops, Roy Rogers and Dale Evans were my favorite, while Wendell Corey was General Hochmuth's favorite. Perhaps this was because Corey was another tall Texan, and about the same age as Hochmuth. He mentioned that Corey had been a television star "hero" of his for a long time, especially for his *Harbor Command* TV series in which he played a Coast Guard Captain. Some of Corey's other many movies and the roles he played were *Rear Window* (a policeman), *Alias Jesse James* (Jesse James), *Cyborg* (a sheriff), and *Waco*, (a preacher). He also starred on the *Westinghouse Playhouse* in the early 1960's with Nanette Fabray.

Corey's visit came in August 1967, just a couple of weeks before I would be going home. I thought I was pretty safe at that point, until Corey told General Hochmuth he wanted to go out with a recon (reconnaissance) patrol! I said to myself, "You've got to be kidding!" and felt sure the General would veto that request. But Corey wasn't and General Hochmuth didn't! He "suggested" I take him out in the bush and let him visit with a recon patrol. I found a patrol just returning from their mission, and took some extraordinary pictures of Corey with this patrol. Corey himself carried a miniature camera pinned to a collar on his utilities. I know he got some great pictures as well. (On other occasions I also accommodated Actors Robert Stack who wanted to ride in an Amtrac (Amphibious Tractor), and Robert Mitchum, who wanted to "go out and see the guys.") General Hochmuth thoroughly enjoyed Wendell Corey's visit, and for a change, his morale was definitely uplifted after Corey's visit to *his* 3d Marine Division.

Sadly, there is no happy ending to this story. Once a week I would climb aboard a helicopter with General Hochmuth to fly to the 1st Army of the Republic of Vietnam (ARVN) Division Headquarters. We would meet with our counterparts on subjects of mutual interest and coordinate matters related to Vietnamese awards presented to Marine Corps personnel. On 14 November 1967, a little over two months after I left Vietnam, General Hochmuth's helicopter crashed on one of those very same trips I regularly made with him. It was reported that it was an operational crash. Perhaps it was, but I would not have been surprised to hear it was shot down, because we flew over hostile areas on those trips. General Hochmuth became the only Marine Corps General to become a casualty of the Vietnam War. For sure, The Corps lost a wonderful man, and an outstanding leader!

Story
by John A. Lundquist

TET 1968 in Vietnam means a lot of different things to all of the Marines who were involved. First of all, we have had time to put this TET offensive in perspective. To me, as I look back, it was a long, drawn-out affair.

I feel that it really started January 21, 1968, with the beginning of the siege at Khe Sanh, continuing through and beyond the TET holidays. The fight, the length and breadth of Vietnam, did not end with the Battle of Hue City. You must include the spring counter-offensive which included the relief of Khe Sanh (Operation Pegasus), a raid into the A Shau Valley and the Battle for Dong Ha City. Most people forget to include what was known as mini-TET, May 5-27, 1968. That was my part.

The Vietnamese had launched that second major offensive for the year on May 5, 1968, signaled by 199 rocket, mortar, and artillery attacks throughout Vietnam. In I Corps, within 24 hours, the airfields at Da Nang, Marble Mountain, Quan Tri, and Chu Lai; the headquarters of both III MAF and I Corps in Da Nang, along with the headquarters of Force Logistics Command; the MACV Compound in Hue; and the command post of the 101st Airborne were all hit. These attacks continued on May 11 and May 13. Marble Mountain's air facility took 20 or 25 rounds.

On May 19, the North Vietnamese engaged the U.S. Army Base at Camp Evans with a single "lucky" rocket attack. Their ammo dump was hit with 12 rocket rounds. The resulting explosions destroyed several helicopters and inflicted varying degrees of damage on a number of other aircraft and 80,000 gallons of fuel went up in flames.

On May 20, MAG-16 at Marble Mountain was hit again. On May 21, Camp Hochmuth at Phu Bai took 150 rounds of mortar fire.

On May 25, Cua-Viet Naval Facility was pounded by 111 rounds of mixed rocket and mortar fire. I can tell you it was artillery – 152mm. We heard each round leave the tube. Sixteen 10,000 gallon fuel bladders went up in flames on May 27.

Although the enemy had once again demonstrated his ability to coordinate wide ranging attacks by rocket, mortar, and artillery against military bases and inflict stinging damage in the process, the May attacks were but a pale shadow of the February TET offensive.

On May 27, 1 fairly serious thrust was made at Tam Ky following mortars with a ground assault. Three hundred houses were destroyed and 50 civilians were reported dead.

My TET '68 starts on May 4, 1968, when we landed in Vietnam about 9 a.m. I had just finished Radio School and 19 days with Staging Battalion at Camp Pendleton. What struck us all was how hot it was. We quickly were taken to a wooden shack with red dusty screens to secure air transport to Dong Ha. We looked so clean and everyone else looked so "salty" with a scattering of men with those thousand-yard stares.

We loaded onto a C-123 for a noisy ride to Dong Ha. Officers and NCOs sat in the web seats on the bulkheads. The rest of us sat in ranks on the floor. The ride was short. We banked over the ocean and we could clearly see the green of Vietnam out the left windows.

When we landed, it became a madhouse. The ramp went down and an NCO ran in saying, "Get out now!" Other Marines threw our gear out the back. The plane never shut down its engines. With motors running, hot air and red dust all over as we tried to find our gear, the plane taxied to the north end of the matted steel air field, turned around and headed back at us. We luckily had our seabags because down the runway it came and took off.

As I walked toward the small square hut on the west side of the airstrip, I heard artillery impacting near by and a jet was dropping napalm not very far away. I said to myself, "Damn! What did I get into?"

I reported to the "air terminal" (that little shack) and was pointed in the direction of the 3d Marine Division Supply for my 782 gear and the armory for my rifle, an M-16. My orders read FLSG-B, H&S Co., Communications Platoon. I walked the road, the length of the airstrip past an eight-sided concrete bunker. I later learned this was an old French bunker and the airstrip was a Japanese airfield during World War II.

I passed through a huge natural depression (the Dust Bowl), past the firehouse (the

combat bakery), and the mess hall to the communications shack. SSgt. Taylor welcomed me aboard, issued me a hooch number, told me to get some chow, and that I was on A-Guard tonight. I wondered what A-Guard was. A PFC said, "You! You're on 'rocket watch.'"

"What the hell is rocket watch," I said. He said, "You'll figure it out." As I looked about the sky for rockets, another Marine laughed and took pity on me. "Got stuck with rocket watch already?" he asked. I answered that I smelled a rat. He said it was good that I'd figured out the usual "newbie" trick. "Get some chow and get back because the Corporal of the Guard is coming with a truck to pick up the A-Guard. You will be on the bunker line for a four hour shift."

After chow, I received a rack, a foot locker, loaded my magazines, got an extra bandolier of ammo, and waited for the truck. About 7 p.m., we were trucked out to the line of bunkers which sat on the railroad track line (I figured the train no longer ran) and the Sergeant of the Guard took us out to the bunkers, dropping two men off at each bunker. I was in Bunker 30, the last one on the east side of Dong Ha Combat Base.

I got the 2 a.m. to 6 am. watch and was told to get some sleep. There was no sleep. Artillery – outgoing and incoming – continued sporadically. The C-130s dropped flares all night. At 2 a.m., I was told to come out, it was my watch. You didn't stand watch in a bunker but in the fighting hole off to the right and below the railroad grade.

Across Highway 1 and the Quang-Tri River artillery fell, red and green tracers arched in the sky mixed with all of the eerie light of the occasional flares. At times, sniper fire opened from across the road but we kept fire discipline. In fact, the order of the day was to get permission to fire. The sky started to lighten. I did not fall asleep. I survived my first night. Welcome to mini-TET.

We rode back to FLSG-B and had chow and as I prepared to fall in the rack I was ordered to SSgt. Taylor's office again. "Pvt. Lundquist, pack your seabag. We are sending you up north." "Up north," I said, "How much further north can you go?" "You are going to Cau-Viet and you will catch a ride by the ramp in Dong Ha at the river."

Luckily, I never unpacked, but the offers of extra magazines from two other guys

in the hooch gave me an uneasy feeling. I retraced my route past the air strip, out the front gate and, with some other Marines who looked a lot saltier than I did, proceeded to the ramp.

I finally found out what was going on. Starting on April 29, elements of 2/4 had found 5,000 NVA from the 320th Division. The Battle of Dong Ha had begun.

The initial six days of heavy fighting centered on Dai Do Hamlet, 1.5 miles northeast of Dong Ha. Heavy fighting continued until about May 16 around Nhi-Ha and involved 3/9 to the west, 3d Battalion, 21st Infantry, and, once again, 2/4. Although greatly outnumbered, the Marines prevented the 320th Division from assaulting the Dong Ha Combat Base.

As I turned to the ramp, I looked west down Highway 9 into the center of Dong Ha. It looked like a Vic Morrow set on *Combat*" – two-story stucco, French-style buildings half blown away. I looked across the ramp over the river and jets still dropped bombs and napalm.

Luckily, we were riding on a Navy PBR (Patrol Boat, River) craft – fast, light and heavily armed. The Navy Chief had us lock and load and lay out on the deck at various angles and we left for Cau-Viet.

You pass near Dai Do as you enter the main river channel. Lots of sniper fire but no B-40 rockets until we were about two miles downstream.

Cau-Viet is about two miles north and 10 miles east of Dong Ha. It sits on the South China Sea and is a Navy off-loading ramp for LSTs, a Seabee base, home for 1st AmTracs, and home of the 7th Separate Bulk Fuel Co. It was my home until September 1968. 1 experienced more than 1,000 rounds of artillery from the DMZ and my last experience of the mini-TET was May 25,1968.

Since my arrival on May 5, we had been frantically building the new bunker. There were four of us radio operators. We handed all radio traffic to Dong Ha and we did it while off-loading Navy AOGs and Shell Oil tankers. It always made my blood boil because a Marine Private made about $130 a month and the Shell Oil guy made $1200 a month (I guess we weren't in it for the money).

Since we were on the sea coast, you could only dig down two feet before you hit water. So, our bunker sides were very thick and had many, many layers of sand bags. About 50 meters from our bunker sat sixteen 10,000 gallon fuel bladders. I always wondered what would happen if we were in the bunker when all that fuel "went up" so close to us. On May 25, I got the answer.

The Russian 152mm field gun has a longer range than the US 155mm and is a bad-ass gun. We were close enough to the DMZ that you could hear the rounds leave the tube in North Vietnam and count the 11 seconds it took to arrive. A whistle over head was a good sign because it meant it was going beyond you. The first 15 rounds were okay, all whistles. PFC Jones and I looked at each other because each whistle got shorter. Finally, no whistles at all – just rounds impacting very close. Yes, they found the range with round 20 and now it was time to fire for effect.

All 160,000 gallons of aviation gas (JP-4, a jet fuel) was on fire. An eerie light roared outside and it started to get hot. It finally got so hot it was time to get out or roast like a turkey in an oven. We heard five more rounds leave the tube. We got up, grabbed the radios, ran to the count of 10, then hit the deck. Man, it was like a movie. Geysers of sand erupted all around. Five more rounds left the tube. Ten more seconds running, hit the dirt. Up again. We made it to the next bunker. After 111 rounds, it was all over. The field was on fire and four hours later we were back in our bunker.

The History of The 3d Defense Battalion Fleet Marine Force, US Marine Force November 1, 1943 - June 13, 1944
by Fred McCrory
The Bloody Tides of Bougainville

It is a long way from Greensboro, Alabama, to Bougainville, but on November 1, 1943, I landed on Torokina Point at Blue 2 with Task Unit 3 on D-Day. Thus began one of the bloodiest battles of World War II, the fierce, deadly invasion of Bougainville, the last stronghold, in the Solomon Islands, and thus began one of the most engrossing combat accounts to come out of the war. A story of a grim and unrelenting battle of the 1st Marine Amphibious Corps, the 3d Marine Division and the 3d Defense Battalion.

When they blew reveille at 5:00 a.m., November 1, 1943, on board the *USS Alchiba*, off the Island of Bougainville, I

just felt it was going to be a long day. D-Days (Debarkation Days) are all long, tough days. This is one day that I had a gut feeling something would go wrong. We had a breakfast of steak and eggs and did not realize this would be our last hot meal for two weeks. We were ready to go over the side of the ship with rifles, full ammunition and a full canteen of water at 7:12 a.m.

As we were going down the nets on the far side of the ship, the first thing that went wrong was, the waves were high and banging the nets against the ship. The LCVPs were rising and falling 3 to 4 feet with the waves, making it difficult to hang onto the nets, much less climb down them to the LCVPs waiting to take us to shore. Lots of men fell from the nets and were severely injured. Finally, my squad made it down safely to the LCVP and circled the ship one time and then headed for shore. The enemy troops ashore, alerted by air and naval gunfire in the period before D-Day were ready for us Marines.

Why were we trying to take Bougainville? A closer air base was needed by us to cut off and close down the main Japanese supply base for their Army, Navy and Air Force located at Rabaul. The closest Marine and Naval Base to Rabaul at the time was Vella LaVella, which was 400 miles from Rabaul. It was obvious a stronger American Air and Naval base nearer to Rabaul was required. There were no existing airfields on Bougainville which would serve this purpose. If we could take a portion of the island and build an airfield at Cape Torokina, it would put us within 210 miles of Rabaul, and our fighters could escort and protect our bombers to help knock out this strong enemy base.

The target for us to land on was on the west coast of Bougainville at Cape Torokina in Empress Augusta Bay. I remember many briefings on the assault of Empress Augusta Bay because my father was named Augusta H. McCrory. Everyone called him Gus

The first thing to go wrong was, the tide tables had been miscalculated. They said the tide would be in and it was actually out. As we passed Puruata Island in our LCVPs on the way to Torokina Point, an enemy platoon was steadily firing on the incoming waves of landing craft. This was our first test of fire. It was not like it was in the movies; this was serious and deadly. The landing boats would play hell trying to reach the beaches because of the low tide. The LCVP I was on had to lower its ramp

about a 200 yards from the beach. This created all kinds of problems for the landing craft as well as those of us who had to run the gauntlet from the time they lowered the ramp until we reached the beaches.

In the meantime, the most formidable enemy gun position I had ever seen was hidden in the thick vegetation along the cape. In this bunker was a 75mm gun which flanked the landing beaches on D-Day. It had a clear shot of our landing boats as they came in range.

The Japs had a determined gun crew and did a lot of damage. They were firing this 75mm gun at us while on the way to the beach and knocked out a great number of LCVPs. Once the ramp was lowered on our craft, enemy fire was hot and heavy. As we waded to our designated landing area, we could see a lot of LCVPs were in shambles. Some boats had crashed into each other and washed ashore in every position imaginable. By the time the day was over, 64 or more LCVPs and 22 LCMs were wrecked and useless. We finally hit the beach and pushed the enemy back, and within days, the Seabees started building an airfield, to be known as the Torokina Point Fighter Strip.

Other things I remember about the overall operation plan to establish and defend a beachhead on Bougainville are: It was under the command of the late great Admiral "Bull" Halsey. Admiral Halsey had requested the 3d Marine Division to take Bougainville. The Division regular infantry regiments were the 3d, 9th, and 21st Marines. The artillery regiments were the 12th and 19th Marines. The 3d Defense Battalion and the 2nd Raider Regiment units, 2nd and 3d Battalions, were part of the initial assault. All landing forces came under the command of the 1st Amphibious Corps (IMAC).

* *"Later on we brought in the corps troops, including the 2nd 155mm Artillery Battalion and two battalions from the 1st Parachute Regiment."* Henry Shaw, retired Chief Historian, HQMC article.

The final thing which went wrong on D-Day was, our intelligence briefing had said in advance of our landing there were about 5,000 Japs on the Island. Actually there were about 29,000! This created a big problem.

Some of the LVCPs got crossways in the surf, and our crated 20mm guns were full of salt water. After landing on the beach, we took them apart and cleaned them one at a time, as others in the group were shooting Japs inland. For about four hours, we didn't know if we would be able to hold the beachhead. Four Jap dive bombers came in low and dropped their explosive cargo, hitting several landing craft coming in while we were still under fire from Jap rifles and artillery ashore.

Another thing that worried me was when I found out, about 16:45, that the task force that brought us in, and had not fully unloaded, got a message to leave at 17:00 D-Day. There was a task force of Japs leaving Rabual, headed for Bougainville, to try to kick us off the beachhead. It really saved our lives and the beachhead when Admiral Halsey sent an American squadron of four cruisers and six destroyers to intercept the enemy task force and kicked the hell out of them.

Fortunately, in the Battle of Empress Augusta Bay, the US Navy defeated the Japanese ships so badly they turned around and fled for Rabual, diverting them from protecting a counterattack on the beaches. However, the Japanese soldiers tried to land without any Naval support and died in the effort.

One "Washing Machine Charlie" Didn't Make It Back To Rabaul November 19, 1943

Between November 1, 1943, and November 20, 1943, official Marine Corps records show that 558 enemy aircraft were shot down during the first 20 days, over and around the invasion of Bougainville.

One of those enemy aircraft was shot down by gun crew #220 of the Special Weapons Group, 3d Defense Battalion, attached to the 3rd Division. The gun crew consisted of gun Captain Fred McCrory, Ignacio Maez, and Benny Satterfield.

We used to call them "Washing Machine Charlie" when a lone plane would come in during the night to drop a few bombs and harass us in general. Their main thing was trying to keep us from sleeping and resting.

On the night of November 19, 1943, "Washing Machine Charlie" was making his nightly run. The island had been alerted with a "Condition Red," and we were ready for the lone enemy airplane. The searchlights had picked him up at about 15,000 feet. The flak was coming up heavy from our 90 mm, 40 mm and 20 mm guns, and

we could hardly believe he was able to dodge the flak. But evidently it got "hot and heavy" for him when all of a sudden he put his airplane into a steep dive.

He leveled out about 200 feet above the water. The searchlights located on the beach picked him up again, and when they did the enemy aircraft was about 500 yards south of our gun crew #220. He was headed north, and on the course he was flying would put him directly overhead in about 20 seconds. We were locked and loaded and ready for him. As soon as the searchlights picked him up, we commenced firing and had led him enough to be sure he would fly into my line of fire. We had loaded the 20mm magazines with one tracer for every four rounds.

I could see the tracers were right in his flight pattern and as the enemy plane got about 50 yards from our gun position, we hit the engine and I could clearly see the pilot in the searchlights. The engine caught on fire and at the time he actually flew over our gun position, he was at about 50 feet high and still burning from the engine. About 600 feet behind us was a coconut grove. I was still firing at him when he hit the top of the coconut trees and crashed about 4000 yards from my gun position. We could see a small fire where he had crashed.

We continued manning our gun position for the night. At the crack of dawn, we went to the crash sight. We had shot down a Nakajima K1.84 Hayate, a single-engine plane. The plane was partially burned and the pilot was dead.

The fuselage was partially burned, and the left wing and the right wing were in fairly good condition. I cut the nameplate off the bottom right wing, with my trusty Kabar. The name plate shows the airplane was manufactured by Aichi Clock Electric Company. It was Aichi #3, serial number 3190, and accepted by the Japanese Navy.

I carried the nameplate and showed it to everybody in the Special Weapons Battalion, and told them that in order to claim downing an enemy plane in the future, they had to produce the nameplate! Fifty-three years later, I still have the nameplate in my archives.

Comments On Bougainville

The Bougainville campaign basically resembled that of Guadalcanal: it had a limited objective – the capture and defense of

a strategic airfield site. The acquisition of a base on Bougainville was part of the overall plan of isolating the highly strategic Japanese naval and air base of Rabaul on the island of New Britain. The initial landing on Bougainville was intended primarily as a Marine Corps operation. Once a beachhead was secured, the Marines were to be withdrawn and replaced by Army troops.

The task of seizing the Cape Torokina region on the island was assigned to the 1st Marine Amphibious Corps, commanded by Lt. General Alexander A. Vandegrift and later by Major General Roy S. Geiger. For this operation, IMAC included the following assault units: 3d Marine Division, Major General Alan H. Turnage; 37th Infantry (Army) Division, Major General Robert S. Beightler; 2nd Marine Raider Regiment (Provisional), Lieutenant Colonel Alan Shapley; 1st Marine Parachute Regiment, Lieutenant Colonel Robert H. Williams; and 8th New Zealand Brigade Group, Brigadier R.A. Row.

The New Zealanders and one battalion of the parachutists were assigned special missions directly related to the Bougainville operation, yet not connected with the actual landing. On 27 October 1943, four days before D-Day, the brigade, along with some US elements, made an assault on the enemy-held Treasury Islands, some 65 miles southeast of Empress Augusta Bay. This had a dual purpose: to serve as a feint to distract the enemy from the main thrust and to neutralize a potential threat to the American lines of communication. The New Zealanders met considerable resistance in the difficult terrain but succeeded in securing the entire area by 12 November.

Another feint was made by the 2nd Parachute Battalion, commanded by Lieutenant Colonel Victor H. Krulak, on the island of Choisenl on 27 October. The Marines stormed ashore destroying all enemy installations within reach. Believing that a much larger force had landed, the Japanese counterattacked but were repulsed with numerous losses. After seizing their limited objectives, the Marines withdrew to rejoin the main force that had landed on Bougainville, having lost only 11 men killed and 14 wounded. No other American forces returned to the island, as Choiseul became one of the many enemy-held islands left behind in the backwash of war.

At 0700 on 1 November 1943, the first wave of the assault force moved ashore on

Bougainville. The initial landing was made by the 3d Marines, 9th Marines and 2nd Raider Regiment, 3d Defense Battalion, less one battalion. Despite prior bombardment by the ships and planes, the invasion force met heavy fire from the defenders. Although this shore fire did not prevent the landing, it did cause much confusion. The situation was further complicated by a heavy surf. As a result, squads. platoons, even companies landed far out of position and in sectors assigned to other units. The dense jungle, moreover did nothing to facilitate reorganization.

Because of the difficult terrain, the beachhead was not expanded very rapidly. Three days after the landing, perimeter was only an average of 1,500 yards from the beach. Following the initial resistance, the advance had been unopposed. The Marines now faced another enemy – the jungle and the swamps. Any advance inland was a matter of clawing, hacking and wading one's way foot by foot.

From the initial landing until the end of the Marine participation in the campaign, the story of Bougainville is one of a beachhead expanding slowly, inexorably against nature and the Japanese. Behind the perimeter, engineers and Seabees struggled to construct air facilities on one of the most unpromising pieces of real estate in the entire Pacific.

The Japanese, for the most part, dug into the jungle and the ridges and waited for the Americans to carry the fight to them. Not until months after the Marines had left did they make a determined effort to oust the invader, and by then it was too late. Only once did the Japanese attempt to throw out the Marines. During the night of 6/7 November, the enemy made an abortive counter-landing at Atsinima Bay, some distance beyond the Marines' left flank, then anchored on the Koromokina River. In the meantime, the Japanese attempted an attack on the perimeter by infiltrating forces down the Piva Trail.

This two-pronged attack was ineffectual. The amphibious landing force was too small to really disrupt the American hold on the perimeter. More important, American naval and air forces thwarted any enemy attempt to send reinforcements to their beleaguered troops. Despite a determined resistance by the Japanese landing force (approximately 500 men), it was practically annihilated after three days of heavy fighting. The attack via the Piva Trail was also stymied after three days of heavy fighting.

By 10 November, two battalions of the 9th Marines reached Piva Village and found that the Japanese had withdrawn. From then on the Japanese operated strictly on the defensive against the Marines and Army units which were gradually building up their strength on the island. The enemy, from his well-placed positions, now began utilizing the tactics of counterattack, sniping, and infiltration, with an occasional Banzai charge to enliven proceedings. In country which gave the defenders every advantage, this made for some bitter and bloody fighting. The Japanese inability to commit sufficient troops for the task at hand, however, insured their ultimate failure.

One particularly bloody engagement was the Battle of Piva Forks , which began on 19 November and ended seven days later. This was a rather bitter and difficult battle in which units of the 3d Marines bore the brunt of the fighting. After engaging the Americans in very close combat, the Japanese broke off the fight, leaving behind more than 1,200 dead, and withdrew into the hinterland. There they set about the preparation of strong defensive positions beyond the range of American artillery. Clashes between Marine patrols and Japanese forces continued for some time, One such action merits special mention.

The last major battle for the Marines on Bougainville was the engagement at "Hellzapoppin Ridge," where some of the toughest fighting of the campaign occurred.

The Japanese were dug in on the steep slopes and crest of the ridge. After the discovery of the Japanese positions, it was found that the only way to dislodge the enemy was by a frontal assault. Between 12 and 18 December, the Marines, primarily the 21st Marines, struggled to gain the ridge. Time and again they would get a foothold, only to be forced to abandoned it a little later. After a series of air strikes on the last day of the battle, the Marines were able to reach the crest. Over 200 of the defenders had died by the time the struggle ended.

Toward the end of December, Army units began replacing Marine Corps personnel and shortly after the first of the New Year most Marines were redeployed elsewhere. Their mission was completed: a precious beachhead had been secured on which American naval and air bases were rapidly being constructed. The price paid by the Marine Corps for the seizure of the Bougainville base sites was 732 killed and

1,259 wounded. The valor and courage displayed by the Marines demonstrated how tough we were.

From the advance bases on Bougainville, American forces disrupted the vital Japanese lines of sea and air in the Southwest Pacific. As a result, thousands of Japanese troops were cut off from their sources of supplies. By early 1944, the enemy's' offensive capability in this area of the Pacific had been effectively neutralized, thus enabling American forces to advance along the northern coast of New Guinea and into the Philippines. The seizure of potential base sites on Bougainville by the Marines had assured other American troops of easier going in the Pacific war.

Military Award Arrives 53 Years Late
by Peggy Sanford

Fred McCrory has a new testament to his World War II fighting days. It came 53 years late, and it comes from the US Government.

McCrory, a former Vestavia Hills City Council president and a former city school board member, received his World War II Combat Action Ribbon in late May.

He wrote to the U.S. Military's National Personnel Records Center in St. Louis, Mo., in January and asked for the ribbon after learning they must be formally requested, McCrory said. Congress approved the ribbons in recent years, he said.

"I didn't know you had to write for it. I thought they would send it to you," he said. "But you had to prove your service. They didn't know who actually saw combat. A lot of people never faced the enemy. They never left the States.

McCrory said the combat action ribbon "means you fought the enemy in World War II."

McCrory has a room full of Marine and World War II memorabilia from his four years of service, from Oct. 1, 1942, to Nov. 10, 1946. Some, like the Japanese flag draped over a chair in his dark-paneled home office, are serious reminders of his World War II combat time with the Marine 3rd Defense Battalion.

The nameplate of a single-engine Japanese plane is another of the somber reminders McCrory has held onto. He collected it after he and two other members of a gun crew on the Pacific island of Bougainville shot down an enemy plane on Nov. 19, 1943.

McCrory also has more traditional reminders of his Marine days, There's the desktop statuette of the famous image of Marines raising the American flag on Iwo Jima, and a fine pencil etching of the flag raising drawn by his son.

His collection also includes photographs, badges, other service ribbons, captain's bars and marine recruiting posters he signs and sends to hospitalized or ailing Marines.

McCrory said he wanted the Combat Action Ribbon 53 years after his military service ended because it is "a valuable and important ribbon."

"It's the most important medal the Marine Corps has, except the Congressional Medal of Honor," he said.

McCrory remains a Marine enthusiast because the Corps represents discipline, integrity and loyalty to each other, he said.

"Once a Marine you're always a Marine."

Leonard F. Mason

Last Name: Mason First Name: Leonard Middle Name: F.

Rank: PFC Award: Medal of Honor Year: 1944 Unit: 2/3/3

Location: Asan-Adelup, Guam, Marianas Islands

The President of the United States takes pride in presenting the MEDAL OF HONOR posthumously to Private First Class Leonard F. Mason United States Marine Corps for service as set forth in the following

CITATION:

For conspicuous gallantry and intrepidity at the risk of his life above and beyond the call of duty as an Automatic Rifleman serving with the Second Battalion, 3d Marines, 3d Marine Division, in action against enemy Japanese forces on the Asan-Adelup Beachhead, Guam, Marianas Islands, on 22 July 1944. Suddenly taken under fire by two enemy machine guns more than fifteen yards away while clearing out hostile positions holding up the advance of his platoon through a narrow gully, Private First Class Mason, alone and entirely on his own initiative, climbed out of the gully and moved parallel to it toward the rear of the enemy position and wounded repeatedly in the arm and shoulder, Private First Class Mason grimly pressed forward and had just reached his objective when hit again by a burst of enemy machine-gun fire,

causing a critical wound to which he later succumbed. With valiant disregard for his own peril, he persevered, clearing out the hostile position, killing five Japanese, wounding another and then rejoining his platoon to report the results of his action before consenting to be evacuated. His exceptionally heroic act in the face of almost certain death enabled his platoon to accomplish its mission and reflects the highest credit upon Private First Class Mason and the United States Naval Service. He gallantly gave his life for his country.

Franklin D. Roosevelt

One Marine's Thoughts of 1942
by Frank Chaboudy

When the 3d Marine Division was formed at Camp Elliott, I was in Ohio on furlough. When I returned to Camp Elliott and the 10th Marines, I was told I was now a member 12th Marines, 3d Marine Division. No change of command – nothing – just a shuffling of papers. I have no idea who or why some men stayed in the 10th and some of us were sent to the 12th. I like to think it was because I was so outstanding!

I think one of my most pleasurable weeks was spent living in a stable at the Del Mar Race Track, where we were sent for R&R before being sent overseas. The horses had only just been removed before we whitewashed the walls and moved in. The smell remained! Each morning we would run the race track just like the other thoroughbreds. Our afternoons were spent at the beach just north of the roped off area reserved for the hotel guest of the Del Mar Hotel. Of course the rope was only a foot high, so before long it was difficult to distinguish who were thoroughbreds from the Del Mar Stables and who were guests of the hotel. We had liberty every night and some of us were able to share it with guests at the hotel.

My claim to fame during my time in the "Old Corps" was that I was one of the first Marines to be stationed at Camp Pendleton. When construction of the barracks was completed, there was a need for someone to clean and wash the windows. I was one of four chosen for this sensitive task. The "Chosen Few" were sent to Camp Pendleton two weeks early to complete the arduous task. We completed it in three days. The remainder of the time we spent exploring the liberty possibilities of the metropolis of Oceanside, California. The rest of the

12th Marines marched from Camp Elliott to Camp Pendleton. I delighted in hearing how difficult the hike had been.

I that was the highlight of my tour of duty at Camp Pendleton, the lowlight followed a 72-hour leave to Los Angeles. Near the end of my leave I found myself short of funds and I was ready to hitch hike back to camp; one of my friends, however, persuaded me to stay the remainder of our leave and offered to pay my return bus fare. The following morning about 10 a.m., as I'm policing the area around the barracks, I see a Marine still in his "greens." I wondered why he was in his liberty uniform at 10 in the morning? As he approached, I recognized him as my friend who had paid my bus fare back to Camp Pendleton. In the confusion of unloading at the bus stop at Oceanside, I had forgotten to awaken him and he had continued onto San Diego. By the time he got back to camp, he was five hours over leave, thereby drawing a two-week restriction. All he said to me was, "Semper Fi, Buddy"!

Christmas Reflections

1941 – World War II – Wake Island – Guadalcanal – Bougainville – Guam – Iwo Jima!

Thank God! Our memories blot out our more traumatic experiences while enabling us to remember the more pleasant times in our lives.

If we could have chosen our time in the history of man during which we would prefer to live, would there be a better choice than 1941 through 1945.

What opportunities we had: To serve our country and out world in her time of greatest peril. To serve with men of greater and lesser stature, but all with the same goal: "The common good for the common man." With these thoughts, let us travel back in time to those opportunistic years. Christmas time 1941 – 1942 – 1943 – 1944 – 1945.

How was a 17-year-old boy hoping to grow into a man to be affected? There were questions to be answered.

Christmastime 1941 – Wake Island had just fallen. All of Camp Elliott was on alert for the Japanese invasion of the west coast of the United States. The 10th Marines spent hours, night and day, sitting in trucks with our meager combat gear; yet prepared to move anywhere on the coast of Mexico to Canada to do our duty; hopefully as well as the Wake Island, Marines! What did it all mean to a young 17-year-old Marine?

Christmastime 1942 – a year has passed; instead of the 10th Marines, it is now the 12th Marines – instead of Camp Elliott it is now Camp Pendleton. Instead of preparing to defend the west coast, we are preparing for duty overseas.

But the scuttlebutt is rampant: We are going to land on Truk! We are going to invade Rabaul. Who ever heard of such islands – were there really such places?

The young marine, living in Chula Vista, searched the harbor for troop transports each and every time he went home – hopefully – fearfully. When would he get to serve?

Christmastime 1943 – Bougainville: the young Marine's first combat is pretty much behind him. Everyone has been changed by the events of the past few weeks. What effect will crying to himself in his foxhole have on the young Marine? The feelings of desertion by family and friends – of not receiving mail from home as the other Marines always did. Can we really develop a hardness to protect our emotions? Can the young Marine truly change his personality?

Christmastime 1944 – the young Marine's locale has changed – even some of his tent mates. The young Marine is now on Guam preparing for a third island invasion. The ever present scuttlebutt is for an easy campaign. Iwo Jima is only a mile long! Should take less then a week – by then the young Marine will have served 30 months overseas and has hopes of returning home. What does the future hold for the young Marine?

Christmastime 1945 – a recently discharged United States Marine – 21 years old – the young boy who had quit high school to become a career Marine now had no marketable skills and little education. Could the ex-Marine succeed in this new world?

Christmastime 2000 – now nearly 60 years later we can look back and give our own answers to each of the questions that were so important to the young Marine during the most exciting time of his life.

We all should feel proud to look back – we answered our country's call. We did our jobs – large or small – to the best of our abilities.

We should feel proud to look back: we sacrificed ourselves for the good of others. We should feel proud to look back: we had the opportunity to work toward that common goal. We do feel proud to look back upon our era of achievements and accomplishments. This old Marine can now look back and whisper to all other Marines, young and old – Semper Fidelis.

Story
by Alfonzo Fanella

Upon returning to Guam from Iwo Jima, the 3d Division rested a short time before getting ready for the invasion of Japan. This engagement was to take place in November 1945.

While our outfit (E/2/21) was on Guam training for the big battle against the Japanese Islands, the two Atomic bombs were dropped on the cities of Hiroshima and Nagasaki. This brought the ending of the war with the Japs.

Thus began the occupation duties of those that did not have enough points to go home. Some members of our company were designated to go to Japan for occupation duty. I was chosen to serve as an interpreter and took a crash course in the Japanese language. We were all excited because we would be spending the next few months in Japan.

But it didn't work out in that fashion. Another unit was sent to Japan and we ended up shipping out to the Truk Islands in the Southwest Pacific.

My thoughts here would be to acquaint others of the significance of these islands, located just north of the equator, were to the United States during World War II.

There were many islands that belonged to the Truk group. Some of these islands were very small – others medium sized – while a few were rather large. Hundreds of Japanese soldiers occupied them. It was decided by our top brass to not invade any of them. Instead the United States Air Force used these islands for target practice.

Of course, there was a negative aspect to this strategy. While these islands afforded our airman excellent target practice, some of these planes were shot down out of the skies by the Japs. It is here that the Japanese soldiers committed the heinous crime of beheading our airmen that were shot down.

A stockade about 30 feet high was erected. We then proceeded to visit the remote islands where these Japanese who committed these atrocities were hiding. We had excellent sources as to which Japanese soldiers committed these awful crimes. They were the natives of these Truk Islands. It would have been a more difficult task for the Marines to round up these criminals without the aid of the natives.

We then transported these Japanese back to our camp, and the stockade became their new home. Besides looking for war criminals, we confiscated hundreds of there rifles and swords.

Our unit headed back to Guam after several months of duty on Truk. Most of us had accumulated enough points to head back to the USA. Consequently, we never did know the fate of those rounded up Japs who beheaded the US airmen. We all agreed that they should have received the maximum sentences for their misdeeds.

Dozens Blast Way To Top of Ridge
by PFC Cyril O'Brien

Guam – When a Marine company was faced with annihilation after it had failed

Five members of our squad while on Truk Islands. Photo courtesy of Alfonzo Fanella

three times to storm the face of Chonito Ridge, a second company took the Ridge from behind.

The second company's advance was up two 60-degree slopes. Its only concealment was ankle high grass. The hills above were fortified each by two enemy defense lines – one on the crest, another on the flat summits.

The Marines of the second company first advanced up the naked slopes but were thrown back before a hundred yards had been covered.

Gathering all available men, they tried to rush the hills again under cover of dusk. A squad leader, wounded in the leg as he lead the advance, shouted to his assistant squad leader, "Take over, Hully!" Then, he attempted to return to cover. Machine gun fire hit him. He tumbled dead to the bottom of the slope.

With only a clip of ammunition per man, the company assaulted again in the morning. This time a lieutenant reached the top of the hill but was killed there by a grenade. An automatic rifleman advanced to within 20 yards of a machine gun nest before the gun cut him down. One man was hit 13 times before he had gone 20 yards. He is still alive.

"They knew there was not a prayer of a chance getting up those slopes," said 1st Lt. French R. Fogle, of St. Mary's, W. Va. "Yet they kept rushing and falling."

That afternoon, the company tried to storm the ridge again. Little more than a dozen of the men reached the top of Chonito. They jumped into a slit trench 25 yards from the Jap entrenchments. In the trench were four men of the first company which had tried to take the hill from the front. They had been there 36 hours.

Three of them were wounded, the fourth was dead. The Japanese showered the trench with grenades. The Marines were battling them away with there hands.

Seeing that they would never make the remaining 25 yards without assistance, the Marines signaled for a mortar barrage. They were willing to risk being knocked out by it themselves.

In the wake of the barrage, the remaining handful of Marines charged into the Jap positions. They found only one Jap alive. His legs had been blown off below the knees. There were not three whole enemy bodies to bee seen. Two enemy officers, sporting new equipment, had apparently killed each other. One had a Samurai sword imbedded in his neck. The other, his sword scabbard empty, had a bullet hole in his forehead. Two Jap rifleman were huddled together, as if seeking by companionship to protect themselves from the flying fragments of the 81s.

The top of the hill was furrowed with shallow spider trenches. They wound aimlessly about the summit like the tracks of a huge worm.

The body of a Marine lieutenant still defied a Jap machine gun nest. Two Japs inside had bullets in there heads. The Marine was kneeling forward, his carbine

E Co. 2nd Bn. 3rd Marines 3rd Division, August 15, 1944. Photo courtesy of Cyril O'Brien

across his lap. The side of his head had been smashed. An American grenade which did not explode, lay between the two Japs.

Artillery and mortar shells also pounded the hill which the company had failed to take. When the barrage lifted, Capt. William E. Moore, of Sierra Madre, Cal., ventured with a patrol to its peak. Not a single enemy gun opened fire.

Here the Captain found the same situation: bodies of the enemy huddled in narrow trenches. Up the slopes Marine dead formed an uneven line. Most of them had their feet dug into the soil as if ready to charge again.

Duo Takes 'Band of Brothers' Literally
written by Cpl. Jason Dequenne
published in *Okinawa Marine,*
December 13, 1996
submitted by Chris Pangalos

CAMP HANSEN - Known for sharing close bonds of friendship, Marines have been frequently called a "band of brothers." However, there are two Marines in Weapons Company, 1st Battalion, 3d Marines, 3d MarDiv., who are literally just that. Cpl. Chris Pangalos and his brother, LCpl. Steven Pangalos, have been inseparable since joining the Corps more than a year and a half ago.

According to Chris, 33, he and Steven, 29, natives of Mahopac, N.Y., a suburb of New York City, never thought they'd one day become Marines. Of course, they ran around the neighborhood as children playing Army with friends, but they also dreamt of becoming professional soccer players. Nevertheless, there they were, at Parris Island, taking the first steps on a journey that has taken them from 1st Recruit Training Battalion, to Bravo Co., School of Infantry (SOI), Camp Geiger, N.C., to their first duty station, 1/3, Kaneohe Bay, Hawaii.

"We never seriously thought of joining the Marine Corps, at least until we were in senior high school," said Steven. "Actually, the first time I ever talked to a recruiter was as at a college fair. I looked at the booth the Marine recruiter set up, but at the time, I just wanted to play soccer competitively and go to college."

According to Chris, he, too, thought of joining the Corps while in high school. He also had a passion for soccer and was the only student from his high school to play on the All-American high school soccer team.

"After high school, I got a soccer scholarship to Keene State College in New Hampshire, where I played for four years and got degrees in public relations and communications," said Chris. "A couple of years later, Steve went to Belmont Abbey College near Charlotte, NC, on a soccer scholarship."

Following college, Chris and Steven played two seasons on professional soccer teams – finally fulfilling their childhood dream.

With two seasons of professional soccer under their belts, they decided it was time to move on, said the elder brother. They quit playing soccer to be with their family, who moved to Charlotte, NC from New York.

"We have an extremely close family. Everyone always knows what everyone else is up to, and we always look out for one another," said Steven. "So when our parents moved to Charlotte, we decided to move there and be close to them."

While living in Charlotte, Chris and Steven started their own business. It was a disc jockey/entertainment company called Rolling Thunder Productions. They provided music, lighting, and entertainment for weddings, parties and conventions as well as video tapes of other special events for clients. Although partners, Chris ran the business while Steven managed a restaurant near Charlotte. It wasn't too long before Chris and Steven started thinking about joining the Marine Corps.

"At that point, we had done pretty much everything we had wanted to do: go to college, play professional soccer and own our own business," said Chris. "The one thing we didn't do was join the Marine Corps. Neither of us wanted to be old men, looking back at our lives saying, 'I did everything I wanted to do except be a Marine.'"

The desire to become Marines came from a sense of patriotism, said Steven. They wanted to serve their country. They also wanted to do something together.

"Because of our age difference and college, we had been apart from one another for about 10 years," said Chris. "We wanted to do something special together and really bond after being apart for so long ... so we joined the Marine Corps."

"Originally, we planned on being reservists," said Steven. "However, we thought about it and decided if we were going to join then we'd do it all the way and be active duty infantry for four years."

At boot camp, Chris and Steven were in the same platoon, which made dealing with the day-to-day stress of basic training a whole lot easier, said Chris. However, that didn't come without its price.

"Right off the bat, we were put in the same platoon at boot camp, and when I got in trouble and was digging sand in 'the pit' I always knew my brother was soon to join me," said Chris. "The D.I.s always sent us out to the pit together. So just when one of us got out of trouble, the other one would get into trouble, and there we were back in the pit together."

According to Steven, all the trips to the pit and the "special" treatment from the D.I.s because they were brothers paid off when they got to SOL.

"When we were on the range at SOL, shooting the SAW (Squad Automatic Weapon), the battalion commander of the school wanted to talk to us," said Steven. "He thought the two of us being together was a rather unique situation. So we talked with him, and he asked us if we wanted to be stationed together."

Eager to accept the offer, the two brothers issued a quick "Yes sir!" and anxiously waited for orders. When they finally got orders to Kaneohe Bay, they were extremely happy.

"When we joined, we were hoping to do this together," said Chris. "However, we never thought we'd be in the same unit. Especially since I'm a machine-gunner and Steve is a mortarman."

According to Steven, being in the Marine Corps has certainly been an experience that's brought him and his brother together. It's also something they can't wait to tell their children and grandchildren about one day.

"This has been really great because we've gotten a chance to bond again, and we're seeing and doing a lot of things together, like seeing Okinawa and serving our country," said Steven. "The best part is I get to do this with Chris, who's not only my brother but also my best friend."

Finding A Friend
written by former Marine Ed German, alias G-man
published in *The Veteran*
submitted by Martin V. D'Giff

The explosion was loud. Splinters and larger fragments of wood rained down on our heads from the blown up trees. Men were digging holes and chopping down jungle vegetation to clear fields of fire and make places to sleep for the night. The pungent smell of the plastic C-4 explosive filled my nose like a thousand matches ablaze at once. It was my first day with Bravo Company, 1st battalion, 4th Marines. We were in the northwest sector of South Vietnam, near the DMZ. I was 18.

When I first saw Marty, he was stooping down, squinting up at me, and opening a can of fruit cocktail. He needed a shave and his youthful face had a couple of creases that reflected some recent pain. After introductions, he asked me, without looking up from his dessert, "So where you from?"

"I'm from New York," I kind of announced.

"Oh, yeah? Well I'm from Brooklyn!" He looked up at me and declared.

"Me too!!" I confirmed.

We shook hands and smiled. Marty is Jewish and I'm black, but there was an instant bond between us. Here we were, two city kids, 18 and 19 years old, meeting on a remote hill up on the DMZ in Vietnam in 1968. Marty, with only three months left in the country, was to be my squad leader.

He was a rough kid, the kind that would choose the Marine Corps, the kind that would read his maps and compass accurately and the kind that had been around New York. He knew the deal and wouldn't tell his men anything that wasn't good for them.

For sure, there was distinct contrast between me and Marty, but there was also the startling contrast between New York City and the Vietnam jungle that strengthened our bond. There were the things that we both knew, like chocolate egg creams, and Katz's Deli on East Houston Street, playing skelly and calling a fire hydrant a "johnny pump." Brooklyn high schools in the mid-'60s were populated by a good mix of Jews, Blacks, Italians, Irish and Puerto Ricans, so we'd been exposed to other cultures long before some of our comrades from the South and the Midwest.

Marty was the kind of guy who'd listen well as you described something, and throw his head way back, open his mouth wide, and laugh, and he did so on this September afternoon up in the Highlands as we joked about being from "the city so nice they named it twice, New York, New York."

Wherever we New Yorkers went, we stuck together and there was a kind of aura about us, and folks from other parts of the US would always gather around and inquirer about the big city. It seemed that we were so much more versatile and experienced. New York was well represented among the US soldiers in Vietnam.

From September through December, we endured the monsoon rains, the heat exhaustion, and the hostile jungle, and Marty learned to appreciate the songs and lyrics of Oscar Brown Jr., my favorite vocalist at the time, whose repertoire I had memorized to entertain during rest in the rear as we drank hot beer. Marty D'Giff had acquired a nickname, "D'Giff de Jew." Once he ordered a white marine from down south to show me how to set up the Claymore mines during my first days with Bravo Company, 1/4. Marty didn't kick the Marine's butt because he'd refused the order, but because he'd called Marty a Jew bastard in the process, and had turned the Claymore around so that the explosive mine faced us instead of the enemy. So, considering the circumstances and the environment, Marty was justified in beating the man with a shovel. It was the only way at that time for him to gain that particular man's respect. The insult was not only disrespectful, but also very dangerous, since we all carried weapons. Outward racism and hatred were treated severely in the combat zone and dealt with immediately with strength and support.

We all supported Marty, because he was a good guy. Most of us were good guys, in that we trusted in our leadership and lived on the same faith that had built America. We regarded our tours of duty as investments in our futures.

As a kid, Marty had lived with his family in the Ocean Hill/Brownsville section of Brooklyn. He played stickball in the schoolyard of P.S. 144, and his parents did some of there shopping at the old market that used to be on Prospect Place, between Howard and Saratoga Avenues. I also played stickball in 144 and walked through the market everyday on the way to school, about nine years after Marty's family moved out of the neighborhood. So I knew where Marty was coming from.

We spent Christmas 1968 at a place called Qua Viet, a beachfront retreat where we enjoyed steaks cooked on a barbeque grill and more hot beers. We surfed in the South China Sea on our air mattresses, and basked under our tents out of the sun, while the sweet breeze filled our nostrils. These

were times when we would reflect and not hold back our tears of self-pity and loneliness.

It was Christmas, but it was 80 degrees and we all wanted to go home. I knew Marty for three and a half months, but war adds potency to short acquaintances. I guess the most striking thing about our Vietnam experience was that for the first time, all military units were integrated with a diversity greater than our country's ever seen. I had never met Mexican-Americans until Vietnam, which also introduced me to the Navaho tribe members, dressed in jungle-green camouflage, with their tribal insignia painted in black magic marker on their helmets.

When Marty left Vietnam it was January 1969. He was on his way back to Brooklyn via Dong Ha, Quang Tri, and Da Nang. But he wasn't as joyful about his departure as one might expect. In a way, he didn't want to leave. He didn't want to go home, because there lay uncertainty and alienation, and because the pain he'd experienced in Nam still gnawed at him, pulling him back, back to his early days in country when he'd lost his best friend Alejandro Diaz from Brooklyn, with whom he'd gone through boot camp. Alejandro had been shot in the face on one of their first patrols and Marty had been with him; he had seen it happen.

Marty went home, but at the airport in California where he'd connect to his flight to New York, he let six planes leave before finally boarding one for the last leg of the journey. It was because nothing at home could ever measure up again. Northing could ever reach the level of emotion felt from the anguish of war, of surviving, of loss, of friendship, laughter, hunger, thirst, and sorrow.

Marty offered to visit my girlfriend for me and he did, and he gave her confidence and letters from me. She later told me that she could tell that Marty was one of my friends. I was glad for him, that he'd done his tour of duty and had survived his part of the war, that he had made it all the way home to the comfort of Sheepshead Bay, family, friends, and fresh food. I couldn't tell how the war had changed Marty, because I didn't know him before the war. This was for his loved ones to measure.

By the beginning of February, our letters stopped. I don't remember why, but I know that I became more involved in the war-survival business, and Marty had to get on with his life, too.

I got a few days off from combat, ten days of R&R partying in Yokohama and Tokyo. I was 18 years old and I had $1,200 to blow on nightclubs, women, and hotels. Needless to say, it was a lot of money in 1969. When I returned to the war, our unit remained in the northwest sector, near the DMZ, patrolling the dense mountain jungles. Then on May 10, 1969, over Mother's Day weekend, I was shot in the back by a sniper while on a squad-sized patrol. Fourteen of us fought our way out of a U-shaped ambush, and my gunshot wound was my ticket home. It was over for me and I was tired of it. Not only had I seen the deaths of my friends, but I had even witnessed a suicide; a fellow marine from the Navaho Indian tribe took his own life as an audience of us stood horrified, watching his thumb on the trigger of his M16, propping up his chin.

Fast forward to 1991: I'm 41 years old now and I haven't seen or heard from Marty in over 22 years. I was sitting at my desk late one night at work, when I got a call. I listened curiously in disbelief and began groping for words to make sensible sentences. It was my old friend from the jungle – Marty D'Giff. I hadn't recognized his name when I saw it in print in an ad in *The Veteran*, a magazine published monthly by the Vietnam Veterans of America in which veterans place ads in The Veteran Locator section, trying to locate old buddies. Marty's ad described his former Vietnam unit and the dates he was there, so I wrote him a short note stating that I was with the same outfit at the same time and "even though I don't know who you are, welcome home and God Bless You." When Marty reached me on the phone, he said: "Whaddya mean you don't know me. It's me ... Marty ... D'Giff de Jew."

Marty was calling from North Lauderdale, Florida, where he now lives with his wife Donna and his two children, Samantha and Dominick. We spoke on the phone for two hours that night, trying to patch together incidents and places, faces and names, and hills and landing zones from 22 years ago. To me it was a miracle that Marty and I were talking, and that we were both basically alright. Marty talked about his first years back in The World – of being home and trying to keep it together – and then about the ten years he spent as a cop on the police forces in Norwood and Walpole, MA, when he finally fell apart. And I told him of my years of denying that the war had really affected me, probably

because I had been conditioned to believe that my reactions were normal, and that my tense, impatient, high-strung behavior was simply who I was. It could never have had anything to do, I believed, with my participation in the war and my suffering and my loneliness. Guys like me and Marty are lonely, even when we're surrounded by our friends and families. That's why Marty put his ad in *The Veteran*, and that's why I was combing the Locator's columns, hoping to find a friend. We're lonely because we're survivors, and we still relate to a world that was just a little bit slower than it is now, just a little bit smaller, a little less sophisticated and a little less cruel.

There was a reunion last fall of New York veterans of the Vietnam War. Approximately 150,000 of us from New York served in Vietnam. Reunions are important to Vietnam veterans, because most of us came home one at a time, and we all have someone from the past that we've wondered about. And some of us are lucky enough to find our someones.

Marty came to New York in November to spend the weekend and to attend the reunion. It was a genuine reunion for him and me. When he found out where Alejandro Diaz is buried on Long Island, he asked me to drive him out there. He hadn't forgotten his old Puerto Rican buddy, who came home with his eyes closed.

Marty helped me stay alive in Vietnam. Thanks Marty. Welcome back.

With B Company, 1st BN., 3d Marines On Mutter's Ridge, Republic of South Vietnam, September 2-12, 1968
by Dennis L. Richardson

Listen up! This is what happened. The way I remember it anyway ...

September 2, 1968 – Monday – Republic of South Vietnam

Seven to eight clicks (kilometers) to the northwest of the "Rockpile," off Route #9, in north central I Corps (Roman number 1 or "I," the northernmost of the five sections that South Vietnam was divided into for military operations and political control), Mutter's Ridge was not just one ridge line. It was more a series of long, generally east–west oriented, finger-like ridges that came down from the north–south running mountains, separating the low coastal

plains south of the Demilitarized Zone (DMZ) near Con Thien from highland flats around Khe Sanh, in the northwest corner of South Vietnam, near the border with Laos. Mutter's Ridge, was named for Staff Sergeant Alan Mutter, USM.C. (killed in action while serving with 3d Bn., 4th Marines in 1967); but that was our American name for the ridge. It was never named as such on any Vietnamese map, not then, and especially not now that we are gone.

1st Battalion, 3d Marine Regiment, 3d Marine Division mounted out for a helicopter assault from their base camp at the "Rockpile." Our mission was to once again search for and destroy North Vietnamese Army (NVA.) units known to be in the Mutter's Ridge area. We had operated from these hills several times before. We had not made significant contact in this area in our previous operations on and around the ridge; they were mostly exercises in hill climbing, sweating and water discipline. To my knowledge, the landing zone (LZ) had not been "prepped," with either artillery or air strikes, prior to lift off. We could clearly see the hilltops from our base camp below, as I assume we could been seen lifting off.

Bravo ("B") Company was the point for the battalion; 3d Platoon was the point for the company and therefore aboard the first CH-46 Sikorsky, tandem-rotor transport helicopters to lift off in the assault. Capt. Frank Tuckwiller, B Co. Commanding Officer (CO), decided to position himself and his forward command element in the second helicopter off. As 3d Platoon Commander, I, therefore, loaded out on the first helicopter. (This was not necessarily tactically sound, as a commander, for most effective command and control, is supposed to be with or near his lead elements, but not with his point. Therefore, I would have normally been behind my point squad and the CO would have been between his 1st and 2nd platoons.) With 14 Marines loaded in each helicopter (or less depending on the altitude, heat and humidity's effect on lifting capacity), and with the CO, Co. Gunny (Company Gunnery Sergeant, senior enlisted Marine in the field), FAO (Forward Artillery Observer), FAC. (Forward Air Controller), their radio operators, the CP (Command Post) radio operators and corpsman (medic) in the command elements. plus myself, my radioman and Platoon Sergeant, there would have been less then 15 or 16 infantryman to secure the LZ from the first two helicopters to land. Because the LZ was a small hilltop, only one helicopter at a time could land, and a hot LZ could mean big trouble for the landing force.

The LZ was very hot! We were in big trouble from the beginning. My bird landed, discharged and left empty under heavy, but so far ineffective semi-automatic and automatic rifles, and a .51 caliber crew served heavy machine gun fire from a hidden enemy on the opposite hill top, about 100 meters to the northwest. We hastily spread out, forming a defensive line to the incoming shooting and started to return fire. The second CH-46 was attempting to land with both forward and rear door gunners putting out heavy covering fire with their .50 caliber machine guns.

The North Vietnamese guns found their mark and the bird hit very hard, bounced, laid over on its side, and then flipped completely the other at least two more times as the huge rotors bit into the ground and beat themselves into pieces. The dead chopper started to burn. The LZ was blocked. The rest of the Battalion was forced to return to base. We were alone and taking a lot of enemy fire. As it turned out we were lucky to have the command group with the company's supporting arms controllers on the ground with us.

The injured and shaken Marines were freeing themselves and their from the crashed helicopter. With our machine gunner down to a severe back injury, other Marines retrieved his M-60 machine gun and quickly put it into service, pouring effective suppressing fire on the enemy-held hill. Capt. Tuckwiller directed the unhurt Marines into a defensive position along the south end of our hill, completing a very open perimeter.

The south end of the hill had a just barely flat enough area that could be used for a medi-vac (medical evacuation) point if it was cleared and defended. The CO set some of the men to that task as we took a count of the wounded. They would have to be evacuated before we could hope for an extraction or a land withdrawal.

Any thoughts of a march off the hill were soon put away. To the northwest and north, the enemy was entrenched on the other hill. The east and southwest were blocked by a steep, cliff-like drop-off. A large enemy force was discovered in the draws moving toward us from the south and east.

We were advised to ready our wounded for a medi-vac attempt. I called to one of my Marines to help me search the wrecked helicopter for injured. The last of the crew

and our Marines were climbing out as we entered. The pilot was shot in the foot with a .51 caliber round and was in bad shape. We managed to free him from the cockpit and pulled him from the bird. I carried and dragged him toward the newly cleared LZ area where the rest of the crew and our injured were staged. We could hear a CH-46 coming up the valley from the southwest.

As the medi-vac chopper popped up over the hill and flared for hover/ wheeltouch only pick-up, the whole world seemed to explode at once. The two .50 calibers from the inboard chopper were firing full automatic, a couple of enemy B-40 rockets (a shoulder-fired, multi-purpose, rocket propelled explosive) flew at the helicopter, there were light and heavy machine gun rounds from the enemy positions spraying the air and digging up the ground all around us. Our own machine gun, all our M-16's rifles and our 40mm grenade launcher were all returning fire at once. In the middle of all this fury, the first pick-up was completed and the medi-vac chopper disappeared over the west edge of our hill.

I returned to the wrecked helicopter to see if there was anything usable that was going to burn up. The two .50 caliber heavy machine guns and their ammo were high on my list. To check the gun for damage, from the forward door, I fired a few rounds at our tormentors across the way. We freed both guns from their mounts, grabbed all the ammo cans we could find, and left the smoking hulk to burn.

I'd had some training on a "50," not as a Marine, but way back in military school. My Plt. Sgt. had none and all the crew of the helicopter were being evaced, so I became a .50 caliber machine gunner. We stuck the barrel in the split fork of a downed tree trunk, as we had no ground mount for the gun. We loaded it just in time for the second medi-vac attempt to get out the rest of our injured.

This time we had spotted the crew-served machine gun position. When they opened up on the incoming helicopter, we surprised them with some heavy fire of our own. The second pick-up was successful and all of our seriously injured were now gone. We were now free to deal with the rest of the enemy.

Capt. Tuckwiller's group had contacted the air attack and artillery support that was made available to us. He was able to call in constant and heavy shelling on the enemy in the draws and on the slopes approaching us from the south and east. He turned the

FAC. over to me to deal with the enemy-held hilltop. We had a lot of explosives and steel dropping on the enemy positions for us.

At one point, we had a flight of two Air Force F-4 "Phantom" attack jets who didn't want to drop their 500 and 1,000 pound bombs on the forward slopes of the NVA hill because they were afraid of hitting us. Our Marine A-4 "Sky Hawk" attack jets had been doing a great job of close air support but had run out of bombs. We repeatedly asked the Air Force F-4 drivers to do the same. If the enemy positions looking down on us weren't silenced, we would stand little chance of a successful evacuation. We did not want to be stuck on our hill for the night. The Air Force drivers still would not their loads where we wanted them to, so I released them and told them to get out of the way. As there was not any more Marine air available, I called for artillery fire, which had been told to stand by while the air support was on station.

I was assigned a couple of Marine 8" guns, some of our biggest and most accurate artillery pieces, for my fire mission. I was told that due our proximity to the target and the gun angle, the 8" guns would be shooting with an inbound trajectory such that the shells would be less than 100 feet over our heads on the last 100 meters to the target. With a bursting radius that could include our forward positions, it was a close call. No room for error, but we didn't have any other choice if we wanted out.

We were to be called a "splash" five seconds before impact, to give us time to get our heads and everything else down. We passed the word and pulled as much of ourselves as we could under our helmets and into our flak jackets.

Those 8" shells sounded like freight trains flying overhead, but the enemy bunker site disappeared in the first two impacts. I called a "fire for effect" and walked the shells up, down and across the enemy held hill for a while.

During the first mission, I got a radio call from 1st Lt. Sandy Hunt, our XO (Company Executive Officer, second in Command, whom I'd known since being enlisted recruits together in San Diego boot camp). He was listening to our battle on the radios from the Bn.3 shop (Battalion Staff section 3, Operations) back at the "Rockpile." He said "they" wanted him to remind me not to chew up any future LZ's too much, if I knew what he meant. I told him that I didn't really have the time to discuss my thoughts about "their" choice of LZ's right at the moment, and that "they" probably didn't want to know anyway, if he knew what I meant. The other hill looked lie a barren, cratered moonscape when we lifted fire, but it was very quiet.

The CO was having similar success with his targets, but he had a lot more to shoot at, and suggested to Battalion that they might well want to extract us ASAP. They were sending two CH-46's right away.

I remember shooting down the slope with my rifle and having a lot of things being shot back up at us, as I was the last man to dive into the last chopper. I landed at Capt. Tuckwiller's feet. He had this really strange look on his face as he looked down at me as if he thought I was acting undignified. I was, and I was still scared to death, plus, I never have liked helicopters; but he never did say anything.

We landed a very short time later back at the "Rockpile" with the rest of the Battalion waiting and cheering from their places along the perimeter. The Operation Officer (S-3), a major, was there at the end of the ramp. He slapped me on the back and said, "Rich, it's great to see you, we had written you guys off!" I was so stunned and shocked, I just glared at him. Capt. Tuckwiller and the Company Gunny firmly took my arms and pulled me away without another word.

Bravo and the air crew had taken no KIA's (Killed In Action) that day. The other guys didn't do so well.

As we took our positions in the line, we could see the hills that we had just come from, Air and artillery were working them over pretty hard. We were going back alright.

September 3, 1968 – Tuesday

We knew the night before that we were going to go back to Mutter's Ridge at first light. We just didn't know the order and the how. The order came as we moved out of the Base Camp lines to the LZ; we were to go last, to be in reserve. The how can as the first birds with the assault force returned from the ridge for another pick-up, the zone was "sweet," no enemy fire. The NVA had decided not to play today. We would not have to fight our way back onto Mutter's Ridge again.

Alpha ("A") Company had landed and was establishing a perimeter on the northern hilltop from which we had taken so much fire the day before. They were to send a Marine over to our hill later with a sou-

venir for me, several linked .51 caliber rounds from the destroyed NVA machine gun bunker.

Bravo landed on the same hilltop to the southeast of Alpha that we had crashed on and fought from. The fire from the crash, plus all the air strikes and cannon fire, had not left much of the downed CH-46. All that remained was part of the tail section, several feet to the rear of the aft cabin door. We settled into own perimeter and waited for the word to start patrolling.

The plan was for the two companies to send out combat patrols, supported from their hilltop positions, to locate the direction of the enemy withdrawal. All the indications were that the enemy had gone north.

After a scheduled supply drop late in the day (our combat load was for extra ammo and only one day's rations for the initial air assault) with our extra food and water, we expected to stay in our perimeters that night and head out north the next morning. The supply drop never came. Mother Nature had something else in store for us.

A tropical storm developing in the South China Sea, east of us, gained unexpected strength to a full-blown typhoon and then turned due west, right at I Corps and us. For whatever reasons, all I'm sure very reasonable and fully justified, our two Marine Rifle Companies on those two small hilltops on Mutter's Ridge did not get resupplied.

For the next five nights and four days, we would not see the sun, the surrounding hills or the valleys below, let alone anything flying. We would only know Alpha Company was still there, less than 100 meters away, because they would tell us they were still there, just as wet and hungry and miserable as we were. We would have all the water we wanted to drink, a first for Mutter's Ridge.

The rain came just as we finished our fighting holes for the night. We were experts at erecting low profile covers over our fighting holes with sticks and our ponchos. No big deal. We had been in the weeds for months on end ... it's raining, so what. Then the clouds came right down on us and opened up. And the wind blew and the rain came at us sideways. We couldn't see more then a few meters. Making it to the next fighting hole was a major undertaking. The ground was a slick, wind driven muck, all but impossible to stand on. Out of sight of your own fighting hole, blinded and not sure of the di-

rection, there was constant danger of sliding over the side of the hill.

All we could do was to hunker down and survive. The priorities were to keep the radios protected, get as warm as we could, and protect as much of our gear as we could. Wet was not an issue. There became degrees of wet. The fighting holes filled with water and stayed full. Huddled shivering against a buddy in a soaked poncho liner under a leaking poncho was better than out in the cold, driving rain. You couldn't put on dry socks, but you could change them for warmer wet socks that you had put inside, under your shirt and flak jacket, pressed against your skin.

Sgt. Hare, my Platoon Sgt., and I made the rounds of the platoon's fighting holes several times a day, checking on the condition of our Marines. We both admonished them to take off their wet clothing off or at least open it up and bare the skin to the open air a couple of times a day. Especially their feet. A testament to their field craft was, that when the storm passed, only two Marines had severe enough cases of immersion foot to be medi-vaced. Surprisingly, they were part of a group that had holed up inside the helicopter wreckage. They had just never taken their boots off. I would have liked to have had them brought up on charges. I settled for severe public chewing out, in front of their buddies whom they had let down and a message to the 1st Sergeant in the rear not to let them enjoy themselves.

The Company CP was established in an old NVA dugout. It was a deep trench like fighting hole with a back room. Enemy soldiers, always wary of our aircraft overhead, had dug in several feet from both ends into the backside of a trench, leaving an overhang. The two holes were connected by a widened tunnel, creating a comfortable, but somewhat claustrophobic for big Americans, cooking and sleeping room. It lasted until the second or third day, when the rain soaked the earth caved in.

The enemy wasn't much of a concern after the second day. We maintained our outpost and watches. Our lines connected with Alpha Company to the north and northwest. We had the protection of steep drop-offs on the east and southwest. The only reasonable approach was up the steep-sloped finger to the south, which was covered by one of the other platoons and a river of flowing water and muck from our hill. Besides, any NVA to the south had to be just trying to survive and were as miserable as we were. Any NVA we might have seen, we would have expected to be surrendering. We almost would have welcomed an attack as a diversion from our torment. An attacking enemy wouldn't have stood a chance, as most of the time we were pretty surly. It was not a fighting time, and the living wasn't fun.

No one could really sleep, it was more of who was really on watch. The rest of the time you were in a kind of zoned out, miserable, and numb daze. I huddled in a four-man hollow trying to share warmth with my Platoon Sgt., radioman and a corpsman.

There wasn't any food for the last two or three days of the storm. What C-rations (Korea era, single meal, canned food – combat rations) we had each carried in our packs were gone if not that first morning, by the end of the second day. We all searched each pocket of our equipment and dug around in old trash pits for anything previously thought to be inedible. The four of us one day,scrounged a single can of cheese and crackers. We each had one, stale round cracker with crusty bland cheese spread on it. It seemed like a banquet.

Sometime during the night of the fifth day, the storm finally spent itself. Sunday dawned clear, hot and steamy; but dry. We were resupplied by chopper by noon. Water (OK, fine!) and cases of C-rations and radio batteries. We each bragged about how many C-ration meals we were going to eat. Most of us couldn't finish one, our stomachs had shrunk so much.

We were told that the typhoon that we had just endured on that hill top in the open was one of the worst storms to hit Vietnam. It got our vote.

With the sun and drying out, came other changes. The resupply choppers had brought in some replacements, new guys, including a 2nd Lieutenant. Sandy Hunt, the XO was relieved and was sent to the rear as a staff officer in the S-3 section. I was promoted to XO and turned 3d Platoon over to the new 2nd Lieutenant.

I had been a platoon commander, in the field, since arriving in country the previous October, over 10 months. My first eight months were with 3d Anti-tanks, as an Ontos (a small tracked vehicle armed with six 106mm recoilless rifles [canons]) Platoon Commander at fire bases and on convoys from Khe Sanh to Con Thien and all the garden spots along the way and back.

I'd had the 3d Platoon of B/1/3 since June. We had been on almost continuous operations in the field, from Di Do near the coast, west to Camp Carroll and the "Rockpile." We were always near the DMZ, with more time on Mutter's Ridge than anyone else.

Units that I was attached to and served with, had been awarded a Presidential Unit Citation, two Navy Unit Citations and three Meritorious Unit Citations for combat actions under fire. I had been injured three time, one counted for the Purple Heart. I was ill enough once to be sent to the Da Nang hospital for four days. I had medivaced quite a few of my Marines for illness and wounds, but, until now, no one in my charge had died. We were good, but we were always very lucky too. Our luck was about to change.

September 9, 1968 - Monday

Mutter's Ridge connects several high spots, one of which was Hill 461 (a surveyed, benchmarked knob, map marked as 461 meters above sea level) about a kilometer northwest of our hilltop LZ's. Hill 461 is just three clicks below the DMZ, and North Vietnam.

A descending sloped finger led off Alpha Company's hill pointing toward Hill 461. Dried out, fed and resupplied, Alpha Company packed up and moved down the finger, looking to re-establish contact with the NVA. Bravo Company followed.

Off the hilltops, the ridges and fingers were still quite green with moderately heavy forest and vegetation, in spite of obvious efforts to defoliate, bomb and shell most of the hiding places of this northern "free-fire zone" (Rules of Engagement: areas of the country, evacuated of all civilians and declared "unpacified," therefore anyone found in the area unidentified as friendly was presumed to be the enemy, and did not require pre-authorization to take under fire). The steepness of the terrain, required our movement be restricted to the high ground and therefore march by column, not exactly the most secure of battle maneuvers, in terms of reaction and support.

The point elements of Alpha Company were ambushed and pinned down on the ridge line trail, in the early afternoon, short of Hill 461.

One of the worst command jobs, especially in the field, can be that of Executive Officer, if the unit has a strong, well-

organized, leader in the Commanding Officer. Other than being the CO's shield holder (a seldom required activity in a modern army) troop cheerleader, record-keeper, supply officer, march prodder, straggler gatherer and "one in wait for the command," there's not a lot of requirements on the position when the company's on the march. I found myself a new XO, with little understanding of what more might have been required of me, no unattended-to specific instructions, but there, available for the CO but out of the way, in a long column of march, moving toward the shooting up ahead, and not in the fight.

For reasons not made clear to me, Bravo was ordered to pass through Alpha's column and take up the attack, still in column, through the ambush site and toward Hill 461. Passing Alpha took most of the rest of the day. By dusk we were being held up under heavy enemy small arms and machine gun fire, just short of a narrow draw at the base of Hill 461. We had taken three KIAs in the approach fighting. The Company was in combat, two or three Marines against two or three NVA at a time. Make contact, push over and through them and move forward a little to their next strong point. Not exactly classic company movement to contact, fire and maneuver tactics. The NVA had, once again, picked the fighting ground.

Nightfall came with no resolution to our efforts to gain a foothold on the hill in front of us. We were not going back and the NVA, for the time being, had decided to be in the real estate business. We moved our dead and wounded back up the trail to the hilltop LZ with Alpha Company, to be medivaced. We called our own 81mm and 60mm mortars for covering fire on the enemy positions.

The enemy was still pinning down our forward elements with heavy rifle, rocket and machine gun fire from hidden positions somewhere on forward slopes of the hill. They were not showing much of their intention to depart; wherever they were and in what number, we couldn't determine. Their strong points were just enough to control the approach to the hill. For our part, we could withdraw, or take one position at a time, but not maneuver.

We were going to be trading fire with them for most of the night, not so much for tactical gain but to harass the other guy and to make sure he knew we had no intention of breaking off and vice versa. With the dense brush and tree cover overhead, direct artillery fire was not that effective, especially as close as we were to each other. It was a long night.

With daybreak, we were able to spot their fighting positions and resume our attack to the base of the hill. There was one particularly tough enemy automatic weapons position near the top on Hill461 that had us pinned down for hours, extracting a heavy price in casualties for every foot we advanced. This particularly courageous NVA soldier had excellent, almost unobstructed fields of fire from a dirt- and log-covered trench near the bottom of a tree, right below the hill crest. Only a blazing weapon barrel occasionally stuck out of the fighting hole. Because we were not yet far enough off the ridge and into the draw at the base of the hill to spread out, we had difficulty massing enough fire to knock out the position or suppress his fire. We started calling him "Super Gook." Every attempt to advance or dash from tree to tree in an attempt to get a better angle of fire was met with incredibly intense and accurate return fire from his hole. In spite of our horrendous machine gun, LAW. (Light Anti-Tank Weapon, a disposable 40mm shoulder-fired rocket), mortar and grenade fire that at the time seemingly obliterated him, "Super Gook" kept up his fire. He was finally silenced, but not before racking up an awful toll in dead and wounded Marines. When we finally took the hill, he and a comrade were found dead in the partially collapsed trench. It was impossible to tell how many times they had been wounded. It was not hard to quietly and respectfully cover over their hole.

As we were spreading out and just about into position for a final rush up Hill 461, the enemy hit us with a shower of their own 60mm and 82mm mortar rounds, tearing into our assault force and shredding them with hot shrapnel. Our senior Corpsman, "Doc" HM2 Alan James, was later awarded the Navy Cross for his efforts in aiding, comforting and protecting our wounded, at times with his own body, during the three-day battle for Hill 461. His efforts during this devastating mortar attack, were noted in particular.

As the mortar fire slackened and we again readied for a dash to the top, we spotted a group of NVA off to the west, breaking out in the open as were we, and headed back top the top. It was a mad-dash foot race to the crest, with the Marines winning and pushing back the enemy soldiers, killing several in close combat. It was an ex-

hausting effort, but we still had to consolidate our new position and prepare for an expected counter attack.

We had suffered seven more KIA Marines that day. Bravo started out for Hill 461 with less then 120 Marines instead of the close to 200 that a fully-manned infantry is supposed to put in the field. With a total of 55 dead and wounded, there was not much more than a reinforced platoon left of Bravo Company when we reached the summit. We needed medivacs, replacements, water, ammunition and rest. We got rain and it was getting dark.

The few standing trees on the crest, not much more than a narrow, razorback high spot on the ridge line, had to be cleared for any helicopter approach, even for a wheels and ramp touch only, as there was not enough room to land.

"Doc" James told us that he had a few wounded that were going to go critical. An LZ was cleared with axes and C-4 plastic explosives.

Capt. Tuckwiller had arranged for a "Spooky" flight (WW II era DC3-, Army/Air Force C47 twin-engine airliner/military transport, converted to flare dropping for lighting up whole battlefields) to help us consolidate our positions and to guide the medivac choppers, who had agreed to make a try at a pick up if they could find us in the dark.

Sometime after it was completely dark, in the eerie light of "Spooky's" flares, a CH-46 came out of the wet, pitch black sky in a slowly descending hover to try and touch its rear ramp against our ridge top for a medivac pick up. The NVA would have none of it. A hail of green tracers from NVA positions all around the hilltop crisscrossed the sky, creating what would seem to be a impenetrable wall of fire all around the helicopter. Our own return fire added a like wall of dancing red streamers, reaching back at the enemy positions. It was like a War God from hell had predetermined a visual scoring system for his hideous enjoyment.

At one point, as the incredibly brave pilot had almost made a touch down, an enemy gunner fired a rocket at the hovering chopper. The yellow fire-streaming rocket went right through the cabin, in one forward side gunner statopm door right behind the cockpit and out the other gunner station door on the other side. As incredible as it was to us on the ground, it must have been unimaginably terrifying to the crew, who were forced to withdraw into

the safety of the black night. Just the sound of an approaching helicopter triggered a repeat performance, with the resulting wave-off and no pick up. The crews had tried real hard, but we would have to make it through the night with our wounded, on our own.

Sometime during the rainy night, the NVA tried one more time to push us off Hill 461. With fixed bayonets, enemy soldiers came up out of the dark of the night and rushed our line at the west peak of the hilltop. Bravo's Marines were ready and met with almost instantly with grenades, rifle and machine gun fire, dispatching the last one as he fell forward stabbing his bayonet into the ground in front of our screaming and shooting Marines.

The rest of the night passed as we crouched in our defensive positions, tense and at the ready, rain soaked and staring into the blank emptiness of the dark. We waited for another attack. There were no more attacks. Only the occasional sharp crack of one of our Marine's M16's as he nervously probed at a sneaking ghost in the dark.

The morning dawned on our scattered, chewed up and exhausted command. It was like finding out that we had defended a rain soaked, muddy trash heap, littered with the rubble left from driving off NVA, plus our own field gear, bodies (theirs and ours), ammo cans, spent cartridges, rocket tubes, soiled battle dressings and ration containers. It was like a visual hangover from a long binge, it was depressing, the nightmare was real after all.

The narrow ridge crest to the north was easily defended with only a few Marines covering a steep drop-off. We pushed our east and west lines out as far as we dared stretch the men, out past collapsed bunkers with dead enemy soldiers, buried and not so buried, sticking out. All along the south sloping crest of the hill top, the rest of bravo spread out gathering itself for the new day. We set about collecting and tagging our dead and wounded for evacuation. We sent a squad-size recon patrol out over the north ridge to give us warning of anymore enemy presence near us. We called for the helicopters to bring us re-supply and carry off our casualties. We were not in a victorious mood, that morning. We were tired beyond description, we were spent, alive, but spent.

While checking our wounded with "Doc" James, one of them, a radio operator from 3d Platoon, Cpl. Thompson, called to me. He was severely wounded by shrapnel in the groin area. He'd been given a lot of morphine and although very upset, he was considerably dopey. He kept begging "Doc" and I to recheck his wound, could we be sure he was still ok? You know, was he intact, was the equipment hurt? He would not calm down, so "Doc" asked me to "consult." We carefully pulled the battle dressing away. There was a lot of blood from tissue damage all around his thighs, a tear in the scrotum that would require some really painful suturing, but the count of his essential body parts was still correct so, we assured him all appeared intact. The young Marine sobbed, relaxed and let the pain killers carry him away, smiling. He was going home, and with all his "equipment."

A single shot rang out to the north. A radio barked. Our recon patrol had taken a sniper hit. More shots. Answering fire from our Marines. Shouts for help over the crest, down the slope. One more KIA.

I went over the side of the hill to help with the body, when the squad was coming back up. Single rounds from the hidden enemy sniper occasionally hit near us; they were wild, not well aimed, considering the body. Maybe the sniper had one lucky shot, maybe our return fire had him rattled. Eventually there was no more firing. We were left struggling to bring our dead brother back up to the "safety" of our perimeter. It was one of the physically most difficult things I have ever experienced. No amount of training could ever prepare someone for the final, desperate act of dragging a dead human being, clawing inch by inch, up a almost vertical hill.

Private Wayne E. Christopher was not any more or less special than any of the other Marines of Bravo Company. He wasn't my favorite Marine, although a most likable and agreeable young man, always eager to take up whatever task he was assigned. He rather reminded me of that famous comedian, Lou Costello, in his face and his stature. I sometimes called him "Lou;" I was never sure if he knew who Lou Costello was. The sniper had ended Wayne Christopher's young life. He was 3d Platoon, the first and only Marine who was mine to die while I was in Vietnam, the "lucky" part of our tour. He was only one of 58,000 US serviceman to die in whatever the dying in Vietnam was

called. Private Wayne E. Christopher, USMC, whose name is among thousands of others on The Wall, panel 44 west, was the eleventh Bravo Company Marine to die in that fight on Mutter's Ridge, and the last.

What had we done? Our jobs, just what we were told to do, that simple. We were to search for and destroy North Vietnamese Army (NVA) units known to be in the Mutter's Ridge area. We found them, engaged them, killed a lot more of them – 49 confirmed — than they did of us. We drove them back north, once again and for now, out of South Vietnam.

The intelligence people from the rear came ou. They poked around the battlefields, looked at the NVA bodies, talked to our survivors, took notes and made some reports. They concluded that we had destroyed an NVA regimental headquarters site and had fought and defeated more than a battalion of enemy troops in well-fortified positions. All that would begin to mean something later, after we had been withdrawn from Hill 461. Right then, it didn't seem to mean much. We were to tired and drained, beat up and hurting to feel much good about anything but breathing.

There were some medals awarded, never really enough, for Bravo's actions during those 10 days: at least two Navy Crosses, Silver Stars, Bronze Stars and 60 Purple Hearts. But the medals really never tell the story of combat, especially with Marines. It's always a story about a few, really good men, in harms way.

Bravo Company's Marines were the finest, the toughest men I could ever imagine knowing. In their everyday existence, they displayed unimaginable courage, physical and moral. I am and will be forever proud to have served with the magnificent young Marines that I shared that time and war with. I honor their lives, their service, their deeds, their courage, and for some, by their death, their memory.

Semper Fidelis Marines

PFC – Clarkson, Gerald J. – 2397456-680908 – A/1/3

LCpl – Dewater, Patrick L. – 2436069-680908 – A/1/3

LCpl – Glegg, James E. – 2415422-680908 – A/1/3

PFC – Rambert, Franklin – 2325173-680908 – A/1/3

PFC – Rea, Billy M. – 2404514-680909 – A //3

Cpl – Campbell, Donald A. – 2128722-680909 – B/1/3

LCpl – Christopher, Wayne E. – 2350592-680911 – B/1/3

Cpl – Cisneros, Roy - 2341534-680911 – B/1/3 (Navy Cross)

PFC – Drivere, Richard J. – 2445541-680910 – B/1/3

PFC – Graveline, Richard P. – 2368916-680909 – B/1/3

PFC – Nunn, Samuel J. – 2346578-680910 – B/1/3

PFC – Porras, Juan – 2377756-680920 – B/1/3

LCpl – Robertson, Merle E. – 2388054-680910 – B/1/3

PFC – Ruchti, Heinz – 2425013-680911 – B/1/3

PFC – Tines, Franz – 2416583-680911 – B/1/3

LCpl – Tyson, Dennis L. – 2380740-680909 – B1/3

Story
by Woodrow W. Easterling

As one who marched from Camp Elliot to open up Pendleton, we look back on our time in the 3d Division with awe and love and deep respect and honor for those we knew and served with.

We all had the desire, as I could hardly wait to get overseas to get after the Japs. First was New Zealand, then to the Canal for more training, and then Bougainville, back to camp at the Canal, then to Guam, then to that hell on earth, Iwo Jima. My God, what a deathtrap to so many young American boys.

They say we're not to live in the past, but all who served there will never forget the death and the black sand. Everywhere you looked was a tunnel, cave, or outcropping of brush that hid Japs , and we were exposed as never before. Never had we seen so much blood and guts, enough to last four lifetimes.

I want to thank the fleet and corpsmen and Division for such an outstanding , and they paid dearly for their efforts. We had the greatest bunch of officers, and they cared about all of us and would have laid down their lives for any private in rear ranks.

I'm now 83 years old and in failing health, but grateful I can be called a Marine. God bless you all. Semper Fi!

Third Marine Division
Association Presidents

+ Gen. Graves B. Erskine Founder, 1949-53

+ LtGen. Edward A. Craig, 1953-57

Col. Chester G. Smith, 1957-58

MajGen. Sidney S. McMath, 1958-60

+ Thomas W. Stone, 1960-62

+ CWO Thomas O. Kelly, 1962-64; 1968-69

Harold J. Melloy, 1964-66; 1967-68

Robert E. Williams, 1966-67

+ Col. Austin P. Gattis, 1969-71

Roy E. Gerken, 1971-73

Gen. Raymond G. Davis, 1973-75

+ Gen. Lewis W. Walt, 1975-76

+ Charles R. Powers, 1976-77

Col. Edward F. Danowitz, 1977-79

Leo A. Farrow, 1979-81

BrigGen. James P. King, 1981-82

Col. Warren H. Weidhahn, 1982-84

Harold K. Noble, 1984-86

SgtMaj. M.W. "Bill" Krueger, 1986-88

Col. Jerome W. Brown, 1988-90

Joe Garza, Jr., 1990-92

LtCol. George R. Gay, 1992-94

+ Henry L. Gardner, Jr. 1994-96

Capt. Ronald R. Burton, 1996-1998

Royal Q. Zilliox, 1998-2000

2dLt. John H. Rine, Jr. 2000-2002

+ = Deceased

Recipients of the General Allen H. Turnage Award

The general Allen H. Turnage Award for Exceptional Service is the Association's highest honor, and is the most prestigious acknowledgement of service to the Association by an individual that can be identified and recognized.

The Association's Board of Directors makes the award in recognition of exceptional service encompassing, "… that which is more distinguished in nature than that normally performed by, or expected of, members, officers and /or friends of the Association."

Since it was first presented in 1974, only the following individuals have been honored with the Turnage Award:

*Albert L. Jenson, 1974	Richard E. Jones, 1988
*I. Robert Kriendler, 1975	Edward F. Danowitz, 1990
*Thomas O. Kelly, 1976	*Harvey W. Tennant, 1991
*Joseph A. Rabun, 1978	M.W. "Bill" Krueger, 1992
Lenny A. Mormino, 1980	Robert B. Van Atta, 1993
Tom Stowe, 1981	Leslie G. LeBlanc, 1995
*Charles R. Powers, 1982	Thomas W. Kelley, 1997
*Russell W. Adamczuk, 1984	Joe Garza Jr., 1998
Bert R. Barton, 1984	* Deceased

General Turnage commanded the 3d Marine Division from September 1943 until September 1944 during its two earliest campaigns of World War II, Bougainville and Guam. At the time of his death in October 1971, General Turnage was the Honorary Life Chairman of the Association.

Association History

In 1949, General Graves B. "Blood and Guts" Erskine, Commanding General of the 3d Division at Iwo Jima, organized a meeting at Camp Pendleton Officers Club to begin the formation of the Third Marine Division Association, with funding obtained through a loan from Marine Corps Headquarters. General Erskine was the Association's first president, and membership quickly rose to 4,700. Interest dropped off considerably during the Korean War, but picked up again when the Association was reorganized under the leadership of Lieutenant General Edward A. Craig, the Association's second President.

The Third Marine Division Association began a membership drive in February 1951. To let potential members know about the organization, a press release was sent to newspapers in the Norfolk, Virginia, area, where the Association was headquartered, and to newspapers and radio and television stations in Washington, Los Angeles, and other major cities throughout the country. The announcement was also carried in the camp newspapers at Parris Island, Camp Lejeune, Cherry Point, Quantico, San Diego, and Camp Pendleton, as well as in the March 1 issue of the *Army, Navy, and Air Force Register*.

Early in 1952, the Association's first newsletter – a three-page, hand-typed letter from General Erskine – was sent to members. In his letter, General Erskine explains the details of forming the Association, names its regional officers, updates members on some of the organization's recent activities, and provides a report on the Association's finances.

In its early days, the Association was in some financial difficulties, brought on, in part, by the deactivation of the Division; however, reactivation of the Division in January 1952 brought new members and enough money to pay off $2,000 of the debt, with hopes of paying off the remainder by the end of the year.

The Association did not hold a reunion in 1952, instead concentrating on building membership and financial support through regional activities. General Erskine also recommended raising the membership fee to $2/year, effective September 15, 1952.

The newsletter reported on several chapter activities. In March 22, the Norfolk area chapter held a "Dagwood" dinner, which was well attended. At the event, Major Richard C. Peck agreed to act as a Special Representative for the Association president at Quantico. A few weeks later, he held a meeting which was attended by 20 individuals, including six new members. The group decided to hold regular get-togethers on the second Monday of each month. The Third Region members held their first meeting, a cocktail party and organization session, at the Hotel Astor in New York City. Seventy-five people attended, including 15 new members, and the meeting was written up in the *New York Times*.

The Association's second newsletter, published in 1953, marked the first time the name *Caltrap* appeared on the masthead. The main news feature was a story about the 3d Marine Division's return to Iwo Jima, this time to participate in amphibious maneuvers.

Caltrap was published on a more regular basis, beginning in 1954, and beginning with the September issue, the newsletter also took on a more formal appearance, with the Caltrap insignia appearing on the masthead for the first time.

The previous year, the Marine Division Associations had discussed holding their annual reunions at the same time and in the same city, allowing men who had served in more than one division the opportunity to attend all meetings. Although a committee had been appointed by the 1st Division Association to study the matter, no firm decisions

BOUGAINVILLE   GUAM   IWO JIMA

3D MARINE DIVISION ASSOCIATION
Headquarters, Fleet Marine Force, Atlantic
U.S. Naval Base
Norfolk 11, Virginia

NEWSLETTER NO. 1

Dear Member:

Without doubt you will be interested in a report of the activities of the Association since the initiation of the new membership drive last February.

As a starting point, a press release was made to newspapers with very good cooperation; All of the papers in the Norfolk area, one in Washington, D.C., two in Los Angeles and at least one in San Diego carried it. Also, the announcement was carried in camp newspapers at Parris Island, Camp Lejeune, Cherry Point, Quantico, San Diego and Camp Pendleton. The announcement was also carried in the March 1st issue of the Army, Navy, and Air Force Register. Similar material was also forwarded to radio and television media in the Norfolk and Los Angeles-San Diego areas; unfortunately, however, there is no definite information available as to its usage by these media.

The release to the various organs in the Norfolk area also mentioned our regional get-together of March 22nd, the week-end nearest the anniversary date of the conclusion of heavy fighting on Iwo Jima. This shin-dig took the form of a "Dagwood" buffet supper with drinks on a pay-as-you-go basis and a very pleasant evening was had by all who attended. In spite of the fact that some of our members at this headquarters were away on temporary duty assignments this affair was attended by thirty members, some of whom travelled from as far away as Camp Lejeune and Washington, D.C. The Quantico delegation is to be congratulated for having the largest representation from any single locality.

At the March 22nd party, Major Richard C. Peck agreed to act as Special Representative of the President at Quantico to organize and direct the activities of the Association in that area. As a result of his efforts a meeting was held in Quantico on 7 April with twenty attending, six of whom were new members. At this meeting it was decided to hold regular get-togethers on the second Monday of each month. This program has been carried through and has brought in a good number of new members. Some of these meetings have been in the nature of outings at the Picnic Grounds in the locality and have been well attended and very much enjoyed.

On June 13th the members of the Association in the Third Region held their first meeting at the Hotel Astor in New York City. This meeting, a cocktail party and organization session, was attended by seventy-five and brought fifteen new members into the fold. Major Ralph Horgan, Vice President for the Third Region, reports excellent cooperation from publicity media in connection with this get-together including a write-up in the New York Times.

were made, which meant that a joint reunion could not be planned for 1954. Later that year, a modified plan was suggested, with each association holding its reunion in Washington, DC, beginning in 1955 and continuing every fourth year thereafter. Each association was to have an independent reunion, with one joint function for all groups and a joint memorial service at Arlington National Cemetery. The combined reunion was scheduled for June 24-26, 1955.

The Association was in the process of reorganizing in order to expand and strengthen the organization. A "test" program for local chapters in New York City and San Francisco had been proposed, with these chapters -- which were to be named after the Division's famous battles or deceased Marines who had been honored for heroic conduct -- functioning under the Regional Vice Presidents. Any member who felt there were enough interested members in his area to form a local post was advised to contact his Regional Vice President or the Association with his recommendations.

The October 1954 edition of *Caltrap* reported that the 1st, Third, 5th, and 6th Marine Division Associations had agreed to participate in a joint reunion in 1955. The organizing committee agreed to a consolidated program featuring separate editorial chapters for each association, the proceeds from advertising pro-rated among the associations according to their attendance. Later that year, the organizing committee agreed to set up a joint convention office and to have joint convention letterhead printed. They also agreed on a joint event – a dress parade at the Marine Corps Memorial site on the Saturday afternoon of the reunion, followed by a brief memorial service.

During 1954, there were some changes in Association leadership. Colonel Ronald R. Van Stockum, Colonel John H. Goodwin, and Lt. Colonel John L. Clark, who was stationed at Camp Pendleton, were appointed Regional Vice Presidents. Retired General Allen H. Turnage was named Honorary President.

In November, the Association began a large membership drive, chaired by Colonel Van Stockum, which was scheduled to end on February 19, 1955, the tenth anniversary of the Division's landing at Iwo Jima. The Association also began offering members an official lapel pin featuring a replica of the famed Caltrap insignia. The pins cost $1.

Hundreds of Marines converged on Washington, DC, in late June 1955 for the Association's first reunion, as well as the first joint reunion of all Marine Division Associations. Group programs and time for individual pursuits were worked into the schedule.

The Association had also scheduled its annual business meeting during the reunion so that members could elect officers, vote on resolutions, and discuss editorial policies for *Caltrap*. Presiding over the business meeting, Lieutenant General Craig reported that membership had increase by 2,863 individuals since June 1953 . The Association's worth was reported as $8,314.66. The acts and proceedings of the outgoing boards and committees, as well as the First Annual Report compiled by the Acting President and the Association's financial report, were accepted. Tentative bylaws were also accepted, pending examination and a report by the Association's Legal Officer. Other business matters included election of a new president, employment of a full-time secretary, and work on incorporating the organization.

Two wartime commanders – General Turnage and General Erskine – gave brief speeches. In addition, Major General James P. Risley, Commander of the 3d Marine Division in Japan, sent a greeting, which was read to the assembly:

"Radio greetings from the Third, from Commanding General, Third Marine Division in Japan. Commanding General, officers, and men, Third Marine Division sends to members of the Third Marine Division Association. Warm regards and best wishes to al the old hands. In Japan, Hawaii, and Okinawa today's division seeks to emulate the high standards you have set for us. We look forward to next year and the hope that many of us can be with you for the 1956 reunion."

General Lemuel C. Shepherd, Commandant of the Marine Corps, addressed the assembled marines and their guests at a memorial service held at the Iwo Jima Memorial.

The Association continued its efforts to attract new members, including Marines on active duty, recruiting more than 2,000 new members, including 703 from the 3rd Tank Battalion and 627 from the 9th Marines. Major General Risley was awarded the first certificate of membership from the Okinawa drive. In October, Colonel Walter Asmuth, Jr., Regional Vice President, Third Marine Division Association in the Orient, began a campaign to sign up new members from among his men who were due to leave for the States and civilian life. The New York Metropolitan Chapter was organized towards the end of 1954, with their first meeting, held at the famous "21" Club. The March 1955 issue of the newsletter reported that membership renewals had increased by 90 percent over the previous year.

The Association's 1956 reunion was held in Chicago, at the Congress Hotel, June 29-July 1, with Captain Charles Zell heading the organizing committee. Hundreds of members from all over the country attended, and there were many individual reunions between World War II buddies who had served together at Guadalcanal, Bougainville, Guam, and Iwo Jima, while younger members renewed acquaintances they had made while serving in Japan and Okinawa.

At the business meeting, the Association elected new officers and selected Directors, Regional Vice Presidents, and members of the Membership Committee. Two amendments to the Association's by-laws were also passed, one making provisions for establishing and administering a scholarship fund and the other establishing Life Memberships in the Association, with dues set at $40. Three resolutions were unanimously accepted: The first endorsed and approved the training and indoctrination methods used at the Parris Island and San Diego Recruit Depots for all men recruited for service in the Marine Corps; the second noted the Association's active opposition to a proposed merger of all branches of the United States Armed Forces; and the third charged the Association with investigating efforts of the Corps or the government to erect monuments or markers at Bougainville, Guam, Iwo Jima, and other sites of battles and campaigns fought by the 3d Marine Division in World War II.

General Turnage was the featured speaker at the All-Marines banquet. Major General T.A. Wornham, Division Commanding General, was unable to attend the reunion, but sent a message to members of the Association from members of the 3d Marine Division overseas, expressing their best wishes for a successful and enjoyable reunion.

In accordance with the resolution passed at the meeting, the Association President contacted the Corps and the American Battle Monuments Commission regarding markers for the Pacific battlefields. The Commission replied that two memorials were being erected in honor of those who served in the Pacific – one at the American Cemetery in Manila, Philippines, and the other at the National Cemetery of the Pacific, Punchbowl Crater, Honolulu, Hawaiian Territories. Because of personnel and budget constraints, the program for marking the battlefields had been delayed.

The Scholarship Fund was started with a donation from Captain Richard McCutchen, who provided $600 from his winnings on the popular television game show *The $64,000 Question*. With contributions from members, the fund stood at $1,176.40 in 1956. Children of all Marines who served with the Division, whether members of the Association or not and whether they served in war or peacetime, were eligible.

Two new Chapters were organized in 1956: the Greater Pittsburgh Chapter, organized by James R. Drew, and the Cleveland Chapter, organized by Charles A. Dietz, Jr.

The Association's third annual reunion was held in San Francisco, July 19-21, 1957, at the Marine's Memorial Club. The club, the only memorial of its kind in the world, was called "The Crossroads of the Corps." The money for purchasing and furnishing the club was raised through donations from Marines, both officers and enlisted personnel, another testament to the Marines' esprit de corps, and membership was free and open to all Marines, with associate memberships for hospital corpsmen and veterans of other services who served with the Marines. The club's manager, Major General Evans O. Ames, had served with the 3d Division's 21st Marines.

At the business meeting, officers, Regional Vice Presidents, and Directors were elected. Two important resolutions were unanimously adopted – one reaffirming faith in God and Country and a rededication of the membership to the defense of the Constitution and the principles for which it stands, and the other expressing dissatisfaction with a provision in some security treaties giving foreign governments the right to exercise primary jurisdiction over United States Armed Forces troops under certain conditions.

In 1957, the Association received its official designation as a non-profit 501 (c)(3) organization, which meant that contributions to the Association, including donations to the Scholarship Fund, were tax deductible.

The prior year, the Association had voted to establish the Third Marine Division Association Rifle Trophy, an annual competition for members of the Division. Contributions from Association members were solicited to fund the trophy. Just prior to relinquishing command of the 3d Marine Division, Major General Shapley accepted the trophy on behalf of the Division. It was delivered by Captain Frank E. Copeland, Association representative on Okinawa. The trophy was presented to Sergeant John B. Funk, H Company, Third Battalion, squad leader of the 3d Division's top squad.

The Association continued to experience growth and prosperity throughout the year. A successful membership drive on Okinawa added 901 new members. Major General Shapley presented a check for $1,840 to Major Charles C. Henderson, Association Vice President for delivery to the Association's treasury. In addition, a donation of $300 was made to the Association.

The 1958 reunion, organized by members of the New York Chapter and chaired by Ralph T. Horgan, was held at New York City's Hotel Roosevelt, July 18-20. Among the highlights of the event was a memorial service held at Yankee Stadium prior to the Yankees-Kansas City game. Sidney S. McCath, former governor of Arkansas who served with the Division's Third Marines, was the speaker for the Saturday luncheon meeting. He stepped in for Lieutenant General R.E. Hogaboom, who was unable to attend due to the crisis brewing in Lebanon.

New officers were elected at the business meeting, and six Regional Vice Presidents were selected, with an additional three to be named later. Five amendments to the Association's bylaws were adopted, dealing primarily with organization structure and matters. Four resolutions were proposed and passed unanimously. The Association also voted that, beginning with the 1958 reunion, profits would be divided, with 80 percent to the Association and 20 percent to the hosting chapter.

Luther Skaggs, Jr., one of five living Medal of Honor recipients who had served with the Division in World War II, was elected president of the Association's newly-formed Washington (DC) Area Chapter.

The Association had new stationery designed in 1958, featuring Caltrap insignia. Caltrap letterhead was entered in a national competition and won an award of merit for Ocean Beach Printing and Publishing in recognition of outstanding craftsmanship in printing.

The Association's newly-organized Washington Area Chapter hosted the 1959 reunion, held at the Mayflower Hotel in Washington, DC, July 17-19.

President Sidney S. McMath presided over the business meeting. It was noted that the Association's mailing list included 2,295 individuals, including 205 still on active duty with the Division and 14 Life Members. Between July 1958 and July 1959, 281 new members had joined, 148 of them currently serving with the Division. The Association's net worth as of the end of May was $5,610.30. The Association's Scholarship Fund had been redesignated as the Welfare Fund, as a new government program provided college educations for the children deceased servicemen and veterans.

Several resolutions were proposed and approved, including one resolving that the " ... basic racial problem and the fundamental constitutional issue involved should be opened up for public discussion and debate without regard to political considerations or religious affiliations." The Association also voted to hold the 1960 reunion in Washington, DC, as part of a concurrent reunion of all Marine associations. In addition, a motion was passed authorizing the Judge Advocate to take steps to incorporate the Association. A proposal to raise annual membership dues to $5 was rejected. The nominating committee's slate of candidates was received. Ralph Horgan was appointed Vice President-at-Large, while Edward A. Galiskis was appointed Regional Vice President, 1st MCR and Recruitment District. Other Regional Vice Presidents were to be appointed at a later date.

The Division's five living Medal of Honor recipients were the Association's honored guests at the reunion. They were also honored at a memorial service held at the Iwo Jima Memorial.

General R. McCall Pate, Commandant of the Marine Corps, presented the keynote address at the reunion. Major General Alan Shapley, Director, Marine Corps Reserve and Recruitment, addressed the Association's Saturday luncheon on the subject of the Marine Corps Reserve.

George J. Smyth, who had been appointed Regional Vice President for the Northern California Region at the 1958 reunion, began efforts to organize a Chapter in the San Francisco area.

With the decade of the 1950s drawing to a close, the Association continued its efforts to recruit new members. Meanwhile, T.O. Kelly, who had been selected to chair the 1960 reunion, was busy with plans for the event, which would be held concurrently with the reunions of the five other divisions the following year.

As the decade of the 1960s opened, the world was in a state of relative peace. In just a few short years, however, that would change dramatically. And, as in World War II, the 3d Marine Division would play a significant role in the conflict.

The Association's 1960 reunion was held at the Mayflower Hotel in Washington, DC, in conjunction with the second Fleet Marine Force Concurrent Reunion. In addition to the Association's activities, there was also a joint dinner-dance at the Sheraton Park Hotel and a special military demonstration at the Marine Corps Schools at Quantico.

More than 100 members attended the Saturday business meeting. Tom Stowe was elected President, the first non-Marine to hold that office. He had been attached to the 9th Marines at Camp Elliot, New Zealand, and Guadalcanal, as head of a Red Cross Unit; he also served with the 9th Marines at Bougainville and also worked as a war correspondent on Iwo Jima and Okinawa. A resolution urging Congress to enact H.R. 11318, equalizing retirement pay for veterans who retired prior to June 1, 1959, and after that date was unanimously approved. The Association also adopted a policy of mailing membership renewal bills on January 1, rather than waiting until April 1, when they became delinquent. Another resolution gave members the choice of purchasing life membership in installments and on a graduated scale based on the age of the member. In addition, the Association voted to reimburse travel expenses to reunions for the Secretary-Treasurer and his wife.

Brigadier General William T. Fairbourn, Director, Marine Corps Reserve, who served with the 12th Marines during World War II, spoke at the Saturday luncheon about the need to keep the Association a healthy, vital organization. The Association launched a new membership drive at the 1960 reunion:

"With the continued wealth of potential members leaving the Division each year, leaving with the same mark of the 3d all of us bear, our Association can become strong. Let each of us then within the Association personally contact a Division man not yet a member. The Division is of age now. So, when we contact a potential member, let us no longer consider whether he is of the old or new Division. There is only one 3d Marine Division. Let us Association members gather in the Division's newest alumni."

The Association's 20 Regional Vice Presidents were also enlisted to aid in increasing membership and forming new chapters. Tom Kelly was appointed chairman of a special membership committee. In addition, a seven-man Presidential Advisory Committee – comprising General Erskine, General Shepherd, Lieutenant General Craig, Colonel McCath, Colonel Kriendler, and Major General Donald M. Weller, the Division's Commanding General on Okinawa – was appointed to provide guidance and counsel on the welfare of the Association.

February 19, 1960, marked the fifteenth anniversary of the landing of American forces on Iwo Jima.

BOUGAINVILLE... GUAM... IWO JIMA...

CALTRAP

OFFICIAL NEWSLETTER OF 3D MARINE DIVISION ASSOCIATION

VOL. VI, No. 3   FEBRUARY-MARCH 1960

Commemorate Marine Assault On Iwo

ARLINGTON, VA., Feb. 19 – Headed by Marine Corps Commandant General David M. Shoup, representatives of five USMC divisions gathered at the Iwo Jima Monument today on the 15th anniversary of the World War II landing of American forces on Iwo Jima (February 19, 1945) to pay tribute to the 5,931 marines who gave their lives in the 26-day campaign, and to plan memorial ceremonies to highlight concurrent reunions of all Marine divisions in the nation's capital June 24-26.

Leading the group in a salute to their deceased comrades, is General Shoup, shown on the right with Major Gerald L. Pines, USMC, Fourth Marine Division and Major Joseph R. Fisher, USMC, Fifth Marine Division. On the left are General Graves B. Erskine, USMC(Ret.), who commanded the Third Marine Division on Iwo; Lt. Gen. Julian C. Smith, USMC (Ret.), general chairman of the Concurrent Reunions, Second Marine Division; and Brig. Gen. James J. Keating, USMC (Ret.), First Marine Division. The Sixth Marine Division was not represented.

Memorial Club Aids Reunion

Members of all Marine Division Associations residing on the West Coast will be interested in knowing that the Marines Memorial club, 609 Sutter St., San Francisco, Calif., is endeavoring to arrange special group transportation by air that will provide substantial savings in travel cost. If you plan to attend the Fleet Marine Force Concurrent Reunion in Washington, D.C., June 24-26, 1960, write the Club, giving your name, address, and be sure to indicate whether you will attend by yourself or with your wife or husband. The early receipt of this information will enable the Club to determine if enough are attending to make it possible to arrange group transportation for those on the West Coast. If chartered plane service is used it is likely that arrangements can be made to board planes for the trip east from San Francisco, Los Angeles, Portland and Seattle.

Assign MarDiv Hotels

Although most of the main events of the 1960 FMF Concurrent Reunions in Washington, D.C., June 24-26, will be joint affairs, each of the five division associations will have separate hotel headquarters. Their locations follow:

1stMarDiv	Sheraton Park Hotel
2ndMarDiv	Washington Hotel
3rdMarDiv	Mayflower Hotel
4thMarDiv	Shoreham Hotel
5thMarDiv	Willard Hotel

Third Marine Division veterans desiring additional information about the concurrent reunions to be held in Washington, D.C., June 24-26, should write to CWO T. O. Kelly, USMC (Ret.), 1418 Valley Crest Blvd., Annandale, Va. He is the 1960 reunion general chairman.

Representatives of the five Marine Corps divisions gathered at the Iwo Jima Memorial to pay tribute to the nearly 6,000 Marines who gave their lives to secure the island. General Erskine represented the 3d Marine Division.

The Association returned to New York City and the Hotel Roosevelt for its 1961 reunion. Bob Williams, who chaired the reunion committee, strived to make the event a family affair, with special programs and activities for wives and children of members and arrangements with the hotel to provide baby sitters.

In his opening remarks at the banquet, General Turnage praised Association President Tom Stowe and his wife, Alice, for their exemplary service and untiring efforts on behalf of the organization. Stowe was made an honorary Life Member of the Association.

The first rumblings of the Vietnam war were being heard at this time, and Major General Alpha L. Bowser, Assistant Chief of Staff G-1, HQMC, seemed to foretell the coming conflict when he opened his remarks by reading these words from greetings sent by General Shoup:

"Today your old outfit stands ready and able in the Far East to take on whatever mission may be assigned."

At the business meeting, new officers were elected. The Association's bylaws were revised to allow executive officers the power to act on Association matters in times when it was impossible to muster a quorum of Board members. Resolutions were approved pledging Association support for President Kennedy's Berlin stand and calling for observance of Veterans Day in all 50 states. In addition, three commendations were made – to General Shoup for his support of the Association, to Reunion Chairman Bob Williams and individuals who assisted him, and to Colonel I. Robert Kriendler for exceptionally outstanding financial support.

The reunion netted more than $8,000 in profit for the Association, with 20 percent going to the host chapter and 80 percent to the Association's treasury.

General Turnage, Tom Stowe, and Colonel Kriendler represented the Association at the funeral of General Randolph McCall Pate, former Commandant of the Marine Corps, who passed away on July 31.

A new Chapter was formed on March 23 in Philadelphia, birthplace of the United States Marine Corps. Dr. John J. Stanton, Jr., who served with the Division's 12th Regiment in the Guam and Iwo Jima campaigns, was elected President of the Philadelphia Area Chapter. Earl B. Gerheim and his wife were contacting all 3d Division Marines in the Detroit area, hoping to organize a Chapter there. On June 8, another new Chapter – this one in Chicago – was formed when 12 members gathered at the home of Ed Chelsea for their first meeting.

The membership drive had recruited 363 new members had been recruited, almost four times the number of new members from the previous year. In addition, renewals increased dramatically as a result of sending out renewal notices on January 1. In addition to the committee's efforts, Lenny "Humpy" Mormino, the Association's Sergeant-at-Arms and a Regional Vice President, undertook a one-man campaign to recruit new members for the Association. By November, he had signed up 105 new members. At year's end, total Association membership stood at just over 1,200, a 75 percent increase since 1959.

The Association appointed 30 Regional Vice Presidents, whose duties included recruiting new members, forming local chapters where practical, and spreading the word about the Association and its annual reunions.

Members of the Association were urged to contribute to a fund to buy 18 etched-glass windows for the Marine Corps Memorial Chapel at the Marine Corps Schools, Quantico. The non-denominational chapel was dedicated in 1957 in memory of those who lost their lives serving with the Corps.

The Association returned to Washington's Hotel Mayflower for a third time in 1962. It was a memorable occasion, coinciding with the twentieth anniversary of the Division's activation. The reunion banquet was an unqualified success. Secretary of Agriculture Orville L. Freeman, who served with the 9th Regiment at Bougainville, gave the keynote address.

To add to the celebratory atmosphere, the night of the banquet was also the forty-second wedding anniversary of General and Mrs. Turnage. The Association presented them with an engraved, sterling silver cake knife in honor of the occasion. The Division's former commanding generals were recognized in a special tribute, and six of them attended the banquet with their wives. Other special guests included Congressman James C. Corman, of California, who served with the 21st Marines at Bougainville, Guam, and Iwo Jima; former Marine Corps Commandant, General Lemuel C. Shepherd, Jr., who served for a time as Commander of the Division's 9th Regiment; Congressional Medal of Honor recipients General Shoup and Colonel Louis H. Wilson, Jr.; and Luther Skaggs, Jr., a Medal of Honor recipient and President of the Congressional Medal of Honor Society. Both General Shoup and General Turnage spoke following the dinner.

At the business meeting, new officers were elected. Tom Kelly reported that 600 new members had joined the Association since July 1960 (Lenny Mormino continued his efforts, recruiting, on average, five new members each month.) The Association paid tribute to Colonel Kriendler for his continued support, and vote of thanks to the Division's Commanding Generals was passed. A patriotic-theme essay contest for Association members' children with a total prize not to exceed $75 was approved. The Association also authorized a committee to investigate and recommend Division veterans or children of deceased veterans eligible for welfare assistance or scholarship aid. Brigadier General Raymond F. Crist was appointed chair of the committee. Both the recently-formed Chicago Chapter and the Philadelphia Chapter presented bids for hosting the 1963 reunion, with Philadelphia winning by a narrow margin.

In addition, the Association made a $100 contribution to the USMC's Historical Museum in Philadelphia and approved financial assistance for newly-formed chapters. The Association also voted to pursue legal incorporation as soon as possible.

A project to consider medical or education assistance to needy individuals in American Samoa was approved, with Harold J. Melloy named chairman of the Samoan Project committee. The 3d Marine Division had a close relationship with the Samoan people, having helped defend Samoa during World War II. Chairman Melloy, who had served in Samoa, was concerned about the deteriorating economic and social welfare of its people. His committee was charged with preparing a report making recommendations to be acted upon at the 1953 reunion.

September 16 marked the Division's twentieth anniversary. Three members of the original 3d Division – Sergeant Major Dave L. Johnson, Sergeant Major Harlan L. Graham, and First Sergeant James F. Esslinger – were still serving with the Division.

In 1963, the the Association's annual reunion was held in Philadelphia for the first time, with the Hotel Benjamin Franklin serving as headquarters..

At the business meeting, officers were elected. In addition, Lenny Mormino was appointed Assistant to the President, and Tom Stowe was appointed Publicity Officer. Resolutions adopted by the Association included a citation to Colonel Kriendler for his invaluable service to the Association, and a salute to General Turnage in honor of the 50th anniversary of his Marine Corps career. Membership dues were raised to $3 to help cover increased costs for postage, stationery, and printing. The Association pledged to support and promote the Marine Military Academy and Prescott, Arizona.

Winners of the children's essay contest were announced. First prize of $40 dollars went to Monica Mocadlo, daughter of Mr. And Mrs. Victor Mocadlo; second prize of $25 went to William Caccia, son of Albert Caccia; and third prize of $10 went to another Mocadlo daughter, Barbara.

Major General Henry W. Buse, who became Commanding General of the 3d Marine Division in 1962, spoke at the banquet about the modernization, training, and capabilities of the Division. He also commented on the distinguished record of the 3d and praised the tradition of brotherhood carried on by the Association:

"Your gathering here symbolizes your desire to help keep alive the spirit which has inspired the Third Marine Division and made it invincible. The continued existence of that spirt and your individual contributions to the overall effort will insure that the Marine Corps will always remain steadfast in its roll as the nation's ready-force."

Colonel Rex R. Stillwell was invited to speak at Memorial Services, held on July 20 at Philadelphia's Independence Hall.

For their Samoan Project, with the Association had decided to raise money to buy books to stock the island's first public library. The goal was to raise $7,500, which would purchase more than 2,000 books as well as some much-needed equipment. The $500 provided by the Association to defray planning and initiation costs for the project was donated to the fund, with committee members choosing to pay their own expenses. By June, more than $1,000 had been raised. His Highness Galumalemana, Prince of Tutuila, American Samoa, F.F. Le'Aupepe, and several other notable Samoans visited the reunion.

The year saw the Washington Area Chapter bestow the Association's first honorary membership on Christian F. Ballman and his wife in memory of their son, Gilbert, who gave his life at Bougainville. In February, Pauline Roberts became the first woman to be given an honorary membership, in recognition of her interest in the Washington Area Chapter activities and her work has hostess of the style show at the 1962 reunion.

The Association kept up its efforts to recruit new members. Marines serving their first tour with the Division were eligible for one-year honorary memberships, while those on second or subsequent tours could join for the reduced rate of $2/year. Association President T.O. Kelly announced in October that rosters of prospects, along with an instruction sheet and sample letter, would be sent to all members. Association President Kelly also appointed 36 Regional Vice Presidents to "spread the word" about the Association and recruit new members.

As the year drew to a close, the Association was incorporated in the state of California, where the Division had been activated. It had been a long process, but was worth the wait. Incorporation added to the Association's already significant prestige and dignity and also protected individual officers from unwarranted legal actions.

The Chicago Chapter, which had failed in its bid to host the 1963 reunion, was selected to host the 1964 reunion, which was held at the Sheraton-Chicago Hotel.

Entertainment included a Friday evening Siva-Siva party, with a performance by the Drum Dancers of Tahiti, in native costume, and South Seas-style food served around the hotel's swimming pool. Lenny Mormino arranged to have grass skirts, sarong, mumus, Aloha shirts, coconut hats, and leis shipped from the South Pacific for the occasion.

The annual Memorial Service was held in front of the hotel, with addresses by Commander W.F. Doyle, CHC, U.S. Navy, and by Father Conway, the Association's chaplain. The Navy Blue Jackets Choir from the Great Lakes Naval Training Center sang, and the color guard, bugler, and firing squad came from the Glen View Naval Air Station and Marine Corps Reserve Station. At the end of the ceremony, the chimes of the Chicago Tribune Tower tolled.

Navy personnel who served with the 3d Marine Division were honored at the dinner dance, and tributes to them were included in the reunion souvenir booklet.

New officers were elected at the business meeting. Certificates of appreciation were presented to Congressman Corman and Judge Advocate Gattis for their efforts on the Association's

REUNION DIGNITARIES - The head table at the 1964 Chicago Reunion. Left to right: Vi and Hal Melloy; Betty and Ed Schubel; Father Joseph J. Conway and Father George M. Kempker; Tom and Alice Stowe; Congressman James C. Corman; Herrett and Tom Kelly; Inez and Al Jenson; Bette and Reg Hameetman; and Ed Gonzalez. (Photo by Flash Foto Co., Chicago, IL)

incorporation. Resolutions were passed eulogizing General Turnage, Colonel Kriendler, and Congressman Corman for their outstanding support of the Association, and another resolution paid tribute to the host chapter and to the reunion chairman, Reg Hameetman, and his staff. Other resolutions urged support for the Marine Military Academy; increased the cost of life membership and initiated a $1/year membership fee for active duty members; recommended reimbursement of reasonable expenses for Association officials; and supported a bill pending in Congress that would make it possible for veterans to have their life insurance reinstated.

As of July 1, membership stood at 1,203, and the Association's assets on May 31 were listed as $5,609.02. More than $10,000 was raised from the sale of souvenir program ads.

Congressman Corman was the featured speaker at the reunion banquet. He noted that the nation – and the Corps – stood at the halfway point between the Japanese counter-attack on Guam and George Orwell's fictional 1984. He also paid tribute to the Navy men who had served with and provided invaluable assistance to the Division.

Chairman Melloy reported that more than $5,300 had been donated to the Samoan Book Fund, all of it used to purchase books for the library. Member Ben Byrer donated a painting he had done, portraying a scene on Bougainville, to be raffled off to raise funds for the project.

In October, President Melloy appointed J.M. Gerarve to chair an Americanism Committee to help promote a feeling of patriotism in the United States and its possessions on national holidays. Chairman Gerarve solicited the assistance of the seven Association chapters by forming committees to assist with the project.

In the November issue of the newsletter, Honorary President Eddie Craig requested the help of all members in supporting the ongoing membership drive, reminding them:

"Let's not lose sight of the reason for our Association's existence. Always remember, we are dedicated to perpetuate the comradeship, history, and traditions of a famous combat division that never knew defeat – the 3d Marine Division. Its reputation and prestige is involved. DON'T LET IT DOWN."

By the end of the year, membership was 1,400. Tom Kelly was determined to double, even triple, that number.

The Association lost one a great friend with the death on December 12 of Brigadier General Raymond F. Crist, Jr. A member of the Washington Area Chapter, he had served as chairman for the first reunion and in 1962 had chaired the scholarship and welfare committees.

The 1965 reunion was held at the Marriott Motor Hotel in Washington, DC, July 22-25. While the reunion was, as always, a festive affair, there was also an air of solemnity surrounding the celebrations, as the Association's brother Marines of the 3d Division were in the thick of the war in Vietnam. The reunion's theme was "A Salute to Industry."

General Wallace Greene, Jr., Commandant of the Marine Corps, was the featured speaker, and he talked at length about the difficulties facing the Marines and other U.S. forces in Southeast Asia. During the banquet, General Greene called Major General Lewis W. Walt, Commanding General of the 3d Division in Vietnam via two-way, short-wave radio, sending greetings from the Association to Marines serving in Vietnam.

General Erskine also touched on the value of freedom and the nobleness of sacrifice during the memorial service at the Iwo Jima Memorial, noting that, "We are not the first generation of Americans to face deadly danger, nor shall we be the last." Lieutenant General Shapley presided over the ceremonies. Music was provided by the Marine Band, and the color guard from the Marine Barracks.

The Committee on Resolutions presented seven items for consideration. The Association chose honoring the active 3d in Vietnam as the theme for the 1966 reunion, limited chapter membership on nominating committees to one, not including the chairman, and approved selecting reunion sites two years in advance. A proposal to limit the Association President to two consecutive terms was defeated.

A final report on the Books for Samoa Project was presented by President Melloy. More than $6,000 was raised and over 2,000 books shipped to Samoa's library. Territorial Librarian thanked the Association in a letter to Melloy, writing, "The books contributed by your Association have been wonderful aids as we have set about enlarging and improving

library service in Samoa." Samoa's acting governor also expressed his thanks for the Association's contribution.

On February 19, a five-man delegation from the Association – Frank Wilder, Tom Kelly, Tom Stowe, Bob Goldstein and Milt Barnes – attended ceremonies at the Iwo Jima Memorial to commemorate the twentieth anniversary of the landing on Iwo Jima. On May 11, Hal Melloy represented the Association at a dedication ceremony for the new Marine Corps museum in Philadelphia.

Andrew Reposky was appointed to chair a fundraising committee for the Marine Military Academy in Harlingen, Texas. The Academy, a high school-level military academy with a Marine Corps atmosphere. The Academy opened in September 1965.

The Association joined in CARE's voluntary Civic Action Program to provide food, clothing, and other essentials to needy civilians in Vietnam. Members of the Association were urged to " ... forego some pleasure and support this cause with a direct donation." All contributions from Association members were for use of the III Marine Amphibious Force's program.

The Association got a boost in membership when the Third Marines' entire 1st Howitzer Battery in Vietnam – 195 Marines in all – joined. Member Winston O. "Wimpy" Solomon, whose son was serving with the 1st, was responsible for recruiting this group.

The Association gathered at the Hotel Roosevelt in New York City for their 1966 reunion, held July 14-17. The theme was "The Combat Active 3d Division."

Major General William R. "Rip" Collins, the featured speaker, praised the Marines of the 3d Division, calling them "truly extraordinary in character," and noted that it was the only Division to be continuously deployed overseas without the presence of dependents. Major General Collins was well prepared to speak on the 3d's readiness, he was commanding the Division and the III Marine Expeditionary Force when they deployed to Vietnam. General Erskine was unable to attend the reunion due to injuries suffered in a taxi accident in New York, so Colonel Kriendler read his address, which paid tribute to the Division's men who had died in battle, at the closing banquet.

President Melloy reported that membership had increased over the last year and was continuing to grow, adding that the war in Vietnam was contributing to increased interest. The Association's income increased by just over $2,000 over the previous year. *Reunion Journal* editor, Major C. Louise Frazier, an active member of Public Affairs Unit 1-1, USMCR, New York City, became the first woman to serve in this capacity.

On the Corps' 191st birthday, the Association presented a check for $650 to the Civic Action Fund. Members also collected toys and soap for gift packages for Marines fighting in Vietnam. Donations for the Marine Military Academy continued to come in. One hundred thirty-nine cadets enrolled for the Academy's second year of classes.

Fifty Association members attended a special Evening Parade on August 25 commemorating the fiftieth anniversary of the Marine Corps Reserve.

Throughout the year, *Caltrap* was filled with news from Vietnam, including reports on the activities of the 3d Division in that war-torn country.

Recruiting efforts continued, with some novel approaches added to the usual methods. Hal Melloy donated 300 decks of personalized playing cards to be distributed to prospective recruits, along with membership information. The cards featured the Marines Corps insignia and Caltrap emblem. Members were also given lists of former 3d Division Marines who lived in their areas and were asked to contact them. The New York Chapter collected donations to sponsor 3d Marines on duty in Vietnam. In December the Board of Directors authorized Association members to sponsor former Third Division Marines for membership in 1967 at the cost of $1.

The year 1967 marked the twenty-fifth anniversary of the 3d Marine Division and the fiftieth anniversary of its oldest regiment, the "Striking Ninth," which originated in World War I. Cherry Hill, New Jersey, was chosen as the site for the reunion.

Lieutenant General Lewis W. Walt, recently returned from Vietnam, was the featured speaker at the reunion banquet. He also spoke at a press conference and at the Memorial Service for the Division's war dead. General Walt noted that Marines had built schools, markets, dispensaries, and roads in Vietnam, and had also aided with relocating hundreds of Vietnamese families, as well as refugees from the DMZ.

During the business meeting, Hal Melloy and T.O. Kelly were nominated from the floor as candidates for President and Vice President, respectively, and won over the nominating committee's candidates. Resolutions passed included one condemning the conduct of draft dodgers as "cowardly and unpatriotic." Other resolutions expressed thanks to those who helped make another successful reunion; recommended a $100 donation to the Nimitz Memorial; stipulated that newly-elected officers would assume office immediately following the reunion at which they were elected; stipulated that the Association President should not appoint Chapter members, other than the Chairman, on nominating and resolutions committees without the concurrence of the Chapter President; recommended that a stenographic record of the annual business meeting be made in future years; called for a standing reunion committee appointed by the President; issued a charter for the new Minnesota chapter. Resolutions that proposed reinstating the scholarship fund and educing the host chapter's share of the net profits from the reunion were rejected.

The Association registered its strong opposition to a proposed monument on Guam honoring Japanese soldiers. The association considered the proposal especially egregious in light of the fact that the American Battle Monuments Commission still had not erected battle monuments for American military personnel who gave their lives on Bougainville, Guam, and Iwo Jima.

Cash contributions, as well as donations of soap, toothbrushes, and toothpaste continued to be solicited for the Civic Action Program. The Association also continued its support of the Marine Military Academy, which was designated a Naval Honor School in 1967. In all, the Association had contributed more than $10,000 to worthwhile civic projects since its founding.

Following the Cherry Hill reunion, membership more than doubled to 3,500 paid members. Many of the new members were on active duty in Vietnam.

Throughout the year, news from the war filled the pages of *Caltrap*. The 3d Marine Division men continued to uphold the reputation for bravery and honor established by their brothers from the Old Breed. Six of the seven Medals of Honor awarded to date were bestowed on men of the 3d Marine Division. And for the second

time in its history, the Division was awarded the Presidential Unit Citation.

The 1968 "Smoky Mountain" reunion was held in at the Mountain View Hotel in Gatlinburg, Tennessee, with some events scheduled across the state line in Cherokee, North Carolina. The theme was "Bougainville," in honor of the twenty-fifth anniversary of the Division's first major battle.

Speaking at the banquet, Major General Louis Metzger said that the United States was winning the war and achieving the objective of freedom for South Vietnam. He also praised both the Old Breed and New Breed members, saying:

"We are assembled in this beautiful part of America to refurbish our memories, to regain the bonds of fellowship, and to show our support of the new generation of marines now engaged in bitter combat in another tropic clime, Vietnam."

The annual memorial parade featured the 2nd Marine Division Band from Camp Lejeune and the Knoxville Marine Corps Reserve Unit, as well as a long column of Division veterans. General Turnage reviewed the parade.

Among the officers elected was Edward F. O'Neill, Jr., Sergeant-at-Arms. O'Neill, whose father previously had held the post, was the first New Breed veteran elected to an Association office.

Several resolutions passed at the business meeting. Colonel Kriendler was again cited for his invaluable service to the organization. Association members reiterated their pride in being "patriotic and loyal defenders of our country and the ideals for which it stand." Other resolutions recommended a donation of $200 to the Civic Action Fund and additional clerical assistance for the Executive Secretary-Treasurer, as needed. Dues were increased to $5/year, $2/year for active duty Marines, and age-based dues for life membership. It was also recommended that the Board appoint three persons to serve on a national reunion committee to advise and assist the President with convention work.

The Board approved the charters for new chapters in Georgia and Florida, and placed the Los Angeles Chapter on one year's probation for lack of activity. Editorship of the newsletter was assigned to the Public Relations Officer, and Tom Stowe was appointed to that position. The Board also agreed to publish an informational booklet on the Association rather than a new edition of the Roster Book. Net profits from the reunion totaled more than $6,300.

More than $12,000 in donations was given to the Association to establish a scholarship fund in memory of Major General Bruno A. Hochmuth, the Division's Commanding General who was killed in a helicopter crash in Vietnam in 1967. In February, the Board endorsed the fund with a unanimous vote. The scholarship funds were to be used to pay for the education of dependents of 3d Marine Division men killed in Vietnam. Members voted against contributing a percentage of reunion proceeds to the fund.

At its meeting, the Board voted to employ temporary clerical help to deal with the overwhelming number of new members. Almost 10,000 new members had joined the Association, large numbers of them from the Division's forces in Vietnam. New chapters were formed in Minnesota, Florida, Georgia, and Indiana.

War news continued to fill the pages of Caltrap, as the fighting in Vietnam continued unabated. Seven 3d Division Marines were awarded the Medal of Honor in 1968, including Private First Class James Anderson, Jr., the first African-American to receive this honor.

The Association suffered two significant losses in 1968. Charter member and former Association treasurer Colonel Morris L. Shively passed away on August 6 at the age of 72. On August 26, shortly after his return from the reunion, Father Joseph J. Conway, who had served both as Division and Association Chaplain died from a heart attack at age 61.

The Association headed for the warm and sunny environs of Bal Harbour, Florida, near Miami Beach, for its 15th reunion, held July 10-13. Wimpy Soloman chaired the organizing committee. The Marine Corps Reserve's 4th Air Naval Gunfire Liaison Company, Force Troops, FMF, offered their support and assistance in making this reunion a special event. The reunion also marked the twenty-fifth anniversary of the liberation of Guam.

Major General Raymond G. Davis, former Commanding General of the 3d Division and a Medal of Honor recipient during the Korean War, was the featured speaker. In his talk, he praised today's Marine as, " ... the smartest, best trained, best equipped, most superbly led, and the most highly motivated Leatherneck who ever went to war," adding, "And he should

be – he is building on a foundation you helped to lay; a reputation which you helped to create."

At the business meeting, Austin Gattis was elected President, Tom Stowe again was named PRO and Caltrap editor, and Association finances were deemed to be in good order with total assets and a net worth of $28,991.80.

The Association voted to allocate $300 to the Memorial Scholarship Fund, as well as 15 percent of the reunion's net proceeds, and to designate that Association funds be donated to one or more Marine Corps civic activities organizations should the Association ever be disbanded.

The Memorial Service, which paid tribute to the Division's 9,000 war dead, was held on the hotel's Cabana Deck, with Chaplain Rabun presiding. Memorial wreaths were dropped into the nearby ocean from a passing helicopter, including one in the form of Caltrap and another in the shape of a cross to honor the memory of Chaplain Conway.

The Board held the largest meeting in its history on August 16 in Washington, DC. President Gattis proposed changing the concept of the presidency to attract a greater number of qualified candidates. He also announced the administration's goals of increasing membership with special attention to active duty Marines in Vietnam, forming regular chapters for officers and enlisted men at USMC bases, and creating and promoting a unifying theme that would appeal to both Old Breed and New Breed Marines. Tom Stowe was appointed Executive Assistant to the President, a position that was approved at the 1968 meeting. A committee was formed to study the by-laws and recommend change. Chaplain Rabun was appointed to head a committee to explore Association services to veterans and their dependents.

Trustees were named for the Memorial Scholarship Fund, which provided grants ranging from $200 to $800 per academic year for dependents of Division personnel killed in Vietnam.

With Major General Ray Davis's help, the Association's first base chapter was formed at Quantico. Former Marines living in the Quantico area were also recruited for membership.

As the war continued in Southeast Asia, three more Marines serving with the 3d Division were awarded the Medal of Honor, bringing the Division's total to 15.

The year 1970 marked the twenty-fifth anniversary of the battle for Iwo Jima. Members of the Association were invited to participate in a reunion trip to Guam, Saipan, and Tinian sponsored by the newly-formed 20th Air Force Association.

The Third Marine Division Association was also making plans to commemorate the anniversary at their annual reunion, which would be a joint celebration with the Fifth Marine Division Association. The two Divisions had a long history together. Men from the 3d and the 5th fought together at Iwo Jima and again in Vietnam.

The January/February issue of Caltrap reported that as of December 31, 1969, the Memorial Scholarship Fund stood at $19,540.91 and that the 1969 reunion had netted $5,963.09 in profits. Still, much more money needed to be raised for the Fund before it started awarding grants; in 1970, most of the eligible children were still too young to be making college plans.

On January 10, the Association lost another good friend with the death of retired Colonel Robert C. Thaxton. A veteran of both world wars, Colonel Thaxton was a charter member of the Association and had chaired the committee that drafted the Association's constitution and bylaws.

The 3d Marine Division in Vietnam was doing more than fighting the enemy. They were also creating a legacy that would continued long after they left – the 3d Marine Division Memorial Children's Hospital. Association President Austin Gattis appointed Colonel William F. Simlik to represent the Association on the hospital's Board of Directors. At their 1969 reunion, the members had voted to make a $500 contribution to the hospital.

At the personal invitation of General Leonard F. Chapman, Jr., the Commandant of the Marine Corps, Association President Austin Gattis officially represented the 3d at the Iwo Jima memorial service at the National Cathedral in Washington, DC, February 19, 1970.

The Association received a new flag, donated in the name of Michael Matthew Melloy, four-month-old son of Past President Hal Melloy. The new Association flag was designed by Ben Byrer and unfurled for the first time at the April Board of Directors meeting.

An April Board of Directors meeting in Washington, DC, refined the proposed major revisions to the Association bylaws for presentation to the Association membership at the July reunion. The bylaws revisions would significantly change the make-up of the Board to include all elected Association officers, the three honorary officers, all past presidents, all chapter presidents, and the Division's Commanding General.

Commandant of the Marine Corps, General L.F. Chapman, Jr., gave his approval for President Gattis to make a 10-day trip to Okinawa in June to visit the 3d Division Marines there in order to spread the word about the Association and recruit New Breed members. President Gattis returned with $3,000 in checks for membership dues. To bolster support among active duty Marines, the Association began publishing more Division news in *Caltrap* and distributing 1,000 copies of each issue to the Division.

Nearly 600 people attended the 1970 joint reunion with the Fifth Marine Division Association was held at the Sheraton Park Hotel in Washington, DC, July 23-26. General Lewis W. Walt, Assistant Marine Corps Commandant, was the featured speaker. Former Japanese Army Major Yoshitaka Horie also addressed the reunion, giving an account of his role in the war. At the memorial service, James D. Hittle, Assistant Secretary of the Navy, spoke of the high price paid in Marine lives to capture Iwo Jima.

At the business meeting, the entire slate of candidates was re-elected to office, and blanket approval was given to all committee chairs and executive officers appointed by the Board. The proposed revision of the bylaws was also approved.

As the new year was ushered in, the Memorial Scholarship Fund was nearing the $25,000 mark. The 3d Marine Division had added $2,200 to its coffers. Another $250 was donated in the name Dr. Radha Widner, an anesthesiologist at a Swiss hopsital. Dr. Widner had become friends with the wife of artist and Association supporter Victor Sparks while treating Mrs. Sparks. After learning about the Association's Memorial Scholarship Fund, Dr. Widner asked Mrs. Sparks to make the donation in her name in lieu of fees for services.

In the February 1971 issue of *Caltrap,* Bill Caipen reported on the reunion trip he and his wife, Rose, had taken with the 20th Air Force Association, saying "It was well planned, and the group received a warm welcome wherever we went."

The Association's fundraising efforts continued to bear fruit. The 1970 reunion's net profit was $11,379, with 75 percent of the proceeds going to the Third Marine Division Association and 25 percent to the Fifth Marine Division Association.

On March 28, Father George M. Kempker passed away. Father Kempker had been the Division's Regimental Chaplain during World War II and the served as Association Chaplain for three terms. Charles R. "Buddy" Powers, who had been Father Kempker's bodyguard at Bougainville, represented the Association at his funeral.

Earl and Lillian Browne, uncle and aunt of Major General Hochmuth, became honrary member of the Association. They had contributed $900 to the Scholarship Fund created in memory of their nephew.

The 1971 reunion was held at the Breezy Point Inn in Pequot Lakes,

CAUGHT OFF GUARD - General Lewis W. Walt (left) presents sterling silver trays and plaques from the Commandant of the Marine Corps to Association President Colonel Austin Gattis USMCR (second from left); Dr. Robert Goldstein (second from the right), General Chairman of the joint committee for the 1970 combined reunion of the 3d and 5th Marine Division Associations; and 5th Marine Division Association President retired Brigadier General Lester Hamel.

Minnesota., with Major General Louis H. Wilson, Jr., as the guest speaker at the banquet. Special guests included Colonel Donald M. Beck, USMC (Ret.), Commandant of Cadets at the Marine Military Academy, who served with the 21st Regiment at Bougainville and Guam, and Cadet 1st Sergeants Richard H. Bauman and Wendell F. Johnson, both student at the Academy. A short documentary film about the Academy was shown at the reunion.

Officers and eight regular members of the Board of Directors were elected at the business meeting. Income from the *Reunion Journal* was anticipated to be around $7,000. The Association's total net worth was listed at $49,195.92. The members voted to transfer $500 from the General Fund to the Memorial Scholarship Fund, which stood at $26,335.33.

The Association went on record with support of a "One Nation Under God Week" to be celebrated annually each May. The idea came from Rev. Joseph A. Rabun, the Association's Chaplain, who sent letters to state and federal official asking for their support.

As the year drew to a close, *Caltrap* reported the death of one of the Division's and the Association's staunchest supporters. General Allen Hal Turnage passed away on October 22 at the age of 80. He was the Division's Commanding General in World War II and the Association's Honorary Life Chairman. General Erskine, Austin Gattis, T.O. Kelly, Hal Melloy, Tom Stowe, and Floyd Bagley, the Association's Judge Advocate, represented the Association at General Turnage's funeral. To honor his memory, the Association created the Allen Hal Turange Award, to be given to an Association member who demonstrates outstanding service and leadership to the organization.

While on a trip to Hawaii with a delegation to the Jaycee World Congress, Franklin A. "Ski" Somosky became a sort of roving goodwill ambassador for the Association. He visited with the Marines at the First Marine Brigade Headquarters at Kanehoe Bay. His mission: recruit new members. In an article in the February 1972 issue of *Caltrap*, Somosky said he hoped to return to Hawaii soon and also visit the 3d Division on Okinawa, adding "I get tired of staying at home and would like nothing better than recruiting Association members by visiting our bases."

The March issue of the newsletter reported that the 20th Air Force

Association would be organizing two Pacific reunion tours. The first, in April, would cover three weeks with stops in the Marshall, Mariana, Caroline, and Hawaiian Islands. The second, in September, would be a 16-day visit to Guam, Saipan, Tinian, Hong Kong, Tokyo, and Hawaii. Association members were invited to participate.

The 1972 reunion was held in Savannah, Georgia, July 19-23, with General Cushman as the featured speaker. Honored guests included General Ray Davis, Major General Carl W. Hoffman, Commanding General at Parris Island, and their wives.

General Cushman praised both the Old Breed and New Breed Marines, saying:

"Today's Marine is better educated, mentally and physically tough, and will no longer submit to brute force without questioning its logic. We are continuing to make Marines the way we always did – no compromises, no promises except one – those who make it through the most demanding training in the world will be Marines, and all that title bestows"

During the reunion, some Old Breed Marines proved they still had what it takes. Nicknamed the "Retread Platoon," the group of volunteers from the Association spent at day at Parris Island reliving their Boot Camp days under the direction of regular Drill Instructors. A short documentary film was made of the Retreads going through their training.

Work on the "One Nation Under God Week" program continued, with support growing throughout the country. At the business meeting, the Board of Directors voted to spend $500 on promoting the program. They also voted to give $300 to the Memorial Scholarship Fund Trustees.

1973 LOUISVILLE REUNION - The Gerkens, Melloys, General Raymond G. Davis, and T.O. Kelly enjoy dinner in the Louisville Downs clubhouse.

The Association's growth – both in membership and finances – continued, with a new chapter forming in Southern California, replacing the Los Angeles Chapter. The 1972 Dedicated Members Page program earned the Association $5,180, with total reunion profits reaching $8,618.

The Association continued its efforts to establish a "One Nation Under God Week," and the April issue of *Caltrap* reported that the Marine Corps League had endorsed the proposed national holiday.

The 1973 reunion was held in Louisville, Kentucky. Brigadier General Edward J. Miller was the featured speaker at the reunion banquet. The banquet programs featured a reproduction of a picture by Johnny Hopper's portrait of three of the Association's most dedicated members – Al Jenson, Tom Kelly, and Tom Stowe – all septugenarians. Retired General Ray Davis was elected the Association's eleventh president, only the second time in history that a four-star general has headed the Association.

Dr. Bob Riley, Lt. Governor of Arkansas, spoke at the memorial service, and Chaplain Rabun read the names of 11 members who had made the final formation. Among them was General Graves B. Erskine, the Association's founder, who passed away on May 21.

One of the highlights was a "Nite at the Races" at Louisville Downs. The featured race was named in honor of the 3d Marine Division, and President Roy Gerken presented a trophy to the winner on behalf of the Association.

Growing and maintaining a strong organization was becoming an even more important issue, as Association membership fell below 1,000 in 1973. At its October 13 meeting, the Board of Directors proposed several organizational changes that would strengthen the association, including reducing the size of the Board and stepping up efforts to recruit young Marines.

The February 1974 issue of *Caltrap* reported that Major General Fred Haynes, Commanding General of the 3d Division, wrote to Association President Ray Davis, stating that he was personally launching a membership drive to recruit Marines under his command.

The newsletter also reported that the former FBI Academy building at the Quantico Marine Base was renamed Hochmuth Hall in honor of Major

1974 REUNION HI-JINKS - Association Chaplain "Jumping Joe" Rabun clicks his heels in mid-air to demonstrate he's still young in body as well as mind and spirit. (Hawkins photo)

General Bruno A. Hochmuth. Executive Vice President Warren H. Wiedham; Lieutenant Colonel Clyde L. Dean, President of the Quantico Chapter; and Past President Tom Stowe represented the Association at the dedication ceremony.

On April 25, the Association celebrated its twenty-fifth anniversary, with a special Silver Jubilee celebration planned for the reunion.

The 1974 reunion was held in San Diego, July 17-21, and attendance was at an all-time high. Lieutenant General Louis H. Wilson, Commanding General, Fleet Marine Force, Pacific, was the featured speaker at the banquet, and Generals Ames, Bowser, Shepherd, Krulak, and Craig were the Association's honored guests.

At the business meeting, new officers were elected. After 17 years as Secretary- Treasurer, Al Jenson passed the torch to Al Nisco. For his many years of dedicated service to the Association, Jenson was presented the first Turnage Award.

The Association voted to grant Honorary Life Membership to all the 3d Marine Division's Commanding Generals and their Sergeant Majors, strengthening ties with all officers and enlisted men who had served with the Division.

The Association lost one of its greatest friends and supporters on August 15, when

Colonel Bob Kriendler, "The Man Behind the Third," passed away. Owner of New York's famous 21 Club, Kriendler had been the Association's principal financial benefactor for man years, chairing the annual *Reunion Journal* for 17 years and raising over $200,000 through ad sales. The following year, his widow agreed to assume chairmanship of the *Reunion Journal*, continuing her late husband's legacy of service to the Association.

In November, the Association entered the computer age, thanks to the Marine Corps Association, which allowed the organization to house its membership records on the MCA's computer and print and mail the newsletter.

Two new chapters were chartered in 1974, the Razorback Chapter in Arkansas and the Massachusetts Chapter, which announced plans to raise funds to construct a Marine Corps Memorial building.

Early in 1975, the Florida Chapter set an important milestone when retired Captain Mary Lou Demmond became the first woman Marine to join the Association. Her husband, Major Jack Demmond, was also a member.

The February 1975 issue of *Caltrap* reported that Vice President Warren Wiedhahn and PRO Tom Stowe attended a November 6 meeting of 15 Marine-oriented veterans organizations to study the formation of a National Marine Corps Council.

ASSOCIATION TRIBUTE - *Association President General Lew Walt places a wreath at the Marine Corps War Memorial during the Memorial Service at the Association's 1976 reunion in Washington, DC. Corporal Wayne R. Comtois and Corporal Robert K. Swininger assisted in the ceremony.*

In keeping with tradition, the Association held its 1975 reunion in the home state of one of its new chapters, meeting in Little Rock, Arkansas, for the first time. The themes of the 1975 reunion were honoring the Marine Corps bicentennial and honoring the memory of Bob Kriendler. Ed McMahon, Johnny Carson's sidekick on *The Tonight Show* and a former Marine Corps fighter pilot in World War II and Korea, served as emcee at the banquet. Major General Herbert L. Wilkerson was the featured speaker, subbing for Major General Haynes, who took ill. Another four-star general assumed leadership of the Association, when General Lew Walt was elected President.

The Association paid tribute to Bob Kriendler at the 1975 reunion's Memorial Service and he was named the recipient of the General Allen H. Turnage Award. His widow, Mrs. Florence Kriendler, accepted the award.

The Association undertook a new activity in 1975, when General Walt proposed raising money to sponsor disabled Division veterans for Life Membership. This effort became known as the Care of Our Own Fund. At the reunion banquet, the first award was made to Captain Buddy Spivey, DAV's 1975 "Man of the Year," who was sponsored by Sea World of Orlando, Florida.

The 1976 reunion was held July 21-25 at the Stouffer's National Center Inn in Arlington, Virginia, hosted by the recently merged Washington and Quantico Chapters. Marine Commandant General Louis H. Wilson was the featured speaker at the banquet, and in his talk he defended the Corps' recruiting and training methods. T.O. Kelly, who served three terms as President, was presented the Turnage Award for his years of service to the Association.

General Erskine's widow established a memorial scholarship in his honor. The first award was presented to Pamela Ohanesian, daughter of Lieutenant Colonel Victor Ohanesian, who was killed in Vietnam. Pamela was a guest at the reunion banquet.

The memorial service was held at the Iwo Jima Memorial. Among the names of those who made the final formation was Luther Skaggs, Medal of Honor recipient, former president of the Congressional Medal of Honor Society, National Commandant of the Purple Heart Association, and first President of the Association's Washington, DC, Chapter, who passed away on April 6.

The November issue of *Caltrap* announced the creation of a new charitable program. Lucy Caldwell, a volunteer nurse in Vietnam, wrote a book about her experiences at the China B.Q.S.O. Navy Hospital in Danang, and wished the profits to be used to benefit wounded Marine veterans and children of Marines killed in Vietnam. Copyright for the book was transferred to the Association, with proceeds from sales to be placed in a Boston bank and made payable to the Association, with interest, in 10 years.

At the 1976 reunion, the Florida Chapter proposed a resolution establishing a patriotic essay contest for high school students; the Association members voted in favor of the proposal. The essay theme was to be "America and What It Means to Me," with prizes awarded of $100, $50, and $25.

The 1977 reunion was held in Orlando, Florida, and it was once again a successful event.

Once again the Retreads Platoon displayed their determination and courage. They participated in an amphibious landing, dubbed "Operation Alligator," on the lake at Sea World.

Lieutenant General Barrow was the featured speaker, and he brought recorded greetings from General Louis H. Wilson, Commandant of the Marine Corps.

Kirby Grant, star of the *Sky King* television program and an honorary member of the Florida Chapter, attended the reunion. The host chapter presented its Semper Fidelis Award to golfer Lee Trevino who had served with the 9th Marines and with Division Headquarters in 1956-1957. Another special guest at the reunion was Lucy Caldwell, who was presented with an engraved plaque in appreciation for her generous gift to establish a fund to aid Vietnam veterans and their children.

Colonel Edward F. Danowitz, who was elected President at the reunion, read the prize-winning patriotic essay submitted by Richard Earl Van Tassell II of Millington, Tennessee.

The Association's first PX opened in 1977, with items such as caps, cufflinks, decals, pins, and shoulder patches available by mail order. Secretary-Treasurer Russ Adamczuk was in charge of the PX.

Efforts to recruit and retain members continued throughout the year. By mid-year, 52 disabled veterans had applied for Life Membership through the Care of Our Own program. In September, Dick Jones, Executive Assistant to the President, began a 30-day, cross-country driving tour to recruit new members. He visited former Marines in Los Angeles, Houston, San Diego, and Milwaukee. He also flew to New Orleans to help with efforts to charter a new chapter in the Crescent City.

The December-January issue of *Caltrap* announced that Constance Erskine, General Erskine's widow, had pledge an annual scholarship grant of $1,000 to be named in memory of her husband. The Association also announced another tribute to the late General, establishing the General Graves B. Erkine Award, to be presented annually to the 3d Division rifle squad with the best competitive record.

At the Board's December meeting, members unanimously approved a charter for the Gulf Coast Chapter, to be headquartered in New Orleans. The Board also proposed amending the bylaws to allow the Board to elect its own chairman, who would be someone other than the Association President. The change was subsequently approved at the reunion business meeting in San Francisco.

In the March issue of *Caltrap*, President Danowitz announced that the Association had received $12,000 from the sale of Lucy Caldwell's book, *Sin – One Way – Economy Class*. President Danowitz paid a personal visit to Mrs. Caldwell following the December 3 Board meeting to thank her for her support. Formal regulations governing the Lucy Caldwell Fund were drafted in February, with Gil Randall appropriated to chair the committee administering the program. The fund was created to provide assistance with medical bills, food, clothing, transportation, education, etc., for needy Vietnam veterans. Progress was also being made on the Care of Our Own Fund, with donations covering Life Memberships for half of the disabled Division veterans enrolled in the program.

The Association's Judge Advocate, James King, was promoted to the rank of Brigadier General and assigned as Director of the Judge Advocate Division, Headquarters Marine Corps.

The 1978 reunion was held in San Francisco, July 26-30, at the Marines' Memorial Club. Marine Corps Commandant, General Louis H. Wilson, was the featured speaker at the banquet. Sergeant Thomas J. Kazee, the 3d Division's "Marine of the Year"; and I/3/9 Rifle Squad, winner of the General Graves B. Erskine Award, were honored at the reunion. Lucy Caldwell was also in attendance, and General Wilson presented her with a Meritorious Service Citation.

The Board of Directors granted a charter to the new chapter formed by the Marine Corps League's Westchester County (NY) Detachment, which became the Association's fifteenth chapter.

Among the names called at the Memorial Service were those of Winston O. "Wimpy" Solomon and Brigadier General Verne Kennedy. Solomon, affectionately known as the "Florida Gator," and his wife had raised more than $15,000 for the Association through the Dedicated Members Page Program. He was a Life Member of the Association and was founder and first President of the Florida Chapter and a member of the Association's Board of Directors. Major General Kennedy had served as a member of the Memorial Scholarship Fund's Board of Trustees.

Chaplain Rabun was forced to resign from his post after 10 years of service due to illness, and the October issue of *Caltrap* announced that Rear Admiral John J. O'Connor, the Navy's Chief of Chaplains, was elected to replace him. Chaplain Rabun was honored at the 1978 reunion with the Turnage Award and was also named the Association's Honorary Life Chaplain.

The Association continued to recruit new members. A campaign to recruit active duty members from the Division was announced to coincide with the Marine Corps Birthday on November 10, with the Division's Commanding General appointing his assistant Chief of Staff for Career Development to spearhead the membership drive.

As 1978 drew to a close, the Memorial Scholarship Fund was approaching the $60,000 mark, with nearly 20 scholarships awarded since 1972.

The April 1979 issue of *Caltrap* brought welcome news from Major General Calhoun J. Killeen, Division Commander on Okinawa, that 304 of his troops had joined the Association as a result of a membership drive. That brought total membership to almost 2,000, including approximately 700 Life Members.

That same issue reported the passing of Lucy Caldwell, benefactress of the charitable fund bearing her name. Memorial services were held at Princeton University on March 10, with Past President and Mrs. Charles R. Powers representing the Association.

The Association its Silver Anniversary in 1979. The reunion was hosted by the Gulf Coast Chapter – the Association's newest – in New Orleans, July 18-22. Earlier in the year, the Gulf Coast Chapter became the first to grant women the privilege of becoming full dues-paying members with voting rights.

Guest speaker at the banquet was General Robert H. Barrow, who became Commandant of the Marine Corps on July 1. He spoke of the continuing need for a strong Marine Corps. Those attending the reunion learned that Sergeant Steven W. Ochs had been selected as the "Marine of the Year" and that E/2/4 had received the Erskine Award as the Division's top rifle squad.

A new feature was added to the reunion – a round table discussion – giving all members to talk about Association activities and the Board the opportunity to hear directly from the members about their thoughts and concerns.

Chaplain O'Connor was unable to attend the reunion due to receiving an unexpected honor bestowed on him by Pope John Paul II. On May 27, he was ordained as an auxiliary bishop in a ceremony in the Vatican, becoming the military vicar assigned to the military ordinariate, headquartered in New York City.

As the year drew to a close, news came that the Philadelphia Chapter, inactive since 1967, would be reborn at the 1980 reunion and serve as host chapter for the 1981 reunion.

At the start of a new decade, the Association was beset with the need to increase both membership and income in order to meet increased operating costs, topics that were both discussed at a February Board meeting. At the same meeting, the Board recommended salary increases for both the Secretary-Treasure and the *Caltrap/Reunion Journal* editor, the Association's only paid officials. The Board also endorsed a recommendation to offer Life Memberships to the surviving BLT 2/4 Marines burned in the Mt. Fuji fire.

The March issue of *Caltrap* reported that President Leo Farrow and New York Chapter Treasurer Harry K. Noble attended a benefit luncheon for the new Marine Military Institute; the luncheon took place at the 1st Marine Corps District Club.

The Association noted another first on May 18, when Delores Bernaden was elected President of the Chicago Chapter, the first woman to hold that office in any Chapter.

The 1980 reunion was held at the Stouffer's Riverfront Towers in St. Louis, July 23-27. The theme was "Honoring Men of the Cloth," and the reunion was dedicated to chaplains of all faiths. The Most Reverend John J. O'Connor, Auxiliary Bishop, Military Vicarate and former Association Chaplain, was the featured speaker. He paid tribute to former Chaplains Father Conway, Father Kempker, Rev. Rabun, and Rev. Thomas.

At the business meeting, the Nominating Committee's slate of candidates was approved unanimously. By-laws were amended to separate the accounting functions of the *Reunion Journal* and the Reunion Committee. The Association's fiscal year was also changed from July 1-June 30 to June 1-May 31. And the objective Lucy Caldwell Fund was modified to allow one-time use to aid current Division personnel injured by catastrophic events and to allow one-time use to aid any needy Association member.

The 1980 Turange Award recipient was "the incomparable" Lenny Mormino. Al Jenson accepted on behalf of Lenny, who was unable to attend the reunion due to family illness. The "Marine of the Year" award went to Sergeant Jonathan D. Hewitt, "C" Company, 3d Recon Battalion;

"Let's All Rally 'Round the Gateway Arch!"

REUNION ENCOURAGEMENT - A photo of the famed Gateway Arch and downtown St. Louis dominated page 1 of the June-July 1980 Caltrap *and advocated maximum attendance at the July 23 annual reunion.*

K/3/5 took home the Erskine Award for the Division's top rifle squad.

Tragedy struck on October 22, when retired Colonel Gerald H. Polakoff, Association Vice President and President of the Southern California Chapter, was killed in an automobile accident. Only a few weeks prior, the Association had lost one of its founding members and its first Secretary-Treasure when Cecil A. Gunsolley passed away on October 5 after a long illness.

Financial problems continued to plague the Association in 1981, as high inflation caused expenses to skyrocket. President Farrow requested all Life Members to make a special contribution of at least $10 to help ease the financial crisis. The Scholarship Fund stood at $60,000 at the end of 1980, including gift of $1,246 in honor of Gerald Polakoff.

At its February 21 meeting, the Board learned that $10,000 would need to be taken from the Reserve Fund to meet the Association's financial obligations. The Board recommended steps to improve the Association's financial position, including reducing the number of *Caltrap* issus from 9/year to 6/year.

The 1981 reunion was held in Philadelphia, July 22-26. The theme was a tribute to the Division's Commanding Officers. The reunion banquet included a roll call of the 29 living and eight deceased Commanding Generals and a special tribute to those attending the banquet. Featured speaker and guest of honor at the banquet was Lieutenant General Adolph G. Schwenk, Commander of the Division and III MAF on Okinawa, 1977-1978. Tom Stowe became the sixth recipient of the Turnage Award. An Association member since 1995, Stowe served as PRO and *Caltrap* editor for 23 years. "Marine of the Year" was Sergeant Carl A. Reynoso, 3rd Recon Battalion.

As the year was coming to a close, the Association's financial health was on the improve. One-third of the Life Members had responded President Farrow's call with contributions of nearly $4,000. The *Reunion Journal* ads and Dedicated Members Page Program added $16,514.48 and $5,649.48 to the coffers, respectively.

The 1982 reunion was held in San Diego. Jacqui Polakoff, wife of late member Gerald Polakoff, served as Assistant Chairman for the event. A student in San Diego, she had made a commitment to remain involved with the Association after her husband's untimely death. The reunion honored Marines who fought and died in Vietnam. The honored guest speaker at the banquet was Major General Kenneth L. Robinson, Commanding General, Marine Corps Base, Camp Pendleton. Four recipients of Hochmuth scholarships attended the banquet as guests of T.O. Kelly. The Turnage Award was presented to Charles Powers, a charter member, who had served the Association as its President, Chairman of the Board of Directors, Reunion Chairman (twice), and *Reunion Journal* chairman.

Some 275 Association members attended the Thursday dedication of the Association-sponsored stained glass window at Camp Pendleton's Edson Range Chapel. The planned Sunday Memorial Service was combined with breakfast and held in the hotel.

At the Board's organizational meeting, the decision was made to expand the membership Committee, dividing it into two sections – one to recruit World War II-era veterans and the other to recruit Vietnam-era Marines.

By the end of the year, the Association was showing signs of returning to financial health. Over 100 new members had joined. The Dedicated Members Page Program had brought in $6,271.31, and the *Reunion Journal* netted a profit of $11,213.31.

The February-March issue of *Caltrap* included an update on the Care of Our Own programs. Six grants totaling $1,800 in all had been awarded to needy veterans who had served with the 3rd Division.

The Association returned to Atlanta for its 1983 reunion, July 20-24, with a theme honoring the Marine Reserves. Lieutenant General D'Wayne Gray was the honored guest and featured speaker at the banquet. The Division's "Marine of the Year" was Sergeant Eric V. Bradford, 7th Communications Battalion. Among those remembered at the annual memorial service was General David M. Shoup, Commanding General of the 3d Division, 1958-1959, and a Life Member of the Association.

At the organizational meeting, a Board of Directors was elected, and individuals were appointed to various positions and committees. Chaplain Tom Kelley requested that the Association sponsor a stained glass window at the new chapel being built at Parris Island.

At year's end, there was again good news for the Association. The *Reunion Journal* made a profit of more than $11,500. And, once again, Lenny Mormino set a new record for the Dedicated Members Page Program: 634 participants, and $6,497.90 in contributions.

The year 1984 marked two important milestones: the fifteenth anniversary of Operation Dewey Canyon and the fortieth anniversary of the landing on Guam.

In the February/March issue of *Caltrap*, Board Chairman Ed Danowitz reported on his trip to visit the Division on Okinawa. Major General Haebel invited Danowitz to accompany him on a visit to the 9th MAB in Korea. They spent the Marine Corps birthday with the troops in the field. On his return to Okinawa, Danowitz talked with Marines about the Association and invited those returning to the States to join. Major General Haebel was preparing a video for the Association members to view at their reunion. Danowitz also visited Camp Fuji and the orphanage supported by the Division for more than 30 years.

The April/May issue of the newsletter reported that Pope John Paul II had named Bishop John J. O'Connor, the Association's Chaplain, Archbishop of the Archdiocese of New York.

Reunion Headquarters for 1984 was the Pittsburgh Marriott Green Tree Hotel, and the event was held July 18-22. The featured speaker and guest of honor was Lieutenant General William R. Maloney, deputy Chief of Staff for Manpower, Headquarters Marine Corps.

For the first time since it was instituted, there were two recipients of the Turnage Award: Russell W. Adamczuk and Bert Barton. Adamczuk was honored for his six years of service as Secretary-Treasurer and his contributions as Chairman of the 1982 reunion. Barton was honored for his service on the Board of Trustees for the Memorial Scholarship Fund since its inception and his guidance as financial advisor to the Board of Directors. A one-year waiver of the rules regarding the Turnage Award was required to make two awards. The Division's "Marine of the Year" was Corporal Randy L. Bird, Intelligence Unit, Headquarters, 4th Regiment.

Among those called for the final formation over the past year were Chaplain Joseph Rabun, who passed away on April 9, and Charlie Powers, a Charter member, Association President 1976-1977, Board of Directors Chairman 1978-79, *Reunion Journal* Chairman for five years, and recipient of the 1982 Turnage Award.

On November 10, 1984, the Guam monument honoring the 3rd Division's Medal of Honor recipient for heroism in the battle for the island, was dedicated. Two members, Luther Tom Cook of the 25th Seabees and Don Hoein, who served with B-1-9, went to Guam for the commemoration of the 40th anniversary of the island's liberation. While there, Cook met Juan T. Evangelista, a Guam native who fought with the Division, and sponsored him for membership in the Association.

The Association's financial picture continued to improve. The *Reunion Journal* realized a profit of more than $14,200, and Lenny Mormino set yet another record for the Dedicated Members Page Program. Also, the Association received 100 shares of Oppenheimer Industries stock, a gift from A.L. Oppenheimer, Chairman and CEO of the company and a veteran of 32 years of service with the Corps.

On March 1, 1985, the Association's window at the Parris Island chapel was dedicated in the memory of General Erskine. The window's three panels depicted a kneeling Marine, along with the campaign ribbons from the Division's past wars, and the Caltrap insignia. Attending the ceremony was Major General Olmstead, along with Chaplain Kelly, and Captain Daisyanne M. Elquist, the first Woman Marine to join the Association as a Regular member. The Board of Directors was told that the cost of the Association-sponsored window was $3,000.

The 1985 reunion was held in San Antonio, July 17-21, with Major General James J. McMonagle, Assistant Deputy Chief for Manpower/Director, Personnel Management Division, Headquarters Marine Corps, as the featured speaker and guest of honor. In addition, he presented a wreath to be placed inside the Alamo on behalf of the Association. The Division's "Marine of the Year" for 1985 was Sergeant David W. Russell, "F" Company, 2nd Battalion, 1st Marines, attached to the 9th Marines.

The October/November issue of *Caltrap* reported on the new plaques that were to be sold to Life Members. The newsletter also announced that Cadet Captain Cody Shane Brothers, a student at the Marine Military Academy, had received a special award from the Association, which continued to support the Academy.

The December 1985/January 1986 issue of the newsletter included an account of the 1985 "Return to Guam" tour. Twenty-three Association members (including wives) had made the trip, which also included visits to Saipan and Tinian.

As the year drew to a close, membership stood at 2,526 – an all-time high.

As more children of Vietnam-era veterans were reaching college age, the February/March 1986 issue of the newsletter noted that more than $100,000 in tuition assistance had been awarded through the Memorial Scholarship Fund.

The Association returned to Washington, DC, for the seventh time for its 1986 reunion. It was the largest reunion ever, with 819 registrants and 755 in attendance at the banquet. General P.X. Kelley was the honored guest and featured speaker at the banquet. The largest contingent of Vietnam-era veterans ever attended the 1986 reunion. They presented a wreath at the Memorial Wall.

Among those who made the final formation and were honored at the annual memorial services was Russell Adamczuk, who passed away on February 27. He served as the Association's Secretary-Treasurer for six years and was a recipient of the Turnage Award.

The bylaw changes previously recommended by the Georgia and Southern California Chapters were tabled pending further study. The Association approved a proposal by Harvey Tennant to create a fund to establish a Division memorial on Guam.

The year brought good news and bad news for membership. Recruitment ads in *The Leatherneck*, *VFW*, *American Legion*, and *Purple Heart* magazines had attracted 111 new members. However, three chapters – Philadelphia, Golden States, and North Central States – were deactivated. Efforts were underway to reorganize the Philadelphia chapter, and by the time of the 1987 reunion, it was once again active. In addition, a new chapter was being formed in Michigan, and an organizational effort was ongoing in North Carolina. The Association continued its efforts to increase membership and set a goal of 3,000 members by May 1987; 125 new members would have to be recruited.

The December 1986/January 1987 issue of *Caltrap* brought news that the Commandant, General Kelley, had given his approval to the Association's "Return to the Pacific" tour, with departure

scheduled immediately following the San Diego reunion.

At its mid-winter meeting, the Board hired Russell Loller as the Association's new PX Officer. A Blue Ribbon Committee, appointed by the Board and chaired by Brigadier General Jim King, studied 13 proposed bylaws changes and recommended action to the Board. Seven of the changes received favorable votes and would be presented to the membership for action at the General Membership Meeting in San Diego.

The 1987 reunion was held in San Diego, July 22-26, with General Al Gray, Commandant of the Marine Corps, as honored guest and featured speaker. At the business meeting, Chaplain Kelley was made a Life Member of the Board of Directors, and formal charters were approved for the Delaware Valley (Philadelphia), North Carolina, and Ohio Chapters.

Immediately following the reunion, 20 former Marines, along with 13 of their wives, departed for the "Return to the Pacific" tour. During their visit to Guam, 17 men who had taken part in the battle for the island were present when Harvey Tennant unveiled the memorial plaque.

The Washington Area Chapter visited Baltimore, MD, on October 17, and the city's mayor declared it "Third Marine Division Day." In turn, the Chapter made the mayor an honorary member.

The February/March 1988 issue *Caltrap* reported that Master Gunnery Sergeant Jim Kyser USMC (Ret) had been named the Association's new PRO/Editor and that retired Colonel Vince Robinson had been named interim Secretary-Treasurer. The newsletter also reported that the Tennessee State Legislature had passed a joint resolution inviting the Association to hold its 1990 reunion in Nashville. The Tennessee Chapter applied for a charter later in the year.

The 1988 reunion was held in Tampa, Florida, July 20-24. The year 1988 marked the twentieth anniversary of the battle for Khe Sanh, and General William Westmoreland, retired Army Chief of Staff and former Commander, Military Assistance Command in Vietnam, was invited to be the Association's honored guest and featured speaker. At the banquet, General Westmoreland made his remarks "off the cuff" and spoke about the attitudes towards Vietnam veterans. The Division's "Marine of the Year" was Sergeant Kenneth Allman, Truck Company, Headquarters and Service Battalion.

GATHERING PLACE - The lobby "refreshment area" was a popular and convenient meeting place for Association members at the 1994 Annual Reunion in Savannah.

There were reports at the business meeting on the Association's charitable programs. The Memorial Scholarship Fund, which was celebrating its twentieth birthday, had provided tuition assistance to a total of 70 children of 3d Division Marines. Three of the Fund's original five trustees attended the reunion. The Lucy Caldwell Fund had made three grants, totaling $2,000, to aid needy Vietnam veterans. And the Care of Our Own Fund had provided Life Memberships to seven Vietnam veterans.

The Association received a letter of thanks for its contribution to the Korean War Memorial sponsored by the "Chosin Few." The memorial was to be erected in Los Angeles. The Parris Island Historical Society Museum also sent a letter thanking the Association for its support. The hat was passed at the Savannah mid-winter Board meeting,

and an additional $434 was collected for the museum.

By the end of the year, membership was approaching the 4,000 mark, and new chapters were being organized in Colorado and Oregon. There was also, for the first time, a chapter on Guam.

The April/May 1989 issue of *Caltrap* reported that four Association members had been recruited by Governor Ned McWherter of Tennessee to work with youth offenders in the state's "boot camp" program.

The Association lost another great friend when General Lewis Walt passed away on March 26. On June 17, the newly-formed Rocky Mountain Chapter held a ceremony to honor the late general and planted a tree in his memory. The Chapter also established a memorial fund in General Walt's name with money going to the Association.

The 1989 reunion, the Association's thirty-fifth, was held in Chicago, July 10-

18, with 200 people signed up to depart for the "Return to Guam" immediately following the reunion. Retired General Robert H. Barrow, former Commandant of the Marine Corps, was the featured speaker.

The last *Caltrap* issue of the decade reported on the "Return to Guam" trip. Ninety-nine men who had served during the battle for Guam were among those making the return trip. In honor of those who had served there, the Association named a Liberators of Guam Committee to work on establishing an academic scholarship fund for the children of native Guam residents, and reflecting the strong bond between 3d Division Marines and the Guamanian population.

The decade of the 1990s started with a call in *Caltrap* for members to submit their stories and recollections, as well as photographs, for a book commemorating the fiftieth anniversary of the activation of the Third Marine Division.

1990 also brought about a major change in the Association's day-to-day administration. Prompted by continuing membership growth, demands for enhanced services to the membership, and to take advantage of available technology to computerize all of the Association's administrative records and activities, and all membership and financial records to provide greater efficiency, continuity and accountability, the Board of Directors approved a full-time Association Manager position to become effective at the installation of officers elected for the 1990-91 term in July. Retired Master Gunnery Sergeant Jim Kyser, who had served as the Association's Editor and Public Affairs Officer since January 1988 as well as the elected Secretary-Treasurer in 1989-90, was named to the position.

Retired Captain Luther A. Bookout presented the Association's annual Marine Military Academy Award to Cadet 1st Lieutenant James B. Rogers at a ceremony held at the Academy on May 10. Cadet Rogers received an engraved plaque and a check for $100.

The 1990 reunion was held at the Sheraton Music City Hotel in Nashville, Tennessee, July 18-22. Lieutenant General Norman H. Smith, Deputy Chief of Staff for Manpower and Reserve Affairs, Headquarters USMC, was the guest of honor. He was the Division's Commanding General from 1987-1989 and praised the "... strong spirit of the Association" in his speech at the reunion banquet.

A highlight of the Nashville Annual Reunion was the appearance of the U.S. Marine Corps Battle Color Ceremony from the Marine Barracks, Washington, D.C. The hour-long Battle Color Ceremony attracted more than 1,000 Association members and spectators to the famed Parthenon in downtown Nashville, and featured the U.S. Marine Corps Drum and Bugle Corps, the Marine Corps Silent Drill Team, and the Marine Corps Color Guard. The Battle Color Ceremony was commanded by active duty Association member Captain James G. Kyser IV; the Association's reviewing official was retired Master Gunnery Sergeant James G. Kyser III, the Association's out-going Secretary-Treasurer. The U.S. Marine Drum and Bugle Corps and the Marine Corps Color Guard also opened the Annual Reunion Banquet, and took part in Sunday Memorial Service.

The Board's slate of officers for the coming year was elected by acclamation. At the meeting, President Joe Garza also named the Executive Assistant to the President, Military Liaison Officers, and Association Historian, as well as the Association Representatives to the Marine Corps Districts and committee chairs.

Sergeant Mark A. Matteson received the "Marine of the Year" award and served as the Division's enlisted representative to the reunion. The Association presented Sergeant Matteson a plaque and an engraved wristwatch in honor of his achievements.

The Turnage Award was presented to Colonel Edward F. Danowitz, USMC (Ret.). A Life Member of the Association, Colonel Danowitz's military career spanned 24 years. He served the Association in various elected and appointed capacities, and was instrumental in the establishment of the Lucy Caldwell Fund.

The Memorial Scholarship Fund received a donation of $1,050 from Pauline Sullivan in memory of her son, Corporal David O. Sullivan, who was killed in action in Vietnam while serving with the 3d Division. Mrs. Sullivan was made an Honorary Life Member of the Association. Eleven scholarships were awarded for the 1990-1991 academic year.

The year 1990 was a good one for the Association's fundraising efforts. The Dedicated Members Page Program had raised more than $22,000, after expenses, with more than 1,300 Association members and friends contributing to the fund. A commemorative

3d Marine Division wristwatch, featuring Caltrap emblem, was offered for sale for $39.95 plus shipping costs, with the Military Time Company donating $6 for each watch sold to the purchaser's choice of the General Fund, Memorial Scholarship Fund, or Liberators of Guam Fund.

Retired General Lemuel C. Shepherd passed away on August 6 at the age of 92. The 20th Commandant of the Marine Corps had been named an Honorary Life Member of the Association on December 3, 1977.

As Operation Desert Shield turned into Operation Desert Storm in early 1991, a number of active duty members, as well as members serving in the Reserves, were called to action.

The 1991 reunion was held at the Stouffer Concourse Hotel in Denver, Colorado, July 16-21. General A.M. Gray, 29th Commandant of the Marine Corps, was the guest of honor and featured speaker at the reunion banquet. President Garza presented General Gray with a bronze replica of the Iwo Jima flag raising in honor of his contributions to the Association and the Corps.

Sergeant Allen H. Watai, Jr., a squad and section leader for the 81mm Mortar Platoon, Weapons Company, 2nd Battalion, Third Marines, was named "Marine of the Year," and was presented an engraved wristwatch and plaque from the Association.

Retired Captain Harvey W. Tennant was presented the Turnage Award. A Life Member since 1982, Tennant was known as "Mr. Third Marine Division Association" for his outstanding work and dedication on behalf of the organization. He was also instrumental in raising public awareness and securing financial support for the 3d Marine Division Monument at Asan Park, Guam.

The Memorial Scholarship Fund received a significant boost with a $50,000 donation from retired Captain G.G. Sweet, made in honor of his friend and fellow Marine, Sergeant Major Harvey Frye. Marines serving with the 3d Marine Division at Okinawa raised $5,000 for the fund.

Three new chapters were chartered in 1991 – Arizona, Hampton Roads (Virginia), and New Jersey; six others – Dallas, Indianapolis, Las Vegas, Milwaukee, Omaha, and Seattle – were in the planning stages.

The year 1992 marked the fiftieth anniversary of the Division's activation, and the reunion was held in the Division's birthplace, San Diego. Six former Commanding Generals, as well as the

Division's current Commanding General, were invited to the reunion banquet.

Officers, as well as three Board members, were elected at the reunion. Membership dues were increased to $20/year; dues for active duty members were set at $7.50/year. Life Member dues were also increased, based on age.

Sergeant Major M.W. "Bill" Krueger, USMC (Ret.), received the prestigious Turnage Award. A Life Member, he served the Association in a variety of leadership capacities and was named the General Erskine Recruiter of the Year for nine consecutive years, from 1984-1992.

Recipient of the 1992 Marine Military Academy Award was Cadet Gunnery Sergeant Jason Arnold.

Fundraising efforts continued. Donations to the Dedicated Members Page Program totaled more than $24,000 after expenses. The Florida Chapter initiated the sale of name badges for reunions, with proceeds going to the Memorial Scholarship Fund; by the time of the 1993 reunion, badge sales had netted $1,000 for the Fund. The chapter also raised $750 for the fund through a crafts sale and prize drawings. And the donations from the 3d Marine Division wristwatch were increased to $9 per sale.

Both the MCRD Museum Historical Society and the Parris Island Historical Society received a donation of $500 for their respective museums from the Association.

The long-anticipated history of the Division, *Two Score and Ten*, was printed and shipped in mid-December.

As the year 1993 opened, President George Gay announced the appointment of key personnel, including chairs for the Membership, Awards, Distinguished Benefactor, Reunion Advisory, and Guam Liberators Fund Committees, as well Marine Corps District Representatives.

Life Member Ray Kelley spearheaded a two-year campaign which raised money to convert an unused Massachusetts National Guard Armory into a shelter for homeless veterans. The New Jersey Chapter sold Association badges to help raise funds for the shelter.

Dixon L. Poole was named the Association's PX Officer and exclusive vendor for Association merchandise. The PX had been suspended temporarily in late 1992.

The New England Chapter raised funds for a bronze memorial plaque to honor those who served with the Division. The plaque was to be placed along the

Memorial Path in the National l Cemetery in Bourne, Massachusetts, coinciding with the Division's fiftieth anniversary.

The 1993 reunion was held at the Hyatt Regency Hotel in San Antonio, Texas, September 22-26. Honored guests included Brigadier General Ray L. Smith, Commanding General of the 3d Division; Division Sergeant Major Joel Williams; and Sergeant Randall Richardson, who was named "Marine of the Year." The Cadet Band from the Marine Military Academy in Harlingen, Texas, provided the official music at the reunion banquet and for the Sunday Memorial Service at The Alamo. At age 96, Al Jenson was still active in the Association and made the trip from his California home to attend the reunion.

One hundred Association members attended the September 23 dedication of the Third Marine Division Association plaque at the Nimitz Museum in nearby Fredericksburg, Texas. Money for the plaque had been raised by the Association's Texas Chapter.

Recipient of the 1993 Turnage Award was Robert B. Van Atta, who was cited for his contribution's to the Memorial Scholarship Board of Trustees, as well as his service on the 50th Anniversary Book Committee. An Association member since 1956 and Life Member since 1979, Van Atta served in both World War II and the Korean War.

Mrs. Myrtle R. Owens, wife of retired Colonel Alfred L. Owens, a Life Member, died on April 25. She bequeathed $25,000 to the Memorial Scholarship Fund in memory of her husband.

The January-February 1994 issue of Caltrap reported President Gay's confirmation of key appointments to Association committees, including the Membership Committee, the Distinguished Benefactor Program, and the Awards Committee. The newsletter also announced that the Dedicated Member Page Program had raised $25,000, with contributions from more than 1,600 members and friends. This figure represents 25 percent of the operating budget for the 1993-1994 fiscal year. On the downside, both attendance and revenues for the San Diego reunion had failed to meet expectations, resulting in no profit from the event.

The year marked the fiftieth anniversary of the liberation of Guam, and on February 16, ground was broken for a U.S. Veterans/ Chamorro Memorial in the War in the Pacific Park at Asan, Guam. The Association was actively involved in the planning and implementation of the "Golden Salute Return to Guam" scheduled for July 16-22.

The September/October issue of Caltrap featured a long article detailing the Return to Guam. Mrs. Florence Kriendler presented the Association with a donation of $1,000 for the Guam Liberators Fund, in honor of the fiftieth anniversary.

Because of the Return to Guam program in July, the 40th Annual Reunion was held August 31-September 4 at the Radisson Plaza Hotel in Savannah, Georgia. Mayor Susan Weiner proclaimed September 4 as "Caltrap Memorial Day," in honor of the Association.

As always, new officers, Board members, and committee chairmen were selected at the meeting. The bylaws were amended to develop a five-year plan for reunions that would reflect the geographic locations of all members and to clarify the responsibilities of the Reunion Advisory Committee.

Brigadier General David F. Bice, recently named Commanding General of the Third Division, attended the reunion. President Gay presented General Bice with his Life Member card and pin at the reunion.

The year 1995 was the fiftieth anniversary of the battle for Iwo Jima, and the Association's Return to Iwo Jima Committee had organized the Honor and Return to Iwo Jima tour, scheduled for March 10-16. The event included a joint American-Japanese memorial service, attended by General Munday, Marine Corps Commandant. Commemorative activities were also held in Washington, DC, February 17-19, with Life Member Thomas F. Hogan representing the Association. On September 2, Association President Henry Gardner represented the organization at a wreath-laying ceremony at the National Memorial Cemetery of the Pacific in Hawaii.

The 1995 reunion was held at the Union Plaza Hotel and Casino in Las Vegas, July 19-23, with Lieutenant General Anthony Zinni as the Guest of Honor. At the business meeting, all officers were re-elected to the second term. Joe Garza was re-elected Chairman of the Board of Directors, and Board members and committee chairman were appointed. Colonel Robert Cohen, Commanding Officer of the 4th Marines, spoke at the business meeting on the "state of the 3d Marine Division." Sergeant Kenneth R. Allen was named "Marine of the Year." In an Association first, member Tom Ryan got married during the reunion.

Sergeant Major Leslie G. LeBlanc was named the 1995 Turnage Award winner. He was unable to attend the reunion due to his wife's illness and was notified by phone from the Board meeting. His award was delivered to his home at a later date. Sergeant Major LeBlanc's Marine Corps career spanned 30 years, including World War II and the Korean and Vietnam Wars. He was active in chapter and national affairs, and had become famous for his personal correspondence with members, affectionately known as "bug" letters.

At ceremonies in Hawaii, commemorating the end of World War II, Past President Gardner laid a wreath at the memorial at the Punchbowl cemetery and offered a prayer for all who had died in the war. He also received personal greetings from President and Mrs. Clinton, as well as from General Louis Wilson. Following the service, Life Member Dr. William W. Putney received the Silver Star he earned for heroism on Guam from General Louis H. Wilson, the Corps' 26th Commandant.

The Dedicated Members Page Program had another record year, raising $27,500 for the Association. And fundraising continued, as always, for the Memorial Scholarship Fund. An August bowling tournament, sponsored by active duty Marines, raised more than $3,500 for the Fund. The total raised for the fund in fiscal year 1995 was $7,220.47.

The Association voted to donate $1,500 from the Liberators of Guam Fund to the University of Guam Library to underwrite the costs of periodical subscription renewals.

On September 16, 1996, Association Life Member Don Gee was named recipient of the Donald L. Dickson Memorial Award by the Marine Corps Combat Correspondents Association. He is the third Third Marine Division Association member to be so honored, following in the footsteps of Jim Kyser in 1982 and Tom Bartlett in 1992.

In March 1995, the Wisconsin Chapter had been formed, with its charter approved at the 1995 reunion. In early 1996, the Chapter requested a name change to the Gunnery Sergeant Alan P. Loper USMC Wisconsin Chapter, in honor of the founder and first president of the Chapter who passed away in April 1995. It was the first chapter named for an individual since the Association was formed.

On January 21, Harvey Tennant, a Life Member and winner of the Turnage Award

Return To Guam 1994

Return To Iwo Jima 1995

passed away. His wife, Margaret, also a Life Member, followed him in death one week later. On February 1, the Association suffered another tremendous loss with the passing of Wayne Goodhart, a former Sergeant-at-Arms who had served as chairman of the Awards Committee and President of the Florida Chapter.

May 2-3, representatives from 28 Marine Corps-related organizations, including the Association, attended a meeting in Washington, DC, to study the formation of a community outreach program that would communicate the Corps' mission, values, and accomplishments to the American public. President Henry Gardner served as the Association's representative to the group. At the reunion, he was appointed to chair the Association's new Community Outreach Committee.

The 42nd Annual Reunion was held at the Adams Mark Hotel in Philadelphia, July 24- 28, 1996. General Charles C. Krulak, Marine Corps Commandant, was the guest of honor. "Marine of the Year" Sergeant Jabe S. Smith was also at the reunion.

The Board voted to separate the duties of the Association Manager and the Public Affairs Officer/Editor, at the request of Jim Kyser, who had suffered two heart attacks earlier in the year. Don Gee was appointed PAO/Editor, and Kyser remained as Association Manager. General Ray Davis was named the Association's new Honorary Life President following the passing of Lieutenant General Edward Craig.

Retired Lieutenant Colonel Richard E. Jones was presented the Association's first Presidential Service Award for his " ... continued and tireless service to the Third Marine Division Association." His contributions included serving as Secretary of the Memorial Scholarship Board of Trustees and as Chairman, Humanitarian Programs. He received the Turnage Award in 1988.

At the Sunday memorial service, Joe Garza tolled the bell as the name of each member who had made the Final Formation in the past year was read. Among that list was the name of Harvey Tennant, who had tolled the bell each year since the ceremony had been introduced.

The January/February 1998 issue of *Caltrap* reported $27,800 in donations to the Dedicated Member Page Program for the previous years. Approximately 1,800 members contributed to the program.

On January 21, 1997, Tom Bartlett, also known as "Mr. Leatherneck," made the final formation at the age of 62. A Life Member of the Association, he served as editor of *Leatherneck Magazine* for 22 years.

Brigadier General J.D. Humble, Commanding General, Marine Corps Recruit Depot/Eastern Recruiting Region, solicited the Association's help with a new program. He asked that members visit the Recruit Depot to " ... share with today's young men and women those values of teamwork, individual responsibility, and integrity that you learned while in garrison, on liberty, and in combat."

The 43rd Annual Reunion was held at the Grand Milwaukee Hotel, in Milwaukee, Wisconsin, July 23-27, 1997. The theme for the event was "Valor and Sacrifice." The guest speaker at the banquet was Colonel Leonard M. Supko, Commanding Officer of the 12th Marine Regiment, representing the Commanding General. The guest of honor was Major General Ray L. Smith, Deputy Commanding General of the II Marine Expeditionary Force and former Commanding General of the 3d Division.

Association Chaplain Thomas Kelley, Captain (CHC) USN (Ret), received the Turnage Award for his many years of service to the Association. Bill Krueger received the Presidential Service Award. He served as Chairman of the Membership Committee for 10 years, and membership increased by 75 percent during his tenure. Sergeant Sandra D. Bassett was named the Division's "Marine of the Year," the first Woman Marine to be so honored. Colonel Supko presented Sergeant Bassett with the Navy-Marine Corps Achievement Medal.

Forty-eight young men and women received scholarships for the 1997-1998 academic year. It was reported that over its history, the fund had raised a total of $362,598. The Association voted to again donate $1,500 to the University of Guam Libarary for subscription renewals.

The Florida Chapter played host for the Association's 44th Annual Reunion, held at the Omni-Rosen Hotel in Orlando, July 29-August 2, 1998. General Davis, a medal of Honor recipient and Association Honorary Life President and Sergeant Timothy A. Hartmann, the Division's "Marine of the Year" were guests of honor at the banquet.

Sunday morning's memorial service breakfast paid tribute to the Third Division's war dead and also honored 112 Association members who had made their "final Formation" since the previous year's reunion.

New officers and Executive Committee members were elected at the business meeting, and Board vacancies were filled. Robert Van Atta was appointed to another term as Trustee for the Memorial Scholarship Committee, and Dean C. Taylor was named Executive Assistant to the President. Four-star General and Medal of Honor recipient Louis H. Wilson, Jr., was made an Association Honorary Life President.

The Bylaws Committee proposed formalization of seating on the Board of Directors to include all honorary officers and Turnage Award recipients. Turnage Award recipients had been seated as Board members and exercised full voting rights since the

PRESIDENT'S TABLE - *Mrs. Ray L. Smith (left), Major General Ray L. Smith (facing camera), Mrs. and Association President Ronald R. Burton, Mrs. and Past President George Gay, Mrs. Annette Loper, Association Chaplain Thomas W. Kelley (back to camera), and Association Manager Jim Kyser at the Milwaukee Reunion Banquet.*

Award was established in 1974 but had not been listed as Board members in the bylaws.

Association members began raising funds for a 3d Marine Division plaque at the Parris Island Museum, with North Carolina Chapter President Jimmie A. Bryant leading the effort. The 3d Division was the only Marine Division without a plaque in the museum. Bryant estimated that it would cost approximately $1,200 to cast the bronze plaque. Additional plaques could then be made for a cost of approximately $500. The Association's Golden Gate Chapter raised more than $600 for the Devil Pups Program through a raffle.

The Association's Web site, www.caltrap.com, was launched in 1998. Designed by Bill Ervin, the site contained a wealth of information about the Association, including its history, and proved a valuable recruiting tool for new members.

As the year drew to a close, membership stood at 5,177.

The last reunion of the 1990s was held at the Doubletree Hotel in Spokane, Washington, July 14-18. Major General James T. Conway, President of the Marine Corps University at Quantico, was the guest of honor. Other distinguished guests included Brigadier General Gordon C. Nash, Commanding General of the 3d Division; Division Sergeant Major R.A. Paradine; and Corporal Dacken W. Albertson, who had been named the Division's "Marine of the Year."

The annual Memorial Service, honoring the Association's dead, was held on Sunday morning on an outdoor floating stage near the hotel. Association Vice President Jack Rine read the 108 "Roll of Honor" names.

Officers and Directors were elected at the annual business meeting. Joe Garza, Jr., was named recipient of the 1998 Turnage Award. A Life Member of the Association since 1989, Garza held numerous elected and appointed offices with the Association and its Southern California Chapter.

The Association suffered the loss of several Old Breed members who had given years of service to the organization. Colonel William Andrew "Iron Man" Lee, an Honorary Life Member since 1990, died on December 27, 1998, at the age of 1998. CWO Thomas O. Kelly, who served two terms as Association President, died of a stroke on March 25, just three days before his ninety-seventh birthday. On July 16, Lieutenant Colonel Albert Jenson USMC (Ret) died of congestive heart failure at the age of 102. He epitomized the dedication

and camaraderie of the Association, serving as Executive Secretary for 17 years. And on September 3, Life Member Art Renkosiak died of a heart attack.

Bert Barton, chairman of the Memorial Scholarship Fund, reported that more than $400,000 had been awarded to eligible children of 3d Division Marines over the 31-year life of the program. The program was initiated in 1968 and the first Memorial Scholarship Fund award was made in 1972. The Florida Chapter continues to sell name badges for chapter meetings and reunions to help raise money for the scholarship fund.

The Association began offering its own credit card to members. The Platinum-Plus Master Card, which bears the organization's name and Caltrap logo, carries no annual fee. Royalties from the credit card will be used for the benefit of members.

On February 20, the fifty-fourth anniversary of the landing on Iwo Jima, an Iwo Jima Monument was dedicated at Camp Pendleton. Joe Garza, Jr., a Past President of the Association, chaired the Iwo Jima Commemorative Committee, which organized the dedication. The ceremony included an outdoor memorial tribute, with a 21-gun salute and the sounding of "Taps." Garza originated the Memorial Tribute in 1988.

Life Member Ed O'Donnell represented the Association at a service held at the Iwo Jima Memorial in Remsen, Iowa. He placed a commemorative wreath at the monument's base February 20 to honor the anniversary of the 1945 landing.

A 3d Marine Division monument was unveiled April 17 at the Chattanooga National Cemetary. The ceremony was attended by Association members David Crowder, Ralph Tate, Dale Quillen, Charles Moore, Page McClelland, Cy O'Brien, Warren Brumleve, Bill Head, Henry Gardner, Robert Wheeler, Harold Weist, Pat Durkee, and Joe Hamilton.

As the decade drew to a close, Association membership stood at 5,231.

As the new millennium dawned, the Association was making plans for its 46th Annual Reunion, to be held in Virginia Beach, Virginia, September 13-17, 2000. The Hampton Roads Chapter hosted the event, with Colonel Jim Phillips heading the organizing team. The year 2000 marked the first time the Association had held its reunion at Virginia Beach.

The theme for the reunion was "The New Millennium, The Changing of the

Guard," as Association President Royal Q. Zilliox explained in his speech:

"With the new Millennium we must look to passing the leadership for our Association from the World War II Marine to those who entered the Corps later. If you fall into this category and are not presently in a leadership position, step forward and state your qualifications."

Navy Captain John T. Nawrocki, skipper of the USS Iwo Jima, was a special guest at the reunion. He was there to promote his ship and to establish a relationship with the Third Marine Division Association and, in particular, with Iwo Jima veterans. Other honored guests included Major General Wallace C. Gregson, Commanding General of the 3d Marine Division; Division Sergeant Major G.J. Amos; and Sergeant Davide F. Sartoni, who was the Division's "Marine of the Year."

At the business meeting, the Association's bylaws were amended, opening Associate membership to all relatives of persons, living or deceased, who are or were eligible for Association membership. A second bylaw change removed the geographic restriction for Association chapter formation, allowing formation of the Association's first Unit chapter – the 1st Battalion, Third Marines. (Association members may belong to more than one chapter.)

A special three-day salute to Korean War veterans, held in honor of the 50th anniversary of the Korean War, also took place during the reunion. Events included a re-enactment of the Inchon landing, a parade, a candlelight ceremony honoring POWs and MIAs, and historical displays. General Ray Davis, one of the Association's two Honorary Life Presidents and Medal of Honor recipient, was the speaker at a dinner honoring Korean War Medal of Honor recipients.

Life Member Robert B. Van Atta, a Memorial Scholarship Fund Trustee since 1968, 1993 Turnage Award recipient, and co-author of *Two Score and Ten*, the 50-year history of the Division, received the President's Distinguished Service Medal from the University of Pennsylvania-Greenwood Campus at the university's 2000 Commencement ceremonies.

A highlight of the Virginia Beach reunion was the playing of "The Fighting Third" Division song, composed in response to a challenge from Brigadier General Gordon C. Nash, Division

Commanding General, at the 1999 Spokane reunion. Nash pointed out that the 3d Division didn't have a song like the 1st and 2d Divisions did, and he'd donate $100 to the Memorial Scholarship Fund if such a song could be composed.

Retired Colonel Edward F. Danowitz and Associate Life Member Mrs. Sara Fopiano responded to the challenge. Colonel Danowitz wrote the lyrics based on the Division's "Courage, Honor, Fidelity" motto, with three verses covering the past, present and future of the Division. An accomplished musician and composer, Mrs. Fopiano set the words to original music, and the completed words and music were mailed to Brigadier General Nash on Okinawa.

He, in turn, gave the music and lyrics to CWO James A. Ford, Jr., Director of the III MEF Band on Okinawa, to have it arranged for the band. On June 3, 2000, "The Fighting Third" was performed by the III MEF Band at the Ginbowan People's Civic Hall, and sung by the combined voices of the Kubasaki and Kadena High School choirs.

Reflecting the "changing of the guard" theme of the 46th Annual Reunion, retired Second Lieutenant John H. Rine, Jr., a Vietnam-era Marine, was elected Association President, and Deane C. Taylor, who served in the Division in early 1960's, was elected Vice President. Vacancies on the Board of Directors and several key committee chairmanships also were filled by other post-World War II members as the Association moved into 2001.

On May 1, 2001, retired Gunnery Sergeant Don Gee — who had served as Editor and PAO since October 1996 — became the Association Manager, replacing retired Master Gunnery Sergeant Jim Kyser who had held the position since July 1990.

The Association — as well as 4th and 5th Marine Division veterans, crew members from the previous ships bearing the USS Iwo Jima name (LPH-2, 1961-1993) and other veterans — was allocated 200 spaces for the day-long June 23 maiden voyage of the Iwo Jima (LHD-7) from Pascagoula, Mississippi, to Pensacola, FL. Most of these slots were filled by Association members and spouses, and many remained in Pensacola for the June 30 commissioning of the USS Iwo Jima that was attended by hundreds of 3d, 4th and 5th Marine Division veterans of the 1945 battle for Iwo Jima.

As the Association readied for the 47th Annual Reunion scheduled for late September in Irving (Dallas), Texas, the tragic events of September 11 did not deter Association members and guests at the annual gathering, but they did prevent the 3d Marine Division Commanding General, Division Sergeant Major, and Division Marine of the Year from attending — the active duty Marines "…were otherwise occupied."

Most Association Officers were elected to second terms, and the trend continued for post-World War II Marines to fill key Association positions. The U.S. Marine Drum and Bugle Corps was in Dallas for the Texas State Fair and provided an evening performance for members at the reunion; and the Guest Speaker at the annual banquet was *Flags of Our Fathers* author James Bradley.

The 48th Annual Reunion in San Diego, CA, scheduled for September 4-8, 2002 celebrates the 60th Anniversary of the 3d Marine Division. The Division was activated September 16, 1942, at Camp Pendleton, California.

Today's Third Marine Division Association comprises 22 area chapters and one unit chapter. The Association's annual reunions allow members to experience the camaraderie of being part of the 3d Marine Division and to renew friendships made during service with the Division. The Association continues to keep members apprised of what is happening in the Marine Corps today, as well as Association news, in the pages of *Caltrap*.

The Association also continues its tradition of charitable work through the Memorial Scholarship Fund, the Liberators of Guam Fund, the Care of Our Own Life Member Program, and the Lucy Caldwell Fund.

The Association welcomes all who have served honorably with the Division or who were attached to units supporting the Division to join the Third Marine Division Association. Associate membership is open to parents, relatives, and spouses of individuals, living or deceased, who are, or were, eligible for regular membership.

OPENING CEREMONY - The Colors were presented in the opening ceremonies for the Reunion Banquet in Virginia Beach.

3d Marine Division
Fleet Marine Force

Commanding Generals

MajGen. Charles D. Barrett	September 16, 1942 - September 14, 1943
MajGen. Allen H. Turnage	September 15, 1943 - September 14, 1944
BrigGen. Alfres H. Noble	September 15, 1944 - October 13, 1944
MajGen. Graves B. Erskine	October 14, 1944 - October 20, 1945
BrigGen. William E. Riley	October 21, 1945 - December 28, 1945
BrigGen. Merrill B. Twining	January 7, 1952 - February 14, 1952
MajGen. Robert H. Pepper	February 15, 1952 - May 9, 1954
MajGen. James P. Risely	May 10, 1954 - June 30, 1955
MajGen. Thomas A. Wornham	July 1, 1955 - July 26, 1956
BrigGen. Victor H. Krulak	July 27, 1956 - September 6, 1956
MajGen. Alan Shapley	September 7, 1956 - July 1, 1957
MajGen. Francis M. McAlister	July 2, 1957 - March 28, 1958
MajGen. David M. Shoup	March 29, 1958 - April 1, 1959
Col. Rathvon McC. Tompkins (Acting)	April 2, 1959 - May 8, 1959
BrigGen. Lewis C. Hudson	May 9, 1959 - June 19, 1959
MajGen. Robert B. Luckey	June 20, 1959 - August 31, 1960
MajGen. Donald M. Weller	September 1, 1960 - August 31, 1960
MajGen. Robert E. Cushman Jr.	September 2, 1961 - June 3, 1962
MajGen. Henry W. Buse Jr.	June 4, 1962 - May 9, 1963
MajGen. James M. Masters Sr.	May 10, 1963 - June 16, 1964
MajGen. William R. Collins	June 17, 1964 - June 4, 1965
MajGen. Lewis W. Walt	June 5, 1965 - March 17, 1966
MajGen. Wood B. Kyle	March 18, 1966 - March 17, 1967
MajGen. Bruno A. Hochmuth	March 18, 1967 - November 14, 1967
BrigGen. Louis Metzger (Acting)	March 15, 1967 - November 27, 1967
MajGen. Rathvon McC. Tompkins	November 28, 1967 - May 20, 1968
MajGen. Raymond G. Davis	- May 21, 1968 - April 14, 1969
MajGen. William K. Jones	April 15, 1969 - March 30, 1970
MajGen. Louis H. Wilson	March 31, 1970 - March 22, 1971
MajGen. Louis Metzger	March 23, 1971 - January 7, 1972
MajGen. Joseph C. Fegan	January 8, 1972 - January 7, 1973
MajGen. Michael P. Ryan	January 8, 1973 - August 31, 1973
MajGen. Fred E. Haynes Jr.	September 1, 1973 - August 22, 1974
MajGen. Kenneth J. Hughton	August 23, 1974 - August 13, 1975
MajGen. Herbert L. Wilkerson	August 14, 1975 - July 19, 1976
MajGen. George W. Smith	July 20, 1976 - July 16, 1977
MajGen. Adolph G. Schwenk	July 17, 1977 - July 10, 1978
MajGen. Calhoun J. Killeen	July 11, 1978 - July 11, 1979
MajGen. Kenneth L. Robinson Jr.	July 12, 1979 - July 24, 1980
MajGen. Stephen G. Olmstead	July 25, 1980 - June 21, 1982
MajGen. Robert E. Haebel	June 22, 1982 - June 8, 1984
MajGen. Harold G. Glasgow	June 9, 1984 - June 3, 1986
MajGen. Edwin J. Godfrey	June 4, 1986 - September 9, 1987
LtGen. Norman H. Smith	September 10, 1987 - September 25, 1989
LtGen. Henry C. Stackpole III	September 26, 1989 - June 27, 1991
MajGen. Michael J. Byron	June 28, 1991 - June 8, 1993
MajGen. Donald R. Gardener (Interim)	June 9, 1993 - August 16, 1993
MajGen. Ray L. Smith	August 17, 1993 - May 4, 1994
BrigGen. David F. Bice	May 5, 1994 - August 4, 1995
BrigGen. Raymond P. Ayres Jr.	August 5, 1995 - July 10, 1997
MajGen. Dennis M. McCarthy (Interim)	July 11, 1997 - October 9, 1997
BrigGen. J.D. Humble	October 10, 1997 - April 1, 1999
BrigGen. Gordon C. Nash	April 2, 1999 - July 10, 2000
MajGen. Wallace C. Gregson	July 11, 2000 - July 26, 2001
MajGen. James R. Battaglini	July 26, 2001 - Present

Division Sergeants Major

SgtMaj. Floyd D. Hudson	1942 - 1943
SgtMaj. Henry G. Schlindwein	1943
SgtMaj. T.O. Kelly	1943
SgtMaj. Kenneth A. McKnight	1943 - 1944
SgtMaj. Henry A. Herrero	1944
SgtMaj. Robert T. Parker	1945
SgtMaj. Arthur L. Poganski	1952
SgtMaj. William W. Holt	1952 - 1953
SgtMaj. Frank Drasil	1953 - 1954
SgtMaj. Harold E. Harper	1954 - 1955
SgtMaj. Chester T. Barker	1955
SgtMaj. Wayne D. Shaffer	1955
SgtMaj. Robert Walker	1955 - 1956
SgtMaj. Donald D. White	1956
SgtMaj Delmas A. Bryant	1956 - 1957
SgtMaj. B.H. LeGrand	1957 - 1958
SgtMaj. Frank Carollo	1958 - 1959
SgtMaj. Mehrl A. Hotchkiss	1959
SgtMaj. J.W. Arnett - 1959	1960
SgtMaj. Butler Metzger Jr.	1960 - 1961
SgtMaj. Russel O. Baker	1961 - 1962
SgtMaj. Emory M. Krotky	1962 - 1963
SgtMaj. Nelton J. Dartez	1963 - 1964
SgtMaj. Herbert J. Sweet	1964 - 1965
SgtMaj. Nicholas D. Parice	1965 - 1966
SgtMaj. Robert E. McIntire	1966
SgtMaj Clyde M. Long	1966 - 1967
SgtMaj. Borge E. Freeberg	1967
SgtMaj. Michael Popichak	1968
SgtMaj. Harlan L. Graham	1968
SgtMaj. Joseph W. Daily	1968 - 1969
SgtMaj. Fernand Violette	1969
SgtMaj. Clyde M. Long	1969 - 1970
SgtMaj. John D. Steely	1970
SgtMaj. Thomas J. Avery	1970 - 1971
SgtMaj. Michael D. Mervosh	1971 - 1972
SgtMaj. Richard G. Benson	1972
SgtMaj. Louis B. Jeffrey	1972 - 1973
SgtMaj. Robert W. Williams	1973 - 1974
SgtMaj. Peter C. Patmalnee	1974
SgtMaj. James H. Staggs	1974 -1975
SgtMaj. Philip M. Rudolph	1975 - 1976
SgtMaj. Robert H. Brueggenjohann	1976 - 1977
SgtMaj. Peter J. Marovich	1977 - 1978
SgtMaj. L.C. Johnson	1978
SgtMaj. Dominick Irrera	1978 - 1979
SgtMaj. William L. Huggins	1979
SgtMaj. Gilbert Mireles	1979
SgtMaj. Robert E. Cleary	1979
SgtMaj. George D. Rogers	1980 - 1981
SgtMaj. Albert L. Ross	1981 - 1982
SgtMaj. C.C. Robinson	April 1982 - April 1983
SgtMaj C.D. Mortis	April 1983 - April 1984
SgtMaj. R.E. Behrend	April 1984 - April 1985
SgtMaj. F.A. Thomas	April 1985 - February 1986
SgtMaj. J.W. Durham	February 1986 - September 1987
SgtMaj. P. McLane	September 1987 - June 1991
SgtMaj. Richard W. Smith	June 1991 - April 1992
SgtMaj. Thomas J. Cruz	April 1992 - August 1993
SgtMaj. Joel S. Williams	August 1993 - May 1995
SgtMaj. John M. Gallegos (Interim)	May 1995 - June 1995
SgtMaj. William R. Hancock	June 1995 - May 1997
SgtMaj. R.A. Paradine Jr.	May 1997 - April 2000
SgtMaj. George J. Amos	April 2000 - March 2, 2001
SgtMaj. Robin W. Dixon	March 2, 2001 - Present

Medal of Honor Recipients, 3d Marine Division

WWII

*PFC Henry Gurke	3d Raider Bn.	Neche, ND	Bougainville
2dLt. John H. Leims	Co. B, 1st Bn., 9th Mar.	Chicago, IL	Iwo Jima
*PFC Leonard F. Mason	Co. E, 2d Bn., 3d Mar.	Middlesboro, KY	Guam
*Sgt. Robert A. Owens	Co. A, 1st Bn., 3d Mar.	Greenville, SC	Bougainville
PFC Luther Skaggs Jr.	Co. K, 3d Bn., 3d Mar.	Henderson, KY	Guam
*Sgt. Herbert J. Thomas	Co. B, 1st Bn., 3d Mar.	Columbus, OH	Bougainville
Pvt. Wilson D. Watson	Co. G, 2d Bn., 9th Mar.	Tuscumbia, AL	Iwo Jima
Cpl. Hershel W. Williams	Co. C, 1st Bn., 21st Mar.	Fairmont, WV	Iwo Jima
Capt. Louis H. Wilson Jr.	Co. F, 2d Bn., 9th Mar.	Brandon, MS	Guam
*PFC Frank P. Witek	Co. B, 1st Bn., 9th Mar.	Derby, CT	Guam

Vietnam

*PFC James Anderson Jr.	Co. F, 2d Bn., 3d Mar.	Los Angeles, CA
*LCpl. Richard A. Anderson	Co. F, 3d Recon Bn.	Washington, DC
HM2 Donald E. Ballard	Co. M, 3d Bn., 4th Mar.	Kansas City, MO
*LCpl. Jedh C. Barker	Co. F, 3d Bn., 4th Mar.	Franklin, NH
1stLt. Harvey C. Barnum	Co. H, 2nd Bn., 9th Mar.	Waterbury, CT
*2dLt. John P. Bobo	Co. I, 3d Bn., 9th Mar.	Niagara Falls, NY
*PFC Bruce W. Carter	Co. H, 2d Bn., 9th Mar.	Schanactady, NY
*PFC Ronald L. Coker	Co. M, 3d Bn., 3d Mar.	Alliance, NE
*SSgt. Peter S. Conner	Co. F, 2d Bn., 3d Mar.	Orange, NJ
*Col. Donald G. Cook	Comm. Co., Hq. Bn., 3d Mar. Div.	Brooklyn, NY
*LCpl. Thomas E. Creek	Co. I, 3d Bn., 9th Mar.	Joplin, MO
*PFC Douglas E. Dickey	Co. C, 1st Bn., 4th Mar.	Greenville, OH
*Sgt. Paul H. Foster	2d Bn., 4th Mar.	San Mateo, CA
1stLt. Wesley L. Fox	Co. A, 1st Bn., 9th Mar.	Herndon, VA
2dLt. Terrence C. Graves	3d Force Recon Co., 3d Recon Bn.	Corpus Christi, TX
*PFC Robert H. Jenkins Jr.	Co. C, 3d Recon Bn.	Interlachen, FL
Capt. Howard V. Lee	Co. E, 2d Bn., 4th Mar.	New York, NY
Capt. James E. Livingston	Co. E, 2d Bn., 4th Mar.	Towns Telfair, GA
*Cpl. Larry L. Maxam	Co. D, 1st Bn., 4th Mar.	Glendale, CA
SSgt. John J. McGinty	Co. K, 3d Bn., 4th Mar.	Boston, MA
Capt. Robert J. Madrzejewski	Co. K, 3d Bn., 4th Mar.	Milwaukee, WI
*Cpl. William D. Morgan	Co. H, 2d Bn., 9th Mar.	Pittsburgh, PA
*LCpl Thomas Noonan Jr.	Co. G, 2d Bn., 9th Mar.	Brooklyn, NY
Cpl. Robert E. O'Malley	Co. I, 3d Bn., 3d Mar.	New York, NY
*LCpl. Joe C. Paul	Co. H, 2d Bn., 4th Mar.	Williamsburg, KY
*Cpl. William T. Perkins Jr.	Serv. Co., Hq. Bn., 3d Mar. Div.	Rochester, NY
*LCpl. William R. Prom	Co. I, 3d Bn., 3d Mar.	Pittsburgh, PA
*1stLt. Frank S. Reasoner	Co. A, 3d Recon Bn.	Spokane, WA
*Sgt. Walter K. Singleton	Co. A, Bn., 9th Mar.	Memphis, TN
*SSgt. Karl G. Taylor Sr.	Co. I, 3d Bn., 26th Mar.	Laurel, MD
Capt. Jay R. Vargas	Co. G, 2d Bn., 4th Mar.	Winslow, AZ
*PFC Alfred M. Wilson	Co. M, 3d Bn., 9th Mar.	Olney, IL

*= Posthumous Award

Veteran Biographies

JAMES H. AMOS, JR., president and CEO of Mail Boxes Etc., the world's largest franchiser of retail business, communication, and postal service centers. Also serves as chairman of the International Franchise Association.

A former Marine Corps captain and veteran of two combat tours in Vietnam, Amos received 12 decorations, including the Purple Heart and Vietnamese Cross of Gallantry.

Author of two books, *Focus or Failure: America at the Crossroads* and *The Memorial*. Recently contributed to *The Entrepreneur's Creed—The Principles & Passions of 20 Successful Entrepreneurs*. Currently working on his third book.

A graduate of the University of Missouri, he was honored as the 1998 scholar-in-residence. Recognized in "Marquis Who's Who in America," "Who's Who in American Executives," "Who's Who in Finance and Industry," "Who's Who in American Authors," and "The International Authors and Writers Who's Who."

Serves on the boards of Mail Boxes Etc., the MBE We Deliver Dreams Foundation, the University of Missouri Advisory Council, and the San Diego Opera.

JAMES N. ANDERSON, JR., born April 18, 1929, in Wilmington, Delaware. Enlisted in the USMC on June 17, 1945.

Parris Island, Coco Solo, C.Z. HQ 4th MCRD, Quantico, Cherry Point; HQCO, 9th MCRS, Philadelphia, Pendleton; Atomic Ordnance at Lejeune and HQBN, 3d Marine Division, Pendleton, Quantico; HQMC, Pendleton, 5th Marine Division; 12th Marines/Vietnam, 4th Marine Division. Retired on November 1, 1968, as 1st Sergeant.

Military awards include the Purple Heart and the Navy Commendation Medal with "V" device.

Married Peggy Schramm (Sergeant, USMC) on May 3, 1952, and we have six sons: James, Mark, Paul, Steve, Eric, and Carl.

Founded Anderson International Trading, 1976, wholesale hardwood plywood company, Anaheim, California. Still active as CEO.

Resides at 1123 Tylee Street, Vista, CA, 92083; phone home, (760) 724-1531, or work, (800) 454-6270.

To all Marines: I maintain a small museum for Marines in Anaheim, California.

GERALD S. ANDERSEN, born on August 25, 1925, in Minneapolis, Minnesota. Joined USMC on June 23, 1944, in Chicago, Illinois. Went to San Diego for boot camp and to Camp Pendleton for further training.

Was sent overseas on November 12, 1944. Landed on Guam on January 1, 1945, and trained there for a month and a half. Was sent to Iwo Jima, where I joined the 3d Marine Division on March 1, 1945. Was with the 3d Division until December 28, 1945, for final taps.

Boarded ship for Tien Tsin, China, where I became part of the Third Amphibious Corps. Discharged on August 14, 1946, at Great Lakes NTS, in the rank of Corporal.

Military awards include the Presidential Unit Citation, Asiatic-Pacific Campaign Medal, China Service Medal, and World War II Victory Medal.

Returned to Chicago, where I met my wife, Rita Stratynski. We have been married for 47 years and have two sons, two daughters, ten grandchildren, and two great-grandchildren. We are both retired now and enjoying our family.

KARL C. APPLE, JR., born March 17, 1925, in Oskaloosa, Iowa. Joined USMC on June 4, 1943. Training locations include: Parris Island, South Carolina; Iona Island NAD, New York; Camp Lejeune, North Carolina; Camp Pendleton, California; Guam, Marianas Islands.

Participated in Iwo Jima campaign as a Machine Gunner with A-1-9, 3d Division. Wounded in action on February 26, 1945, and was sent to hospital in Guam. Discharged on February 18, 1946, from Great Lakes NTS, in the rank of Corporal.

Military awards include the Purple Heart, Presidential Unit Citation, American Campaign Medal, Asiatic-Pacific Campaign Medal, and World War II Victory Medal.

Returned to Pittsburgh, Pennsylvania, and married high school sweetheart, Florence Leitholf. Firstborn, Craig, died at age of one month; daughters are Lindsay and Joan.

Retired from Fullerton (California) Fire Department with 27-1/2 years of service. Employed as firefighter, fire inspector, fire and arson investigator. Now active in backpacking, photography, canoeing, and enjoying retirement.

LA VERNE L. ARNOLD, born October 22, 1943, in Kalamazoo, Michigan. Enlisted in the USMC on September 4, 1963. Training locations include: MCRD San Diego, California; Camp Pendleton, California; Camp Courtney, Okinawa. Participated in Vietnam Campaign; HQ CO, HQ Battalion, 3d Marine Division, Da Nang, 1965-1966. Returned to MCRD San Diego, completed Drill Instructors School, and assigned to 1st Recruit Battalion.

Military awards include the Presidential Unit Citation, Good Conduct Medal, National Deof

the armed forces. Honorable discharge, rank of Sergeant (E-5), September 3, 1967.

Married Cynthia Emery of Whittier, California. Children include daughters Amy and Heather, and son Lance. Graduate of Mt. San Antonio College and University of Phoenix.

Currently Administrative Director of Respiratory Services at Los Robles Regional Medical Center, Thousand Oaks, California. Active in genealogy research, military history, travel, and ornamental horticulture.

LONNIE W. ASPINWALL, enlisted in the USMC on August 4, 1954. Training locations included Parris Island, South Carolina, and Camp Pendleton, California.

Shipped to Kobe, Japan, on the *General W.M. Black* on March 3, 1955. Assigned to the A-1-9, 3d Marine Division, FMF, as a barman at Shinodayama. A few paces outside the main gate

was Shinodayama Village, where we pulled liberty. June 1, it was sayonara Shinodayama. The first elements departed Kobe, Japan, aboard the *USS Magoffin*, arrived and disembarked at Buckner Bay, Okinawa, June 5, and embarked onboard an LST, ship to shore by AmTracs, June 7. Was on maneuvers from beachhead to Camp Naponja. This was our permanent base until after the first of the year. Liberty rights was Koza (Four Corners) and Futenama. We relocated to Camp Sukiron after the first of the year.

I was promoted to Corporal on May 1, the day we shipped out for the U.S.A. on the *Gen. Hough J. Gaffey*. Corporal's Warrant was mailed to me from TISF, California, while home on leave.

Now retired from Rayonier Paper Mill, Jessup, Georgia, as G.M.3 millwright with 38 years and 4 months of service. Go to Florida each year for baseball spring training, enjoy hunting and fishing.

JEROME W. AUMAN, born April 30, 1921, in Ridgway, Pennsylvania. Joined the USMC on September 8, 1942. Training locations include Parris Island, South Carolina, and New River, North Carolina.

Shipped overseas on December 2, 1942, from San Diego, California, aboard the *USS Day Star*,

arriving at Pago Pago, Samoa, on December 27, 1942, and transferred into "H" Company, 2nd Battalion, 22nd Marines, FMF into the heavy 30 caliber water-cooled machine guns. August 1, 1943, transferred into H&S Btry., 2nd Def. Bn., M.P. Co. On American Samoa, August 10, 1943. October 10, 1943, promoted to PFC. Embarked onboard the *MS Boschfontein* at Tutuila, American Samoa, March 24, 1944, and arrived in San Francisco, California, April 18, 1944. After a 30-day leave to come home, had to report back to Camp Pendleton, Oceanside, California. Into H&S Btry., Arty. Bn. Training Center, May 26, 1944. Was a cannoneer on 75 and 105mm Howitzers. July 13, 1943, was once again shipped overseas aboard the *USS Barnstable*, leaving San Diego, California, July 22, 1944. Arrived in Honolulu, Hawaii, July 30, 1944, and transferred into A Btry., 5th 155mm Bn., 5th Amphibious Corps. On September 9, 1944, sailed from Hilo, Hawaii, aboard the *USS Catskill* and disembarked on October 21, 1944, at Leyte, Philippine Islands. Participated in the liberation of the Philippine Islands from October 21, 1944, to December 12, 1944.

On December 13, 1944, sailed from Leyte, Philippine Islands, aboard USS LST #71. December 19, 1944, arrived at Guam, Marianas Islands. April 4, 1945, transferred into the K Btry., 4th Bn., 12th Marines, 3d Marine Division. Embarked onboard the *USS Bollinger* (APA- 234) on November 1, 1945. Arrived at San Diego, California, November 14, 1945. From San Diego, shipped to U.S. Naval Training Center, Great Lakes, Illinois, and was discharged on December 11, 1945.

Retired from Automatic Turning & Machining after 30 years of service. Now active in gardening, woodworking, photography, and attending Marine Corps reunions.

ALBERT H. BAIRD, born July 6, 1922. Joined the USMC on November 16, 1942. Was discharged on September 28, 1945. Training locations include: Parris Island; Camp Lejeune; Camp Pendleton; American Samoa; Auckland, New Zealand; and live training at Guadalcanal and Guam.

Participated in Bougainville and Guam campaigns with "F" Company, 19th Marines; Iwo Jima campaign with "F" Company, 3d Pioneers, attached to the 9th Marines. Was a Squad Leader and Demolition Man.

Dedicated my awards to my buddies, some of whom are still over there.

Most memorable experience was the chaos on the beach at Iwo, when we were detached from the 3d Marines and sent to try to get food and ammo through the wreckage on the beach while taking artillery, mortar, and rifle fire.

Returned to Trafford, Pennsylvania, and married Emma Colloso; had four children: Cecelia, Albert, Aimee, and Hugh. Now have eight grandchildren.

Worked as a locomotive engineer for 43 years. Retired from Con-Rail. Last run was the Broadway Limited.

Now active serving as a local and county school director. Enjoy golf, travel, and surf fishing.

MAXWELL E. "DOC" BAKER, born November 16, 1930, in Shenandoah County, Virginia. Graduated Calvin Coolidge High School, Washington, DC, and enlisted in the USN in 1949. Boot camp and Hospital Corps School at Great Lakes, Illinois. Field Medical Service School at Camp Lejeune in 1951 and Camp Pendleton in 1967.

Served as senior company corpsman with Easy Company, 2nd Bn., 3d Marines, at North Camp Fuji, Japan, from June 1954 to May 1957. Life member of 3d Marine Division Association. Also served five tours of duty with the 1st Marine Division, including tours in Korea and Vietnam.

Military awards include the Navy Commendation Medal with "V" device (2), Combat Action Ribbon, Good Conduct Medal (8), Korea Service Medal with three stars and combat operations insignia, Vietnam Service Medal with 10 stars and FMF insignia, RVN Civil Actions Medal (personal award), Republic of Korea War Service Medal, plus several unit awards.

Retired as Master Chief Hospital Corpsman in 1979 at Quantico, Virginia, after 30 years of service. Returned to family's ancestral homeplace in Virginia's Shenandoah Valley near Strasburg, Virginia, to find it long abandoned and in deplorable condition. Over the next several years, he restored it to the verge of showplace status. Visitors welcome!

ROBERT J. BANKS, born April 14, 1926, in Bayonne, New Jersey. Raised and educated in Elizabeth, New Jersey. Enlisted in the USMC on June 29, 1944, in New York, New York. Parris Island, July and August 1944; Camp Lejeune, North Carolina, September and October 1944.

Replacement draft to Guam, Marianas Islands, November 1944. Invasion of Iwo Jima, Volcanos Island, February 24, 1945. There joined Co. F, 2nd Bn., 21st Marines until the 3d Division disbanded, September 1945. Occupation of Truk, Caroline Islands, September 1945 to February 1946. Occupation of China, Hq.Co. 2d Bn., 22nd Marines, 6th Marine Division. Stationed at airfield outside of Tsing Tao until August 1946. Discharged at Great Lakes, Illinois, August 22, 1946, in the rank of Corporal.

Married Mildred Gallagher on April 13, 1948; four children: Linda, Robert, Mary Lou, and Raymond. Was on the Elizabeth (New Jersey) Police Department's homicide squad for 25 years. Retired in the rank of Sergeant in 1982 and relocated to Tennessee. Worked in the Federal Court, Knoxville, Tennessee, as Special Deputy, U.S. Marshals. Retired for good in 1991.

JOSEPH W. BELL, Sergeant, #462103, September 14, 1942, through October 17, 1947, born April 4, 1925, in San Antonio, Texas. Joined the USMC on September 14, 1942. Training locations include: Boot camp, San Diego, California; Scout and Sniper School, Camp Pendleton, California, Papakura, New Zealand, and Guadalcanal.

Served with Fox Co., 2nd Bn., 9th Regiment,

from November 7, 1942, through February 24, 1945. Participated in the Bougainville, Northern Solomon Islands, Guam, and Iwo Jima campaigns.

Military awards include the Purple Heart for wounds received July 25 and July 26, 1944, Fonte Ridge, Guam; Gold Star in lieu of second award for wounds received February 24, 1945, on Iwo Jima; Good Conduct Medal; American Campaign Medal; Asiatic-Pacific Medal with four stars; World War II Victory Medal; Presidential Unit Commendation Ribbon with two stars for Fonte Ridge, Guam, and Iwo Jima.

Married Ruth Anne Hamilton of Philadelphia on September 3, 1947 (deceased 1970), and we have three wonderful children: Joanne, Joseph Jr., and James W.

Used the G.I. Bill to acquire B.A. degree, Accounting. Worked seven years in public accounting and 25 years in real estate and concrete products manufacturing. Retired in September 1980.

ROBERT E. BENNING, born October 2, 1923, in Evanston, Illinois. Enlisted in the USMC on February 18, 1942. Schools attended: Radio, San Diego; Combat Intelligence and Scout Sniper, Camp Elliot. Served in the 2d Scout Company, then the 3d Scout Company from its inception. Principal military duty: intelligence man — radio operator.

Participated in the landing and battle to re-

take Guam. Received gunshot wounds in both legs. Temporarily regained consciousness as a red tag was being placed on his wrist. The corpsman called out, "This one is alive." His dog tag had been clipped, and he had been placed with the dead. He was then transferred to the hospital ship the *USS Solace*, where his left leg was amputated.

He arrived in California at Mare Island Naval Hospital via Pearl Harbor and the *Sea Star*. Here he met his wife, Yeoman Patricia Cook, WAVES. They were wed at the Mar Island Naval Chapel on September 6, 1945.

Discharged May 21, 1946, in the rank of Platoon Sergeant. Military awards include the Purple Heart, USMC Good Conduct Medal, American Campaign Medal, Asiatic-Pacific Campaign Medal, and the World War II Victory Medal.

Settled in Napa, California, he served as Assistant County Treasurer for seven years. He then was elected for six consecutive four-year terms as County Auditor. He retired in 1978 with 31 years of service.

He has four children and seven grandchildren. His wife and he continue to live in Napa, California.

JACK M. BENTIVEGNA, born August 28, 1922, in York, Pennsylvania. Enlisted in the USMC on June 16, 1942. Trained at Oceanside, California, and St. Margarita Canyons. Assigned to 1st Corps Tank Battalion, M4 (Sherman) tank, Oceanside, California. Served on Guadalcanal,

Guam, and Iwo Jima with "C" Company, 3d Tank Battalion, 3d Marine Division. Was a Platoon Sergeant. Discharged on June 16, 1946.

Military awards include two Presidential

Unit Citations, American Campaign Medal, Asiatic-Pacific Campaign Medal, two Battle Stars, Good Conduct Medal, World War II Victory Medal, and Combat Ribbon.

After discharge, returned to York, Pennsylvania, and married my sweetheart, Anna (Judy) Vaughn, who waited for years for my return. We had four children: Leonard, who is a dentist; Helena, who manages dental offices; Sandra, who owns York's leading restaurant; and Jackie, who is a postal worker. I was in the restaurant and bar business for 30 years, then became an aide to Governor Milton Shapp of Pennsylvania. Retired in 1978 and have been living the good life of retirement for nearly 25 years. To pass time, I daydream of battles that were.

ANDREW A. BERNARD, Phm 2/C U.S. Navy Corpsman, born August 9, 1920, in Lawrence, Massachusetts. Enlisted in the USMC on February 26, 1942. Trained at Newport (Rhode Island) Training Station and then transferred into FMF, Camp Lejeune, American Samoa, New Zealand, and Guadalcanal.

Served in "M" Company, 3d Battalion, 3d

Regiment, 3d Marine Division, from May 1942 through September 1943. Transferred to Regimental Headquarters, September 16, 1943 through December 15, 1943. Made initial landing on Bougainville, November 1, 1943, second wave. Discharged from service in August 1945.

Military awards include the Silver Star Medal, Navy Unit Commendation, Combat Action Medal, Asiatic-Pacific Campaign Medal, American Campaign Medal, and World War II Victory Medal.

Married to Mary Hopkins, March 1944. Married for 57 years. One son, Richard. Operated my own dental lab for 20 years. Worked as a dental salesman for 17 years. Became a dental consultant, professional relations manager. Re-

tired in 1985. Enjoy fly fishing for trout and salmon, golf, and reading.

GEORGE H. BIXLER, born January 11, 1921, in Hanover, Pennsylvania. Joined the USMC on June 16, 1942. Served with C-1-21, 3d Marine Division, as Machine Gunner. Also served as acting Section Leader on Guam and senior NCO on Iwo Jima, in charge of machine gunners.

Training locations include Parris Island,

South Carolina; New River, North Carolina; Camp Elliot, California; Camp Pendleton, California; and New Zealand.

Participated in campaigns at Guadalcanal, Bougainville, Guam, Marianas Islands, and Iwo Jima. Wounded and contracted malaria in Guam hospital.

Military awards include the Purple Heart, Presidential Citation, Navy Citation, Asiatic-Pacific Campaign Medal, World War II Victory Medal, and citation from General Erskin. Discharged in September 1945 in the rank of Sergeant.

Returned to Hanover, Pennsylvania, to marry Gladys Edwards and have three children. Opened a plumbing and heating business in 1944 and retired in 1986 after turning the business over to my two sons. I have three grandchildren and two step-grandchildren. I enjoy fly fishing.

Memorable experience: I was on Iwo Jima when the flag was raised. Unfortunately, there are too many unhappy experiences during that period.

SGT. MAJOR THOMAS J. BLAGG, born in Oklahoma City, Oklahoma. Joined the USMC on September 26, 1963. Promoted to PFC in boot camp, Platoon 277, MCRD, San Diego, California, and selected to be the company guide, "H" Company, 2nd Battalion, Infantry Training Regiment, San Onofre, California.

First duty station was "A" Company, 3d AmTrac Battalion, FMF, 1st Marine Division (Rein), Camp Pendleton, California. Promoted to Lance Corporal and caught a rotation to Okinawa. Three weeks at Camp Schwab, Okinawa, then received orders to 3d Marine Division, Military Police Company, Camp Courtney, Okinawa. Upon arrival received orders to the Ryukian Armed Service Police (RASP), Camp Buckner, Okinawa. During my year at Camp Buckner, various units of the RASP (a combined service unit) were receiving orders to South Vietnam. At end of tour, requested and received a six-month extension to go to South Vietnam with first available unit.

Assigned to MP Company, HQ Battalion, 3d Marine Division. Landed with the 7th Marines at Chui Lai and participated in Operation Star-Lite. After Star-Lite, transferred to Danang, from where I participated in Harvest Moon and Blue Marline before extension ended.

Received orders to "A" Company, 2nd AmTrac Battalion ForTrps, FMFLant, Camp Lejeune, North Carolina, 2d Marine Division. While at Courthouse Bay, participated in Apollo and Gemini programs at Cape Kennedy, Florida. During this time, also did Caribbean cruise with H&S Company, CARIB 1-67, 2d Battalion, 2d Marine Division, Gru 1.

December 1977, joined Delta Battery, 2nd Battalion, 14th Marine Regiment, NAS Dallas, Texas. December 1990, 14th Marine Regiment activated for Desert Shield/Desert Storm. Served as Watch Chief in the Combat Operations Center.

Separated from 14th Regiment in 1991 and became a Marine Advisor to Navy Mobile Construction Battalion 22, NAS Dallas, Texas, followed by assignments as the 3d Brigade Senior Enlisted Advisor, 3d NCB, Port Hueneme, California, and as the 2nd Brigade Senior Enlisted Advisor, 2d Navy Construction Brigade, Norfolk, Virginia. Transferred to Alpha Company, 4th Reconnaissance Battalion, San Antonio, Texas. Promoted to Sergeant Major. Next duty station was the Senior Enlisted Marine Advisor to Admiral T.J. Gross, Deputy Commander, Contingency Engineering Group, Naval Facilities Engineering Command, Washington, DC. From March 1999 to present, Sergeant Major, 14th Marine Regiment, NASJRB, Fort Worth, Texas.

Military awards include the Combat Action Ribbon.

Married to high school sweetheart, Judith Lee (Patterson); two children: daughter, Caroline Elizabeth Blagg, and son, Thomas Andrew Blagg, as well as daughter-in-law, Lori Malone Blagg. Currently Vice President of Connect Specialized Transport, Inc., and Vice President of CST Logistics, Inc.

FRANCIS X. BLAND, born November 15, 1924, in Lima, Ohio. Enlisted in the USMC on December 14, 1942, in New York City.

Served with the 2nd Defense Battalion, Samoa, 1943; 14th Defense Battalion, New

Caledonia, Guadalcanal, and Guam, 1943-1945; V-12 detachment, Yale University, 1945.

Military awards include the Pacific Service Medal and World War II Victory Medal. Discharged on November 16, 1945, in the rank of Private First Class.

Memorable experiences include four months on various troop transports in th South and Central Pacific; working and training in the swamps of Guadalcanal; combat landing and operations at Guam.

Married Marguerite Grinnan, a World War II WAVE, in 1947. Had 10 children from 1948-1960. Now also have 10 grandchildren and two great-grandchildren.

Graduated from Yale University, 1949, B.S. in Geology; graduate assistant instructor, University of Kansas, 1949-1950. Geologist with Chevron USA in Gulf Coast, 1941 through 1985. Retired as Division Exploration manager, 1985. Moved to Durango, Colorado, in 1987 and have worked as a volunteer for the Colorado Division of Wildlife for the last 10 years.

DAN PETER BOZIKIS, born May 7, 1922, in Crystal City, Missouri. Joined the USMC on August 31, 1942, in Cleveland, Ohio. Trained in San Diego, California, Platoon 474, Pendleton, Defense of New Zealand and Guadalcanal.

Participated in Bougainville and Guam campaigns under Capt. Fowler and Lt. Howell Heflin

(former Senator), 3d Platoon of A-1-9, 3d Marine Division. Slightly wounded on Hand Grenade Hill, Thanksgiving Day, November 25, 1943. Received the Purple Heart on August 5, 1944, for the Battle of Finegayan, where heavy opposition and bloody fighting ensued. Injured during Guam push, October 25, 1944. Sent to Hawaii. Surgery on knee, December 2. Sent to Great Lakes Naval Hospital in Illinois and received medical discharge as a Corporal, September 20, 1945.

Married Ethel "Butch" Ahamnos, June 23, 1946, in Chicago. Three children: Demetra, Peter, Tina. Three grandchildren: Austin, Brysen, Brittany Coccia. Moved to California, 1957. Happily married almost 50 years. Lost Butch to breast cancer in 1996.

Worked 38 years as bread salesman and supervisor in Teamsters. Involved as president and board member with St. Anthony's Greek Orthodox Church. Enjoying retirement with grandchildren, family, friends from church, and my best buddies from "A" Company at reunions.

P.E. BRANDON, born June 29, 1935, in South Dakota, and moved to Oregon in 1942.

Joined the Marines, January 1953, going through Boot Camp at San Diego, joining "B" Company, 1st Battalion, 3d Marines, 3d Marine Division, at Camp Pendleton. His first platoon leader was Lt. Cheatham, who was awarded the Navy Cross in Vietnam and retired a three star General.

Brandon was in several commands before joining the 3d Marine Division again in 1967 as

Company Gunnery Sergeant of "F" Company, 2d Battalion, 4th Marines. He served in the 1st and 2d Marine Divisions. Spent almost three years as a DI, Parris Island. Brandon was an all-Marine football player for the Marine Corps and Navy, and rode bulls at the Camp Pendleton rodeo. Brandon was wounded six times in Vietnam, awarded four Purple Hearts. He spent several months in the hospital to recover from 43 holes and was retired after 20 years.

Since retiring, Brandon owned several business. Gunny's Gym was picked "gym of the year" in 1986. He is the author of the book *Gunny* and presently owns a Northwest asphalt company. Married to the former Shirlie Bird since March 9, 1956. Three children: Jan, Russell, and Rita; five grandchildren: Derrick, Tanner, Kayle, Crissanda, and Tine. Brandon lives in McMinnville, Oregon.

CLARENCE E. BROOKES, born November 14, 1917, in Cortland, New York. Enlisted in USMC, June 5, 1941, Syracuse, New York. Boot at Parris Island; Norfolk Naval Air Station to October 1942. Volunteer, 4th Raider Battalion. Trained at Camp Pendleton, California.

Overseas, February 9, 1943, to New Hebrides, train rubber boat landing, Espirita Sahto. Did

patrol for Jap coast watches on many islands in the area. Then to Guadalcanal. First combat, June 30, 1943. Carried the Boys 55 Cal anti-tank rifle. Injured on cargo net, pinned between *USS McKeon APO* and *Higgins* boat, both knees hurt. Back to the Canal, then to New Georgia. Took part in Bairoko Harbor attack. Returned to Canal, then New Caledonia and New Zealand.

Returned to New Cal and Guadalcanal. Transferred to "A" Company, 1st Battalion, 9th

Marines, 3d Marine Division. With 3d just 10 days. Sent to Navy hospital. Had knee surgery, February 3, 1944. Returned to 3d Marine Division, A-1-9, about the time the 3d Division returned to Canal from Bougainville.

Went to Guam and trained for Iwo Jima. While on liberty on a fishing trip in Guam, December 2, 1944, three of us killed four Japs and captured one. Wounded on Iwo Jima, March 6, 1945. Evacuated to Guam. Right knee problem made worse at Iwo. Put knee in cast and sent to hospital in Hawaii, then by hospital ship *Rickie* to the States. After furlough, stationed Brooklyn Naval yard until discharge on September 12, 1945.

Retired from New York Environmental Conservation Department on April 2, 1975. Raised and sold Christmas trees after retirement. Both knees were replaced in 1992 and doing fine.

FRANK D. BROWN, born April 8, 1923, in Cheyenne, Wyoming. Joined the USMC on July 11, 1942. Training locations: San Diego Marine Corps Base, Camp Elliott, Camp Pendleton. Attended Radio School at San Diego Marine Corps Base. Joined the 3d Tank Battalion, 3d Marine Division, and served in Companies "D," "B," and "A." Trained in New Zealand and Guadalcanal.

Participated in the invasions of Bougainville (wounded on November 19, 1943, sent to hos-

pitals on Choisel, Guadalcanal, and New Caledonia), Guam, and Iwo Jima. Selected for the V-12 program and sent to Colorado College, Colorado Springs, Colorado. Was discharged on July 28, 1946, at Great Lakes NTS in the rank of Sergeant.

Military awards include the Purple Heart, Good Conduct Medal, Asiatic-Pacific Medal with three Battle Stars, American Theater Medal, and World War II Victory Medal.

Graduated from Colorado A&M College in June 1949 with a B.S. in Light Construction and Marketing. Married Marilyn Lamb of Hamilton, Ohio. We have three children, sons Tandy and Richard and daughter Christy Lyn. Retired from the Illinois Department of Transportation as Civil Engineer in 1986. Now active in volunteer work for seniors, play French horn in the American Legion band, and active in church affairs.

EUGENE A. BUTTS, born April 4, 1926, in Cateechee, South Carolina. Joined the marines on July 4, 1942. Boot Camp at Parris Island, South Carolina. Served at Portsmouth, New Hampshire; San Diego, California; Samoa. Joined the 3d on Guadalcanal. Participated in

campaigns at Bougainville, Guam, and Iwo Jima; Korea, 1951-1952; San Francisco and Camp Lejeune. Retired in 1964 as Gy. Sergeant.

Military awards include the Presidential Unit Citation, American Campaign Medal, Asiatic-

Pacific Campaign Medal, and World War II Victory Medal.

Married to the late Ardella Wheeler; second wife is Shirley Hamilton. Own a rental business in Jacksonville, North Carolina. Still in touch with the Marines at Camp Lejeune and with retired Marines in the area. Sometimes meet at 3d Marine Division reunions. Play music in a community band and an 18-piece dance band for a hobby.

JAMES R. CANNON, born October 2, 1936, in King George, Virginia. Enlisted as tank driver, 176th RCT, VANG., 1953. Graduated from Stafford High School, 1954.

Enlisted in the Marine Corps on August 6, 1954. Received Boot Camp, Parris Island, South

Carolina, and ITR at Camp Pendleton, California. Served with B-1-9 at Shinodyama, Japan, and Camp Napunja, Okinawa, 1954-1956. A-1-3, Danang area, Vietnam, Staff Sergeant, 1965. Returned to Quantico, Virginia, for 7th WOSC. Was commissioned Marine Gunner (O3), 1966. Attended Basic school, appointed temporary 2nd Lieutenant, 1966, and returned to Vietnam, serving with Echo 2/3.

Received Gold Medal at 8th & I Parade, 1963, from CMC General David Sharp for "Best Squad Leader in the Corps." Also awarded Silver Star for extraordinary heroism and conspicuous gallantry during the "Hill Fights" near Khe Sanh, May 1967; Bronze Star with combat "V" at "AP Vinh An," South Vietnam, July 1967; and two Purple Hearts, May 3 and 4, 1967, Khe Sanh, Vietnam.

Became 1st Commanding Officer of the Marine Communication Detachment aboard the *USS ATT Whitney* (LCC-20), 1970. Retired as Major while serving as Assistant Director for Reserves 6th District in downtown Atlanta, Georgia, December 1977. Today, helps vets and travels.

2ND LIEUTENANT DANIEL F. CASEY, born July 20, 1922, in Gleasonton, Pennsylvania. Joined the USMC on January 13, 1940. Training locations include Parris Island, South Carolina; Portsmouth, Virginia; and Quantico, Virginia. Became an officer on January 12, 1944.

Served aboard the *USS Wichita, USS Wasp, USS Quincy, USS Tuscaloosa, USS Idaho, USS Washington*, and *USS Massachusetts*. Partici-

pated in the naval engagement at Casablanca, Morocco, and naval actions in the Aleutian Islands. Served at Iceland and on convoy duties in the North Atlantic. He served with the 34th Replacement Draft and joined the 9th Regiment on March 2. He was killed in action on March 6, serving with A-1-9.

Military awards include the Navy Cross, Purple Heart, American Defense Service Medal with Fleet Clasp, European-African-Middle Eastern Campaign Medal, Asiatic-Pacific Campaign Medal, and World War II Victory Medal.

GEORGE A. CAVANO, enlisted in the USMC on April 12, 1942, in Grand Rapids, Michigan. Boot camp at San Diego Recruit Depot. Joined Reg. Weapons Company, June 1942, Camp Elliot. Moved to Camp Pendleton, June 20, 1942.

Sailed on January 24, 1943, to Auckland, New Zealand, *Mt. Vernon*. Sailed on June 29, 1943, to Guadalcanal with HQ CO, 3d Battal-

ion, 9th. Bougainville, December 27, 1943. Guam, June 17, 1944. Evacuated around September 24, 1944. Alea Hospital, Hawaii. Navy gun factory, Washington, DC; Naval Observatory, Washington, DC; Headquarters Marine Corps, Washington, DC; Camp Robert Small, Great Lakes Separation Center. Discharged on April 11, 1945, Great Lakes.

Spent two years in active reserves at Anacosta Naval Air Station and HQ Marine Corps in Arlington.

Moved to southwest Florida, and met and married Betty Marshall from Philadelphia, Pennsylvania, on October 22, 1948. Retired from Florida Power and Light Company on February 28, 1974, after 30 years of service. Now living in Punta Gorda, Florida. One son, George, and one daughter, Kerry Oliver; two grandchildren.

FRANK R. CHABOUDY, born January 5, 1924, in Akron, Ohio. Moved to Chula Vista, California, in 1939. Enlisted in the USMC on June 17, 1941, at Marine base, San Diego, California. Completed Telephone Lineman school, assigned to C-1-10, Camp Elliot. Transferred to H&S-1-12 when 3d Marine Division formed. Transferred to Camp Pendleton prior to overseas duty in New Zealand. Unit transferred to Guadalcanal in 1943. Battles included Northern Solomon Islands, Bougainville, Guam, and Iwo Jima.

Military awards include the Navy Unit Commendation with Star, Good Conduct Medal, American Defense Medal, American Campaign

Medal, Asiatic-Pacific Campaign Medal with four Stars, and World War II Victory Medal. Discharged on September 17, 1945, Marine base, San Diego.

Returned to Chula Vista. Completed high school at Sweetwater Adult School, 1946. Graduated from San Diego State College, 1950; Master's degree, 1956. Retired from San Diego City Schools after 34 years as an elementary teacher and principal. Married Bente Christensen, 1948; daughters Anna and Susan, both school teachers. After retirement became certified USPTA tennis professional and has served as the tennis professional for the City of Chula Vista for the past 16 years.

LUCIEN CHUISANO, born May 14, 1911, in Freeport, New York. Enlisted in the USMC on September 22, 1942, in New York. Served with 2H, 21st Marines, 3d Marine Division. Mortar Platoon, jeep driver, and company clerk. Stationed at Parris Island, South Carolina; Camp Elliot, California; and New Zealand.

Participated in action against the enemy on Bougainville, Solomon Islands, November 11, 1943 to December 28, 1943; Guam, Marianas

Islands, July 21, 1944 to December 6, 1944. Late replacements; received last-minute orders to Iwo Jima (trying hard to have it printed on my discharge certificate). For two months, we were a defense outfit, protecting New Zealand against the Japanese forces. On October 1, 1944 received the following citation from Colonel A. H. Butler: "Chuisano, Louis F. 21st Marines while in combat against Japanese forces at Guam was responsible for the submission of information of material intelligence value. The information submitted afforded the Regimental Commander a more complete and comprehensive estimate of the enemy situation and enabled the regiment to carry out its assigned mission successfully and with the least cost of life." Received the Purple Heart; discharge paper states: July 30, 1946, wounded on Guam, July 26, 1944, A.E. O'Neil, Colonel, U.S. Marine Corps. Returned to the States and was stationed at Parris Island with the Rifle Range Detachment, Marine Barracks under Lt. Colonel J.E. Dentsh, until my discharge on October 20, 1945.

When I had time, I would do drawings and illustrations for the officers and enlisted men, at their request, to send home in their victory mail.

I have had several one-man art shows in New York and in Greensboro, North Carolina. I'm retired now, and playing golf and doing artwork.

PETER A. CIPRIANO, born April 18, 1921, in Brooklyn, New York. Upon graduation from the U.S. Naval Academy, Class of 1944, with graduation date of June 9, 1943, I was commissioned a 2nd Lieutenant. Training locations included Flight Observer, Jacksonville, Florida; Marine Barracks, Quantico, Virginia; and The Infinity School, Fort Benning, Georgia. Served with HQ CO, 3d Marine Division, and HQ CO, First Battalion, 21st Marines, 3d Marine Division. Resigned in January 1947 in the rank of 1st Lieutenant.

Memorable experiences: Upon landing on the beach of Aguna, Guam, I made reconnaissance in a cave in the vicinity of our landing area and secured two American flags. These flags were the first American flags to be recaptured from the Japanese during World War II. One is in the library at the U.S. Marine Corps University at Quantico; the other is in my possession to be used at my funeral. While on Iwo Jima, myself and two "volunteered" men from my battalion moved to the line company to swap their bad radio for one of our good ones. En route, I spotted a Japanese soldier illuminated by flares and fired twice in his direction. The next morning, we revisited the area of the incident and spotted a Japanese soldier who must have killed himself by holding a grenade to his chest. I examined him and picked from him a Japanese flag, which I am holding in my possession.

Currently, I am President and CEO of an engineering and construction firm. I am also President of a real estate development and man-

agement company.

LUTHER LLOYD CLAIBORNE, Sgt. (EP), born September 26, 1922, in Roseville, California. Attended Roseville High and Placer Junior College. Employed as fingerprint classifier at FBI headquarters in Washington, DC, in 1942. Influenced by the bombing of Dutch Harbor, enlisted in the Marine Corps on August 12, 1942. Training at San Diego, California, Boot Camp, Platoon 647; Camp Matthews Rifle Range; Camp Elliott for organization of the 3d Marine Division, HQ CO, D-2 Combat Intelligence Section. Served in Bougainville, November 1 to December 21, 1943; Guam, July 21, 1944 to February 14, 1945; Iwo Jima, February 24 to March 29, 1945.

Discharged October 6, 1945, in San Francisco. Returned to work for the FBI in DC and married Janice Jenkins on December 16, 1945.

Returned to Roseville, California, in 1946, to enter construction field as apprentice carpenter; employed in all areas of construction and cabinetmaking. Retired as building trades supervisor form the State of California in 1985. Busy with church activities and visiting family: daughter, Dr. Brenda Claiborne, and her husband, Dr. Paul Farnsworth, San Antonio, Texas; daughter, Edith, and husband, Rance Savage, and their five children in Shepherd, Montana; son, Howard, and his wife, Marie (Washburn), with one daughter in Denver and one son, U.S. Marine LCPL Howard (Dallas) Claiborne, stationed at MCAS, Miramar, California.

WILLIAM DUFFIE CLEMONS, born April 30, 1920, in Oklahoma City, Oklahoma. Served with the 45th Infantry Division, Oklahoma National Guard, 1937-1940; U.S. Marine Corps, 1940-1971. FMF units include: 1st Defense Battalion, Pearl Harbor; 16th Defense Battalion, Johnston Island; 1st Provisional Marine Brigade, Pusan Perimeter, Korea; 1st Marine Division, Signal Battalion, Korea, and HQ Battalion, Vietnam; 3d Marine Division, 4th Marines Japan, and 3d FSR, Okinawa; 2nd Marine Air Wing, MACS-6, Cherry Point; 3d Marine Air Wing, MACS-1, Yuma, Arizona.

Military awards include the Bronze Star with "V," Combat Action Ribbon with two Stars, Good Conduct Medal with four Stars, Presidential Unit Citation with two Stars, American Defense Medal with one Star, Asiatic-Pacific Service Medal with one Star, Pearl Harbor Commemorative Medal, American Service Medal, World War II Victory Medal, National Defense

Medal with one Star, Korean Service Medal with four Stars, Vietnam Service Medal with three Stars, United Nations Medal, China War Memorial Medal, Korean Presidential Unit Citation, Republic of Korea War Service Medal, two Vietnam Presidential Unit Citations, and the Vietnam Cross. Retired CWO-4.

Married Virginia (Jenny) Morris in 1943. Three children, four grandchildren: son Wendell, Major, USMC (Ret.); grandson Nathan, four

years, 11th Marines; son Richard, architect; daughter Cynthea, married former Cpl. Major, Grenadier Guards, Independent Parachute Brigade, and Special air Service, United Kingdom. Duffie graduated from San Diego State University, 1978, B.S. in Botany.

MANUEL CEPEDA CONCEPCION, JR., born November 22, 1941, in Agana, Guam. Joined the USMC in June 1960. Training locations include MCRD, San Diego, California; Camp Lejeune, North Carolina; Guantanamo Bay, Cuba; Hq. Company H&S BN, MCB, CamPen (audiovisual); Okinawa; Marine Barracks, Vallejo, California.

Served with "E" Company 2/5, 1st Marine Division, Vietnam; H&S Company 2/8, 2nd Marine Division, Camp Lejeune, North Caro-

lina; H&S Company, 81mm PLT, 3/3, 3d Marine Division, Okinawa.

Memorable experiences include Drill Instructor School, San Diego, California; NCOIC Special Services, Camp Smith, Hawaii; Embarkation NCO aboard *USS Guam*. Retired, June 1980, in the rank of Gunnery Sergeant.

Military Awards include the Bronze Star Medal with Combat "V," two Purple Hearts, Combat Action Ribbon, Vietnam Cross of Gallantry with Palm Medal, Republic of Vietnam Meritorious Unit Commendation Civil Action Colors, National Defense Service Medal, Vietnam Service Medal with six Stars, Presidential Unit Citation, Rifle Expert Badge (fifth award), Pistol Sharpshooter Badge, Good Conduct Medal with five Stars, and Vietnam Campaign Medal.

Married to Orilda Damian, RN, BSN, employed at the San Francisco Veterans Administration Medical Center for 29 years; four children, six stepchildren, 13 grandchildren, and one great-granddaughter. Currently employed at Hertz Rental in San Francisco, California, as a small tool mechanic. Life member, 3d Marine Division, Disabled American Veterans; member of the Golden Gate Chapter, 3d Marine Division, American Legion, and Fleet Reserve Association. Looking forward to second retirement so my wife and I can travel, spend more time with our families, and garden.

PAUL S. COUNSELMAN, born June 13, 1925, at Franklin, Pennsylvania. Enlisted in the USNR, February 15, 1943. Completed Corpsman school at Great Lakes, Illinois, July 2, 1943. Transferred to USN hospital at San Diego, California. August 14, 1943, USN hospital, Santa Margarita Ranch, Oceanside, California. November 11, 1943, transferred to Fleet (???) Force, Camp Elliot, San Diego, California (field medical school). February 24, 1944, 2nd Battalion, 21st Marines, 3d Marine Division, FMF.

June 3, 1944, embarked and sailed aboard *USS Elmore* from Guadalcanal, British Solomon Islands. July 21, 1944, disembarked and partici-

pated in landing on enemy-held beach at Guam, Marianas Islands. Actively engaged in patrolling against enemy Japanese on Guam, August 11, 1944, through November 3, 1944. February 11, 1945, embarked aboard *USS President Jackson* at Guam. February 21, 1945, disembarked and participated in action against the enemy at Iwo Jima. Was wounded on February 27, 1945, and again on March 8, 1945. May 15, 1945, transferred to 2nd Battalion, 12th Marines, 3d Marine Division, FMF-ITF. September 25, 1945, transferred back to port of entry U.S.A., USN/R5, Shoemaker, California. January 15, 1946, duty at Atlantic City, New Jersey, U.S. Naval Air Service. February 21, 1946, discharged at Bainbridge, Maryland, as Hospital Apprentice First Class, USNR.

Military awards include the Purple Heart Medal with Gold Star, Bronze Star Medal, World War II Victory Medal, Asiatic-Pacific Campaign Medal, American Campaign Medal, and Good Conduct Medal.

Returned to Franklin, Pennsylvania, and married high school sweetheart, Helen, July 5, 1952. We had three daughters. Helen died on December 6, 1990. I have two daughters remaining, four grandchildren, and four great-grandchildren. Retired from Franklin Steel afer 36

years and am still working on my golf game without much success.

DANIEL J. COVIELLO, born March 24, 1949, in Greenwich, Connecticut. Joined USMC on December 27, 1967. Training at Parris Island, South Carolina; Camp Lejeune, North Carolina; and Camp Pendleton, California.

Arrived in Vietnam on June 6, 1968. Assigned to Battery E, 2nd Battalion, 12th Marines. Reassigned to MP Company at Dong Ha,

then again to 1st Searchlight Battery. Rotated home on June 26, 1969. Discharge in July in the rank of Lance Corporal.

Returned to Harrison, New York. Became a police officer with the Harrison (NY) Police Department, 1971. Retired and remarried, 1993. Moved to Matthews, North Carolina. Own and operate a die-cast toy car business called "Pocketcruisers."

JEFFREY A. DEMENT, born June 28, 1946, in Joliet, Illinois. Joined USMC on January 25, 1966. Trained at Camp Pendleton, California. My wife, Carolyn, and I were married on May 28, 1966. We have two children, Michelle and Jeffrey, Jr.

Served in Vietnam, July 1966 to August 1967, with the 2-26 and 1-3. Participated in more than 15 operations, including: Colgate, Bear

Claw, Hickory, and Buffalo. Wounded in action during Operations Colgate and Buffalo. Discharged on January 30, 1968, in the rank of Corporal.

Military awards include the Purple Heart Medal with one Star, National Defense Service Medal, Vietnamese Service Medal with one Star, Vietnamese Campaign Medal, Presidential Unit Citation, and U.S. M-14 Rifle Sharpshooter Medal.

Thirty-three year member of IBEW Local 701 in DuPage County. Served as a Trustee for the Village of Plainfield from 1983-1999. Member of Plainfield United Methodist Church, American Legion Post 13, VFW, DAV, Plainfield Chamber of Commerce, and

Plainfield Historical Society. I enjoy volleyball, tennis, and golf. Looking forward to spending more time traveling.

MARTIN V. D'GIFF, born May 25, 1949, in Brooklyn, New York. July 12, 1967, Bravo Company, 1st Battalion, 4th Regiment, 3d Marine Division. December 1967 to January 1969, Parris Island, South Carolina; Camp Lejeune, North Carolina; Camp Stone Bay, North Carolina; Camp Pendleton, California; Lake Meade, Nevada; Portsmouth, New Hampshire, Naval Disciplinary Command. My whole tour of duty is very memorable.

Military awards include the Combat Action Ribbon, National Defense Medal, Vietnamese Cross of Gallantry, Vietnamese Cross of Gal-

lantry Civil Action, Vietnamese Service Medal with Silver Star, and Vietnamese Campaign Medal.

I retired from the Norwood Police Department, Norwood, Massachusetts, in 1982. Went to work for the United States Postal Service in 1983 and am still presently employed.

GEORGE W. DIGUARDI, Master Sgt.1952-1972. 1952, Parris Island Boot Camp, Crane Ammo Depot Ind., M.P. 1953, Korea, D-2-1, Boulder City, machine gunner. 1954, Norfolk Navy Base, M.P. Camp Lejeunne, 2nd Mar. machine gunner. 1955-56, Paris Island, D.I. 1956-1958, Camp Lejeunne, H&S-2-2, 81 Plt. 1958-1961, Quantico, Va. marksmanship instructor. 1961, H&S-1-5, 81 Plt. 1961-1962, Okinawa, H&S-3-9, 81 Plt. 1962-1964, Camp Pendleton, H&S-2-1, 81 Plt. 1964-1966, Camp Lejeune, H&S-1-6, 81 Plt. Dominican Republic, 1966-1967, Viet Nam, H&S-3-9, 81 Plt. 1967-1969, Wilmington, Deleware, I&I Staff, Staff gunny. 1969-1970, Okinawa, HQTS. Co. HQTS. Battalion, 3d Marine Div. Company Gunny. 4th Marines Rifle & Pistol Team. 1970-1972, Quantico, MCDEC Rifle & Pistol Team, NCOIC. Marine Corps Rifle & Pistol Team, Camp Perry. Retired.

During a tour on Okinawa in 1961-1962, I was the ammo Sgt. of the 81 Plt., H&S-3-9. Four years later, having arrived in Vietnam, I was as-

signed to the same 81 Plt. as Plt. Sgt. During a thirty day stint on outpost Con Thien and having kept the entire area lit every night with illumination, 3-9 and supporting units were able to repel several NVA attacks. To the members of that outstanding 81 Motar Plt., Simper Fi.

THOMAS C. DOLSON, born January 2, 1934, in Chicago, Illinois. Graduated from the University of Idaho and commissioned 2nd Lieutenant, USMC, in February 1956.

Served in 3d Marine Division as Lieutenant (ATA Platoon Commander), 1958; Captain (CO of F/2/9), 1963-1964; Major (S-3 of 3/3 then S-

3 3d Marines), 1968-1969; Lt. Colonel (CO of 2/4), 1976-1977.

Combat awards include the Legion of Merit with "V," Navy Commendation Medal with "V," Vietnamese Cross of Gallantry with Gold and Silver Stars. Retired in November 1978.

Married Judith Jordan, July 14, 1962. Have two sons, Thomas, Jr., and Michael, and two grandsons, Elias and Avi.

From November 1978 until July 1999, held positions as Chief Operating Officer or Chief Executive Officer with five different industrial-manufacturing firms located in Texas, New Jersey, New York, Michigan, and Alabama, respectively. Last position held was President of firm with eight facilities on three continents.

Retired in Florida; playing tennis, traveling, and visiting with Marine pals from the past.

JOSEPH DuCANTO, began his long fruitful life in 1927 as an orphaned child in mid-central New York State. Leaving the orphanage at four years of age as a county welfare case, he spent his young school years in several foster homes within Oneida, New York.

Early in 1944, at age 16, he enlisted in the U.S. Marine Corps during World War II. Recruits were supposed to be at least 17 years old

and five feet, four inches tall. DuCanto was one year too young and one inch too short, but no one questioned him when he said he was 17. After Basic training at Parris Island, South Caro-

lina, he was shipped overseas and assigned to the 21st Regiment, 3d Marine Division. He served as a member of the Pioneer-Engineers during the Guam and Iwo Jima campaigns. His platoon was led by former Notre Dame quarterback and Heisman Trophy winner Angelo Bertelli.

DuCanto spent 36 days on Iwo Jima. His job was to work on the beach, taking in equipment and bringing out casualties. The intense shelling caused him to suffer a 40-60 percent hearing loss. He celebrated his eighteenth birthday while on Iwo Jima. In a 1995 magazine article, he described the landing at Iwo Jima.

"When we hit the beach, there was so much wreckage, it was hard to get in. They'd had 2,000 casualties the first day, more than at Omaha Beach in Normandy. There were bombs and sniper fire everywhere. There was no cover, because every place was visible [from Suribachi]."

Following World War II, he served with the 1st Marine Division, assigned as an Engineer with the 1st Battalion, 7th Marines, in North China.

DuCanto was discharged from the USMC in September 1946. He enrolled at Syracuse University, then transferred to Antioch College because of its excellent work/study program. He graduated from Antioch in 1952 and was awarded a full scholarship to the University of Chicago. Following his graduation in 1955, he began his law practice in Chicago, which continues to this day, beginning his practice in the field of labor law. Today, he is a member of the nationally renowned matrimonial law firm of Schiller, DuCanto and Fleck. He has served as President of the American Academy of Matrimonial Lawyers. In 1982, he founded Securatex. The private detective and security firm serves five Midwestern states and employs more than 600 people.

DuCanto has long been a supporter of educational, charitable, and civic causes. He has produced an outstanding body of legal educational materials and has lectured throughout the country to numerous law schools and legal continuing education groups. He has also served as an Adjunct Professor at Loyola University School of Law in Chicago. He has been a consistent and generous supporter of the institutions with which he has been connected and an unfailing supporter of Marine causes for more than half a century. He was a 2000 Semper Fidelis Honoree.

DuCanto and his wife Patricia live in River Forest, Illinois. They have three sons: Anthony, a former Marine; James, a medical doctor; and Lance Corporal William, currently serving with First Force Recon, 1st Marine Division.

ROBERT L. DUNIGAN, born May 25, 1938, in Brooklyn, New York. Joined the USMC in January 1957. Training locations include Parris Island, South Carolina; Platoon 26; Camp Lejeune, North Carolina, and Camp Pendleton, California, staging area. Assigned to FMF.

Served as Radio/Telegraph Operator, Field

Artillery Fire Control C/4/12, 3d Marine Division, Okinawa, 1957-1958, Camp Hague. Also participated in two separate joint maneuvers on Luzon,

Philippines, Fall 1957 and Spring 1958, as well as ready reserve force, South China Sea, during French evacuation of Indo-China, December 1957.

Discharged from active duty at Marine Barracks, Brooklyn Navy Yard, January 1959. Final discharge, January 1963, USMCR, in the rank of Corporal.

Joined the New York Police Department, October 1962. Retired due to line-of-duty injury from Motorcycle Division, October 1976. Second career as insurance investigator. Currently retired. Three children, Taryn, Katie, James, and a fourth, Robert Michael Dunigan, with wife and great love of my life, Diane, given to me by God at age 58. Currently residing in Tinton Falls, New Jersey. Life member of Marine Corps League and Devil Dog Society.

GUSTAVO A. ESQUIVEL, born September 17, 1949, in Fabens, Texas. Training at San Diego, California, and Camp Pendleton, California. Served in Vietnam from July 1968 to October 1969 with "A" Company, 1st Battalion, 3d Marines, and "F" Company, 2nd Battalion, 9th Marines. Was a grunt. Wounded on November 14, 1968, on Hill 461, Mutter's Ridge, in the DMZ, Quang Tri Province, while serving with A/1/3. Participated in numerous operations in Vietnam and also participated in Operation Dewey Canyon in the Ashu Valley in Laos.

Military awards include the Purple Heart, Good Conduct Medal, Combat Action Ribbon, National Defense Service Medal, Navy Unit Commendation Ribbon, Vietnam Service Medal with four Bronze Stars, Marine Corps Marks-

man Rifle Badge, Republic of Vietnam Campaign Medal, and Republic of Vietnam MVC Gallantry Cross.

Married Ramona Portillo, September 1970. We have three daughters, Veronica, Rachel, and Rose, and one son, Gus, Jr. Also have one granddaughter, Amorette Little Feather Esquivel, and one grandson, Stephen.

I am a disabled veteran, rated at 100 percent permanent. Living in Anthony, Texas, about 20 miles northwest of El Paso, near the border of Texas and New Mexico.

ALFONZO "BUFF" FANELLA, born March 1, 1922, in Donahoe, Pennsylvania. Joined the USMC on August 30, 1943. Upon completion of Boot camp at Parris Island, South Carolina, I became a drill instructor for one year, from November 1943 to November 1944. Transferred to Camp Lejeune, North Carolina, for combat training.

In early 1945, shipped out to Guam, Marianas Islands. Joined the 3d Marine Division. Participated in Iwo Jima campaign as a Rifleman with E/2/21. Discharged on April 26, 1946, in the rank of Corporal.

Military awards include the Asiatic-Pacific Campaign Medal, Good Conduct Medal, American Campaign Medal, and World War II Victory Medal.

Upon returning home, completed my college education. Taught school and coached football and basketball. Later was appointed Postmaster of Indiana Post Office 15701. Have been retired for 14 years. Am now deeply involved in keeping in physical shape, playing golf, and very active in politics.

JOHN FEDYSZYN, born June 14, 1949, in Dunkirk, New York. Joined the USMC in May 1967 at Parris Island, South Carolina. Was part of Platoon 1001. From Boot camp, spent time at Camp Lejeune, North Carolina, then off to Camp Pendleton, California, for Telephone Communications school. After staging battalion, was sent to Okinawa to be retrained as a Field Radio Operator.

Arrived at Da Nang, South Vietnam, on December 17, 1967. Was assigned to Charlie Battery, 1st Battalion, 12th Marine Regiment, 3d Marine Division, stationed at Camp JJ Carroll near the DMZ. Upon arrival, I was assigned as

a Field Radio Operator on a forward observer team whose duties were to call in artillery to

support various grunt units walking patrols along the DMZ. As different patrols came up, we would be assigned to those outfits as needed. Spent time walking patrols with various units including the 3d, 4th, 9th, and 26th Regiments. Did patrols along the DMZ, Rockpile, Khe Sahn, Hill 881, South Con Thien, Giolinh, A3, A3a, and Con Thien.

Participated in Operations Lancaster, Dye Marker, Lancaster II, Rice, Pegasus, Scotland II, Dual Blade, Robin South, and Kentucky. Wounded May 1968, Operation Rice, near Quang Tri.

Military awards include the Meritorious Unit Commendation with Ribbon Bar, National Defense Medal, Vietnam Service Medal with four Bronze Stars, Republic of Vietnam Meritorious Unit Citation (Gallantry Cross Color), Republic of Vietnam Campaign Medal, and Purple Heart. Discharged at Treasure Island, California, January 1969, in the rank of Corporal.

Returned to Dunkirk, New York, and married Darlene Wolfe. Have four children and two grandchildren, JJ and Jordyn Elizabeth. Employed as an electrician and retired in April 2000. Enjoying retirement at the Villages of Lady Lake, Florida.

HOWARD JOHN FIX, born May 7, 1924, in Kearney, Pennsylvania. I enlisted in the Marine Corps on April 21, 1943, at Pittsburgh, Pennsylvania. I left for Boot camp at Parris Island, South Carolina, on May 7, 1943. After Boot camp and leave, I was sent to Lakehurst Naval Air Station, New Jersey, in July 1943 for duty in a guard company.

In October 1944, I left Lakehurst and went to New River, South Carolina, for several weeks of combat training, then on to Camp Pendleton, California, for several more weeks of training. Following training, we left the States for Guam.

I was assigned to "A" Company, 9th Marines, 3d Marine Division.

After a short period of training on Guam, I took part in the battle of Iwo Jima. After being wounded, I was sent back to Guam, and after being hospitalized was assigned to the Fifth Field Depot until the war ended and I came home. I was discharged on February 26, 1946, at Great Lakes, Illinois, in the rank of Corporal.

Military awards include the Purple Heart, Good Conduct Medal, American Campaign Medal, Asiatic-Pacific Campaign Medal, Bronze Star, and Presidential Unit Commendation Ribbon.

After returning home, I married my high school sweetheart and worked at a Chevrolet garage for 10-12 years, then went to work at an auto parts store for several years. I then went to work for a paving contractor, and set-up and ran blacktop plants for the next 20 years. When they sold out, I went with another contractor and worked for 15 years before retiring.

EUGENE "BILL" FLECK, born in Detroit, Michigan, and attended St. Alphonsus elementary and high schools in Dearborn, Michigan. After graduation, worked for Ford until 1942, when he enlisted in the USMC. Boot camp at San Diego, California, then to Camp Elliot, California, where the 3d Marine Division was forming. Assigned to "C" Company, 9th Regiment.

In February 1943, left for New Zealand, where Bill trained as a coast watcher and scout. After five months of intensive training, made a brief stop on Guadalcanal before participating in the invasion of Bougainville. During the fight-

ing for Hand Grenade Hill, Bill was wounded. He spent five months in hospitals on Bougainville, Guadalcanal, New Caledonia, and in Oakland and San Diego Naval Hospitals. After release, stationed at the Marine Corps base, San Diego, then Camp Pendleton, then Hawaii. He was slated to go back with the 3d for the invasion of Japan, but the war ended. Discharged in November 1945 in the rank of Corporal.

Worked for Ford for a while, before becoming an apprentice metal model maker. He continued as a model maker until retirement in 1962. Bill married his wife Molly, now deceased, on May 28, 1949. He has two children, Dennis and Debbie, and four grandchildren.

CARL S. FOGELGREN, born February 9, 1949, in Miami, Florida. Joined the USMC on April 7, 1967. Training locations were Parris Island, South Carolina; Camp Geiger and Camp Lejeune, North Carolina. Ordered to Vietnam, January 1968. Stationed at Dong Ha, Vietnam, with "C" Company of the 11th Engineer Battalion. Returned to the U.S. in February 1969. Stationed at Vieques Island, Puerto Rico, Camp Garcia, August 1969 to February 1970.

Military awards include the Purple Heart, Meritorious Unit Citation, Presidential Unit Citation (Army), Good Conduct Medal, Combat Action Ribbon, National Defense Medal, Vietnamese Cross of Gallantry, Vietnam Service Medal, and Vietnam Campaign Ribbon. Discharge on May 7, 1970, in the rank of Corporal.

Returned to North Miami Beach, Florida, where I retired from the police department after 23 years. I am currently an investigator for Prudential Property & Casualty Insurance Company. Married to Diedre with a daughter, Debbie, and a son, Dennis (former Marine, 1994- 1998).

HOWARD FORNOF, born May 20, 1936, in Universal, Pennsylvania. In march 1953, I joined the Corps. Attended Boot at Parris Island, Platoon 100. After Boot, was assigned duty at HqCo, MCRDep., then to USNRet. Command, Norfolk.

Re-enlisting March 1955 for the 3d Marine Division! Staging at CamPen, then assigned to Foxtrot, 2nd Battalion, 3d Marines, located at Mt. Fuji, Japan. Participated in the Iwo Jima campaign of 1956 as the Company Supply Sergeant. Displaced from Japan to Camp Sukiran, Okinawa, 1957.

Returned to States in 1957 and married the former Margaret Tancraitor from Swissvale, Pennsylvania, 1958, while in the 5th Marines at CamPen. I then changed fields to 01 and after duties with MCBase, CamPen, MCRDep SDiego, Seagoing aboard the *USS Kittyhawk*, 3d MAW El Toro, NBCWS Yuma and Iwakuni, I returned to HqCo, MCRDep PI, as Admin Chief and First Sergeant, retiring in September 1972.

Returned to Arizona with family and in February 1973, to work for Marine Air Federal Credit Union, where I am currently serving as the Vice President and Yuma Regional Manager. I'm active in the Marine Corps League and serve as CO of the Territorial Young Marines.

CONRAD MURPHEE FOWLER, Colonel, USMCR Retired, born September 17, 1918, in Montevallo, Alabama. Joined the Corps in May 1941, 6th R.O.C., Quantico. Commissioned November 1, 1941. Joined A-1-9, San Diego, March 1942. Company Commander in New Zealand, April 1943 to February 26, 1945.

Served on Guadalcanal, Bougainville, Guam, and Iwo Jima. Awarded Purple Heart with Gold Star, and Silver Star with Gold Star. Returned

to States in April 1945. Transferred to Reserves in April 1946.

Attended University of Alabama, 1937-1941, 1945-1946. Received B.S. and LLB degrees. Practice

law six years, was District Attorney six years. Probate judge and chairman, Shelby County Commission, 18 years, ending January 3, 1977. Commanding Officer, Volunteer Training Unit, Birmingham, in 1960s until retirement to Reserves, July 1, 1970.

Employed by West Point Pepperell, Director of Public Affairs; later Vice President, 1977 to 1989. Received three Presidential Appointments to serve as a member of Advisory Commission on Intergovernmental Relations, 1967 to 1977. President, National Alumni Association, University of Alabama, 1969 to 1970. President, National Association of Counties, 1970 to 1971. Chairman, Alabama Constitutional Commission, 1970 to 1976. President, American Lung Association, 1981 to 1982. Inducted into Alabama Hall of Fame, 1981.

My wife, Virginia Mott of Atlanta, and I were married June 15, 1945. Our sons, Conrad, Jr., and Randy, each graduated from the University and each is a an attorney with a successful practice. Conrad was a fine split-end. He played under Coach Bryant and lettered in 1968, 1969, and 1970. We have four grandchildren.

Most days are busy since retirement in 1986. In fact, my "quarterback" wants me to get a regular job so I can get a day off occasionally.

JAMES E. FRANCHETTI, born October 18, 1946, in Richmond, California. Enlisted in the Marines on June 23, 1965, completing boot camp at MCRD San Diego, California. Assigned to various locations, including: Camp Lejeune; Camp Pendleton; MCSB Albany, Georgia; MCAS Beaufort, South Carolina; Cherry Point, North Carolina; and to the 3d Marine Division, 1st Battalion, 4th Marine Regiment, from November 1967 to December 1968.

Served with the 4th Marines with Battalion S-4 (Forward). Participated in numerous operations and was wounded in action on June 4, 1968, on LZ Robin. Returned to duty with the 4th Marines until December 1968. Corporal Franchetti earned a combat promotion to Ser-

geant, the Purple Heart Medal, Naval Achievement Medal with Combat "V," the Vietnam Campaign Medal with three Stars, and the Vietnam Cross of Gallantry with a Star device (personal award).

After six years of active duty, he began a career with the U.S. Department of Justice, Immigration and Naturalization Service, working his way to a second line Supervisory Special Agent position that oversees and directs investigations into the smuggling of human cargo for profit, sex, and slavery. Mr. Franchetti earned his Master's degree at Golden Gate University in San Francisco and is presently an active member, Chief Warrant Officer 2, CID Special Agent, in the United States Army Reserve.

JAMES LESLIE GADBURY, born February 27, 1923, at Monticello, Illinois. Joined the USMC in January 1942. Training: Boot camp at San Diego, Camp Elliot, and Camp Pendleton, California; New Zealand; Guadalcanal. Campaigns included Bougainville, Guam, and Iwo Jima. Was a Machine Gunner in "C" Company, 9th Marines, from its beginning, March 4, 1942, until April 23, 1945, in the rank of Corporal.

Military awards include the Asiatic-Pacific Campaign Medal with four Bronze Stars, Presidential Unit Citation with Bronze Star, Navy Unit Commendation, Good Conduct Medal, World War II Victory Medal, American Campaign Medal, and Combat Action Medal.

Returned to States in May 1945. Stationed at 8th & I Street Marine Barracks in Washington, DC. Spent five months assisting sculptor Felix DeWeldon, a Navy Seabee at that time, building the first statue of the Iwo Jima flag-raising. One of the original flag-raisers and I unveiled it at the ceremony celebrating the Marine Corps' 170th birthday on November 10, 1945. Discharged in January 1946.

Met Norma Gregory while attending Illinois State University. Married 51 years; have five children and 14 grandchildren. We enjoy our family, outdoor sports, and reunions with "C" Company members. We're at home in Monticello, Illinois, following our 38 years of teaching and coaching.

JAMES EDWARD GILLEY, born August 11, 1923, in East Stone Gap, Virginia. Enlisted in USMC on June 24, 1942. Eight week boot camp. Arrived at Camp Lejeune, North Carolina, approximately August 24, 1942. Joined "F"

Company, 2nd Battalion, 3d Marines. Boarded train same day and left San Diego, September 1, 1942, for American Samoa. Volunteered for 3d Marine Raiders Battalion in Samoa, and Consolidation of British Solomons, February 21, 1943, to March 24, 1943. Hospital at Oakland-Norfolk. Returned to Solomon Islands, October 6, 1944, with "B" Company, 9th AmTrac, attached to 6th Marine Division. Okinawa, Ryukyu Islands battle, April 1, 1945, to May 30, 1945. Wounded, Okinawa, May 30, 1945. Flown to hospital, Guam.

Military awards include the Purple Heart, Presidential Unit Citation, Asiatic-Pacific Campaign Medal with two Battle Stars, American Campaign Medal, and World War II Victory Medal. Discharged June 24, 1946, as a Corporal.

University of Tennessee and Stetson University, DeLand, Florida, with B.A. and M.A. in 1950 and 1951. Joined the Federal Bureau of Investigation as Special Agent, 1951, conducting investigations in Missouri, Ohio, and Virginia. Approximately 400 arrests as case agent. Supervisor instructor for first line police offices (sergeants and lieutenants) and hostage negotiator. Retired in 1978 and formed my own corporation for investigations.

Married Virginia H. Legg in 1946; will celebrate our 54th this year. Daughter Paula is employed by the FBI.

EUSEBIO F. "FELIX" GONZALES, born May 18, 1923, in Oakland, California. Joined the United States Marine Corps on April 20, 1944. Boot camp, MCRD San Diego, California; training: Camp Pendleton and Guam. Special qualifications: automatic rifleman.

Arrived on Guam in November 1944; joined C/1/21, 3d Marine Division. Although the island was secured, I participated in several jungle patrols and on one occasion was fired on.

I participated in the Iwo Jima campaign,

landing on the Island, D-Day plus two. March 8, 1945, my platoon came under a heavy mortar barrage. Everyone dove for cover. I was on the extreme left flank, close to the edge of a bluff,

and I could see this Nip with his knee mortar lobbing mortars on my platoon. I fired at this Nip and hit him with the first round. The mortars ceased, and he dove for cover among some jungle brush. I was wounded at 2 a.m., March 13, 1945, from a Japanese ammo dump that blew up. We happened to be dug in on top of it. I was placed in an underground cave hospital.

Upon release, I joined my outfit and returned to Guam. After VJ Day, I was sent to Tien Tsin, China, and served with the 7th Service Regiment, 1st Marine Division, and placed in charge of a PX section. Discharged from the Marine Corps at San Diego in the rank of Corporal.

Awarded the Purple Heart, American Campaign Medal, Asiatic-Pacific Campaign Medal with Bronze Star, World War II Victory Medal, China Service Medal, and Navy Unit Commendation Ribbon Bar.

Returned to Winters, California, and met and married Phyllis Yankee of Sacramento. We have two daughters, Linda and Patricia, and one son, Phillip.

Retired in 1986 as manager of a construction company. Now active as a docent for the California State Railroad Museum and their Amtrak program.

FRANK P. GOODWIN, JR., born August 6, 1925, in Roxbury, Massachusetts. Joined the Marine Corps on August 6, 1942. Trained at Parris Island, South Carolina; Camp Lejeune, North Carolina; Camp Elliot, San Diego, California; Camp Pendleton, California; New Zealand; and Guadalcanal. Participated in Bougainville and Guam campaigns as a scout; I/3/21. Wounded at Guam on August 4, 1944. Returned for surgery to Russell Island, then to San Diego Naval Hospital and Chelsea Naval Hospital, Massachusetts. Resumed duty, June 1945, at Charlestown Navy Yard, Boston. Discharged on November 23, 1945, in the rank of PFC.

Military awards include the Purple Heart, Presidential Unit Citation, American Campaign Medal, Asiatic Campaign Medal with two Battle Stars, World War II Victory Medal, and Combat Action Ribbon.

Most memorable experiences took place twice on Guam when we got into hand-to-hand combat. Also when wounded in the battle south of Finegayan Village.

Returned to Malden, Massachusetts, and married Barbara Dow, who I met in high school. We have five children, Tom, Jean, Frank, Phyllis, and Carol, and four grandchildren. Active in Scouting as a Scoutmaster and Explorer advisor and now committee chairman for 42 years. Mountain climbing, skiing, camping. Enjoying retirement immensely.

WALLACE HAGLUND, born April 11, 1924, in International Falls, Minnesota. Joined service in 1942. Navy Corpsman; served with the 3d Medical Battalion, 9th Marines. Served on Guam. Retired industrial arts teacher. Also a clockmaker for more than 30 years.

In 1995, Haglund returned to Guam to present a gift dedicated to the Navy corpsmen who were killed on Guam. The gift was a handmade clock, with a plaque that reads: "Dedicated to the U.S.N. Hospital Corpsmen of the

Third Marine Division – Killed in Action on Guam – 1944. The gift was accepted by Governor Carl Guitierrez and Lt. Governor Madeleine Bordallo on behalf of the people of Guam. The clock may be displayed in the Guam Museum. In appreciation for his gift, the governor of Guam made Haglund a member of the Ancient Order of the Chamorri, the highest award a non-native of Guam can receive. To receive this award, the nominee must have contributed substantially to the betterment of the community, or have demonstrated real and sympathetic interest in the people of Guam, its history, cultures, traditions and problems.

CHARLES W. HALL, born June 30, 1928, in Fulton County, Georgia. Enlisted in the USMC in October 1945 and received boot training at Parris Island, South Carolina, Platoon 640.

Shipped overseas to "G" Company, 2nd Battalion, 8th Marine Regiment, 2nd Marine Division, in replacement draft #92 as a BAR man. Shipped again to "A" Company, 1st Battalion, 4th Marine Regiment, 6th Marine Division.

MOS Machine Gunner under Corporal Bomar from Texas. Transferred to "K" Company, 4th Battalion, 3d Marine Regiment, 1st Marine Division, while at Tsing Tao, China.

Stateside, he served at Parris Island, South Carolina, and Camp Lejeune, North Carolina,

then shipped to A-T Company, 1st Marine Regiment, 1st Marine Division, in Korea.

Stateside again and served at Camp Pendleton, California. Transferred to MCS Depot, Albany, Georgia, and Camp Lejeune, North Carolina.

Attended basic and advanced automotive schools at Camp Lejeune. Shipped to missile school at Huntsville, Alabama. After school, back to Albany, then to recruiter school at Parris Island. Served in Recruiting in Atlanta, Georgia. Then shipped to Okinawa and on to 9th MT Battalion in Dong Ha, Vietnam.

Ships traveled on: *USS Comet, Gage, Renville, General Black,* and *General Breckenridge.*

Retired as Gunnery Sergeant 3516 from USMC in 1968. After retiring, he attended college and worked as a high school vocational teacher. Married Betty J. Ford in December 1953 in Dekalb County, Georgia. They have three children, Edith, Glenn (served in the Marines), and Trace. Retired in 1988.

FRANCIS E. "FRANK" HALL, born April 20, 1923, in Ridgefield Park, New Jersey. Joined the Marines on August 12, 1942. Saw combat as First Scout at Bougainville, Guam, and Iwo Jima.

Stations included Parris Island, South Carolina; New River, North Carolina; Camp Elliot and Camp Pendleton, California; Warkworth, New Zealand; Guadalcanal; Guam. Promoted

to Corporal, November 1944. Discharged on August 28, 1945, after six months in Naval Hospital, Corvallis, Oregon, following Iwo Jima. Military awards include the Purple Heart, Asiatic-Pacific Campaign Medal with four Battle Stars, Presidential Unit Citation, and Navy Unit Commendation.

Received B.S., Industrial Engineering, Farleigh Dickinson University. Thirty years as editor for magazines; was Editor-In-Chief, *Machinery* magazine, then Procedures and Standards Writer, GPU Nuclear (Three-Mile Island); concurrently Associate Adjunct Professor, CCNY (24 years), Councilman, Township of Teaneck, 29 years; Mayor, six years. Seven children, two grandchildren.

Since retirement, Secretary, Third Division NJ; Commandant, Gooney Birds, MCL; producer/host, MCL cable television program; writer, newsletters; author, Teaneck 100 Year Book.

SGT. JIMMY GILBERT HAMPTON, born May 8, 1920, in Kaw, Oklahoma, and his brothers, **SGT. JOHN ROBERT HAMPTON**, born February 2, 1914, in Coldwater, Oklahoma,

and **SGT. HARRISON OLIVER HAMPTON**, born February 23, 1923, in Kaw, Oklahoma. The three brothers enlisted in the USMC together on September 23, 1940, at San Diego, California, before World War II. John was 26 years old, Jimmy was 20 years old, and Harrison was 17 years old.

All three brothers trained at the US Marine Base, La Jolla Rifle Range, and at Camp Elliot, California. John and Harrison also trained in Iceland.

After they completed training, Jimmy's name

was picked out of a hat, when men were needed to form the 3d Marine Division. Convinced there was going to be a war and that it would be best if he and his two brothers were not in battle together, Jimmy, even though given the option to transfer back with his brothers, decided to stay with the 3d Marines. He went with them to Camp Dunlap, Niland, California, 120 miles east of San Diego, to Imperial Valley Desert. John and Harrison went to Camp Pendleton. All three brothers went to New Zealand, John and Harrison with 2/F/10 and Jimmy with 4/M/12. All three were also shipped to the Solomon Islands. John and Harrison were at Guadalcanal; Jimmy was at Puruata Island, Bougainville, and Guam; Harrison was also at Tarawa and Saipan-Tinian. John was returned to Hawaii. Jimmy was injured at the invasion of Guam. While he was being carried for burial, a corpsman realized he was still alive and ordered that he be evacuated to a hospital ship. He was later sent to Hawaii and then to San Francisco, California, September 1944, and was discharged on January 13, 1945.

Sgt. Jimmy G. Hampton was discharged at Oakland, California, in 1945. He married Norma A. (Angie) Childers on February 14, 1943, at Yuma, Arizona, one week before going overseas. Upon discharge, he returned to Imperial Valley until 1985. In addition to farming a VA-purchased farm for 16 years, he was a heavy equipment operator with the Imperial Irrigation District for 28 years, retiring at age 62 and now living in Visalia, California. He and Angie raised a family of three daughters: Norma M. Smith, two grandsons, Josh and Justin; Susan K. Shepley, two grandsons, Brian and Brad; and Denise a Hampton, one granddaughter, Robin. All are residents of Visalia, California.

Sgt. John R. Hampton was discharged in San Diego, California, in 1946. He lived in Drumright, Oklahoma, and Van Buren, Arkansas, where he died in 1995.

Sgt. Harrison O. Hampton was discharged in San Diego, California, in 1946. He married in 1947 and had one son, Joe L. Hampton, one daughter, Linda (Warstler) Owings, and four grandchildren: Oregon State Trooper Lieutenant Travis Hampton and Malissia, Brent and Meridith Warstler. They lived in Drumright, Oklahoma; Clovis, California; and moved to Portland, Oregon, in 1985, where they lived until his death in 1998. His wife, Mary, and most of his family still live in Portland.

The uniforms Jimmy's gun crew wore during the battle at Bougainville would not have passed inspection at the San Diego Marine Base. These were survivor uniforms at the time. There was no way of drying out this one change of clothes, as it rained every few hours from the time of landing, being just three degrees off the Equator.

Men were hot and galled. Ribs, arms, and legs gaunt from lack of food, and at the mercy of millions of malaria-carrying mosquitos, battling for their lives, their loved ones, and our country's freedom. Above all, we still stand proud 57 years later to say that in the final word of this battle, it allowed us to fulfill our Marine destiny to be the best of men, and realizing that all soldiers in the time of battle cannot have too many friends.

WAR IS HELL! From which there is no return. If one should try to forget, the forever returning nightmares spring back to reality the battles fought and the friends lost. A lifetime spent trying to recover from that Hell, regardless of the path taken, does not let us ever understand why some lived and some died. Only God knows. We were three brothers who were allowed to live, and hope our lives made a difference.

EDWARD HARP, born November 17, 1935, in Highland Park, Michigan. Enlisted in the Marine Corps on November 30, 1955. Training locations included San Diego, California; Camp Pendleton, California; Middle Camp, Fuji, Japan; Camp Sukiran, Okinawa; and Quantico, Virginia.

Participated in PACTRAEX, 3d Marine Division landing maneuvers in the Philippine Islands, 1957. Participated on the Camp Sukiran,

Okinawa, baseball team during 1957, competing in the Far East Forces Baseball League.

Military awards include the Presidential Unit Citation and Good Conduct Medal. Discharged on November 28, 1958, from the Marine Corps Schools, Quantico, Virginia. Achieved the rank of Corporal.

Returned to Detroit, Michigan, and married office sweetheart, Marilyn Yeo. Two grown children, Jeff and Laureen, and two grandchildren,

Joseph and Olivia. Retired in 1996 from Federal-Mogul Corporation as an engineer with 30 years of service. Retirement activities include playing golf, stamp collecting, traveling, and working as a ranger on a golf course.

CHESTER C. HARRIS, born November 13, 1924, in the small village of Limestone, near Danville, Pennsylvania. Chester was inducted into the USMC on April 23, 1943. After boot camp at Parris Island, South Carolina, he was stationed at Hingham, Massachusetts. Chester's duty there was guarding ammo dumps. He was sent to Guam in the summer of 1944, where he carried the BAR on patrol. He later received orders to go to Iwo Jima. After floating around for two days in Higgins boats, they went ashore. On February 24, 1945, he was in a shell hole when a shell exploded in the air, wounding Chester, his lieutenant, and three other Marines. He was taken to the hospital in Saipan, then to Hawaii for R&R, then back to Guam. After the war ended, he was discharged in January 1946.

Chester married Alveretta Michael on December 23, 1947. He has two daughters and eight

grandchildren. He is a retired welder, and enjoys bowling and woodworking. He now serves in God's infantry.

MASTER GUNNERY SERGEANT ALBERT DANIEL HEMPHILL served 30 years with the 3d Marine Division, earning a Silver Star for gallantry in action in World War II with the 21st Marines against Japanese forces on Guam, Marianas Islands, July 28, 1944.

When his First Battalion Company C lost radio and telephone communications with tanks,

Gunnery Sergeant Hemphill volunteered to advance under hostile fire and re-establish contact.

From an exposed position, he transmitted signals from the tanks to his Company Commander and, when fired upon by an enemy machine gun, he located the enemy, returned to his company, and then led a rocket team forward to

destroy the machine gunners, personally accounting for three of the enemy, sustaining shrapnel wounds to his shoulder and back. He was awarded the Purple Heart.

Other awards and commendations earned include: the Presidential Unit Citation and Bronze Star for service on Iwo Jima in 1945 and for service with the 1st Marine Division in Korea, where he was wounded in action on Wonju, July 6, 1951; the Navy Unit Commendation; the American Campaign Medal; the Asiatic-Pacific Campaign Medal; the Good Conduct Medal; and the World War II Victory Medal.

Master Sergeant Hemphill was born in Tylertown, Mississippi, October 16, 1922. He enlisted in October 1939 and received training at Parris Island, South Carolina; Camp Lejeune, North Carolina; Camp Pendleton, California; and Guam in the Marianas Islands.

After Korea, he served as a Drill Instructor at Charlestown Navy Yard in Massachusetts, where he met and married his second wife Phyllis.

After retirement from the Marines in 1969, he began a new career as Chief of Security at Norwood Hospital, Norwood, Massachusetts. His hobbies included hunting, fishing, and gardening.

Master Sergeant Hemphill died of cancer on September 21, 1990, and was buried in Fox Hill Cemetery, Billerica, Massachusetts, with a full USMC Honor Guard in attendance.

ALBERT DAVID HERNANDEZ, born September 15, 1948, in East Los Angeles, California. Moved to Baldwin park, California, in 1955. As a 17-year-old attending Baldwin Park High School, joined the USMC on the 120 day delay program. Left for boot camp (MCRD) on July 5, 1966. Stationed in Kaneohe Bay, Hawaii, as a rifle coach. Volunteered for combat duty in Vietnam.

Joined "L" Company, 3d Battalion, 4th Marines, in Okinawa as a replacement. Arrived in

Vietnam on Mother's Day 1967, and departed Vietnam in March 1968.

Military awards include the Presidential Unit Citation, Vietnam Service Medal, Vietnam Campaign Medal, Combat Action Ribbon, National Defense Service Ribbon, Good Conduct Medal, and the Navy Commendation Medal with combat "V" for heroic achievement on January 18, 1968, in RVN. Discharged on July 3, 1968, as a Sergeant E-5, under two years.

Currently employed by McMaster-Carr Supply Company in Santa Fe Springs, California, for

22 years. Now active in target shooting, wild boar hunting, camping, and being a grandpa to Charlene (daughter) and Dino Velasquez's kids, Celina, 10, and twin boys Dominic and Damien, 5.

FRED HESS, born June 5, 1923, in Enid, Oklahoma. Graduated from high school in 1942, Telluride, Colorado. Enlisted in the USMC in 1942. Basic training in San Diego, California, rec. depot. Served with "C" Company, 3d Tank Battalion, 3d Marine Division. Joined the 3d Marine Division on Bougainville. Sent back to Guadalcanal, new camp, and began training with the 3d.

His machine gun unit was sent to the Marianas, Guam and then to Iwo Jima. Fred's

brother, with the 5th Marine Division, was there, too. His unit sustained heavy casualties, and no one seemed to know him. During a bombardment, Fred crawled in a foxhole. The name "Hess" was on his leggings. A voice from the dark asked if he was Fred Hess. It was his brother Jim. Both were at the front and both brothers returned alive. Fred mustered out as a Line Corporal in 1945.

Fred married his wife Margaret in 1947; they had five children. He was a rancher, artist, and masonry contractor. He was a life member of the 3d Marine Division. Fred passed away on March 21, 1999.

FRED J. HESS, born September 28, 1920, in Clutier, Iowa. Enlisted in the USMC on September 22, 1942. Trained in San Diego; Camp Elliot; Tank Mechanic school, Fort Knox.

Went overseas in July 1943 to New Caledonia, then spent 11 months at Guadalcanal before taking part in the invasion of Guam, July 1944, and Iwo Jima, February 1945. Served as a Chief on a tank maintenance crew.

Among the military awards he received are the Good Conduct Medal, Presidential Unit Citation, Pacific Theater Medal, and two Battle Stars. He was discharged at Great Lakes NTS on December 12, 1945, in the rank of Sergeant.

After returning home, he took employment with the County Road Department for 37 years. Married Dorothy Mareda in August 1948. Dorothy died in April 1979. They had one daughter,

Donna. Fred married Marie Yuska in January 1981. He had two stepdaughters, Mary and Judy, and several step-grandchildren and step-great-grandchildren. After retirement, he developed heart disease and succumbed to cancer on August 15, 1999, after a two-year battle.

DEAN S. HIRST, born May 17, 1946, in Garden City, Michigan. Enlisted in the U.S. Navy, Kansas City, Kansas, August 1954; honorably discharged, August 1962. Training locations included NTC Great Lakes, Illinois; Naval Hospital, Charleston, South Carolina; Camp Pendleton, California (Field Medical Service School – MOS 8404); November 1956, cold weather training, "Pickle Meadows." Married high school sweetheart, Marjorie, November 1954; no children.

Duty assignments include: 3d Marine Division, January 1957, Camp Sukiran, Fort Buckner, Okinawa. Senior Corpsman Hm3 with "A" Company, 1st Battalion, 9th Marines. Took part in massive amphibious training exercise, Dingalin Bay, Republic of Philippines, after which the Division moved to North Camp Fuji, Japan. Participated in the "Fuji Hill Climb." Division moved back to Okinawa, West Camp Hague, tent camp – Napunja, 1958. Rotated stateside to 1st Medical Battalion, Camp Pendleton, California. Released to Reserves, August 1958.

Attended Missouri State, Warrensburg, under GI Bill. Graduated with B.S. in education, double majors, French and Social Studies. Taught high school French and Ancient History until 1962, when I entered the San Francisco Police Department. Was forced into disability retirement due to injuries sustained on the job as of May 1, 1970. Went on to obtain commercial pilot's license, instrument and seaplane ratings, and CFI for anything, single engine land and seaplane. Operated two flying services until forced into permanent retirement, 1984, due to numerous surgeries connected with injuries sustained while with SFPD.

Enjoy amateur radio (call sign KM6RE), reading, working around property – and growing old!

HENRY F. HOUSEMAN, born April 10, 1932, in Kalamazoo, Michigan. Enlisted in USMC on December 31, 1952. Training locations include MCRD San Diego, California; Camp Pendleton, California; Japan; Okinawa; Iwo Jima; and MCAS Cherry Point, North Carolina.

Participated in the 1953 reactivation of the 3d Marine Division and subsequent deployment

to Japan. Served with 3-4 Naval Gunfire Team. Discharge on December 30, 1955, from 2nd

MAW (Cherry Point) in the rank of Sergeant.

Military awards include the Republic of Korea Presidential Unit Citation, Korean Service Medal, United Nations Medal, Good Conduct Medal, National Defense Medal, and Cold War Victory Medal.

Graduated from Western Michigan University and married Patricia Jones. Second born, David, died at age seven. Daughters are Sara and Rachel, and granddaughters are Nicole and Danielle. Retied from Portage (Michigan) Public Schools and Michigan Association of Community and Adult Education with 33 years of service. Now enjoying an active retirement in Fort Myers, Florida, doing volunteer work and traveling. Ultimate goal is to visit all seven continents, having already traveled in more than three dozen countries on seven continents.

GERALD A. JOHNSON, enlisted in the USMC, January 3, 1952. Boot camp at San Diego, California, 16th Platoon, 6th Recruitment Battalion. Went to Driver's School at the Seabee base at Port Hueme, California, for 13 weeks. After finishing Driver's School, went to Camp Pendleton, California. Was assigned to "C" Company, 3d Engineer Battalion.

Went to Japan with the 3d Marine Division in August 1953. My duties while in "C" Company,

3d Engineer Battalion, included truck driver, motor transport dispatcher, and bulldozer operator. Was stationed at Camp Gafu for most of my overseas tour. I was sent back to the USA in October 1954. After a 30-day leave, I was assigned to the Barstow Supply Center, Barstow, California.

Military awards include the Good Conduct Medal, National Defense Service Medal, United Nations Medal, and Korean War Medal. I was discharged at Barstow on January 3, 1955, in the rank of Sergeant. Following discharge from active duty, I served five years in the inactive Reserves.

My present occupation is as a highway contractor, building roads for the State of South Dakota. I've been building a company moving dirt for 37 years.

CLARENCE L. "SHORTY" JUNE, born August 14, 1925, in Bell, California. Enlisted in the USMC on March 8, 1944. Training included boot camp at MCRD San Diego, California, Platoon 238; Camp Elliot, California; Camp Pendleton, California, for infantry training at tent camp #2. After completing training, shipped overseas to Guam on July 22, 1944, as replacement in "I" Company, 1st Platoon, 3d Battalion, 21st Marine Regiment, 3d Marine

Division. On Guam we spent most of our time in the jungles, mopping up remaining Japanese stragglers.

February 1945, regiment sent to Iwo Jima as reinforcements for 4th and 5th Divisions.

Wounded on February 28 and again on March 6; none of these injuries was serious. Hit by rifle or machine gun fire on March 9, resulting in the amputation of my right leg. Spent 14 months at Aiea Heights Naval Hospital, Hawaii, and Mare Island Naval Hospital, California. While are Mare Island, married my high school sweetheart, Jenne M. Effertz; she passed away on November 1, 1998.

Military awards include the Purple Heart, Combat Action Ribbon, Asiatic-Pacific Campaign Medal with two Stars, American Campaign Medal, Iwo Jima Medal, World War II Victory Medal, and Presidential Ribbon with one Star. Discharged in April 1946 in the rank of Corporal.

Attended Southwestern Law School, Los Angeles, under the GI Bill. Went to work for the Veterans Administration in 1948. Retired in 1980 from the VA Medical Center, Long Beach, California, where I was Chief of Prosthetic and Sensory Aids Service, at GS 14 level.

GEORGE W. KISER, born October 11, 1925, in Berkeley, California. Enlisted in the Marine Corps on February 4, 1493. After boot camp in San Diego, and primary training, I was shipped to Guam as a replacement on August 12, 1944. We were held in reserve until the island was secured on August 15.

I was then sent to "C" Company, 9th Marines, 3d Marine Division, on August 16, 1944. I saw two days of combat action on Iwo Jima before I was wounded by mortar fire. I lost my leg and was shipped home in 1945.

I married my beautiful wife and attended San Jose State College in San Jose, California, graduating in 1949 with a B.A. in Chemistry. I was a plant manager in Berkeley, California, for about 20 years. I then worked as a broker in real estate for 25 years and have recently retired. My wife Barbara and I have two children, seven grandchildren, and four great-grandchildren. We now live in Pittsburg, California.

WILLIAM A. KARPOWICZ, born February 10, 1924, in Muskegon, Michigan. Began his military career with "G" Company, 2nd Battalion, 126th Infantry Regiment, 32nd Army Division, Michigan National Guard, 1939. Joined the Marines in 1942. Subsequently shipped to the

Pacific, where he served from February 1943 until April 1945. Participated in campaigns at Bougainville, Guam, and Iwo Jima. Wounded in action on July 21, 1944, while serving as an infantryman with "K" Company, 3d Battalion, 21st Marine Regiment, during invasion of Guam.

Military awards include the Purple Heart, Marine corps Achievement Medal, Asiatic-Pacific Campaign Medal with three Stars, American Campaign Medal, World War II Victory Medal, Presidential Unit Citation with one Star, and a Unit Commendation. Discharged from active duty in 1945 in the rank of Corporal.

After discharge, returned home and married his high school sweetheart, Genevieve Tapek. They have several children: Kenneth, Patrick, Denise (passed away in 1980 at age 25), and William, Jr. Retired from the Grand Rapids Police Department in 1981 after 38 years of service to his community. Now active in numerous veterans group, a Polish cultural group, and his local church.

MASTER GUNNERY SERGEANT JAMES G. KYSER III, USMC (Ret), born October 24, 1933, in San Francisco, California. Enlisted in USMCR on December 22, 1952; requested active duty from the 35th Special Infantry Company, July 1953. Honor graduate, Platoon 307, MCRD San Diego, California. Duty stations: MCAS El Toro, California; Marine Barracks, Pearl Harbor, Hawaii; Marine Barracks, 8th & Eye, Washington, DC; 1st Marine Brigade; 1st Marine Division; 3d Marine Division; Marine Corps Schools, Quantico, Virginia; Office of the Assistant Secretary of Defense (Manpower); Military Assistance Command Vietnam; Headquarters Marine Corps.

Honor graduate, Defense Information School (Journalist); Graduate, Defense Information School (Radio/TV Broadcast Specialist).

Awards: Joint Service Commendation Medal with Oak Leaf Cluster (second award), Navy Commendation Medal, Army Meritorious Unit Citation, Marine Corps Good Conduct Medal (six awards), National Defense Service Medal with one Star, Vietnam Service Medal with three Stars, Republic of Vietnam Cross of Gallantry Meritorious Unit Citation with Palm, Republic of Vietnam Civic Action Unit Citation with Palm, Republic of Vietnam Campaign Medal, Expert Rifle, Expert Pistol. Freedoms Foundation editorial award, 1968, 1969, 1970; Navy CHINFO Silver Anchor Award, 1968; USMCCCA Donald L. Dickson Award, 1982.

Married Virginia L. Detweiler, 1957; daughter Susan; son James G. IV. Retired USMC December 31, 1973. B.A., University of Maryland, 1967; M.S., American University, 1983. Advertising Manager, American Petroleum Institute, 1974-1978; Director of Advertising, Association of American Railroads, 1978-1988; Editor/PAO, Association manager, Third Marine Division Association, 1988-2001. President, U.S. Marine Corps Combat Correspondents Association, 1977-1979; President, Association of Railroad Advertising & Marketing, 1983-1984.

EDWIN D. LAMPMAN, born June 15, 1923, in Hoboken, New Jersey. Enlisted in the USMC on November 23, 1942. Training at Parris Island, South Carolina; Camp Lejeune, North Carolina; Samoa, Marianas Islands; Guadalcanal. Served with 1st Sep. Eng. Co., Samoa, Marianas Islands; "C" Company, 19th Marine Regiment, 3d Marine Division, with 0 5/06 Marvin (Plt. Co.); Casual Company, Quantico, Virginia. Discharged on September 23, 1945, in the rank of Corporal.

Retired from Republic Aviation; supervisor on FS4F, RF84F, F84G, F105. Also worked at Fairchild Aviation; supervisor, A10A Warthog; inspection and repair 119, 123, DC6, 130 Hercules. Partners in senior citizens travel trailer and mobile home communities. Widower; five children and oodles of grandchildren.

ELMER GEORGE LAWLESS, born December 25, 1925, in Whitfield County, Georgia. Enlisted in the USMC on May 9, 1944. Training at Parris Island, South Carolina; Camp Pendleton, California; and Guam. Served with Platoon 295, 7th Battalion, 3d Marine Division, as a telephone man. Participated in action against the enemy at Iwo Jima, Volcano Islands, and occupation of China.

Military awards include the Good Conduct Medal and Ser Lap Button. Discharged on June 13, 1946, in the rank of Corporal.

Returned to Dalton, Georgia, and married Charline Priesly on December 28, 1946. We have no children. Retired from the dry good business and hardware business in 1992 after 46 years of service. I am working part-time at Shawn Chapman Funeral Home. Enjoying traveling, working in my yard, and locating my Marine buddies that I served with. One of them is Doris K. Smith. We served together on Guam. We had not seen each other since 1947 until March 2000. He has been married to Nona Smith for 35 years and is now living in Cartersville, Georgia.

CHARLES W. LEASE, JR., born August 18, 1947, in West York, Pennsylvania. Joined the Marine Corps on September 9, 1965, and received an honorable discharge on May 19, 1971, in the rank of Corporal E-4, which was earned in Vietnam. Training locations included Parris Island, South Carolina; Camp Lejeune, North Carolina; Camp Pendleton, California; South Vietnam; Okinawa, Japan; HQMC, Arlington, Virginia.

Participated in various campaigns and battles in Danang and Khe Sanh, South Vietnam, as a Combat Military Policeman and M-60 Machine Gunner with Charlie Company, 1st Battalion, 3d Marine Regiment, 3d Marine Division.

Military awards include the National Defense Service Medal, Vietnamese Service Medal with two Stars, Vietnamese Campaign Medal (with device), Presidential Unit Citation, Good Conduct Medal, M-14 Rifle Expert Badge, 45 cal. Pistol Expert, MCI-Corrections, MCI-M-60 Machine Gun, Cold War Medal, South Vietnam Commemorative Medal, Armed Forces Expeditionary Medal, and Combat Action Ribbon.

After discharge, attended NVCC, received A.A. in Law Enforcement; GMU, received B.S. in Criminal Justice; GWU, received MASS in Forensic Sciences with minor in Law. Spent 15 years in law enforcement and 15-plus years in beverage sales. Will start law school in September 2001 under VA Vocational Rehabilitation. Presently retired on disability through SSA and VA due to PTSD related to experiences in Vietnam. Married four times. Recovering alcoholic after 12 DWI charges. Have held over 20 jobs and presently single after four divorces and two beautiful children, a daughter, 31, and a son, 12. Intend to go back to work after law school, representing veterans with their claims, but am enjoying retirement at the present time.

REGINALD E. LEMAY, born July 27, 1925, in Manchester, New Hampshire. Joined USMC on October 13, 1943. Training included boot camp, Parris Island, South Carolina; Camp Lejeune. Served in campaigns on Guam and Iwo Jima. Duties: Message Center Code Decoder, 3d Marine Division, HQ 21st Marines. Wounded in action by machine gun, left side of neck and head, in campaign on Iwo Jima.

Military awards include the Purple Heart, Asiatic-Pacific Campaign Medal, American Campaign Medal, World War II Victory Medal, and Presidential Citation. Discharged in Bainbridge, Massachusetts, on January 2, 1946, in the rank of Corporal.

Returned to Manchester, New Hampshire, and married my beautiful sweetheart, Marie A.

LaFreniere, on March 2, 1946. We had three sons and one daughter. My wife was diagnosed with Alzheimer's Disease in 1978 and died on Valentine's Day, February 14, 1998. We were married for 52 years. She was the love of my life. I was a building contractor in New Hampshire and a building contractor superintendent in Florida. Now retired.

ROBERT L'HEUREUX, born July 31, 1943, in Meriden, Connecticut, and graduated from Platt High School in 1961. Enlisted in the Marines in May and completed boot camp at Parris Island, South Carolina, September 1961. After ITR, he was stationed at Camp Lejeune and Camp Pendleton.

In January 1964, PCS'd to Okinawa and was assigned to E/2/12. In February 1965, reported

to MACS-6 at MCAS Beauford and deployed with the squadron to Camp Schwab, Okinawa. In October 1966, was reassigned to Vietnam, where he served with D/2/11 until November 1967. Reassigned to the 1st Battalion, 6th Marines, at Camp Lejeune until May 1968, when he again returned to Vietnam and was assigned to B/1st LAAM Battalion. When 1st LAAM redeployed to CONUS, he was reassigned to MASS-2 and was attached to the 3d Marine Division at Dong Ha. Redeployed with the 3d Marine Division to Okinawa in 1969. Discharged in March 1970. Enlisted in the Army and served 20 years, most of the time with Special Forces.

Presently working as an instructor with the Department of Defense. Married to the former Kazue Asato. They have one son and one daughter.

JOHN R. LILLEY II, born March 18, 1929. Attended schools in Worcester, Massachusetts, graduating from Clark University in 1950. Served with the USMC from April 1947 to June 1980, retiring as a Colonel. Following enlisted service, commissioned in June 1950. Served 10 months in combat, Korea, as a Rifle Platoon

Leader with E/2/, WIA. Served 13 months in combat, Vietnam, with 3d Marine Division as CO, 3d Engineer Battalion, and Assistant G-4/Commander LZ Stud/VCB.

Military decorations include the Silver Star, Defense Superior Service Medal, Bronze Star with "V," Defense Meritorious Service Medal,

Purple Heart, and Combat Action Ribbon.

Following USMC retirement, was Executive Secretary, Emergency Mobilization Preparedness Board, an instrumentality of the National Security Council, August 1981 to October 1985. Served as Director of Security, Federal Emergency Management Agency, retiring from federal service at level four of the Senior Executive Service in November 1993.

Married Nathalie Veronica Roche in 1953. They have two grown children, Russell and Barbara, and five grandchildren; reside in Catharpin, Virginia.

Life member, 3d Marine Division Association and 1st Marine Division Association.

JOHN A. LINDQUIST, born April 24, 1948, in Milwaukee, Wisconsin. Joined the USMC on October 23, 1967. Training locations include San Diego, California, and Camp Pendleton, California. Vietnam, May 4, 1968, to May 25, 1969, including 880 convoys to Vandergrift Combat Base. I was a Radio Operator with FLSG-B H&S Company, Communications Platoon, 7th Motors, H&S C Co. Communications Platoon, and 7th Separate Bulk Fuel Platoon. My daughter, Jessica K. Lindquist, was born on June 9, 1968, while I was at Cau, Vietnam.

Military awards include the National Defense Service Ribbon, Vietnam Service Medal with three Stars, Republic of Vietnam Campaign Rib-

bon, Navy Unit Commendation Ribbon with Bronze Star, Republic of Vietnam Meritorious Unit Citation, Republic of Vietnam Meritorious Unit Citation (civil action), and Combat Action Ribbon.

Returned to the city of Milwaukee and married the lovely Ann L. Bailey. Employed by the City of Milwaukee since 1974 and am now an

Operating Engineer. I'm active in my union and in the 3d Marine Division Association.

ALAN P. LOPER, enlisted in the USMC at U.S. Marine Corps Recruiting Station, Jacksonville, Florida, at age 17. Training at Parris Island, South Carolina; Assigned to Platoon 35, 4th Recruit Training Battalion. Transferred to Camp Lejeune, North Carolina; assigned as Ammunition Carrier, "I" Company, 3d Battalion, 6th Marine Regiment, 2nd Marine Division. Following leave, sent to Treasure Island Naval Base, Oakland, California, before embarking aboard *USS President Jackson* for Pearl Harbor, Hawaii; assigned to Marine Barracks, U.S. Navy Base, as Security Guard. Transferred to Itami, Japan, then to Inchon, Korea. Assignments and duty stations from March 1955 to January 1957 included: Squad Leader, Heavy Machine Gun Platoon, Camp Pendleton, California; Unit Diary Clerk, Weapons Company Office. Discharged on January 22, 1957; re-enlisted the following day. From February 1957 to June 1966, served in various administrative, security, recruiting, and platoon leader assignments. Duty stations included: Marine Corps Air Station, Miami, Florida; Headquarters USMC, Washington, DC; Marine Security Guard School; American Embassy, Oslo, Norway; HMX-1, Marine Corps Air Station, Quantico, Virginia; NCO, Security Section, Naval Air Station, Anacostia, DC; Security Platoon, Marine Corps Air Station, Quantico, Virginia; Recruiters School, HQ Company, MCRD, Parris Island, South Carolina; Marine Corps Recruiting Station, Minneapolis, Minnesota; Marine Corps Recruiting Sub-Station, Rochester, Minnesota; Headquarters and Service Company, 3d Battalion, 8th Marine Regiment, 2nd Marine Division; Platoon Leader, "I" Company, 1st Platoon, 3d Battalion, 8th Marine Regiment; "L" Company, 3d Battalion, 8th Marine Regiment.

July 5, 1966, arrived in Danang, Vietnam. Assigned to "C" Company, 3d Platoon, 1st Battalion, 9th Marine Regiment, 3d Marine

Division. Participated in numerous operations, including: Macon, Swanee, Deckhouse V, Chinook II, Prairie II, Prairie III, Bighorn, Prairie IV, Hickory, Cimarron, and Buffalo. Wounded in action during Operation Bighorn.

Upon return from Vietnam, July 1967, administrative assignments and schools, including: Camp Pendleton, California; Parris Island, South Carolina; and Futema, Okinawa. Reassigned to Vietnam, September 16, 1970, to De-

cember 27, 1970, HQ Company, Headquarters Battalion, 1st Marine Division. Following return to States, assigned to various administrative duties at Camp Pendleton.

Retired in July 1972 in the rank of Gunnery Sergeant. Transferred to Fleet Marine Corps Reserve in inactive, retired status until permanent retirement, February 1983.

Military awards include the Purple Heart, Naval Achievement Medal with Combat "V," Combat Action Ribbon, Good Conduct Medal with Silver Star, National Defense Service Medal with Bronze Star, Korean Service Medal, United Nations Service Medal, Presidential Unit Citation with three Bronze Stars, Meritorious Unit Commendation Medal, Armed Forces Expeditionary Medal, Vietnam Service Medal with three Bronze Stars, Republic of Vietnam Campaign Medal with 1960 Device, Republic of Vietnam Meritorious Unit Citation (Gallantry Cross Medal Color with Palm), Republic of Vietnam Meritorious Unit Citation (Civil Actions Medal, First Class Color with Palm), and Republic of Korean Presidential Unit Citation.

Following retirement from USMC, graduated from college with degree in business. Worked for Northwestern Mutual Life Insurance Company, retiring as Manager, f Policy Owners Service Department. He and his wife Annette had six children. Al passed away at age 59.

He was active as a loaned executive for the United Way, the Marine Corps Badger League Detachment, Devil Dogs, and 1/9 Network. He enjoyed golfing, woodworking, music, and church activities. He was the founder and president of the Third Marine Division Wisconsin Chapter, which was renamed in his honor following his death.

THOMAS H. MACHAUER, born August 2, 1920, in New York. Entered the U.S. Marine Corps on April 5, 1943. Boot camp at Parris Island, South Carolina. Afterward was assigned to Charleston Navy Yard, South Carolina, for duty. Shortly after was sent to Camp Elliot, California, for training as a mortar man in 60mm mortars. Transferred again to the 5th Marine Division on the west coast. Trained with the 5th, then transferred again to a replacement outfit and was sent overseas to the 3d Marine Division, B/1/9, Baker Company, 1st Battalion, 9th Regiment, Rifle Company (infantry).

Fought on Guam and Iwo Jima, 1944 and 1945. Wounded on Iwo Jima, Motayama Airfield #2, February 25 and 26, 1945. Evacuated by hospital ship to Guam, then to Aiea Naval Hospital, Ha-

waii, then to a California hospital, and finally to Newport, Rhode Island, hospital. Medically and honorably discharged on October 31, 1945, in the rank of PFC.

Military awards include the Presidential Unit Citation with Battle Star, Purple Heart with Gold Star (in lieu of second Purple Heart), Combat Action Ribbon, Asiatic-Pacific Campaign Ribbon with two Stars, American Theater Campaign Medal, Good Conduct Medal, and World War II Victory Medal.

Married for 54 years to Marie Urgo of Queens Village, New York; one daughter, Joan; one granddaughter, Kathy, and one great-granddaughter, Ashely. Life member of the 3d Marine Division, DAV, and Military Order of the Purple Heart; member of Survivors of Iwo Jima (Long Island).

LEONARD FOSTER MASON, born February 22, 1920, in Middlesboro, Kentucky. Joined the USMC in 1942. Training at Camp Lejeune, North Carolina. Served with the 2nd Battalion, 3d Marines, 3d Marine Division. Held the rank of PFC. Killed in action on Guam on July 21, 1944. Now serving in God's heavenly Marine Corps. Military awards include the Medal of Honor and the Purple Heart.

For his bravery, destroyer DD852 was named the *USS Leonard F. Mason* in his honor. His parents and his son Larry commissioned the ship on June 28, 1946.

WAYNE MASSEY, born November 19, 1924, in Mullin, Texas. Joined the USMC on May 26, 1943. Boot camp completed at San Diego, California. Served with marine Air Group 45 in the Western Carolines, 1944-1945. Assigned as Adjutant of VMF-311 in the Republic of Korea, 1952-1953. Joined the 3d Marine Division on Okinawa in December 1958 and assigned to 1st Battalion, 3d Marines, 3d Force Service Regiment and JTF-116 (in Japan). Duty in Vietnam, 1966-1967, as Adjutant of 3d Marine Division. Retired on February 1, 1972, in the rank of Lt. Colonel.

Military awards include the Legion of

Merit, Bronze Star with "V," Presidential Unit Citation, Vietnam Service Medal with two Stars, Vietnam Honor Medal 1st Class, Vietnam Cross of Gallantry with Palm, Korean Service Medal, and Korean Presidential Unit Citation.

Since retirement, have been employed in real estate management, sales, and construction in California and Texas. Presently own and operate construction and real estate companies in Fredericksburg, Texas.

CECIL MATHENEY, born in Meridian, Mississippi, in 1926. Graduated from Sumter County High School, York, Alabama. Enlisted in the USMC in January 1944. Sent to San Diego for boot camp. Joined 21st Marines, F/2/21st, as a replacement at the end of the Guam campaign. Landed at Iwo on February 21. Witnessed first flag raising from above second airfield.

Wounded on February 24 while cleaning out a machine gun nest in 5th Division Sector. Went to a hospital ship for a week, and returned to his

company nears third airstrip and sulphur mines. Wounded again on March 6. Sent to Guam hospital. Went back to duty and returned to States three days before the Japanese surrendered.

Discharged at Pensacola, Florida, January 1946. Married his high school sweetheart. They have two daughters and three grandchildren. Owned an automobile appraisal service for many years. Also owned a Ford dealership in the Jackson Metro area. He is now semi-retired in Jackson, Mississippi. He has attended all Iwo reunions.

DONALD R. McBRIDE, born March 19, 1925, in Valley Junction, Iowa. Joined the USMC ON August 10, 1942, at Des Moines, Iowa. Trained at MCRD San Diego, California; Camp Pendleton, California; Auckland, New Zealand; Guadalcanal; and Guam. Shipped overseas in January 1943. Participated in campaigns at Bougainville, November, 1943, and Guam, June 1944. Returned to the States in December 1944. Discharged at the Marine Barracks, Klamath Falls, Oregon, on October 8, 1945.

Returned to Des Moines, Iowa. Employed at a tire manufacturing facility, 1945-1947. Lived in Ashland, Oregon, logging and dairying, 1947-1953. Returned to Des Moines, Iowa, employed at tire manufacturing company, 1953-1958. Credit Union Consultant and Data Processing Specialist for the Iowa Credit Union League, 1968-1990. Retired in 1990, spending

six months in Iowa and six months in Arizona with my wife Margie. Hobbies are traveling and gardening.

CHARLES C. McCAIN, born February 22, 1922, in Oklahoma. Joined the USMC on September 25, 1940; discharged on November 11, 1946, in the rank of Gunnery Sergeant. Boot camp at San Diego, California. Served with 3/M/9 and 3/K/9, 3d Marine Division from first formation, 1942, to final formation, 1945.

My story is a post-war story. After I retired from the Los Angeles County (California) Sheriff's Department in 1972, my wife Laura and I set sail from Los Angeles on June 2, 1972, on our 33.5-foot sloop *Camelot* for a five-year trip around the world.

We anchored in front of the Pt. Cruz Yacht Club, Honiara, Guadalcanal, in May 1974, where we stayed for three weeks before heading to Papua, New Guinea. My specific story occurred at the Yacht Club at a party the evening prior to our departure.

The Number 1 bar steward "Joe" approached my wife apprehensively to ask that she relay a message to Mr. Charley (me). The stewards were not permitted to initiate social conversations with Anglo-Europeans (white people). She suggested he tell me himself and that she would bring me to their area.

When I arrived, the four stewards were standing at attention. "Joe," the spokesman, said, "We want to thank you Marines for saving our country from the Japanese!" They had tears running down their cheeks, and I found some running down my cheeks as well.

In that these stewards ranged in age from 18-20 years, all they knew of t he war was what they heard from their parents and grandparents. I twas a very humbling experience, especially since we never gave them any direct financial aid after the war.

I gave each a hug, something they never previously received from a white person. See what you Marines did before we got there! They will always remember!

JERRY E. McCALL, born April 10, 1949, in Morganton, North Carolina. Joined the USMC on August 30, 1967. Training locations included Parris Island, South Carolina, Platoon 1035, November 2, 1967; Camp Lejeune, North Carolina; Camp Pendleton, California.

Served with C/1/3, 3d Marine Division, South Vietnam, under the command of Lt. William "Rich" Higgins, whom the Navy destroyer

USS Higgins is named after. Participated in the Tet Offensive.

Military awards include the National Defense Medal, Vietnamese Campaign Medal, Vietnamese Service Medal, and Combat Action Ribbon. Honorably discharged at the rank of Lance Corporal on April 30, 1969.

Returned to Morganton, North Carolina. Married to Marcia Garrison; have two children, Jerry Wayne McCall and Libby R. Steffey, and two stepsons, Dustin and Obie Carswell. Retired from Morganton Department of Public Safety, Morganton, North Carolina, with 27-1/2 years of service. Employed as patrol officer, firefighter, criminal investigator, patrol sergeant, criminal investigator sergeant, patrol captain, criminal investigator captain, and major. Now active in camping, golfing, and enjoying retirement.

WILLIAM C. McINTYRE, born March 25, 1927, in Florence, Alabama; raised in Birmingham. Joined the USMC at Shreveport, Louisiana, on September 1, 1942, at the age of 15. Training locations included boot camp at San Diego Recruit Depot; advanced training at Camp Pendleton, where I was assigned to Battery A, 3d Special Weapons; Camp Elliot, California; New Zealand; and Guadalcanal.

Participated in Bougainville campaign with Battery A, 3d Special Weapons Battalion, 3d

Marine Division, and as a BAR rifleman, "G" Company, 2nd Battalion, 3d Marines, during the Guam campaign. Wounded in action on July 27, 1944, Guam campaign; sent to Naval hospital, Honolulu, Hawaii, then Naval hospital at San Diego, California, and subsequently to Corona Naval Hospital, Corona, California. Discharged from hospital on December 15, 1946.

Military awards include the Purple Heart, Presidential Unit Citation, American Campaign Medal, Asiatic-Pacific Campaign Medal with two Battle Stars, World War II Victory Medal, and Combat Action Ribbon.

Returned to Birmingham, Alabama, and in 1949 married Virginia Register and had there children, William Kristopher, Jean Cheryl, and Lloyd Keith. Married for second time in 1988 to Caroline Macy; no children from this marriage. Moved to Orlando, Florida, in 1960 with the Martin Marietta Corporation and retired in 1988 with 28 years of service as a Contracts Manager. Now active in traveling in our motor home and spending the summers in the mountains of North Carolina.

GERALD F. "JERRY" MERNA, born April 1, 1930, in New York City. Raised in his youth by Dominican nuns. Successfully completed three careers in past 53 years, receiving two degrees from George Washington University by attending night school. Raised two children, Linda and Gerald, and has been happily married to high school sweetheart Dorothy (Sedlak) from Piermont, New York, for over 49 years. They have two grandsons.

First career as a Marine, enlisting on 17th birthday, April 1947. Attained rank of 1st Lieutenant after coming up through enlisted ranks

to Master Gunnery Sergeant throughout 22-plus years of service. In Korean, 1952-1953, same time as brother, Sergeant Jim Merna, later joined by brother, Corporal Richard Merna. ATA Leader, Weapons Company, 1st Battalion, 5th Marines. Platoon Sergeant with Easy Company, 2nd Battalion, 5th marines, on Outpost VEGAS. In 1966, commissioned as Mustang 2nd Lieutenant, serving 13 months with 3d Marine Division in Vietnam.

After the Marine Corps, Jerry began his second career in 1968, 18 years with the U.S. Postal Service. Rose steadily to higher management positions, ultimately directing the efforts of over 4,000 Northern Virginia employees, responsible for 150 post offices. Was also the Executive Assistant to the Postmaster General, an SES appointment and one of only 30 officers within the 850,000 strong USPS.

Jerry's third career, that of advertising director, and later VP, for two large defense associations in the Washington, DC, area. Directed worldwide advertising activities for AFCEA's journal, *Signal* magazine. Then became VP for PR & Marketing for NDIA's national *Defense* magazine.

Currently serving as Publications Consultant to NDIA, residing in Potomac Falls, Virginia, with his wife Dorothy.

HERBERT J. MERTES was born on a farm near West Chicago, IL on September 14, 1916 to Bernhard and Emma (Schultz) Mertes, the youngest of sixteen children. On August 29, 1935, he joined the U.S. Army, served with "K" Company, 2nd Inf. at Fort Brady, MI until August 29, 1938. About a week later on September 8, 1938, he enlisted in the U.S. Marines. Training locations were San Diego, CA; Cavite, Philippines; Shanghai, China with "E" Company, 2nd Battalion, 4th Marines.

After spending 14 months in China (where baseball became a part of his life) he was sent back to Quantico, VA. In March of 1943 he was

sent to the South Pacific area and participated in the landing on Bougainville and was wounded on Nov. 24, 1943 (3d Bn. 3d Marines).

He received a Purple Heart and Gold Star for wounds received in action in the Asiatic Pacific area on July 22, 1944 (Guam and Okinawa landings). After 17 months overseas, he returned to California Oakland Hospital. He was discharged December 2, 1945.

He joined the West Chicago Police Department in 1946 and was Police Chief until 1951 when he joined the DuPage County Sheriff's Department. He spent about 30 years in police work and retired in 1982.

Herb and his wife Betty were married in Washington, D.C. on March 3, 1943 just before he was shipped overseas. They had three sons, two daughters, and eight grandchildren.

Herb loved all sports. Besides baseball, he played on the Marines football team while in Quantico... then there was hunting, fishing, golf, billiards and swimming. Plus, there was his love for cooking and playing cards and lots of family get-to-gethers.

MIKE D. "IRON MIKE" MERVOSH, born June 19, 1923, in Pittsburgh, Pennsylvania. Graduated from South High School, Pittsburgh, in 1942, and Mira Costa College, Oceanside, 43 years later.

Having served in combat in every enlisted rank, with Infantry units from Private to Sergeant Major, he began his military career by en-

listing in the Marine Corps in September 1942.

Following recruit training at Parris Island, South Carolina, and Infantry training at New River, North Carolina, he was one of the first Marines activated in the forming of the 4th Marine Division at Camp Pendleton, California. It was the only Division that left the States and went directly into combat in World War II and the first to land on Japanese mandated islands. While with the 4th, participated in battles of Roi-Namur, Marshall Islands, Saipan, Tinian, and Iwo Jima.

Between battles, while afloat and located on the island of Maui, he won the Division middle Weight Boxing Championship; forced to retire because of wounds received in Saipan and Iwo Jima. Boxing record stood at 32 wins (18 KO's) and 4 losses.

His World War II military decorations include two Purple Hearts and the Navy Commendation Medal for heroic actions on Iwo Jima. Remained with the 4th until its deactivation after World War II at Camp Pendleton, California. Upon his retirement, he was last enlisted member of the 4t to leave its ranks.

While in Korea with the 1st Marine Division, Sergeant Major Mervosh was awarded the Bronze Star and his second Navy Commendation Medal for heroic actions while serving with "G" Company, 3d Battalion, 5th Marines.

After two tours in Vietnam with th 1st Marine Division, he was awarded his third Navy Commendation Medal and third Purple Heart.

Between wars he served in five different Marine Divisions, making countless operations and deployments in the Atlantic, Pacific, Caribbean, and Mediterranean. He served with the 3d Battalion, 9th Marines, 3d Marine Division, 1971-1972.

Formal schools included Infantry Weapons, New River, North Carolina; First Sergeant's Course, Parris Island, South Carolina; Recruiters and Drill Instructors School, Parris Island South Carolina (twice). He also had two tours of recruiting duty and two tours on the drill field.

During his 19-1/2 years as a Sergeant Major, he served as a battalion, regimental, brigade, station, base, and division Sergeant Major. His final assignment was as the Fleet Marine Force, Pacific Sergeant Major, 1971-1977, the largest field command in the Marine Corps. His date of rank of February 14, 1958, as Sergeant Major made him the most senior enlisted man in all the Armed Forces when he retired on September 1, 1977, at Perl Harbor, Hawaii, after 35 years of faithful service.

Sergeant Major Mervosh's personal decorations span three wars – World War II, Korea Vietnam – and include 11 personal combat awards with 13 battle stars, 10 unit citations, and numerous other campaign and service awards.

Sergeant Major Mervosh an his wife Margaret reside in Oceanside, California.

JOSEPH G. MIHALEK, born October 20, 1935, in Palmerton, Pennsylvania. Enlisted in te USMC on June 16, 1953. Training, summer of 1953, Parris Island, South Carolina, Platoon 181. Served with the 2nd Marine Division. Engineer School Battalion, Court House Bay, Camp Lejeune, North Carolina; 1st Marine Division, Camp Pendleton, California; "A" Company, Engineers, 3d Marine Division, Japan; HQ 2nd Battalion, 7th Marines, 1st Marine Division, Camp Pendleton, California.

Military awards include th National Defense Service Medal, Korean Service Medal, United Nations Service Medal, Good Conduct Medal. Discharged on June 15, 1956, in the rank of Sergeant.

Memorable experiences: Boot camp, different places I would never have had a opportunity to see.

Owned my own real estate and appraisal company for 38 years. Now enjoying my retirement with my grandchildren, fishing, and traveling.

DONALD J. MILLS, PFC, born November 16, 1920, in Great Falls, Montana. Joined the U.S. Marine Corps on July 7, 1942. Trained in San Diego; Camp Elliot; Auckland, New Zealand; and Guadalcanal. Served with the 3d Signal Company, 3d Marine Division. Landed D-Day on Bougainville and Guam. Held in reserve for Iwo Jima. Wounded at Bougainville.

Returned home on August 5, 1945, my first furlough, and married my high school sweet-

heart Jean Durkee on August 18, 1945. Then the Jap war ended. Drove to Washington, DC, bought a 5¢ paper; found an apartment and Jean found a job (good 5¢ worth). Discharged on October 2, 1945, from 8th & I Street, Headquarters for Marine Corps.

On October 10, 1945, started climbing poles for Northwestern Bell Telephone Company. Ended up 37-plus years later in Engineering; retired in 1982. Raised three sons and a daughter. Now enjoying seven grandchildren. We've been blessed with a good life. Semper Fi.

WILLIAM A. MOORE, born January 29, 1930, in Swissvale, Pennsylvania. Joined the USMC on February 25, 1949, with twin brother Jim and completed boot camp in Platoon 24. On active duty with the Corps for 19 years, 7 months. Served as Personnel Officer with the 11th Engineer Battalion and as Adjutant/Personnel Officer, Headquarters Battalion, 3d Marine Division, in Vietnam, from November 1966 to November 1977. Served in the 1st Armored Amphibian Tank Battalion, FMFPac in Korea from September to November 1950 and December 1951. Commissioned 2nd Lieutenant in May 1966. Retired as 1st Lieutenant, March 1979.

Units served with include: 2nd Tank Battalion; 1st Armored Amphibian Tank Battalion; I&I Staff, Pittsburgh, Pennsylvania; Officer Procurement Office, Pittsburgh, Pennsylvania; VMA-114, H&S

Company, MAG-24, VMA-533, Med cruise; MABS-24; *USS Boxer* LPH-4 (Marine detachment); FMFLant; Headquarters Marine Corps; VMA-121, 13th Marines, 11th Engineer Battalion, HQ 3d Marine Division; MC Supply Center, Barstow.

Military awards include the Navy Achievement Medal with "V" for Vietnam service, Ko-

rean Service Medal with two Stars, Vietnam Service Medal with two Stars, Good Conduct Medal with four Stars, and Presidential Unit Citation with two Stars. Retired from the Corps on September 30, 1968.

Completed four-year apprenticeship in machinery repair, U.S. Navy Aviation Depot, San Diego, 1972. Worked in civil service until retirement in December 1988. Worked part-time for six years between then and now; now fully retired. Married hometown girl JoAnn on November 13, 1954. We have four sons: Bill Jr., Tom, Mark, and Jeff. Recently moved to new home in Sun City, California.

HARRY J. MORSE, born February 12, 1926, in Copenhagen, New York. Joined the Marine Corps on May 23, 1942, at the age of 16. Sworn in on the stage of the Hippodrome Theater in Baltimore, Maryland. The movie playing that day was *The Halls of Montezuma*.

Boot camp at Parris Island, then to New River, North Carolina, where the 3d Regiment

was being formed (B-13). Shipped out from San Diego to American Samoa. Made PFC. Eight months later went to Auckland, New Zealand. Joined 3d Division. Guadalcanal, Efate in New Hebrides, landing on Bougainville on November 1, 1943, as a Machine Gunner in the first wave at Cape Torokina. Became Squad Leader at Piva Forks (D/1/3) after losing a number of our Marines in that engagement. The 3d Regiment was on the front lines for 52 consecutive days and was awarded the Navy Unit Commendation. Back to Guadalcanal Hospital with filariasis. Sent to hospital in Noumea, New Caledonia, then to hospital in Oakland, California, February 11, 1944. Next day, I turned 18, ready for the draft. Duty in the U.S. until 1948.

Sent on Mediterranean cruise, returning in 1949. Discharged on June 17, 1949, in North Carolina.

Stopped in Baltimore, Maryland. Married Anna Raab. Bought a farm in Copenhagen, New York. Raised three children: Margaret, Harry Jr., and Victoria. Retired from farming and construction. Now spending winters in the Florida sun.

JAMES A. MUNDELL, born October 16, 1921, in Amarillo, Texas. Joined the Marine Corps on December 16, 1941, in Houston, Texas.

After attending Life Magazine's Photographic School, he served as a combat photographer in the Pacific Theater of Operation until the end of the war.

In addition to achieving the rank of Technical Sergeant and rifle marksman, he also re-

ceived a Purple Heart in Iwo Jima, the Bronze Star in Guam, and a special commendation from Brigadier General Robert Denig, Director of the Division of Public Information, USMC, for his photographic work.

He served in the Marine Reserve until 1950, and enjoyed a long career in television news, where he was considered a pioneer, working for all three major networks.

He retired in 1995, when he and his wife Susie moved to Lampasas, Texas. He died in July 1997. He is survived by his wife, two daughters, and a grandson T.J.

JIMMY DON MURPHY, born December 3, 1948, in McKinney, Texas. Raised in Hughes Springs, Texas. Joined the USMC, March 1968. MCRD San Diego, California, Platoon 162; ITR, BITS, and Staging, then to Vietnam, August 1968.

Was with Mike Company 3/3, 3d Marine Division, MOS 0331 Machine Gunner. Was in 2nd

Platoon Guns. Was on the Search and Destroy Mission, March 24, 1969, when Ronald L. Coker was awarded the Medal of Honor. I extended my tour in Vietnam in 1969, went home for a special 30-day leave, came back, Mike Company 3/3 was gone to Hawaii. Joined Mike Company 3/4, 3d Marine Division, stayed with them until we pulled out of Nam and sent to Okinawa.

Military awards include the Naval Unit Commendation, Meritorious Unit Citation, Presidential Unit Citation, National Defense Service Medal, Good Conduct Medal, Combat Action Ribbon, Vietnam Service Ribbon, and Republic of Vietnam Campaign Medal. Reached the rank of Sergeant. Discharged in 1976.

Returned to Hughes Springs, Texas. Worked for the City as a utility superintendent and police officer. Today I sell used construction equipment and am also a Texas Constable. I will never forget the people that I was with in the 3d Marine Division, for they were the BEST.

FRANKIE X. NOE, born August 19, 1948. Training at Parris Island, South Carolina, Platoon 289, June 1967 to August 1967.

Was in Vietnam from November 1967 to December 1968; second tour from January 1969

to July 1969. Served with "C" Company, 11th Engineer Battalion. Discharged on April 16, 1970, at the Marine Barracks, Quonset Point, Rhode Island, in the rank of Corporal.

Have been with the Stoughton (Massachusetts) Fire Department for 21 years and am still on the job. Two children: Tara, age 26, and Vincent, age 21, who is in the USMC. Living in Stoughton, Massachusetts. E-mail address is as follows: fxncat@aol.com

HARRY J. O'DELL, born April 2, 1940, in Rockwood, Tennessee. Joined the USMC on March 6, 1966. Training locations: boot camp, MCRD San Diego, California; Camp Pendleton, California; Camp Lejeune, North Carolina.

Joined Kilo Company, 3/9, RVN, on November 7, 1966. Wounded on April 30, 1967, Hill

881S, RVN. Spent 66 days on the *USS Repose*. Returned to Kilo Company and was wounded a second time on July 30, 1967, at Gio Linh, RVN. Medi-vac to *USS Sanctuary*, then to Great Lakes Naval Hospital, Illinois.

Duty stations while in RVN include: An Hoa, Ba Long Valley (old French fort), Cam Lo,

Camp Carroll, Dong Ha, Khe Sanh, Hills 861 and 881S, Gio Linh. Discharged on June 20, 1968, in the rank of Corporal.

Military awards include the Purple Heart with Gold Star, National Defense Medal, Vietnam Campaign Medal, Vietnam Service Medal with Bronze Star, Good Conduct Medal, Republic of Vietnam Gallantry Cross with Palm, Presidential Unit Citation, Combat Action Ribbon, FMF Ribbon, Overseas Service Ribbon, six commemorative Medals, and expert rifle badge.

Married my wife Beverly and raised three children. Now a retired mason, I enjoy fishing and my grandchildren. Resides at 16949 Lovers Lane, Three Rivers, MI 49093.

LOREN CARL OTTO was born September 4, 1943 on the family farm in Belle Plaine, Minnesota. Joined USMC upon graduation from high school at 17 years old. Basic training at San Diego was followed by Artillery Surveyors School at Camp Pendleton, CA.

After six months with the 11th Marines at Camp Pendleton, transferred to the 12th Marines

on Okinawa, Japan. Served with HQ-2-12 as an Artillery Surveyman and traveled throughout the Far East on field exercises as the Corps was preparing for action in Viet Nam. Following an enjoyable and successful initial tour of duty of thirteen months, extended another nine months to finish out enlistment before return to CONUS.

Retirement to Oregon has found new opportunities at sole proprietorship. Also the opportunity to become active in the local detachment of the Marine Corps League and the local Toys-For-Tots program.

ROBERT M. PALMER, born December 8, 1924, in Anoka, Minnesota. Joined the USMC on September 9, 1942. Boot camp at Parris Island, South Carolina. Assigned to the 19th Marines in October 1942, New River, North Carolina. Participated in campaigns at Guadalcanal, Bougainville, Vela Vela, Munda, Guam, and Iwo Jim during World War II. Also served in Korea in 1950 and in Korea in 1963.

Duty assignment include: Supply & Plumbing instructor, Court House Bay, North Caro-

lina; Asset Maintenance Officer, Camp Lejeune, North Carolina; Maintenance Officer, Camp Smith, Hawaii; Special Operations Officer, 3d Force Service Regiment, Okinawa.

Retired from the USMC as a Chief Warrant Officer-3 in 1968 after 24 years of service.

Military awards include the Purple Heart, Presidential Unit Citation, American Campaign Medal, Asiatic-Pacific Campaign Medal with four Stars, Good Conduct Medal, World War II Victory Medal, National Defense Service Medal, Korea Service Medal, and Vietnam Service Medal.

Also retired from Aetna Life & Casualty Insurance Company as a Service Engineer after 17 years of service. Presently enjoying retirement in Florida.

CHRIS M. PANGALOS was born February 24, 1963 in Kingston, NY. Joined the USMC along with his younger brother, Steve, on June 5, 1995 and they served together in every unit from boot camp until being honorably discharged on June 4, 1999.

Training locations include Parris Island, SC; Camp Geiger, NC; MCB Kaneohe Bay, HI;

MCB Camp Lejeune, NC; Okinawa, Korea, Japan, Greece, Puerto Rico, Italy, Spain, Tunisia, Albania and France.

Awards include National Defense Service Medal, Sea Service Deployment Ribbon (w/star), Meritorious Unit Commendation (w/star), Armed Forces Service Medal, Armed Forces Expeditionary Medal, NATO Medal, Navy/Marine Corps Achievement Medal.

Chris served as a Machine Gun Squad Leader with Heavy Guns, Weapons Co., 1/3 before being transferred to Weapons Platoon, Fox Co., 2/2 where he served as the Machine Gun Section Leader of the Battalion's Helicopter Assault Company. Chris now owns a Disc Jockey Entertainment Company (Rolling Thunder Productions) and also works as a Professional Sales Representative for the pharmaceutical firm, Merck & Co., Inc.

STEVE PANGALOS was born November 16, 1967 in Mt. Clemmons, MI. Joined USMC along with his older brother Chris on June 5, 1995 and they served together in every unit from boot camp until being honorably discharged together on June 4, 1999.

Training locations include Parris Island, SC; Camp Geiger, NC; MCB Kaneohe Bay, III; MCB Camp Lejeune, NC; Okinawa, Japan, Greece, Puerto Rico, Italy, Spain and Tunisia.

Awards include National Defense Service Medal, Sea Service Deployment Ribbon (w/star),

Meritorious Unit Commendation, Good Conduct Medal.

Steve served as a Mortar Man with 81's, Weapons Co., 1/3 before being transferred to Weapons

Co., 2/2 where he served as the Battalion's FO (Forward Observer) for 81mm Mortars.

Steve now works (along with his brother Chris) as a Professional Sales Representative for the top pharmaceutical firm in the world, Merck & Co., Inc.

SALVATORE JOHN PARISANO was born July 20, 1924 in Philadelphia, PA. He joined the USMC on May 12, 1943. He served in the 3d Joint Assault Signal Company, Field Signal Battalion, and later, the Headquarters Battalion.

In two major campaigns, Sal disembarked under enemy gunfire at Guam on July 21, 1944

and fought there until August 10. He also disembarked under enemy gunfire at Iwo Jima on February 23, 1945 and fought there until March 16. Sal was discharged at Great Lakes, IL at the rank of Corporal on January 1, 1946.

He returned to Philadelphia and married Rita Del Rossi on May 29, 1954. They moved to Lindenwold, NJ where their five children were born: Gay, Janice, Nancy, Michael and Lisa. Sal passed away on December 4, 1978 and is buried in Eglington Military Cemetery in Clarksboro, NJ. His daughter, Gay Raab, is a Third Marine Division Association member.

JOHN A. PETERKOVICH was born February 1, 1924 in Lyons, Illinois. He enlisted in the USMC March 1, 1943. He underwent basic training at MCRD San Diego, CA with duty at Bremerton and Oak Harbor Navy Base in the state of Washington.

He participated in campaigns Guam and Iwo Jima and was wounded in the Guam Campaign action. He was discharged December 24, 1945 from Great Lakes NTS with corporal rank.

He returned to Cicero, IL and in September of 1946, he married Esther Kuklik. Their son, John, was born March 8, 1950.

Peterkovich was employed as a mechanical

design engineer and retired from Genisco Tech. Corp. after 25 years of service.

He was past commander of V.F.W. Post 1485 and past president of the So. CA Chapter of the Third Marine Division.

BURNETT POTASKI enlisted in the Marines May of 1943 and presently resides in Linwood, Massachusetts ; mailing address is P.O. Box 752, 01525-0752. The following is his account of Iwo Jima.

"My 21st birthday is a day I'll never forget. It was the day I landed on Iwo Jima- my first battle.

We encountered two and a half hours of ar-

tillery and mortor barrage. We finally reached the edge of the second air strip. After about seventy-five rounds, the machine gun received a direct hit and killed the number one and two gunners.

The concussion blew me over on my back and I lost my helmet. I soon found out that I was one of the lucky ones when I found a piece of shrapnel the size of a silver dollar lodged in my trenching tool which I was carrying on my back.

Later that night I killed three Japs who were trying to get through my position. I gathered papers and maps from them which I turned in to HQ. I later found out what they learned from the papers and maps: the attack that had been planned by the 21st Reg. was postponed for a period of time. I believe they must have been important. I never heard anything.

I saw two Japs run into a bunker; I ran up to it and threw in two grenades. Cushman's Pocket was a mess. We were surrounded by Japs. Bombing and artillery could not open it up. We called for a tank; thank God one came and it opened an area for us so we could move up. I killed one with my KA-BAR, wounded the other one, but he escaped.

In the final charge by the Japs, we killed them all with machine gun fire, BAR and rifle fire. That last charge was the end of the hostilities.

After the island was securer, Sax and I would go on daily patrols. On the third day, we located a Jap cave. We entered and went down into it about fifty feet; we heard some voices and left in a hurry.

We returned with a Jap prisoner and an interpreter. It resulted in the surrender of seventeen Japs."

WILLIAM A. PUMMILL was born July 30, 1921 in Crocker, Missouri. Joined the USMC on the 28th day of August 1942. Basic training and communication school at San Diego, California.

Joined Regimental Weapons Company,

Ninth Marines at Camp Pendleton, California in November 1942. On December 24, 1942 Regimental Colors received from M. Gen. Barrett C.G. 3d Marine Division.

Sailed for New Zealand on January 23, 1943. Left Auckland for Guadalcanal June 29, 1943. Made landing at Cape Torokina, Bougainville November 1, 1943. Returned to Guadalcanal December 30, 1943. Embarked for Guam June 2, 1944. The Guam invasion was delayed. Invaded Guam July 21, 1944 and on August 10, 1944 Guam was declared secure. On February 17, 1945 embarked for Iwo Jima. Debarked Iwo Jima February 24, 1945. Iwo Jima declared secure March 14, 1945. Returned to Guam then to USA on rotation in April, 1945. Transferred to USMCAS, Cherry Point, North Carolina and was honorably discharged October 18, 1945 having achieved rank of corporal.

In 1982, I retired from American Airlines and am presently enjoying playing golf and traveling with my wife Helen.

VERNON D. RANDALL born June 25,1944 at Camp Verde, AZ. Joined USMC March 28, 1963. MCRD San Diego and Field Wire School, Camp Horno. Units served with: Communications Platoon, H&S Co. 2/1, 3/3, 1/9, Hdqtrs Co. 10th, Comm. Sch. Bn. Camp Pendleton, 313, and 3/27.

Landed in Chu Lai May 1965 with 3/3; participated in Operation Starlite, campaigns in

Danang with 1/9 returned home in February 1966. Rejoined 3/3 in August 1967 at Dong Ha. Participated in operations at the Rockpile, Dong Ha Mt., Gio Linh, A-3, Cua Viet River, and Cam Lo. Promoted to Sergeant E-5 while along the delta of the Cua Viet river in June 1968 by Bn XO. Had the honor of serving under Lt. Col. Jim Marsh and Sergeant Major Neal King. Returned home September 1968. Discharged March 1, 1969.

Awards include National Defense Medal, Viet Nam Service Medal, Viet Nam Campaign Medal, Presidential Unit Citation, and Viet Nam Cross of Gallantry- w/bronze star.

Returned to Clarkdale, AZ March, 1969

married and attended Northern Arizona University. B.S. History, MEd Educational Leadership. One son, Raymond.

Taught high school in Alaska and Arizona. Faculty Advisor at Prescott College. Was an educator for twenty years. Now an Inspector for the Cliff Castle Casino at CampVerde, AZ. Enjoy fishing, hunting, camping, hiking, photography, and my granddaughter.

R. JOHN RAPSYS, born in 1936 in Kaunas, Lithuania. Hometown is Chicago, Illinois. MCRD San Diego, January 1954. Corporal, S-2, 9th Marines, Camp Sakai, Osaka, Japan, 1954. Camp Napunja, Okinawa, 1955. Marine Barracks, NAS Port Lyautey, French Morocco, 1956- 1957, where he made Sergeant.

Served in the U.S. Navy, 1959-1963, aboard

carrier *USS Independence* (CVA-62); Atlantic, Mediterranean, and Caribbean (Bay of Pigs and Cuban blockade during missile crisis).

Military awards include: USMC Good Conduct Medal, Navy Expeditionary Medal, Armed Forces Expeditionary Medal, two National Defense Service Medals, Korean Service Medal, and United Nations Service Medal.

Graduated from Northwestern University under Korean GI Bill. Worked as ad agency copywriter and copy chief. Later as press officer, writer-editor, and chief speech writer for U.S. EPA in Chicago. Retired in 1999 after 29 years total Federal service.

Avid traveler and photographer; visited 106 countries worldwide. Besides English, fluent in Lithuanian and German. Also speaks French and Spanish. Was married to the late Vida Dudenas for 33 years. Children: Ramona, Anthony, and Aldis. Two grandchildren.

Member VFW, American Legion, 3d Marine Division Association, USS Independence Association, and Port Lyautey Alumni Association.

JACK J. RASMUSSEN, born August 19, 1923, in Monticello, Utah. Served in the USMC from January 4, 1942, to January 9, 1946. Training locations included boot camp, MCB San Diego, Camp Pendleton, and South Pacific with 3-L-9 as a Rifleman and Rifle Team Leader until May 26, 1945; as a Drill Instructor, MCB San Diego until honorable discharge. Campaigns included Bougainville, Guam, and Iwo Jima.

Military awards include Purple Heart presented by Admiral C.W. Nimitz, Letter of Commendation presented by General G.B. Erskine, and Asiatic-Pacific Campaign Medal with four Stars.

Enrolled at Snow College, Ephraim, Utah, and

Utah State University, Logan, Utah, obtaining a B.S. degree in Soil Science. Married my sweetheart LaRee Christensen on September 1, 1948; still my sweetheart. Employed by Soil Conservation Service, USDA, as Soil Scientist. A change from digging foxholes as a Marine to digging soil pits for analysis and scientific study. Retired from SCS in 1982 as Washington State Soil Scientist and started private consulting. We enjoy being active skiing, jogging, mushrooming, travel, and being an active former Marine (MCL).

JEFFREY C. REDLICK, born October 11, 1948, in San Mateo, California. Joined the USMC on December 1, 1965. Training locations included MCRD San Diego; Camp Pendleton, California; Camp Lejeune, North Carolina. Served with the 13th Engineers Battalion, 5th Marine Division; 1st Searchlight Battery, 3d Marine Division; 3d Engineer Battalion, 3d Marine Division; 5th Engineer Battalion, 5th Marine Division; Marine Air Control Squadron-3.

Memorable experiences: When in the 1st

Searchlight Battery, we were told that this was the first unit of Xenon, infrared, Mule mounted searchlights in the history of the Marine Corps. We left for Vietnam via the *USS Paul Revere* on May 30, 1967, from San Diego, California; we arrived in Danang, Vietnam, on June 27, 1967. We were deployed in the I Corps area of Vietnam. I was the first Marine to drive one of our new searchlights in the Vietnam war.

Military awards include the National Defense Service Medal, Vietnam Service Medal, Vietnam Campaign Medal with device, Presidential Unit Citation, Good Conduct Medal, Combat Action Ribbon, Meritorious Unit Commendation Ribbon, Republic of Vietnam Meritorious Unit Citation Gallantry Cross Medal, Republic of Vietnam Meritorious Unit Citation Civil Actions Medal, and Marine Corps Marksman Rifle Badge. Discharged on September 2, 1969, in the rank of E-3.

Living in Northern California with my wife and daughter. Employed at Cisco Systems, Inc. as a Support Manager for the Intel Corporation worldwide.

DONALD R. REICHART, born November 18, 1952, in Milwaukee, Wisconsin. Joined the Marine Corps in September 1970. Training at MCRD, San Diego; further training at Camp Pendleton as O311. Short stint with the 5th Marines, also at Camp Pendleton. TAD. to MPs, El Toro Air Station, then to the 3d Marine Division at Okinawa with FMF 7th Fleet.

Went to Vietnam, South China Sea, for six months. Was called to take action during Easter offensive 1972, but after further recon lost chance to see action. Ended up taking aboard ARVN troops and sending them in with our help. Last duty at Edson Range as PMI.

Military awards include the Vietnam Service Medal with one Star and Good Conduct Medal; Meritorious Sergeant while with the 3d Marine Division FMF. Discharged on September 22, 1973, in the rank of Sergeant.

Presently self-employed as electronic service consultant in Milwaukee, Wisconsin. Divorced with four children: Michael, Crystal, Tina, and Joe.

DENNIS L. RICHARDSON was born September 20, 1944 Aurora, IL. He enlisted in the USMC June 21, 1965. Training: MCRD, San Diego; Hawk Missile School Huntsville, AL; OCS/TBS Quantico, VA.

3d Mar Div Vietnam, October, 1967. PltCmdr A/3d Anti-tanks (Ontos) at Khe Sahn,ConThien , operations on Rt. 9.

June, 1968, B/l/3, Platoon Commander, XO, CO.; a t Leatherneck Square, Dong Ha, Rockpile, Camp Carrol, Mutter's Ridge (@DMZ).

Returned Camp Pendleton, November, 1968, CO I/3/27 and L/3/28. 1970, USMCR, 3d ANGLICO, Long Beach, CA. Discharged Captain, May 31,1977.

Awards include Bronze Star ("V"), Purple Heart, Navy Achievement Medal ("V"), Combat Action Ribbon, PUC, NUC, MUC, Organized Reserve Medal, National Defense Medal, RVN Service Medal (5 stars), Vietnamese Cross of Gallantry , RVN PUC, RVN Campaign Medal, Naval Parachutist wings, Expert Rifle and Pistol Badges.

Married 1969 to Susan, a nurse, and have 3 sons in Orange CA. He's a lumber broker.

Interests include woodworking, reading, gun collecting, Cowboy Action Shooting.

LAWRENCE H. ROANE, JR., born December 5, 1933, in Danville, Virginia. Graduated from R.J. Reynolds High School, Winston-Salem, North Carolina, and 5th Recruit Training Battalion, PISC. Assigned as a Field Radio Operator and served with Shore Fire Control Party, 3d Battalion, 6th Marines, and as Team Chief, Tactical Air Control Party, 1st Battalion, 1st Marines, in Korea and Camp Pendleton, California. Was honorably discharged a Permanent Sergeant in 1956. Received a letter of Exemplary Service from Lt. Colonel L.N. Holdzkom, CO 1st Battalion, 1st Marines.

From 1956-1960, attended North Carolina State College of Agriculture and Engineering in Raleigh, North Carolina. At the invitation of CMC, returned on extended active duty in 1961 as a Sergeant serving with Mortar Battery and "H" Battery, 3d Battalion, 10th Marines, as Comm Chief and supported 2nd Battalion, 6th Marines, during the Cuban crisis, 1962.

From 1963-1964 served with Radio Platoon, 1st Communications Company (Provisional), HQBN 3d Marine Division, Camp Hauge, Okinawa. January 2, 1964 to July 3, 1964, was the senior member of a five-man team of communicators in Vietnam operating, and maintaining a Naval High Frequency Contingency long-range communications network supporting Marine Task Element 79.3.36 during operation "Shoefly." In August 1964 reported to Parris Island, South Carolina, and served at Weapons Training battalion as a Primary Marksmanship Instructor and Junior/Senior Drill Instructor at "C" Company, 1st Recruit Training Battalion. Received a meritorious mast from Lt. Colonel R.J. Perrish, CO 1st Recruit Training Battalion.

In May 1967, reported to Camp Pendleton, California, and took a company through staging in preparation for deployment to Vietnam. Served in Vietnam from July 1967 to February 1969 as Platoon Sergeant, Radio Platoon Communications Company, 5th Communications Battalion; Comm Chief, 1st Amphibian Tractor Battalion (Cau Viet), and 1st Battalion, 3d Marines. Last operation "Taylor Common." For this period of service in RVN was awarded the Naval Commendation with "V" Combat Action Ribbon and Republic of Vietnam Gallantry Cross with Silver Star. Spent a short tour of Inspector/Instructor duty with the 7th 105 Howit-

zer Battery, Waterloo, Iowa, as Comm Chief from May 1969 to November 1969. Took another company through staging at Camp Pendleton and reported to the 3d Reconnaissance Battalion in January 1970. During May-August 1970 was the 3d Marine Division Representative on Joint Service Duty with the U.S. Army Strategic Communications Command, Okinawa, until suddenly reassigned to the 3d Engineer Battalion at Camp Schwab. A serious accident had occurred in the NTA where the engineers were building up the training facilities, and there were not reliable communications between the construction site and Battalion. HQ solved this problem and department Okinawa for a third tour in Vietnam in November 1970. Served with MAG-11 as Radio Chief and Airborne Radio Operator, MASS 3, as Comm Chief for operation Dewey Canyon II, Lam Son 719.

During three tours in RVN received two Presidential Unit Citations, five Naval Unit Commendations, five Meritorious Unit Commendations, and Vietnam Service Medal with one Silver and two Bronze Stars. As units returned to CONUS in June 1971, rejoined the 3d Reconnaissance Battalion at Ona Point, Okinawa. Participated in numerous operations, including one involving the *USS Greyback* out of Subic. In August 1972, reported to Parris Island, challenged DI School, and went to work as a Senior DI at "B" Company, 1st Recruit Training Battalion. Other assignments were: Chief Drill Instructor, Special Training Branch; Operations Chief, RTR; Sergeant Major, Weapons Training Battalion, 1st Recruit Training Battalion; and Depot Communications Chief. May 1976 to February 1979, served on Inspector/Instructor duty with HQ 2nd Battalion, 23d Marines, in Encino, California, as Communications Chief and Maintenance Management Officer. Awarded a Certificate of Commendation from Major General Marc A. Moore, CG 4th Marine Division. March 1979 to march 1980, served in Okinawa with Communications Squadron 18, 1st MAW, as Operations Chief, Facilities Controller, Education/Training Officer. During April to December 1980, served in Communications/Electronics Headquarters, 3d MAW, El Toro, California, as Communications Chief. Transferred to the Fleet Reserve as a Master Gunnery Sergeant with 22 years of active service. Awarded a Certificate of Commendation from Major General L.J. LeBlanc, Jr. CG 3d MAW.

Earned an Associate of Science degree from Moorpark College and a Bachelor of Science degree from California State University, Northridge. Employed by US Department of Agriculture Forest Service, Kaniksu National Forest, Idaho, and Angeles and Los Padres National Forest in California, and retried from the U.S. Postal Service. Relocated to Beaufort, South Carolina, 1994, and is a life member of the 1st, 2nd, and 3d Marine Division Associations; South Carolina Chapter, 1st Marine Division Association; Parris Island Chapter, Drill Instructor Association; Marine Corps Association; BPOE; and Wolf Pack Club.

MICHAEL P. RODRIGUEZ Michael P. Rodriguez was born and raised in Kansas City, Missouri. He joined the U.S. Marine Corps on October 11, 1967 and left for boot camp on October 31. He began his training with recruit platoon 2208, MCRD, San Diego, CA. After boot training in January 1968, he was assigned to Foxtrot Company, 2nd ITR and in February 1968 to Unit 4668, BITS, 2nd ITR, both at Camp Pendleton, CA for infantry training as a rifleman. As a member of Unit 4195, 4th Replacement Company, Staging Battalion, he was flown to Vietnam on May 10, 1968.

In Vietnam he was assigned to Bravo Company, 1st Battalion, 3d Marine Regiment, 3d Marine Division located at Quang Tri in Quang Tri Province.

He participated in operations in the Gio Linh, Cua Viet and Jones Creek areas; the building of the McNamara Line on the Trace; Leatherneck Square; Mutter's Ridge and Hill 461 in Quang Tri Province in 1968. He operated from bases at Gio Linh, Cua Viet, Dong Ha, Camp Carroll, Rockpile and LZ Stud.

In December 1968, the 1/3 and 3/3 Battalions were attached to the 1st Marine Division for operation Taylor Common in Quang Nam Province with the 5th Marine Regiment to form Task Force Yankee. The 1/3 Battalion's forward base was located at An Hoa and assaulted its mountainous triple canopied jungle objective southwest of An Hoa. From December 1968 to mid-February 1969, 1/3's part of the operation continued. During this time he was wounded on January 21, 1969 and medevaced to Da Nang and rejoined Bravo 1/3 in February. Bravo 1/3 and the rest of the 3d Marines returned to Quang Tri Province in mid-February, 1969 and rejoined the 3d Marine Division. In March 1969 from Vandergrift Combat Base (formerly LZ Stud), he participated in operation Maine Crag southwest of Khe Sahn to the Loas border. His last operation in the Vietnam War was at Virginia Ridge below central DMZ in May, 1969. While a member of Bravo 1/3, he served as a rifleman in the 3d platoon and as a squad leader of the 1st platoon and 3d platoon 'guns' respectively (M-60 machine guns). He left Vietnam on June 3, 1969 upon completion of his tour of duty.

From June to August, 1969, he was assigned to H & S Company, S-1 Section, 2nd ITR, Camp Pendleton in the adjutant locator section as a clerk in updating assignments of the Corps personnel throughout the world.

In August, 1969, he transferred to Security Company, Marine Barracks, Naval Station, Treasure Island, San Francisco, CA where he served as Brig Guard until he was honorably discharged on January 30, 1970 as a Corporal.

He returned to Kansas City, Missouri and joined the Kansas City, Missouri Police Department in July, 1971. He served as a Police Officer until he retired on December 7, 1996 with 25 1/2 years of service.

He married the girl from across the street, Sherry Fifer. They have a son, Mark, and a daughter, Rebecca.

BILLY R. ROHNER was born January 14, 1923 in Baker Ore. He joined the USMC on November 12, 1940. Training locations include San Diego Recruit Depot, Camp Elliot, CA. Served with D Battery 2nd Battalion 10th Marines at Camp Elliot, CA, 1941. Radio School San Diego 1941. To 3d MAR DIV September of 1942. Served with H&S-4-12th Marines September 12, 1942 to May of 1945, as radio operator Camp Dunlap, Niland, CA.

Arrived Whangarei, New Zealand on March 11, 1943. To Guadalcanal June 1943. Participated in invasion of Bougainville November – December of 1943. Also consolidation of nothern Solomon I.S December of 1943 – January of 1944. Assault and capture of Guam M.I. July and August of 1944. Capture of Iwo Jima February – March of 1945 (36 days). Arrived back in states June of 1945. Discharged at Philadelphia, PA December 5, 1945 as PFC.

Returned to Stockton, CA. Retired after 38 years with Southern Pacific Railroad. Met my wife, Betsey Ross, there in 1946. Have 3 sons and one daughter, 9 grandchildren and one greatgrandson. Two sons served in U.S. Navy, two grandsons served in USMC. Married 54 years.

WALTER R. ROOSE, JR., Sgt, USMC, born December 17, 1921 Hartford, CT. Enlisted May 6, 1942, Springfield, MA. Recruit training, Parris Island, SC; Radio School, Quantico, VA; tanker training, Camp Lejeune, NC; Camp Pendleton, CA; Warkworth, New Zealand; and Guadalcanal, British Solomon Islands.

Member B Co., 3d Tank Bn, 3d Marine Div, October 1942 – March 1945. Participated in the invasion of Bougainville, Solomon Islands, No-

vember - December 1943; assault and capture of Guam, July – August 1944; assault and capture of Iwo Jima, February – March 1945.

Wounded in action, March 10, 1945. Hospitalized at U.S. Naval Hospital, St Albans, Long Island, NY, 1945 – 1947. Awarded Purple Heart Medal. Honorably discharged as sergeant at Marine Barracks, U.S. Naval Base, Brooklyn, NY, April 6, 1947.

Retired from Sandia National Laboratories, Albuquerque, NM, after 25 years as Technical Information Specialist. Resides in Albuquerque with wife of 52 years, Virginia. Four sons, one daughter; seven grandchildren.

A memorable experience on Iwo Jima: On March 10, 1945, was radioman/loader in a Sherman tank, reconnoitering at the northern end of Iwo Jima. When we drove too close to a huge shell hole, that loose volcanic ash gave way and the tank slid sideways, halfway down into the crater, at about a 35 degree angle. It was not possible to drive the tank out, so radioed back to Command Post for a tank retriever.

Since our tank was helpless, and because of enemy activity in the area, I volunteered to take our Thompson submachine gun and get out to protect the tank, and the crew inside, against the possibility of a Japanese attack with either satchel charges or "Molotov cocktails." (Speaking of this years later, our tank driver, Larry Ward, told my wife that at one time he stuck his head out of the driver's hatch for a moment "and promptly got my hair parted!")

My being already out in the open in no-man's-land when the tank retriever showed up, its crew was happy to let me do the hooking and unhooking of the tow cables myself. Although working alone, I was covered by several riflemen of the 21st Marines in the vicinity. Small arms fire was constant. (When was it not, on Iwo?) Right after the retriever tank had sped away, a Japanese Nambu machine gunner got off a burst, one round of which caught me in the hip and dropped me to the ground.

Tank commander Jack Bush and gunner Ben Allenby promptly scrambled out of the turret and managed to swing me from the ground up onto our tank sponson. Then, risking their lives out in the open, held me there while Larry Ward sped our tank-as-ambulance back to our Command Post.

MICHAEL R. RYAN was born August 5, 1925 in St. Louis, MO. Joined USMC August 10, 1942. Training locations include San Diego, Camp Mathews, Camp Pendleton, New Zealand. Participated in Bougainville, Guam Cam-

paigns, rifleman and runner. Wounded in action late July 1944. Sent to hospital in Hawaii. Discharged August 10, 1946 from Camp LeJeune, NC.

Awards include Purple Heart, Presidential Unit Citation, American Campaign, Asiatic-Pacific, Good Conduct, Combat Action Ribbon, World War Victory Medal.

Returned to St. Louis, attended University of Missouri. Graduated Bachelor of Science degree. Married Margaret Gerhardt – son Michael, daughter Annmarie and four grandchildren. Retired Elder Mfg. Company after forty-one years of service. Employed as a salesman, regional salesmanager and vice president.

Now active in church work, zoo ambassador, science center, and enjoying retirement.

JEROME L. SAIDMAN was born in Baltimore, MD August 29, 1924. Moved to Washington, D.C. 1932. Joined the USMC November 20, 1942. After "Boots" trained at the Submarine Base New London, CT, Camp LeJeune, Camp Pendleton, and Guam. There he joined E-2-21 and later transferred to H&S Co. 21st.

Landed on Iwo Jima and was wounded Feb-

ruary 24th. Treated in hospitals at Guam, Seattle, Washington and Portsmouth, VA. Discharged October 3, 1945 as corporal.

Awards include Purple Heart, Presidential Unit Citation, WWII Victory Medal and Asiatic-Pacific Campaign Medal. Returned home and attended Georgetown University. Married Adele June 1947. Have 3 married children and 8 grandchildren.

Operated a chain of dry cleaning stores for 46 years. Did volunteering at a nursing home and local police department. Now retired and enjoying family.

W. G. SANDBURG, known variously, at various times, by various people as *Walter Gustave, Jr.* (baptismal pastor); *Wall* (parents, siblings and relatives); *White* (high school classmates); *Pumpkin* (teen-aged girlfriend); *Shitbird* (Marine Corps drill instructor); *Sand* (Marine Corps squadmates); *Sandi-san* (Naka-cho cho-sans); *Walt* (other acquaintances); *Whiteman* or *Whitelocks* (longtime buddies Armo, Sam and Schauss); and, most recently, *Grandpa* is born 5 June 1935 in Goodman, Marinette County, Wisconsin. He attends school in Peshtigo, Marinette County, Wisconsin.

Upon high school graduation in May 1953, he enlisted in the Marine Corps for a 4-year hitch and is ordered to report for training – "boot camp" – July 11, 1953 at MCRD (Marine Corps Recruit Depot, San Diego). There, he serves as a squad leader in Platoon 199, the honor platoon of the recruit training battalion series. Upon graduation he is Pfc. (Private First Class) Sandberg.

He is assigned to a "casual" company, Camp

Pendleton, California, from which he is ordered aboard a troop transport, the U.S.S. *General W. H. Gordon*, San Pedro, California, along with about 4500 others, destination unknown.

He is disembarked at Kobe, Honshu, Japan, December 24, 1953 and assigned to HQ Co, HQBn, HQ 3dMarDiv, Camp Gifu, Honshu, Japan. As a member of a supply unit, his duties consist mostly of manhandling bulky crates of sundry materials from pile-to-pile in a huge warehouse.

As a respite from this inexacting duty, he volunteers to attend the divisional ABC (Atomic, Biological and Chemical Warfare) school from which he graduates as an ABC specialist, MOS (Military Occupational Specialty) 5711 and becomes an instructor at the school.

During this time (1953-1955), he is awarded the Rifle Expert badge, National Defense Service Medal, Korean Service Medal and United Nations Medal.

In May 1955 he is accepted into the NROTC (Naval Reserve Officers Training Corps) and ordered to transfer from the 3dMarDiv to NAPS (United States Naval Academy Preparatory School) USNTC (United States Naval Training Center), Bainbridge, Maryland.

Upon graduation from NAPS, he is honorably discharged from the Marine Corps, August 17, 1955 at Marine Barracks, USNS (United States Naval Station), Annapolis, Maryland and immediately sworn in as a Midshipman USNR (United States Naval Reserve), with orders to report to the detachment commander, NROTC, University of Wisconsin-Madison.

Subsequently, he resigns his NROTC commission. On August 17, 1961 he is honorably discharged (his second) from the USMC reserve (inactive).

In 1956 he attends the Wisconsin Institute of Technology-Platteville. In 1957 he begins work in sales and advertising for a major tire company.

During the next 20 years, he writes several hundred freelance articles and stories for local, regional and national publications and a book about hunting, fishing and other outdoor-related subjects.

He marries Carol Kroll, Clintonville, Wisconsin on November 28, 1958 in Beloit, Wis-

consin. The marriage produces twin daughters, Lisa and Lori, and seven grandchildren: Tom, Becky and Katie Haas and Billie Jo, Barbi, Matt and Brandi Robinson.

On September 30, 1998 he retires from a mid-sized Wisconsin electric and natural gas utility after working more than twenty years in public relations and lobbying.

He is a life member of the Third Marine Division Association and the National Rifle Association, and a member of the Marine Corps Heritage Foundation, Marine Corps League, Marine Corps Association and the Gunny Loper (Wisconsin) Chapter of the Third Marine Division Association.

STEWART W. SAYLOR, born October 30, 1921, in Berlin, Pennsylvania. Enlisted in the USMC on August 17, 1942, at SDHS Baltimore, Maryland. Training at Court House Bay, Camp Lejeune, North Carolina. Served as Winch Operator, Barrage Balloon, 6th Squadron, New Caledonia. Also served in New Zealand and the Solomon Islands. Participated in action against the Japanese on Bougainville. Discharged on August 26, 1946, at Camp Pendleton, California, in the rank of Corporal. Now retired.

EDWIN S. SCHICK, JR, born November 9, 1923, in Orange (town), Orange County, California. Enlisted in the USMC on December 17, 1941, at Los Angeles, California.

Following recruit training at Marine Corps Recruit Depot, San Diego, he served at Camp

Elliot, and arrived with the first contingent at Camp Joseph H. Pendleton in September 1942.

While serving as a Sergeant with the 12th Marines in the Pacific Theater, he received a battlefield commission to 2nd Lieutenant five days prior to his participation in the invasion of Guam. He saw service in the Korean Conflict, serving with the 11th Marines and as an advisor to a Korean regimental combat team during the 3d Korean Winter Campaign. Tours at Camp Pendleton and Twenty-nine Palms punctuated the period after the Korean Conflict until he landed at Guantanamo Bay, Cuba, in 1962, with the 5th Marine Expeditionary Brigade. Following a school tour at Quantico, Virginia, he served a three-year tour at the Pentagon with the U.S. Navy, doing Amphibious Warfare Gaming.

A high point of his career came during Vietnam service from 1967 to 1968, when he returned to the same 12th Regiment in which he had served as a Sergeant, to become a Com-

manding Officer. Current official publications state that during this period, the 12th Marine Regiment (Reign) became the largest artillery regiment in the history of the U.S. Marine Corps.

From 1968 to 1978, he served as the Senior Marine Advisor to the Commandant of the Chinese Marine Corps in Taiwan.

Colonel Schick joined the I Marine Amphibious Force (IMAF) at Camp Pendleton in August 1971, and served as its Chief of Staff for six different Commanding Generals.

His personal decorations include the Legion of Merit with Combat "V," Bronze Star Medal with Combat "V," Purple Heart Medal, Combat Action Ribbon, Presidential Unit Citation with three Stars, Navy Unit Commendation with two Stars, Marine Corps Good Conduct Medal; American Campaign Medal; Asiatic-Pacific Campaign Medal with three Stars; World War II Victory Medal; Navy Occupation Service Medal; National Defense Service Medal with one Star; Korean Service Medal with three Stars, Armed Forces Expeditionary Medal, Vietnam Service Medal with four Stars, Republic of Vietnam Gallantry Cross with Palm (Personal Award), Korean Presidential Unit Citation, Republic of Vietnam Gallantry Cross with Palm (unit award), United Nations Service Medal, and Republic of Vietnam Campaign Ribbon.

Colonel Schick transferred to the Retired List of Marine Corps Officers after more than 33-1/2 years of dedicated service. He retired on July 1, 1975, at Camp Pendleton, California.

He and his wife Virginia are enjoying life in Yucca Valley, California.

JOSEPH M. SEEGER, born May 25, 1943 in Sayre, PA joined the USMC January of 1966. Boot camp, Parris Island, SC; ITR, Camp Gieger, NC; RTO school, MCRD, San Diego; staging, Camp Pendleton, CA. Joined H&S Co, 3/4, first week December 1966 at Dong Ha Combat Base, RVN and assigned out to K Co. 3/4 as battalion net radio operator last week December 1966 through October 1967, then back to H&S Co, 3/4 until rotated out of Vietnam first week of January 1968. Spent last 12 months in USMC assigned to comm/center, MCAF Futema, Okinawa. Discharged January 10, 1969 from Marine Barracks, Naval Station, Treasure Island, San Francisco, CA with rank of corporal.

Awards include Purple Heart, Combat Action Ribbon, Presidential Unit Citation, Good Conduct Medal, Vietnam Campaign Medal, Vietnam Service Medal, National Defense Service Medal, Rifle Expert Badge.

Returned to Washington, D.C. until relocated to Los Angeles, CA. Retired from Los Angeles Co. Sheriff's Department with 25 1/2 years of service, last 10 years in Homicide Bureau.

Residing in Anacortes, WA.

RUSSELL L. SEVERSON, born March 4, 1926, in Whitehall, Wisconsin. Enlisted in the USMC on December 18, 1943. Training locations include Recruit Depot, San Diego, California, January 18, 1944; Rifle Sharpshooter, Camp Matthews, California, April 6, 1944; Light Machine Gun and Automatic Weapons, Camp Elliot, California, May 1944.

Served with the 63d Replacement Battalion. "I" Company, 3d Battalion, 21st Regiment, 3d Marine Division, Central Pacific area, July 15,

1944, to April 19, 1945. Landed on Guam, Marianas Islands, August 1944. Actively engaged in patrolling against the enemy until November 1944. Western Pacific area, Iwo Jima, Volcano Islands, February 21, 1945, with the 21st Marines. Wounded on February 24, 1945. Arrived at Guam aboard *USS Pinckney*, February 28, 1945. Flew to Pear Harbor, then to Great Lakes Naval Hospital. Discharged on August 2, 1945, in the rank of Private First Class.

Military awards include the Purple Heart, Presidential Unit Citation, Combat action ribbon, American Campaign Medal, Asiatic-Pacific Campaign Medal, and World War II Victory Medal.

Memorable experiences: Saw the flag raising on Mt. Suribachi. Had the honor to serve with a great bunch of guys and still correspond with some of them.

Married on July 28, 1953; three sons, two daughters, and nine grandchildren. Retired in 1989. Enjoys hunting and fishing. Life member of the 3d Marine Division Association; member of Wisconsin Chapter, 3d Marine Division Association.

ROBERT F. SINGER, born February 11, 1948, Brooklyn, NY. He entered the USMC on September 1, 1966, and underwent recruit training at the USMC recruit depot, Parris Island, SC.

In a career that spanned over 30 years, he served in eight infimtry battalions in the 1st, 2nd and 3d Marine Divisions, and held every

billet from basic rifleman to battalion sergeant major. He also served as a security guard and combat air crewman in the 1st Marine Aircraft Wing.

Special duty assignments included drill instructor at OCS Quantico, VA; Embassy duty in Cyprus, Tanzania and Belgium; inspector/instructor duty at CO-I, 3d Bn., 25th Marines; barracks duty in the Republic of the Philippines; and recruiting duty in Buffalo, NY.

Last two billets held prior to retirement were Sergeant Major of the 11th Marine Expeditionary Unit home based at Camp Pendleton, CA and Sergeant Major of the II Marine Expeditionary Force at Camp Lejeune, NC.

From October 1968 - April 1969 served in the anti-tank company (ONTOS) of the 3d Tank Battalion in Vietnam. Joined the battalion as an 0351 anti-tank assault man and had to be trained on the job and in the field during combat operations. Progressed from loader to driver and was an ONTOS commander when the company was deactivated From April 1969 - July 1969 served in H&S Company, 2nd Battalion, 3d Marines in the 106 recoilless rifle platoon/50 caliber machine gun platoon. During this period was briefly attached to Fox Company under 1st Lt. R. P. Ayres, Jr., a real professional, who years later would command the 3d Marine Division. Remembrances of that period are a mixture of good and bad, but mostly of the privilege of having served with outstanding Marines and Corpsmen in tough combat conditions. The memories of their courage under fire and loyalty to each other will last forever.

From 1975 to 1976 served in Fox Company, 2nd Battalion, 4th Marines, 3d Marine Division on Okinawa, as a platoon sergeant and rifle platoon commander.

Retired from the USMC on October 1, 1996. During 21 months service in Vietnam was a member of both the 1st and 3d Marine Divisions and 1st Marine Aircraft Wing. Was awarded the Purple Heart, Combat Action Ribbon, Combat Aircrew Wings and the Presidential Unit Citation. Campaign service medals are the Vietnam Service Medal w/7 stars, Southwest Asia Service Medal w/star, Marine Corps Expeditionary Medal (Rwanda), and the Armed Forces Expeditionary Medal (Somalia).

Presently employed by the Commonwealth of Virginia as a Veterans' employment specialist.

IRVIN "SMITTY" SMITH was born November 13, 1942 in Rawl, WVA. After getting married June 3, 1962 moved to Columbus, Ohio working at Capitol Mfg. Co, 153 W. Fulton St. for almost 5 years. Came home from work one night, letter from the Gov. greeting we need you. Period. So "Smitty" joined the first one to call, USMC. We have a special, Irvin, two years in and out.

Enlisted at Cincinnati Ohio December 18, 1965. Went to west coast MCRD San Diego, CA. Cut from 12 weeks to 10 weeks of training February 3, 1966 - April 6, 1966. Home to my wife just long enough to get her pregnant.

Smitty got orders for Vietnam Bit and ITR MCB, Camp Pen. CA.

on a commercial plane, pilots were on strike. Damn scab took me to Vietnam of all people.

Stopped in Alaska overnight, on to Japan. Next stop, Okinawa. Layed next to the air strip several hours. Hot. Smitty didn't know, but Vietnam was hotter.

Da Nang air strip now. Day or so later, Dudy Station LY- my hill, ran night patrol there. M.O.S. 0311 rifleman. Grunt out beating the bush, looking for Charlie, V.C.

DON E. SPICER, born August 29,1949 in Laurel, DE. Joined the USMC in September 1967 and trained at Parris Island, Camp LeJune, 29 Palms and Camp Pendleton. Sent to Vietnam March 1968 as a Forward Air Observer 1st Battalion, 3d Marines Third Marine Division. Wounded at Mutter's Ridge on May 19, 1969 and sent to Japan and later Philadelphia Naval Hospital with shrapnel and gunshot wounds. Medically discharged January 1, 1970 with Rank of Corporal. Awards: Navy Commendation Medal with Combat "V", Purple Heart, Combat Action Ribbon, Good Conduct Medal, National Defense Service Medal, Vietnam Service Medal with three Bronze Stars, Republic of Vietnam Meritorious Unit Citation (Gallantry Cross Color) and Republic of Vietnam Campaign Medal.

JOHN H. STERLING was born in Cedar Rapids, Iowa, February 19, 1940. Graduated University of San Francisco. Entered OCS February 1963. Training.- included FAC School Coronado Naval Training Center, All weather bombing OJT with Marine Air Support Squadron -3, El Toro MCAS. Exercised air support with Brigade at Kaneohe, Hawaii. Served with 2nd Recruit Training Battalion MCRD, San Diego, as a Recruit Training Series Commander.

In 1968 and 1969 Republic of Vietnam, attached to 3d Marine Division at Dong Ha, Camp Carroll, Vandegrift, Hill 55 controlling tactical air strikes. In summer 1968, at LZ Veghel, A

Shan, supported U.S. Army 101st Airborne operations as tactical strike controller. Now a Captain, finished tour in RVN as Marine Air Support Squadron -2 Operations Officer (forward) at Dong Ha. After Vietnam, trained air strike control officers at Roosevelt Roads, Puerto Rico.

In 1970-1971 served as C.O. of "C" Company, 4th Tank Bn. Boise, ID. A Landscape Ar-

chitect, owns and operates Sterling Nursery Co. in Boise, Idaho. Married, Lynne, Daughter Aileen.

JAMES L. SWAIN was born October 3, 1924 in Ontario, California. He joined the USMC on December 3, 1942 and began training at the San Diego Marine Recruit Depot, then to Radio School, Camp Elliott, Camp Pendleton, Boat Basin, Oceanside. Left to go overseas on September 21, 1943 and joined the 3d Signal Company, Headquarters Battalion, Third Marine Division on Guadalcanal in October of 1943.

Participated in campaigns in Bougainville,

Consolidation of the Northern Solomon Islands, Guam and Iwo Jima. Discharge from the Corps in December of 1945.

After one year of college, he worked for Bank of America at various locations and positions and later retired after 35 years as Assistant Vice President, Division Head of Corporate Security for Southern California. In 1982 was named Corporate Security Officer for First Interstate Bancorp overseeing the Security Programs for the First Interstate Banks in the thirteen western states. Retired from that position in 1989. Moved to Las Vegas, Nevada in 1991 to play golf and for the wife to bowl in three of four leagues a week.

The photo was taken on the island of Guam in mid-1944. In the background is the Headquarters Battalion Area.

JAMES DONALD TAYLOR, born January 24, 1921, in Wenatchee, Washington. Joined the United States Marine Corps on September 16, 1942, at Seattle, Washington. Basic training

at San Diego; additional training at New Zealand and Guadalcanal.

Participated in battles at Bougainville,

Guam, and Iwo Jima. M-3-9 Machine Gunner, K- 3-9 Machine Gunner. Wounded on Iwo Jima as a 3d Marine Division Machine Gunner. Sent to hospital on Saipan with other wounded. After a furlough in June 1945, there was guard duty at El Centro, California. Discharged from Sands Point Naval Station, Seattle, Washington, on October 16, 1945, in the rank of Private First Class.

Military awards include the Purple Heart, Presidential Unit Campaign Medal, American Campaign Medal, Asiatic-Pacific Campaign Medal, and World War II Victory Medal.

BILL R. TERRILL, born September 26, 1924, in Omaha, Nebraska. Enlisted in the USMC on July 14, 1943. MCRD San Diego, California; Marine Corps Base, San Diego, 1st Guard Battalion; 60 mortar training, Camp Elliot, California; awaiting transfer overseas, Camp Pendleton, California; Transient Center, Pearl Harbor, Hawaii. Joined "K" Company, 3d Battalion, 9th Marines, 3d Marine Division,, at the end of the campaign for Guam. Participated in battle for Iwo Jima and was wounded on February 25 while taking the second airstrip.

Military awards include the Good Conduct Medal, Purple Heart, Presidential Unit Citation, American Campaign Medal, Asiatic-Pacific Campaign Medal, and World War II Victory Medal. Discharged on December 29, 1945, Mare Island, California, in the rank of Corporal.

Married Toni Morrill on January 2, 1946, in San Diego; three children: Bill Jr., Kathleen, Suzanne. Retired from Beatrice Foods Company, Dairy Division, after 40 years as General Manager of the Western Division. We are now living in Port Angeles, Washington, where we enjoy a quiet lifestyle in a beautiful little port town.

RALPH THIEMT, born July 18, 1930 in Chicago, IL, completed school in Columbus, Ohio and enlisted in 1948. Upon completing recruit training at PISC, he was assigned to MB, Naval Torpedo Station, Keyport, WN as a company clerk. In 1949 he was transferred to NTC, San Diego as a student in the Court Reporter Course. Proceeding to Camp Pendleton, he was assigned to the Base Legal Office and while there he had a bit part in the film "The Sands of Iwo Jima". The latter part of 1950 he was assigned to the first enlisted Naval Justice Course under the Uniform Code of Military Justice at

Newport, RI. In 1952 he was the Wing Legal Chief in Pohang, Korea.

During the next 14 years he served as the

Force Legal Chief, Camp Geiger, Chief Investigator with the CID Department at Edenton, NC, State Department Duty in The Hague, Netherlands, Wing Legal Chief, 2dMAW, Cherry Point, and was the first Legal Chief to serve in Vietnam being assigned to the 3dMarDiv Forward in Danang in 1965. Subsequently, he was assigned as Base Legal Chief, Quantico.

Promoted to Warrant Officer in June 1966, he assumed duty as the Adjutant, Marine Corps Air Station, Quantico. He was eventually reassigned to 1stMAW Danang where he served as Adjutant, Marine Wing Headquarters Group. He returned to the states in October 1969 and served as Adjutant, MACS-5, New River and retired November 1970.

January 1971 saw him accepting a position as Postal Supervisor, Ft. Myers, FL. Retiring therefrom in 1986, he assumed duties as Manager, Mail Services for Charlotte County, Florida, a position he held until he retired in December 1996. He recently worked eight months for the Census Bureau.

He and his wife, Mildred Holloway of Durham, NC, have two daughters. He is presently acting as a court appointed legal guardian and is active in various veterans and church activities.

Awards include Bronze Star w/combat "V", Navy Commendation Medal w/combat "V", Navy Achievement Medal w/combat "V", Combat Action Ribbon, Presidential Unit Citation, Navy Unit Commendation, Good Conduct Medal w/5 *, State Department Service Award, Navy Occupation Service Medal, National Defense Service Medal w/2 *, Korean Service Medal w/4 *, Vietnam Service Medal w/4 *, RVN Gallantry Cross w/Palm, United Nations Service Medal, Republic of Korea Presidential Unit Citation, and RVN Campaign Medal.

EUGENE J. THOMAS was born June 23, 1925 in Cumberland, OK. Moved to Texas in 1927. Joined USMC July 1, 1942. Basic training in San Diego, CA. More training on Samoa where he joined E/2/3 and was given the name "Coathanger" after a 20 mile march in the rain. Also trained on New Herbidies, New Zealand and Guadalcanal. Participated in landing on Bougainville on November 1, 1943. Stayed until December 25, 1943. Returned to states and served in San Francisco. Discharged July 8, 1946 from Treasure Island with the rank of corporal. Returned to Dallas, TX. Married Jeanie

Petersen, wife of 50 years. Have two sons, Dwayne and Michael. Was in grocery business for 15 years. Sold out and moved to Paris, TX where he had bought a ranch. Bought a chemical and paper supply company. Retired in 1989. Now live on the Coathanger Ranch and raise Gelbview cattle.

WILLIAM F. TILSON, born October 17, 1917, in Evanston, Illinois. Joined the USMC in 1939. Served in Iceland, 1939; Paris Island, South Carolina; Quantico, Virginia; Bougainville. Was a Platoon Sergeant. Discharged in August 1945. Passed away on December 15, 2000.

STANLEY A. TSIGOUNIS, born October 14, 1922, in Youngstown, Ohio. Was a student at Colgate University when a Marine detachment came to the campus to recruit college kids. We were gung-ho. Before you knew it, I raised my right hand and joined the Marines. A safe place to be in time of War. Colgate University was awarded the V-12 (Navy and Marines) and V-5 (Navy aviation), a program which permitted new recruits to stay in college in uniform, under the direction of the military for a short period of time. We could continue our studies and receive military.

In 1943, all those enrolled in the Marine

Corps boarded the Cannonball Express from Hamilton, New York, to Parris Island for boot camp. Upon completion of boot camp, we were sent to Camp Lejeune as officer candidate applicants. On our hats was a pin, OCA. Other Marines on base thought we were officers and saluted as they passed by.

The Marines had heavy losses at Tarawa, and the Brass decided they needed officers in a hurry. They put the OCAs through 14 weeks of hell; those who passed were given their Bars, seven days of leave, and shipped overseas. I was sent to the 3d Marine Division on Guam, assigned

to "K" Company, 3d Battalion, 21st Marines. In February 1945, I was given the honor, with my platoon, to load the KA ship in Agana.

The 3d Division was to be held in reserve in the Iwo campaign. We arrived at Iwo on the PA *Bolivar* on D-Day. D plus 1 we boarded the landing boats; spent most of the day on the water with battleships firing over our heads. The water was rough and most of the Marines were seasick. Fortunately, we returned to our ship. Next day we boarded again; this time we went ashore. We moved up to the edge of Motoyama #2. The following day at 9:15 a.m., we launched our attack. By 11 a.m., I was severely wounded; lost half my men. Evacuated to the hospital ship *Solace* and sent to the Army hospital on Saipan. Flew on a PB2Y from Saipan to Pearl Harbor Naval Hospital. Month later, boarded the *Maxonia* for the return to San Francisco.

Received the Purple Heart, Presidential Unit Citation, Navy Commendation Medal, World War II Victory Medal, Asiatic-Pacific Campaign Medal, and other awards and citations. Retired in November 1945 in the rank of 2nd Lieutenant.

Today at age 78, I'm still active as a real estate developer. Residing in Sarasota, Florida.

LOUIS W. TUER, born November 14, 1923, in Liberty, Texas. Joined the USMC on May 11, 1942. Training included MCRD San Diego, California; Radio School, San Diego. Assigned to HQ Battalion, 12th Marines, Camp Niland, Brawley, California.

Transferred to 3d Signal Company, Radio Platoon, 3d Marine Division. Arrived in New Zealand aboard the *USS Lurline* on February 14, 1943. To Bougainville in June 1943 after practice landing at New Hebrides. Wounded on Bougainville by bomb shrapnel; hospitalized in New Caledonia. Rejoined 3d Signal Company and took part in Guam and Iwo Jima campaigns. Returned to U.S. on escort aircraft carrier *Cape Esperance*. After a stopover in Hawaii, 30-day leave, arrived in Liberty, Texas. Married high school sweetheart on May 23, 1945. Stationed at Philadelphia Navy Yard; Camp Robert Small; and Great Lakes Naval Training Station, one of three men to operate the teletype.

Military awards include the Purple Heart, Presidential Unit Citation, American Campaign Medal, Asiatic-Pacific Campaign Medal, World War II Victory Medal, and Good Conduct Medal. Honorably discharged on May 12, 1946, with 20 percent disability.

One son, Gary Louis, and one daughter, Renee Marie. Retired from Occidental Petroleum after 35-plus years. Was a Boy Scoutmaster for a number of years in Rockport, Texas. Now living in Wildwood, Texas, a retirement community, and attempting to enjoy golf. Have been a Master Mason over 50 years and a Past Master almost 50.

GREGORY A. VANDERGRIFF was born April 14, 1950 in Chattanooga, Tennessee. Volunteered November 12, 1968. Boot camp and training at MCRD San Diego, CA.

Served in Vietnam as a "Grunt" with B-1-3,

3d Div. Wounded twice on May 25, 1969 on "Hill 174" on "Mutter's Ridge" 300 meters from DMZ.

Awards include Bronze Star with Combat V, Purple Heart with one Gold Star, Combat Action Ribbon, National Defense Service Medal, Vietnam Service Medal with 2 Bronze Stars, Republic of Vietnam Meritorious Unit Citation (Gallantry Cross Color with Palm), Republic of Vietnam Meritorious Unit Citation (Civil actions, First Class Color with Palm), Republic of Vietnam Campaign Medal.

On March 28, 1998 General Raymond G. Davis, USMC, (Ret.) (Medal of Honor Recipient) pinned the Bronze Star Medal with combat V plus a second Purple Heart after almost 29 years, before almost 700 people.

Married for over 30 years to Charlotte and still living in Chattanooga.

ROBERT E. WALKER was born October 21, 1922 in Walla Walla, WA Joined USMC January of 1942 Seattle WA. Training at Marine Base, Camp Elliot San Diego CA, Niland CA, Camp Pendleton CA, New Zealand and Guadalcanal. Combat, November 1, 1943 Bougainville; July 21, 1944 Guam. Served as "Forward Observer" lst Bn. B battery 12th Marines.

Awards include Presidential Unit and Naval Unit Citations, Marine Good Conduct, American and Asiatic-Pacific Campaign Medals, WWII Victory Medal, Combat Action Ribbon.

Discharged Mare Island Shipyard January 5, 1946. Returned to Yakima, WA and the Republic Publishing Co., the local newspaper. Served apprenticeship pressroom, moved to *Seattle Post Intelligencer* 1953 and retired 1984. 42 years in the newspaper business. 2 daughters 5 grandchildren 8 great-grandchildren. Had a good life.

GERALD W. WALLACK, 1332868 USMC, born April 14, 1933 in New Haven, CT. Entered the U.S. Marine Corps Platoon Leaders Class while at the University of Miami in Coral Gables, Florida in 1952. Completed Platoon Leaders Class in 1954. Graduated from the University of Miami in 1955 with a BBA degree. Entered the regular Marine Corps in 1956 as a sergeant. Training location while in the Marine Corps were Quantico VA, Parris Island SC, Camp Pendleton CA.

Was a member of H&S btry, 1st Bn, 12th

Marines, 3d Marine Division FMF at South Camp Mt. Fuji, Japan. Discharged in 1958. Has been a school teacher from 1959 to the present.

Married and lives in Meriden, CT and Ogunquit, Maine.

RICHARD "WASH" WASHBURN, born February 21, 1923, in Aurora, Colorado. Left college to join Marine Corps, November 24, 1942. Boot camp at San Diego, Rifle instructor at Camp Matthew's, Camp Elliot weapons training, Camp St. Louis, New Caledonia, joined the 3d Division, returning from Bougainville on Guadalcanal. Machine gun Platoon, Guam Liberation.

Spent February 21, my birthday, on Iwo Jima;

"K" Company 21st Regiment. On February 24 wounded in right shoulder. I was carrying my machine gun, which took the brunt of the hit, saving my life. On way to aid station, Jap shot me through the neck. Evacuated to *USS Solace*, moved to island and stateside hospitals, finally to US Naval Hospital, Norman, Oklahoma.

Received two Purple Hearts, and Medals, ribbons awarded to unit during time served. Discharged November 30, 1945. Corporal.

Returned to Colorado State University; completed degrees. Worked for US Forest Service 31 years. Retired as Principal Research Entomologist.

Married to Dorothy, reside in Lockeford, California. Sons, Jerry, David, and daughter, Jennifer. President, Golden Gate Chapter, 2000-2001. Semper Fi.

RICHARD S. WEEKS was born January 26, 1923 in Randolph, Maine. Joined the USMC July 16, 1942. Training at Parris Island SC, Camp LeJeune NC. Was in G-2-21 Marines. Went to Camp Elliot, Camp Pendleton CA to New Zealand and more training at Guadalcanal.

First combat at Bougainville. After that, land-

ing at Guam and got wounded in arm by shrapnel that first night and was hospitalized. Went to Iwo Jima and was there for nine days – got shot in arm. Finally got back to the U.S. and was awarded the Purple Heart, Presidential Unit Citation, Navy Unit Citation. Was discharged from Brooklyn Navy Yard in August 29, 1946 as a CPL.

Married my lovely wife Connie and had two

sons, two daughters and five grandchildren. We have been married for 56 years, going for 60. Worked for the V.A. Center at Toqus Marine for 31 years and then retired. Have been carving for my own enjoyment and am also into amateur radio. My call is K1HAR. Had this call for 42 years.

JOHN P. WELSH, born December 13, 1920, in Philadelphia, Pennsylvania. Joined the USMC in July 1942. Training at Parris Island, South Carolina; Tent City, North Carolina; Camp Dunlap, California; Camp Elliot, California; Camp Pendleton, California; New Zealand; Guadalcanal. Served with "D" Battery, 12th Marines. Transferred to "C" Company, 21st Marines, December 1942.

Participated in campaigns at Bougainville,

Guam, and Iwo Jima. Caught malaria when we left the Canal for Guam. Wounded and caught dengue fever at Guam. Aboard hospital ship *USS Bountiful*, dreamed they cut off both my legs to stop the pain from the dengue ... and I was happy. Went to Navy hospital on Banika, Russell Islands. Upon release from hospital, went to Guadalcanal to await ship back to Guam. Caught malaria for the second time. Got back to Guam in time to be promoted to Corporal and go to Iwo. Wounded at Iwo. Back to hospital on Guam and Navy hospitals at Daly City, California; Norman, Oklahoma; and Fort Eustace, Virginia. Marine Corps Quartermaster, Philadelphia, Pennsylvania.

Received the Purple Heart; entitled to all other Division awards. Discharged on October 4, 1945, at Philadelphia, Pennsylvania, in the rank of Corporal.

After discharge, returned to school. Finished three years of high school in 14 months. Graduated from LaSalle College, 1950. Married my pre-war sweetheart, Dorothy Sutton, 1946. We had five children. Three boys: John, Jim, and Tim; two girls: Joan Ann and Dorothy Irene. Now have ten grandchildren and ten great-grandchildren.

After college, worked at the Naval Aviation Supply Office (ASO), Philadelphia Pennsylvania. Navy Supply Systems Command, Washington, DC, 1968; prepared support briefings for the Admiral and Executive Board. Naval Weapons Engineering Support Activity, Washington, DC, 1971; Logistics Manager; Lamps, helicopter/destroyer program. Naval Air Development Center (NADC), 1973; same program. NADC, 1975; Assistant Project Director for logistics on Carrier Tactical Support Center (CV-TSC), later known as Anti-Submarine Warfare Module (CV-ASWM). Retired in January 1980 with 34 years of government service. Now a member of the

Knights of Columbus. Enjoy gardening, fishing, and whatever else I can poke my nose into.

MAX O. WETZEL was born May 9, 1921 in Peerbrook, WI. I enlisted in the Marine Corps August 6, 1942. After boot camp at San Diego, our platoon spent one month of mess duty at the recruit depot. November we went to very new barracks in Camp Pendleton for training.

Col. Lemuel C. Shepherd held a formation and

instructed us that we were a part of the ninth regiment. I became a member of a machine gun squad, G. Co., 2nd battalion, 9th regiment, 3d Division.

January of 1943 we shipped to New Zealand. June of 1943 we moved to Guadalcanal. November of 1943 we landed at Bougainville. Back to New Zealand after received by the Army. July of 1944, liberated Guam and set up camp there. February of 1945, the Battle for Iwo Jima.

I received a Meritorious Service Citation for leadership after assuming the duties of section leader for the remainder of the campaign when our officer was wounded.

After Iwo, I was sent back to the states on the point system and finished my tow at Indian Head, Maryland. I made the three campaigns without getting wounded and was a member of G-2-9 all the while I was overseas. I was discharged October 10, 1945 with the rank of corporal.

RAY V. WILBURN, born July 1, 1919, in Wolfe City, Texas. Joined the USMC on October 19, 1939. Training locations included boot camp, 1939, San Diego Recruit Depot; Sergeant Major School, 1960, Parris Island, South Carolina.

Served in the 3d Marine Division, 1952-

1954, 4/12; 1961-1962, 1/3. Units served with included Artillery, Infantry, Aviation, Communications, PMO, Instructor/Inspector Staff, Guard Detachment, and Medical Battalion.

Military awards include the Legion of Merit with Combat "V," Meritorious Service Medal, Combat Action Ribbon, Presidential Unit Citation with three Stars, Navy Unit Commendation, Meritorious Unit Commendation, Good Conduct Medal with nine Stars, American Defense

Service Medal, American Campaign Medal, Asiatic-Pacific Campaign Medal with five Stars, World War II Victory Medal, Navy Occupation Service Medal, National Defense Medal with one Star, Korea Service Medal with three Stars, Vietnam Service Medal with four Stars, United Nations Service Medal, Republic of Korea Presidential Unit Citation, Republic of Vietnam Gallantry Cross Unit Citation, Vietnam Presidential Unit Citation, Republic of Vietnam Campaign Medal, and Republic of Korea War Service Medal. Retired on March 4, 1971, Marine Corps Base, Twenty-Nine Palms, California, in the rank of Sergeant Major.

Memorable experiences: World War II (Gavutu, Guadalcanal, Tarawa, Saipan, Guam, General MacArthur's Repatriation Team, Occupation of Japan, 1945); Korea; Vietnam (TET Offensive, 1968).

Worked as Advertising Manager for local newspaper. Now enjoying retirement.

JERRY A. WILLIS, born November 13, 1946 at Ft. Benning, GA. Joined USMC July 1, 1965. Training locations include: Parris Island, SC; Camp Giger, NC. Served with A-1-6, 2nd Div. Camp LeJeune, NC; Marine Barracks at Keflavik, Iceland, October 1966 1967; C-1-3, 3d Div. in Vietnam, December 1967-May 1968 as fire team leader and squad leader with 1st plt., 2nd squad. Participated in the combat operations: Kentucky V. Napoleon, Oscelola 11, Jeb Stuart, Napoleon /Saline. WIA May 4, 1968, at Thuong Do, Vietnam, med-evaced to US. Discharged April 30, 1969 from B-1-2, 2nd Div. Camp LeJeune, NC with rank of corporal.

Awards include Purple Heart, Combat Action

Ribbon, Navy Meritorious Unit Commendation Ribbon, Navy Unit Commendation Ribbon, Marine Corps Good Conduct Medal, National Defense Service Medal, Vietnam Service Medal, Rep. Vietnam MUC Gallantry Cross, Republic of Vietnam Campaign Medal. Returned to Columbus, GA, married to Mildred Merkle. Employed with USPS.

WILLIAM JAMES WILSON, born August 13, 1919, in Fairport, New York. Joined USMC on March 29, 1944 (966121). Training at Parris Island, South Carolina; Camp Lejeune, North Carolina. Guam, Marianas Islands, joined 21st Regiment, 1st Battalion, 3d Marine Division. March 22, 1945, combat against the Japanese, 19 days. March 12, 1945, wounded in action. Returned to States. Brother Douglas, Ensign, U.S. Navy; brother Ralph, Medic, U.S. Army.

Military Awards include Sharpshooter M-1

Garrand, test score 300-plus; Light machine Gun (604), rated "Gunner," score "excellent;" 3d Division Patch, World War II Victory Medal, Iwo Jima Victory Medal, Navy Unit Commendation, Asiatic-Pacific Campaign Medal with Bronze Star, Combat Action Ribbon, and Purple Heart. Honorable discharge on January 25, 1946, in the rank of Private First Class.

Married Jane Lawson, November 6, 1940, in Jamestown, New York. First daughter, Johanna, 1-1/2 years old, and second daughter, Jennifer, born when I was on Guam. Returned home and blessed with three more children. Our five children brought forth 10 grandchildren and 13 great-grandchildren. Forty-eight years of marriage ended when Jane died in her sleep. Worked over 40 years in school bus transportation and equipment management. Twelve years ago, married Jacqueline Osborne, widow of bomber pilot James Osborne. Now writing a story, beginning in 1620 when ancestors arrived on the *Mayflower* until present. Blessed with a large family and good health.

LUTHER R. "RAY" WISBY, born March 21, 1922, in Palo Verde, Arizona. Joined the USMC on November 12, 1940, in Stockton, California. Training at MCRD San Diego, California; Camp Elliot, California; Camp Dunlap, Niland, California. Returned to San Diego for embarkation, February 22, 1943, to Auckland, New Zealand.

Served in F-2-10 from January 18, 1941, to

April 11, 1941; K-4-10 from April 11, 1941, to November 1, 1941; M-4-10 form November 1, 1941, to September 1, 1942; M-4-12 from September 1, 1942, to February 1, 1944; I-3-12 from February 1, 1944, to April 13, 1945; USMCR MD, USNT, and DC, Farragut, Idaho, June 30, 1945; Western Recruiting Division, San Francisco, California, March 8, 1946; WCR&R CTR MCB, San Diego, California, November 14, 1946.

Participated in Bougainville, Guam, and Iwo Jima campaigns in artillery (105mm Howitzer). Discharged on January 21, 1947, in the rank of Sergeant.

Military awards include three Presidential

Unit Citations, American Campaign Medal, Asiatic-Pacific Campaign Medal, Good Conduct Medal, American Defense Medal, World War II Victory Medal, and Combat Action Ribbon. Received Letter of Commendation from Major General Roy S. Geiger, USMC, for action in Piva area, Bougainville.

Returned to wife and firstborn son in Stockton, California; two more sons were born. Retired from Southern Pacific Transportation with 36-1/2 years of service. Enjoying retirement fishing, hunting, and RV-ing. Also enjoy visit with old buddies at 3d Marine Division Association reunions.

PAUL V. WODICKA Three Marines still keep in contact even 58 years later. The 3 men went into the forming of the 21st Marines of the Third Marine Division in late 1942.

Harry Bailey, East Hampton, CT; Chester

Stempel, Millers Falls, MA; Paul Wodicka East Hampton MA were all formed into Heavy Weapons 2-H-21. They were together until Wodicka was wounded on Guam in 1944 and Bailey and Stempel wounded on Iwo Jima. Bailey and Wodicka were both in 81M.M. Morters and Stempel a machine gunner. They continue to meet with their wives at least once a year.

Bailey was dye maker in CT and Stempel a carpentry contractor in MA. Wodicka was service station owner in MA. All were discharged in late 1945 and had been from Parris Island, SC; Camp LeJeune, NC; Camp Pendleton, CA; New Zealand; Bougainville; Guam and Iwo Jima for Bailey and Stempel.

JAMES M. WOODLEY, JR. was born July 23, 1934 in Baird, TX. He has resided in Sulphur, Louisiana since 1944. Joined USMC May 20, 1954. Went through boot camp at Parris Island, then to the 2nd ITR Camp Pendleton, then to North Camp Fuji Japan as rifleman with Fox-2-3. He then transferred to Camp Pendleton with the game warden section MPCo MPBn MCB.

Woodley was discharged in May of 1958

with rank of sergeant. He returned to Louisiana and married Marietta Spees. They have 3 children and 7 grandchildren. Woodley is a graduate of NcNeese University. He retired as Chief Firearms Instructor and Regional Director of Probation and Parole, Louisiana Department of Corrections.

RONALD W. WROBLEWSKI, born February 22, 1945 in Charleston, WV. Joined the USMC April 10, 1963. Went to Parris Island, SC on June 6, 1963. Stationed at Camp LeJeune, NC and Vietnam (1965- 1966). Separated from USMC on October 4,1966.

Married high school sweetheart, Geraldine Blankenship. Two sons: Gary Allen (teacher) and Ronald Lee (accountant). One granddaughter: Erin Shea

Disabled veteran but very active in veteran's organizations. Has organized many parades and other activities usually connected with veterans. Co-founder of the West Virginia Marine Corps Coordinating Council, Inc. in 1996 and serving as its first President.

Conceived and organized our Nation's first Marine Day. A tribute to the men and women of the United States Marine Corps – past, present and future. Attendance was nearly 12,000 from 15 different states.

Was three-time Commandant of the Huntington Detachment #340, Marine Corps League, past Vice Commandant - Department of W.Va., Marine Corps League, Kentucky Colonel, Admiral, Cherry River Navy, five-time Worshipful Master of Crescent Lodge #32, A.F.& A.M.

Life member of Marine Corps League, Second Marine Division Association, Third Marine Division Association, USMC Jarhead Network, Veterans of Foreign Wars Post #1064 - Huntington, WV, Disabled American Veterans Chapter 52- Kenova, WV.

Member of Royal Arch Masons #46, Knight Templer-Huntington Commandry #9, Scottish Rite of Freemasonry, S.J., USA Huntington Shrine Club, Beni Kedem Temple of Charleston, WV, Military Order of Devil Dogs, Marine Corps Association, Vietnam Veterans of America - Chapter 628, Vietnam Veterans Inc., America Legion, Veteran's Committee for Civic Improvement, and West Virginia Veterans Coalition.

Awards: "Distinguished Citizen Award" Department of West Virginia, Marine Corps League; "Commandant of the Year" award Department of West Virginia, Marine Corps League; "Distinguished West Virginian" awarded by Governor Cecil H. Underwood.

GENE YEARWOOD, born June 29, 1920 in Jackson Co., Georgia, joined the USMC November 7, 1939. Training locations include: Paris Island, S.C.; Hilton Head, S.C.; Hawaii; Midway Island; Guadal Canal and Guam. Participated in the defense of Pearl Harbor, T.H., on December 7, 1941; of Mid-way Islands from June 3, 1942 until June 7, 1942. Participated in action against the enemy at Guam, Marianas Islands from July 21, 1944 until August 15, 1944 with the Third Marine Defense Battalion as a Rifle Sharpshooter. Discharged December 13, 1945 from Camp Lejeune, N.C. with the rank of Corporal.

Awards: Issued Honorable Service Lapel

Button at Camp Lejeune, N.C. on December 13, 1945; awarded Good Conduct Medal on November 6, 1942; awarded Good Conduct Medal Bar (1st Period) November 6, 1945.

Resides in Jefferson, Georgia as a retired carpenter and farmer. Has been instrumental in getting a monument placed at the Jackson County Court House honoring fallen veterans from Jackson County. Is very active in the Pearl Harbor Survivor Association, and continues to work with schools and organizations to learn about Pearl Harbor, the price of freedom, the value of staying in school and getting an education.

Index

NOTES

Printed in the USA
CPSIA information can be obtained
at www.ICGtesting.com
JSHW060055150824
68134JS00032B/2739